PEOPLE
vs.
PROFITS

PEOPLE
vs.
PROFITS

Columns of Victor Perlo: 1961-1999
Volume I: The Home Front

Edited by Ellen Perlo
Stanley Perlo
Arthur Perlo

INTERNATIONAL PUBLISHERS, New York

Acknowledgments on p. vi

Library of Congress Cataloging-in-Publication Data

Perlo, Victor.
 People vs. Profits : Columns of Victor Perlo / edited by Ellen Perlo, Stanley Perlo and Arthur
Perlo.
  p. cm.
 Includes index.
 Contents: 1. Home front—
 ISBN 0-7178-0736-3 (cloth : alk. paper)—ISBN 0-7178-0730-4 (pbk. : alk. paper)
  1. United States—Economic conditions—1945– 2. United States—Social conditions—1945–
3. United States—Politics and government—1945–1989– 4. United States—Politics and government—
1989– 5. Economic history—1945– 6. Marxian economics. I. Perlo, Ellen. II. Perlo, Stanley. III. Perlo,
Arthur. IV. Title

HC106.5.P457 2003
330.973'092—dc21   2003044954

Table of Contents

ILLUSTRATIONS

Acknowledgments

We want to express our thanks to:

Members of the Economics Commission of the CPUSA for their encouragement, suggestions, and especially for their commitment to continue the "People Before Profits" column. Vic would be pleased.

Professor David Eisenhower and Wadi'h Halabi, whose advice and expertise we called upon time and again.

Joelle Fishman, whose involvement in all aspects of this work was invaluable.

Jesse Bourdon, computer maven whose skill greatly facilitated preparation of this work. And he designed and produced the cover.

Peggy Lipschutz and Seymour Joseph, cartoonists extraordinaire, for their wicked thrusts at 'authority' that so neatly complement these columns.

The Victor Perlo Collection

The Victor Perlo Collection consists of the majority of Perlo's works, including books published in seven different languages. The collection is also comprised of monographs, manuscripts, correspondence, photographs, and personal and family memorabilia.

The Perlo Collection is housed in the J. Glenn Beall Archives of the Lewis J. Ort Library at Frostburg State University. All material is open and available for research. Access is by appointment only; and arrangements to visit the collection can be made by contacting the Ort Library. Information about the collection can be found at the Ort Library's web site at http://www.frostburg.edu/dept/library/myersup/html

Nat De Bruin
Archivist
Lewis J. Ort Library

Foreword

The Ideas of Victor Perlo Are Alive Today

Soon after I became editor of the *People's Weekly World*, Victor Perlo asked me if we would be interested in featuring his weekly column, "People vs. Profits." Vic had been writing this column for many years and had a devoted following. I warmly greeted his offer.

Right up until a few days before he died, Vic delivered that column to us on deadline. His wife Ellen served as his research assistant, copy editor, and designer of the many graphs appearing with his work. She told me that Vic considered the column his most important assignment.

Vic's columns ranged from the federal budget and the Pentagon war budget to the superprofits squeezed from the labor of African Americans and other victims of racist oppression, to the ruthless downsizing by transnational corporations.

He did not rely on assertions of opinion. He marshaled an awesome body of data to prove his case. That scholarly devotion to factual accuracy permeates his columns.

Vic's writings confirm a broad historic truth: that "unpaid labor" stolen from workers is the engine that drives capitalism. Capitalist exploitation generates mass poverty, racism, and war, even as it creates the enormous wealth that could banish these social ills forever. He argued with passion and persuasion that socialism, in which the working class owns the means of production, is the only system capable of resolving these contradictions.

As editor, I read many letters from our readers thanking us for carrying "People vs. Profits." We have toiled to continue carrying the column since Vic's death, a living memorial to him. (We have yet to find an economist who can fill his shoes.)

The contradictions he exposed are now hitting with devastating force: Enron thievery, a war for oil against Iraq, global corporations and the ultra-right running amok. I often wish Vic were still with us, hammering away at these greedy corporate parasites.

With the publication of this book, we can read a selection of his columns once again. They are as fresh as the day he wrote them. They provide deep insights into the dangers and opportunities we face as a people and a nation in the struggle for peace, equality and socialism.

Tim Wheeler

Notes on Editing and Selection of Columns

Of the more than 3,000 columns produced over the 39 years Victor Perlo wrote for the Communist Party paper, we have over 1,000 in our personal files. From these, our selection was based on several factors: relevance to conditions and events of the time; abiding historical importance; exposure of exploitation, racism, anti-labor trends, military excesses, corruption, etc.; analysis of economic conditions and of the policies and factors that shape them; identification of the state/financial/military elite and their control of the government apparatus.

The editors have not tampered with Perlo's work except for obvious typos or other printing errors, and to standardize the style which over the years depended upon several copy editors. Vic periodically addressed several subjects of special interest. As the years passed, each column presented new data and perspective, but also some repetition. Therefore, segments of some columns have been deleted or combined to reduce duplication of content.

The reader will note the evolution of terminology from Negro, to black, to Black, to African American in accordance with political fashion observed by the Party paper and society at large. We have left these and analogous designations in their original form.

Compared to the abundant material on racism in the United States, there is relatively little on the oppression of Hispanics: citizens and immigrants, legal and undocumented, from Latin America. The statistical basis for the study of this subject was scarce in Perlo's lifetime. Before 2000, there was no "Hispanic" or comparable category in the Census.

Except when they occur within a quote, notes in square brackets have been added by the editors for identification or clarity. Dollar figures [in square brackets] have occasionally been converted to their equivalence as of December 2000.

Introduction

Victor Perlo (May 15, 1912–December 1, 1999) was more than a top-notch Marxist economist, internationally respected and honored. He was a prolific and popular author (of 13 books translated into a dozen languages), journalist, lecturer, teacher and participant in forums, conferences and on planning committees. His legacy—books and pamphlets, columns and articles (in newspapers and magazines, domestic and foreign), lectures, reports and conference presentations—is voluminous and historically valuable, especially relevant to economists, historians and political activists today.

Vic took his work and associations seriously. But of all his interests and regardless of other commitments, no matter where he was, his column for the newspaper of the U.S. Communist Party was at the top of his agenda for almost 39 years, from April 1961 through most of November 1999—until just two weeks before his heart gave out.

This commitment made sense. He believed that socialism is the inevitable solution to the trials and injustices that capitalism—and then imperialism—have imposed on humankind. Thus it was logical that he write for the newspaper of the U.S. Communist Party, the political organization whose program he espoused, that he joined. He was elected to membership on its national committee and to its national board, and he served as chair of its Economics Commission.

Vic wrote more than 3,000 columns and articles for the paper, which started as *The Worker,* became *The Daily World,* then the *People's Daily World,* and is now the *People's Weekly World.* But regardless of the name changes, the content has remained true to the proposition that socialism is the answer for the overwhelming majority of the world's population.

The selected columns cover the terms of eight U.S. presidents: John F. Kennedy, Lyndon Johnson, Richard Nixon, Gerald Ford, Jimmy Carter, Ronald Reagan, George Bush, Bill Clinton. They afford a clear overview of the socio-economic and political history of the United States, primarily, but also of the entire world over almost 40 years of intense activity, changes, scientific advances and unmatched military adventurism.

The expansion and accelerating power of state monopoly capitalism—the control of the U.S. Government by the financial/industrial/military complex and the monopolists who run them; the role of the USA, the leading imperialist nation, advancing and protecting the worldwide operations of the transnational giants—are traced and documented. The victories and defeats, successes and failures of groups, movements, countries, coalitions, ideologies, and of pacts and treaties are analyzed.

Tremendous changes, and not only technological ones, have taken place over the 39-year period. But the same problems remain or recur; the same scandals still crop up. And the same causes are responsible; and the same solutions are still valid!—practical, focused solutions, realizable within the system. An uncanny number of columns written in the '60s, '70s, '80s and '90s could be printed today and be as relevant as they were then. They also project fundamental, lasting solutions that may be attained by decisive action to change the social and economic system.

PEOPLE
vs.
PROFITS

Economic Situation

4/16/1961

What Kind of Recovery?

Almost everybody agrees the country should get out of the recession and start a faster economic growth. But how?

Big business says cut their taxes and stimulate investment. The AFL-CIO says raise consumer incomes and mass markets. President Kennedy seems to favor the business way, but makes concessions to the union way to relieve the most acute suffering.

The union campaign is very weak. The approach of the leaders is wrong: they tacitly accept the business position.

Not everybody wants the same kind of recovery. For capitalists, recovery means the increase in profits above all. For workers recovery means jobs for the unemployed, higher real incomes, more paid leisure, and social security. The propaganda that the fates of labor and capital are automatically joined economically is a fiction. Payrolls, employment, and corporate profits do usually move up or down together, but the proportions can vary enormously. And other parts of the picture are in direct opposition.

Recovery with higher living costs means more profits but lower real wages for many workers. But recovery with a shorter workweek at uncut pay means more employment, more total labor income, and less profits for many employers.

Every capitalist cycle that goes up will surely go down. If labor lets capital set the terms for recovery unopposed, its slight recovery gains will be more than wiped out in the next downturn. Workers will end up worse off than before. That happened in the "New Era" of Coolidge and Hoover, and in the last Eisenhower cycle.

Labor struggles ushered in the Roosevelt New Deal. Business spokesmen wailed that it was bringing "reform" and not "recovery." Statistics, cited by Roosevelt, showed that everything recovered substantially, including corporate profits. But the balance was favorable to labor.

Comparing the New Deal peak year 1937 with the 1929 peak, personal incomes of workers were down 7%, farmers 6%, and capitalists 27%. Since the cost of living went down more than 7%, the real income of the working class was restored. But not profits.

Other New Deal reforms—the 40-hour week, minimum wages, Federal Power and Rural Electrification—all cut profits in ways that benefited the people. The government also directly provided millions of jobs to the unemployed, partly at the cost of higher taxes levied on upper incomes.

All of these things were done hesitantly, partially, in the midst of the most bitter struggles. They made a dent in the misery of labor without ending it. There was not enough "reform," not enough of the people's type of recovery.

The recovery the American people now need is a much more vigorous, far-reaching, uncompromising New Deal-type recovery. That is where the main argument should be pitched.

The people need a national health service, decent social security benefits. They need a 35-hour week with 40 hours pay. They need a minimum wage that provides a $4,000* [$23,114] a year minimum living standard. They need the incomes of Negroes to be raised to those of whites. They need a shift of the tax burden from their shoulders to the wealthy. These measures will increase people's income and welfare, but not corporate profits. They may not stimulate private investment. Who cares?

American workers do not need more steel mills, auto factories, and more automation in existing factories at this stage in our history.

We need **government** investment in schools, hospitals, roads, vacation facilities, low-cost housing, and natural resource development. All this must be done on a really massive scale to eliminate in a specified time the substandard aspects of American living standards, on a sufficient scale to provide jobs for all the unemployed in constructing and operating the new facilities.

Mr. Kennedy and his advisors have dramatized the shortcomings in American life. But so far their programs to reduce them are trivial. They are giving priority to stimulating **private** investment.

Our kind of program will mean real, lasting growth for America economically. Labor must realize that to get it means a real political battle against big business. And above all it means a real labor battle for peace, because such a program will never be organized and financed on a sufficient scale until the cold war and its military budget are scrapped.

*$4,000 (1961) = $23,114 (2000)

7/4/1965

The Coming Vietnam War Budget

I believe the Johnson administration plans to add billions to the military budget. The U.S. has multiplied its military budget in every war, and afterwards retained part of the higher level:

Number of Times Military Budget Multiplied

War	During War	Retained Afterwards
1812	7	2
Mexican-American	4	2
Civil War	32	2
Spanish-American	3½	2
World War I	26	2
World War II	75	11
Korean War	4	3

The U.S. is now passing from armed intervention to outright war in Vietnam, where its casualties have already surpassed the Spanish-American War total. On the record, a major military budget rise is probable.

Don't be misled by statements about the weapons not being needed for this limited war. They weren't "needed" in the Spanish-American or Korean Wars either, and only a fraction were used in the two world wars. The United States is a rich country. Our government has always used the occasion of war to hand out lavish armament orders to the most powerful business interests, far beyond the scale called for by technical military requirements. It would be naive to expect the Johnson administration to do otherwise.

After most U.S. wars the military budget was doubled. But after World War II it remained at 11 times the prewar level; and after the Korean War it multiplied 3 times again to 33 times the pre-World War II level. Thus large-scale militarism has become a major peacetime economic factor. The powerful permanent military-industrial complex that has arisen is obviously using the Vietnam War as an excuse to press for another multiplication of their profits and power.

During the cold war Democratic administrations have increased the military budget most. Truman made a virtue of it, and adopted a formula of prosperity through armaments. Johnson's policies follow Truman's, even if he is somewhat more adept at disguising his aims. I think recent statements of economic confidence by Johnson and his entourage are not mere pap. I think they are based on secret assurances that pending big military orders will overcome the very real dangers the economy faces.

Johnson is a veteran political poker player. He and his aides have flatly denied each step of military escalation before taking it, just as they have covered their intentions of increased war spending. In January Johnson issued his second slightly declining arms budget.

After the bombing of North Vietnam started in February, the Budget Bureau assured Congress that the extra-large $650 million contingency appropriation in the budget was enough to take care of the stepped-up fighting. But on May 4 Johnson asked Congress for $700,000,000 extra for the Vietnam War, ignoring the earlier near-promise of his Budget Bureau. Signing the appropriation soon afterwards, he promised the Pentagon a "blank check" for whatever it needs for Vietnam.

Hanson Baldwin wrote: "Military officials are agreed that the 'blank check' the President promised last week to American fighting men in Vietnam will be filled out again . . . The $700,000,000, as one informed source put it, 'just scratched the surface' of what is needed." (*The New York Times*, 5/23/65). Press comment suggests the military aims to put 300,000 men in Vietnam. *Fortune* writes: "If a decision were made to add, say, 300,000 men to replenish the nation's strategic forces, that could mean another $1.5 billion just for pay and upkeep (arms, if needed, would add more)." Also, "just over the horizon" may be $24 billion in five years for the Nike-X anti-missile system, and "almost as much altogether for a variety of other programs." (June 1965)

This would amount to $10 billion per year, close to the $9 billion package the *National Observer* reported last December the Joint Chiefs of Staff wanted to add to the arms budget.

1/22/1967
Stormy Economic Weather: Who Carries the Umbrella?

The prolonged economic rise virtually came to a halt in the second half of 1966, as the consumer economy turned downwards. There is little joy in business.

The real issue among capitalists is how most effectively to make labor pay for the Vietnam War, mainly through inflationary borrowing and higher prices, or mainly through higher taxes. They will certainly try also, through legislation and executive orders, to nearly freeze wages and severely limit strikes. Up to now labor has paid the entire cost of the war, from which capital has profited so hugely.

Now the *World Journal Tribune* cries that corporate profits may fall 10-15%. The capitalists are searching for ways to avoid this, to squeeze still more from a situation that has passed beyond the gravy stage of war escalation.

Business economists say the administration made a mistake not raising taxes in 1966. They mean not raising them enough. For the big shell game of 1966 was the major tax increase put over on labor almost unannounced. Taxes withheld from wages were sharply hiked both for the federal income tax and for social security. Such withholding rose $8.6 billion, or one-third, in the last 6 months of 1966 over the same period of 1965. Collections of other individual income taxes, mainly from property income, went up only $0.3 billion; and corporate tax collections only $1.5 billion, despite the great profit upsurge.

5/16/1972

Pentagon Costs Soar as Economy Stumbles

President Nixon, the Pentagon and the war profiteers are secretly plotting to increase the military budget by tens of billions of dollars to support their escalation of the Vietnam War. This will badly damage the U.S. economy and drastically worsen conditions for over 90% of the American people. It will mean huge extra profits for the munitions makers, unless the people halt Nixon in his tracks.

The Pentagon announced, May 11, that it will demand supplementary appropriations of more than $500 million in the remaining month and a half of this fiscal year, and a billion more next fiscal year, for bombs, shells and aviation gasoline to supply Nixon's escalated bombing and mining campaign. It will also demand an unspecified amount of extra funds to replace destroyed aircraft. That's in addition to the multi-billion dollar step-up already in Nixon's 1973 fiscal year budget.

When Johnson started his major escalation in 1965, the Pentagon initially announced that only a "little" extra money would be required—a "mere" billion or two. But it ended up getting an extra $30 billion a year for the Vietnam War. Nixon and his gang have the same thing in mind.

The May 11 statement uncovers only the first fraction of what they want. Assuming the $500 million ammunition and petroleum will last the rest of fiscal 1972, continuation of consumption at the same pace in the next fiscal year will cost $4 billion, not $1 billion.

The Pentagon had good reason not to give a dollar figure for aircraft replacements. Because of the vastly improved Vietnamese air defenses and their ground successes, U.S. planes and helicopters are being shot out of the sky at a record rate, besides being destroyed on the ground. A minimum of 10 per day are being lost through military action directly, through accidents, through multiple damages in combat rendering the craft unserviceable for future use. That's 300 per month.

The workhorse of the U.S. Air Force is the McDonnell Douglas F-4 Phantom fighter-bomber. The 1971 selling price was $5 million. As much again must be added for armament, avionics, spare parts and engines, making a total outlay of $10 million per plane. Considering other types costing less, and the supercostly B-52s, we may take the $10 million as an average. At 300 planes per month, that comes to $3 billion per month!

Not to speak of the vast arsenals captured by the liberation armies from the puppet forces, or turned by the puppet soldiers against their U.S. military masters.

If the U.S. continues the air war at its present intensity, plane replacement alone will run to over $30 billion per year, and the total cost will go much higher.

The stock market crashed the day after Nixon's escalation speech. But McDonnell Douglas didn't lose anything. And then it started up, gaining 7% in the remainder of the week. President James S. McDonnell says he expects profits to continue upward and Phantom production to double by the end of 1973. Thiokol, a leading manufacturer of aircraft shells, also gained 7%; other munitions makers gained.

If this budgetary escalation goes through, it will mean:

- A big increase in taxes, imposed on workers first of all.
- A further cut in spending for public services and people's well being, a further increase in poverty and hunger, in dilapidated housing and non-teaching segregated schools.
- A tightening of the Pay Board lid on wages, more anti-strike injunctions, more urgent attempts to pass strike-prohibiting and anti-union legislation.
- A fresh international dollar crisis and, in the opinion of most business experts, a setback to the weakly recovering economy.

Every worker affected by soaring living costs and restricted wages faces a cut in real wages that makes earlier losses seem like a joke. Thus 60 million workers and non-managerial employees have a direct bread and butter interest in stopping Nixon's escalation and preventing additional military appropriations.

Every Black, Chicano, Puerto Rican, Indian, Asian; every poor white, pensioner, welfare client; every person needing government-aided low-cost housing, medical care, food stamps; every person striving for a job through government-aided training programs; every student needing a government loan, more federal school aid, and help for desegregation—all stand to lose essentials for decent living, for a chance in life, and, in many cases, for survival.

At least 100 million people in these categories have a vital material interest in stopping Nixon's escalation and cutting off more Pentagon billions.

Every private or public hired wage and salary employee, every professional, every small businessman and farmer, faces financial burdens from a new surge in prices and taxes; therefore 200 million Americans have a direct pocketbook interest in stopping Nixon's escalation and preventing additional military appropriations.

Besides the overriding moral-political interest.

This means all America has an urgent cause to demand of Congress: Stop pussyfooting with "conditional" fund cutoffs.

No supplementary appropriations. Not a cent. No replacements. Cut off all outstanding Vietnam War appropriations immediately. Let the bombs already dropped be the last. Let the planes used up be the last. Let the additional Vietnamese civilians murdered in the past weeks by Nixon's marauders be the last.

Tens of millions should convey the message by wire, phone, letter and demonstration.

• • •

12/21/1974

Inflation Is a Rip-Off

Who's to blame for the 12% inflation? According to establishment propaganda, it's never the fault of business, of private monopolies. For years, labor was blamed, even though the workers' share of the value they created steadily declined. But since the 1971 wage freeze, workers' losses have been so fast and so obvious that employers have had to find a new scapegoat.

They looked abroad, blaming their class enemy overseas instead of at home. Their accusations are given constant publicity by all the media, and are spearheaded by the most aggressive reactionaries—William Buckley, Jr. and Senator Henry Jackson. The principal foreign targets are the "Russians" and the Arabs.

When the USSR bought grain here in 1972, the Soviets were blamed for the increase in the world price of grain and, in an endlessly contrived chain, for the soaring price of bread, meat and finally everything else.

However, a year ago the main target shifted to the Arab lands. When oil-producing countries raised their prices, this was blamed for all increases in the price of gasoline, fuel oil, electric power and, finally, pretty near everything else in the United States. And the shrillest shrieks of the politicians and press are against "Arab oil blackmail," actually giving the impression that only the Arabian countries have raised the price of oil. This device has a double aim: to incite hatred for all of the oil-producing countries and, **particularly**, to build up antagonism against the Arab people and their liberation struggles, to try to win support for U.S. imperialist assistance to Israeli aggression.

All these charges are false. It is corporate profiteering and higher taxes on workers that accounted for more than 50% of the inflation during the past year.

Let's look at the facts about wheat.

In the current crop year, according to U.S. Agriculture Department compilations, the combined U.S. net exports to all countries will come to about 100 million tons. The USSR is importing, net, exactly 1.5 million tons, or 1.5% of the total. Japan is importing 18.8 million tons; Western Europe, 14.7 million tons; and the remainder is scattered throughout the world.

Why don't *The New York Times* and the television newscasters blame Japan or West European countries for imbalances in world grain markets, if any? Obviously, because they are interested not in the truth, but only in using the Soviet Union as a diversionary lightning rod for resentment against the profiteering of the food monopolies.

Especially in bakery products, where the price of bread has risen by up to 10 cents a pound in the last few months, and double that over the past two years; and the price of even the plainest cakes and pies has risen to luxury levels. Do you know that the wheat in a pound of bread today costs only 5 cents? And that that is the same as a year ago? Even the price of flour, with an added miller's margin, has gone up only a half cent. It is obvious from these data that it is not only dishonest to blame the USSR, but also to blame farmers, or foreign buyers in general, or anybody except the chain of profiteering monopolies standing between farmer and consumer.

And now let's consider oil. First, are the producing countries justified in charging $10 a barrel, instead of the $2 they were getting a couple of years ago, and the $1 a barrel in the 1960s? Absolutely, if only to make up for the trifling, inadequate amounts the oil monopolies paid for their oil for decades.

Working people in the United States who support the struggles of workers for better wages and farmers for better prices in this country and in other countries should support the struggles of the people of oil producing countries for better prices for their oil.

U.S. officials support the U.S. oil companies, which are now getting just as high a price for most of their domestic oil as producing countries are getting for their oil; they support the demands of the U.S. oil companies for a complete end to all limits on the price of oil and natural gas. The official policy of the Treasury Department and of bourgeois "oil economists" is to force down the price of imported oil while helping U.S. companies to get a higher price for domestic oil.

But aside from the issue of the justice or injustice of a $10 price for imported oil, what has it to do with inflation in the United States?

I made exact calculations of this for the recent Baghdad oil seminar. The increase in the price of imported oil since 1967 has been enough to account for a rise of one and a quarter points in the consumer price index, or one-fortieth of the increase that actually took place. Over the past year, the rise in the price of imported oil was enough to account for a consumer price increase of 1.13%, or one-tenth of the gain that took place—and that includes not only petroleum-product prices, but also electric power and other second-stage derivatives.

And since Arab countries supply only about one-fourth of the oil imported by the U.S., their price increase could account for only three-tenths of a point rise in the consumer price index over the past year.

Let us consider meat. Prices have remained about at the extreme high reached in the spring of 1973, despite a steep decline in farm prices. Here's a headline in the December 4 issue of the *Wall Street Journal*: "Live Cattle, Wholesale Beef Prices, Plunge to 2-Year Low as Supplies Exceed Demand."

I went through the wholesale cash price lists: butter down 10 cents a pound from a year ago; eggs down 4 cents a pound; broilers down 29 cents; wheat down; most fats and oils down; cotton down 33 cents a pound; wool down $1.05 a pound; copper scrap down 35 cents a pound; rubber down one-third; hides nearly by half; old newspapers, down 90%.

Isn't it time for the cost of living to come down too?

Now let's see what have been the really big factors in inflation. I calculated the increase in corporate cash flow profits and interest paid per unit of production, and the increase in taxes collected from the people per unit of production over the past year. These were about equal to each other, and together accounted for a consumer price increase of 6.82%. That is more than half the increase in the index— or six times as much as can be accounted for by the increase in the price of imported oil.

All of the facts I have presented show how timely was the demand raised at the November 16 demonstrations for a radical rollback of prices. Even now, as admitted at this month's National Association of Manufacturers meeting, companies are raising nominal prices all along the line in anticipation of a price/wage freeze. As the inflationary price boom runs out of steam, because of raw material price collapses and declining markets, they seek the freezes to clamp down on contracted wage increases and to bolster super-high list prices. And, as ever, they will use these wholesale list prices to put over continuing consumer price increases, for a million different items, despite the so-called freeze.

It is up to the people to force a different outcome.

• • •

6/14/1975

Shortage of Capital—For What?

There is a big campaign among government and big business spokesmen to convince the public that there is a shortage of capital and investment in this country, calling for major concessions to the corporations in order to provide funds for such investment. It is claimed that without that, there will not be enough equipment to employ all the country's workers. The *Wall Street Journal* quotes businessmen as saying:

"The U.S. just hasn't been investing enough in new factories and equipment to provide the jobs needed by a growing work force and the expanded supplies of goods needed to avoid inflation . . . Too much emphasis has been placed on promoting consumption and too little on saving and investment . . ." (May 9).

The Chase Manhattan Bank claims a $1.5 **trillion** (a trillion is a million times a million) shortage of new capital in the next decade. Treasury Secretary William Simon ups the ante to $4 trillion, but focuses the blame more on excessive government non-military spending than on consumption.

They all call for lower taxes on business, ending all restrictions on prices, increasing government subsidies and giveaways to business, and curbing wage increases. The self-serving character of these arguments is clear enough. But their lack of merit has to be exposed.

Actually the share of investment in the economy has been growing at the expense of consumption, and this has been associated with a worsening economic situation. Consumer expenditure declined from 64.6% of the gross national product in the 1968-70 cycle to 62.9% in the 1970-73 cycle and 62.7% in 1974. Non-residential equipment and structures spending increased from 9.4% in the earlier cycle to 10.2% in the most recent cycle and 10.7% in 1974.

Interestingly, the *Wall Street Journal* checked up and found that a number of bank economists were stymied when they found similar figures. Thus economist Frederick Deming of the Chemical Bank: "I was planning to make a speech about the capital shortage, so I asked the staff to work up the figures. I found that it was hard to document a case that there's a pressing need for capital spending." First National City Bank's Leif Olsen found that capital spending had "its two best years" in 1973 and 1974—and look what happened! (May 21).

The idea that lack of capacity impedes full employment is idiotic in light of official facts. Manufacturing facilities are now operating at a post-war low of two-thirds capacity, whereas official unemployment is under 10%. That means that existing unused capacity is three times that required to absorb unutilized labor. If operations were raised to 100% of capacity, and all the officially admitted unemployed were hired, there wouldn't be enough workers, even allowing for reasonable increases in productivity, and non-excessive overtime and speedup. Needless to say, big business doesn't want to cut unemployment anything like that much.

What about the alleged shortage of money capital for investment?

The share of corporate cash flow plus interest in total corporate product has been holding steady over the long pull, even without a full accounting, and the share of labor in manufacturing value added has declined drastically, suggesting that surplus funds accruing to the owning class have increased proportionately. In fact, the share of that surplus hidden away in expense account rackets, in bribery of domestic and foreign officials, squandered in advertising, in a supernumerary corporate bureaucracy, etc., has been expanding enormously.

Simon argues that increased government deficits are draining too much from the private capital markets, and thereby justifies his demands for slashing social programs. In fact, increased government spending for goods and services has been concentrated in state and local governments, while the huge deficits are piling up in the federal budget. That's **mainly** due to the rapid erosion of the effective taxation of corporations and upper-income individuals under successive revisions in tax laws and IRS regulations.

At that, even with huge government borrowing, there is no real shortage of capital; but there is banking manipulation to force a very high rate of interest, and more and more capital diverted into ways that do not contribute to the national economy.

Corporations are investing increasingly abroad rather than at home. Plant and equipment spending by U.S. business abroad amounted to 13.7% of their domestic spending in 1966, and a projected 25.6% in 1975. Despite all the hullabaloo about "Project Independence," U.S. oil firms plan to invest as much abroad as in the U.S. this year.

Vast sums are frittered away owing to the anarchy of capitalist production. Thus, most of the world's drilling rigs are used in the U.S. by operators taking "long chance" gambles on land with poor prospects. Many billions go to increase armament capacity. More are spent on superfluous government buildings, duplicating office and commercial buildings. Even so, there is plenty of capital, given the relative limitation of the ultimate consumer market in the United States, which results in turn from the success of big business and its government in holding down real income of the masses.

There is, however, a real shortage of capital, running into hundreds of billions, if not trillions, of dollars, in areas of no interest to private industry.

That is in provision of millions of low-cost integrated housing units, mass transit, health, educational, cultural and recreational facilities. The need for such social capital, to be invested and owned publicly for the benefit of the whole population, is much greater and more urgent than any objective requirement for private capital. And these funds have to be mobilized in exactly the opposite way to that demanded by big business and government propagandists—by taxing the **hundreds of billions** annually of now untaxed capital gains, expense account spending, exempted profits and property income of all kinds; and all of the surplus value generated by labor of workers here and abroad and now appropriated with little or no tax by the corporations and individuals in the upper brackets.

• • •

02/01/79 & 08/30/79

The Recession Profiteers

Most establishment economists accept the obvious: the much predicted recession is here. And they agree on what to do to end it—nothing now!

As for the social cost, the capitalists couldn't care less. Millions of workers will lose their jobs. Hundreds of thousands will have their cars or appliances repossessed, or will be evicted from their homes. Social services will be slashed even more than at present. The small employment gains of Blacks and other oppressed peoples during the boom will be more than reversed.

Big business and its economists, Republicans and Democrats, welcome the recession, because they hope it will:

- Sharply increase unemployment, increase competition for jobs, slow down wage increases, make it easier to enforce speedup, curtail safety and health protection, "take-away" other labor gains.
- Lead to lower imports, while stimulating exports, and thereby improve the balance of payments and strengthen the dollar.
- After some delay, moderately reduce the 13% inflation rate.
- Establish a higher rate of profit from which the next recovery will take off.

They hope that the U.S. recession will not be reinforced by one in Western Europe and Japan, as in the severe 1973-75 crisis. Yet they fear that it will not be a mild "downturn."

They recognize that the recession was set off by the reduction in real wages, which cut mass purchasing power and consumer expenditures. But they are looking forward to a recovery next year based not so much on a revival of consumption as on a profit-fueled investment boom.

They are stressing two propaganda themes as causes of recession and "stagflation":

- "Excessive government regulation." This is directed only at **particular** regulations, won by mass pressure, which in the smallest degree hamper monopoly profiteering, such as environmental and workers' health and safety regulations; equal employment rules; public utility and transportation regulation. They are lobbying for a big **expansion** in regulations to increase their profits. These include tens of billions in subsidies to energy monopolies, record tax breaks, tightened restrictions on wages and unions.

- "Low productivity." It's a lie, as I have demonstrated in several columns. The argument goes that because of "low productivity growth," mass living standards must decline. And that's a pretense at reasoning.

While the recession is on, they are accelerating foreign investments, taking advantage of the continued boom in some capitalist countries and the increasingly aggressive Washington military/diplomatic posture, designed to clear a path for U.S. corporations.

I wrote that they propose to do nothing, now, to stop the recession. Why? To do nothing is a definite policy with predictable results:

- To maintain high interest rates. The replacement of William Miller by Paul Volcker as chairman of the Federal Reserve Board was meant to make sure of that. Usually, soon after economic activity starts to decline, interest rates drop. This helps weaker companies survive, and helps create conditions for the next revival of economic activity. But the most powerful monopolies want the recession to run its course, so they are able to pick up the pieces of weaker firms forced out.
- So as not to provide any additional funds, or programs, to ease the plight of the unemployed, nor to provide jobs; nor to change the racist "first to be fired" rule.
- So as not to cut the tax burden on workers, nor to end the many government measures that jack up prices and increase the inflation rate.
- So as not to end the wage/price guidelines, which are having no effect on consumer prices but are holding down wages.

But the administration and Congress are collaborating in one immediate, active measure to counter a recession, which almost every U.S. administration in the last 40 years has used: **increased military spending.**

Jimmy Carter and the anti-SALT forces are shamefully collaborating to go ahead with the $30 billion MX program, appropriate supplementary billions for the military, set a long-term program going beyond the menacing 3% "real" increase already in effect. These steps are supposed to have a stimulating economic effect, as well as their primary military/political impact. Any short-term stimulating effect is more than canceled out by the lasting inflationary impact, the diversion of resources from socially necessary programs, and the slowing of technological and scientific progress in the civilian economy.

The establishment is also almost unanimous in accepting the perspective of a permanent slow-growth, high-inflation economy; i.e., "stagflation," which fits in with their propaganda favoring higher and higher unemployment and lower living standards.

Everybody concerned with his welfare, and that of the country, should actively oppose this perspective. Only mass struggle can change the outlook: to win positive government programs providing millions of jobs, with emphasis on affirmative action quotas for Blacks, Hispanics and women; for direct action to curtail monopoly profits and prices; for shifting the tax burden from labor to the monopolies; for slashing the military budget and spending tens of billions on housing, mass transit, health, and other social needs of the people; for ending international runaway shops and expanding trade on a basis of equality with socialist and developing countries.

• • •

9/20/1979

'Slow Growth' Reasoning

The Joint Economic Committee, accepting the prospect of continued "slow productivity growth," claims that this will mean lower living standards for workers generally, and especially for oppressed peoples. Slow growth in the 1980s, they say, will mean "protracted and rising unemployment and under-employment for Blacks and other minorities. It means a reduced standard of living and a time of such severe shortages and high prices for energy that people will look back nostalgically and enviously at 1979 . . . Blacks, Hispanics and other minorities fare poorly even under a moderate growth scenario for the 1980s." (*Midyear Economic Report*, p. 3).

Now, leaving statistics aside, I ask: Should slow growth mean a reduced standard of living for the masses? Should it mean even worse discrimination against Blacks?

No way! The argument is advanced to provide a reason for the worsening conditions of workers generally, and especially Black, Chicano, and other nationally oppressed workers. The warning that the sufferings will get much worse during the 1980s signifies the intentions of employers to make them much worse. It seeks to shift the blame from the employers to the workers, whose productivity is being measured.

It seeks to convince people that these sufferings result not from an employer offensive, not from the systematic violation of civil rights laws and elementary social and economic human rights, but from objective, unavoidable economic laws.

There is no such economic law!

If we assume a proportional "fair" distribution of values created between capital and labor, the real wages of workers should go up in proportion to the rise in productivity per worker.

An increasing share of production is going to the military. This reduces what is available for improving living standards.

Living standards have been stagnating, and recently deteriorating, not because of a decline or slowing in productivity growth, but because of a rapid redistribution of income from labor to capital. The fraudulent figures on productivity are invented to excuse and cover up this real reason for the reduction in workers' living standards.

Between 1970 and 1978, productivity in manufacturing, accurately calculated, advanced 30%. Even by the biased method of the Bureau of Labor Statistics (BLS), it went up 24%. The BLS figure for the rise in productivity was 14% for the entire private economy. But real take-home pay of private economy workers, again according to the BLS, rose only 2.5%, and for manufacturing workers about the same percentage.

But corporate profits after taxes, also in "real" terms—that is, in constant prices—increased 95%.

That is just part of the dramatic shift of income from labor to capital since World War II. In 1947, the share of production workers in value added by manufacture was 40.7%. In 1976 it had fallen to 26.9%, barely one-fourth of net output. This means that in 1947 capital got $1.46 for every dollar labor got. But by 1976, capital got $2.71 for every dollar labor got. Labor would need a 50% wage gain, without any hike in productivity or prices, merely to restore its share of 30 years earlier.

Capitalist economists present a false picture of relationship among wages, prices, and productivity. They say, sometimes, that workers get a "fair" share if their wage increases match the rise in living costs, but they do not allow for higher productivity. Other times they say workers get a "fair" share with increases proportional to productivity gains, but without cost-of-living adjustments.

Either way, workers never get ahead in living standards and will often fall behind. And they always fall behind in their share of the total product. But that's exactly what capitalist economic policy is all about—to augment the share of capital at the expense of labor, that is, to increase the rate of exploitation of labor.

To preserve labor's share, workers need higher wages—equal to the combined rise in productivity and living costs. Thus, if productivity goes up 4%, and living costs 8%, a wage increase of 12% is necessary. Generally, if this is achieved, profits will also go up 12%. In other words, labor's share and the rate of exploitation of labor will stay the same. But whenever this happens, whenever wages approach the combined increase of productivity and prices, capitalists scream "soaring labor costs," which, they charge, are causing inflation and unemployment.

Does that mean that higher wages, equal to productivity and price increases combined, are sufficient, or "fair"? By no means. The division of the product between the worker and the capitalist can never be "fair." The boss always gets a surplus over and above anything he might earn by his managerial labors—assuming that he manages the business himself. Otherwise he would not be in business.

From labor's viewpoint, it is **always** right to try to reduce the rate of exploitation, by increasing the share of wages in the total value of the product. This can be done by winning raises in wages that exceed the combined growth of productivity and living costs.

14

09/27/79

Parren J. Mitchell (D, MD), the only Black member of the Committee, refuted the main line of the Joint Economic Committee report in its "additional views." Instead of tax breaks for monopolies he calls for $10 billion of added federal spending and $25 billion in tax reductions for workers and small business to cope with the recession. He wrote:

"A projection of a mild recession translates into deeper depression in the Black community. Where are the economic policies designed to assist the victims of the last-hired, first-fired, cyclical variation of the economy? What do we do to negate the fact that Black teenage unemployment has not been below 30% for the last ten years? We must refocus our economic system to reflect the needs of people. We must channel Federal resources to meet the needs of the working poor, the unemployed, and the elderly."

• • •

11/8/1979

The 1929 Syndrome

Paul Volcker, chairman of the Federal Reserve Board and the hatchet man from Wall Street, laid down the hard line to the American people: Your living standards must be cut; real wages must go down; unemployment must go up. And he acted: to raise interest rates and curtail credit, which were the catalyst that set off a sharp drop in the stock and bond markets, wild fluctuations in gold and dollar prices.

This was in October 1979, 50 years after the great stock market crash that signaled the start of the worst economic crisis in the history of world capitalism.

There is fear in the land. People ask: Will it be 1929 all over again?

This is understandable. The conditions for a new economic crisis were ripe at the beginning of 1979. Everything, including the Volcker actions, indicates that the crisis is about to enter an acute phase, with sharply declining production and mass layoffs.

Government policy today is like the Hoover policy of 1929. It seeks to counter the worsened contradictions of capitalism by braking the economic activity that gives rise to them. And it seeks, like Hoover, to do it in a way that disregards the fate of workers, farmers, small businesses, and homeowners, but does everything to protect and increase the profits of monopoly capital.

However, there is a difference between the Hoover and Carter administrations' propaganda. Hoover advocated the "trickle down" theory—give subsidies to big business and some will trickle down to the people. He promised the masses "prosperity around the corner."

In the Volcker-Carter version, nothing is meant to trickle down. The people are directed, instead, to make further sacrifices in living standards so that capitalism's health may be restored. We are offered nothing but more austerity for the indefinite future.

The Volcker policy sets out to deal with super-inflation and a huge negative balance of payments in ways that are not only in arrant disregard of the people's human rights, but are economic alchemy, not science. It seeks to cure supposedly inadequate productivity by slashing production. It sacrifices $300 billion of national income in a probably futile attempt to right a $30 billion deficit in the balance of payments.

It does these things not from sheer stupidity, but as a class solution, which does nothing to curtail the freedom of big capital to profiteer from the nation's problems. It slashes the average American's living standard faster than before so that the 5% at the top can get richer than ever, so that the priority of guns over butter can be carried still further toward the brink of nuclear catastrophe.

It is a racist solution, which adds to the suffering of the millions of unemployed and underpaid minorities; which seeks to formalize wage and job discrimination, legalize and strengthen de facto segregation. It is an anti-labor solution, which seeks to further undermine collective bargaining and put unions in a straitjacket.

But the current economic crisis does not portend a repetition of 1929.

The stock market cannot fall as far because it is not nearly as high, in relation to profits and dividends.

Production will not fall as far because:

The working people have won many protective measures that, for the majority, will provide sufficient funds for food, for at least a year or two. This will make more difficult mass evictions and the eradication of small savings through bank failures. People have larger and more militant unions and other mass organizations, which will fight for jobs, for social insurance funds, for affirmative action, for other protective measures.

The ruling class have adapted to their vulnerability by developing a system of state regulation and intervention in the economy, which provides stimuli to brake and reverse a serious decline in production. The Carter administration is expected to use these devices in the 1980 election year.

The most conspicuous stimulus already in use is surging military spending. The revelation that Carter plans to hike the 1981 military budget by $20-$25 billion is mainly to further the aggressive plans of U.S. imperialism. But it is also Carter's main instrument for checking a developing crisis before the election. A frightfully irresponsible course that, if permitted, will slash living standards, worsen inflation, and multiply the risk of war.

Other major capitalist countries are not in a crisis, nor does one seem imminent in West Germany, Japan, etc. Their relative prosperity provides a certain support for the U.S. economy, unlike the situation of 1929, when there was a world crisis of capitalism.

Yet, when all is said and done, the crisis can be very severe. People should not be pacified by official assurance that the "downturn" will be "mild."

8/30/1980

Carter's Secret Economic Weapon

Carter has a secret program for reviving the economy: converting it to a wartime basis.

It isn't just Carter, of course. It's also the Republicans and the hawk majority in Congress. Carter and Congress have leapfrogged the military budget since January 1980 so that fiscal 1981 "national defense" budget authority now stands at $182 billion, an increase of $54 billion over the corresponding figure for fiscal 1979.

The escalation of weapons' procurement is even more frightening. At $52.8 billion, it is more than double the figure for fiscal 1976, the last pre-Carter year, and double peak weapons spending in the Vietnam War period.

Such a military program may have a certain short-term stimulating effect on the economy, but not enough to create a boom or reduce unemployment to tolerable levels. Also, it must be connected with the attempt to put over the draft and increase the numbers under arms. But it will only worsen the economy in every way in the not-so-long run.

The main danger, however, is that this enormous military budget is waiting for a war to "happen."

With any of the aggressions in the Pentagon's contingency plans, the consequences—military, political and economic—go beyond the bounds of predictability, except that they will be somewhere in the range between terrible and catastrophic. Wall Street senses that, and hence its nervous reaction.

But while some business groups favor a sane policy, for most of them the nervousness is just a twinge in a continuing chauvinistic, adventurous, profit drive. The United States no longer has the reserves to mount the currently projected military buildup without the imposition of severe sacrifices on the people. The longer organized mass resistance is delayed, the more will be the losses sustained by the great majority of the population. And the struggle on economic issues can buttress the most urgent problem—the struggle for survival against nuclear war.

• • •

10/2/1980

A Phony Cure

Big business has promoted a major campaign over the long-term deterioration in the U.S. economy. It demands the "reindustrialization" or "revitalization" of America.

The problem goes beyond the current recession. Presidential domestic adviser Stuart Eiszenstat says, "There are too many aging plants and equipment. We are losing our technological edge. There has been a general decline in innovation."

Business Week writes:

"U.S. industry's loss of competitiveness over the past two decades has been nothing short of an economic disaster . . . The decline in the U.S. position in the 1970s alone amounts to some \$125 billion in lost production and a loss of at least two million industrial jobs . . . even business shares some of the blame for the decline."

But it places the main blame on "government" and labor.

Let's distinguish between fact and hokum. It's true that thousands of plants have closed down, throwing millions of workers out of their jobs. It's true that imports are taking an increasing share of U.S. markets, while U.S. exports are losing foreign markets over the long run (despite a current surge).

It is not true that rising taxes and wages have slashed profits and the "incentive" for capitalists to invest. Between 1970 and 1979 corporate profits after taxes went up nearly four times, at a compound annual rate of 16.3%, while real wages and the effective corporate tax rate were declining.

It is not true that "excessive government regulation" is the culprit. The scope and scale of government subsidies and pro-monopoly regulation have mushroomed, reaching new heights in the Synfuels Act.

It isn't true that the country is saving too little, over and above current consumption. What is true is that a larger share of that saving, in comparison with other countries, is going for military purposes, and a smaller share for productive investment. Even so, the share of fixed capital investment in the domestic gross national product has been maintained; and total capital investment, domestic and foreign, of U.S. corporations compares favorably with that of its rivals.

What is true is that there has been an explosive expansion in capital investment abroad; that the biggest multinationals have concentrated on building or buying plants elsewhere, while shutting down their "aging plants and equipment"—and sometimes not so aging—in the United States. Between 1970 and 1980, foreign plant and equipment outlays by U.S. multinationals shot up 241%, and in the single recession year 1980, by 26%, as compared with a 140% rise in domestic outlays in the 10-year period.

The largest investors are the oil monopolies. Despite all the propaganda about achieving "energy independence," they are investing more abroad this year than they are in the United States. The auto companies have **tripled** their foreign investments in the last two years, and are spending about as much now to build new plants in Mexico, Brazil, and various other countries as to downsize and robotize their remaining plants in the United States.

It is not true that the U.S. lags in research and development, but it is true that half of all U.S. government spending for R & D is for military purposes, while hardly any of the corresponding spending by West Germany, Japan, etc., is for military purposes.

Even in the old basic industries, technology isn't standing still, and investment goes on. But it is of a type that disregards totally the human side, the requirements of the workers who have built up these industries. The tendency is to curtail or stop output in large, centralized plants and to distribute production in relatively small, scattered, specialized plants with maximum automation and a minimum number of workers. Thus the Westinghouse Corporation announces its intention to build scores of plants, each employing no more than 500 workers.

The U.S.-owned auto companies are developing "world cars" with components manufactured in low-wage centers all around the globe, connected with promotion of sales in these places; and operations in the United States are limited increasingly to final assembly of cars to be sold in this country. Hundreds of thousands of U.S. autoworkers will be permanently displaced by this process, if it goes ahead unchecked.

It isn't true that U.S. firms cannot compete on export markets. What is true is that they prefer to fill export orders from foreign plants, and have multiplied their sales of this type five times in the last ten years.

It isn't true that U.S. commitment to free trade prevents discrimination against imports. It doesn't prevent gross discrimination against imports from socialist countries and nationally owned products from developing countries.

The basic problem, then, is not the deterioration of American industry. It is its distorted development; its moving outside our shores; its militarization; its rapidly increasing gain in profits at workers' expense.

What is required is not the "reindustrialization" or "revitalization" of American industry in general, but the restoration and improvement of the condition of the American working class, which alone can provide a healthy foundation for a new stage in the development of U.S. industry.

• • •

12/11/1980

Reaganomics

What is Reaganomics?

Its main features are: a very big further increase in the military budget, reductions in the civilian budget, a 30% cut in individual income tax rates in three years, cuts in corporate taxes, and a balanced federal budget. Its secondary features are: a tight money policy, less government regulation of business, and a freeze on federal government hiring.

These are the published proposals of Reagan's economic program, but there are also secret parts of it, to be kept in reserve.

Stripped of detail, there is one guiding principle to Reaganomics: to use all the power of government to help big business and the rich increase their profits, and racial discrimination, at the expense of the living standards, health and safety of the population, in an economy geared to rapid preparation for wars of aggression.

Some progressives object to the term "Reaganomics." They say Carter was going in the same direction, so why present Reagan's program as something new. That is, of course, true. And what's more, most of the liberal Democrats are falling over themselves to accommodate to the new regime. But I still like the term and think it's on target because the direction is clearer, the tempo is much faster: Within the official establishment only the Congressional Black Caucus, in the main, continues to resist.

There is a qualitative change presaged under Reagan: overt government support of capital versus labor, war versus peace, racism versus equality.

Let's see what it all means. First, as to the primary aims of Reaganomics—they're economic nonsense. That is, there can be big increases in the military budget, cuts in civilian outlays, big cuts in taxes on the rich and corporations—but there cannot be a balanced budget at the same time. If the Reaganites put over the rest of their published program, the already huge budget deficits will grow, and will probably pass $100 billion in a year or so.

Read the *Wall Street Journal*, or *Forbes*, or *Business Week*. Read the statements of Reagan's own economic advisers. They all concede the inconsistency of the elements of the program. In effect, they are saying that there is no prospect for a rapid easing of the economic situation. They now say that inflation will be faster under Reagan than Carter supporters were projecting—at least for the first year or two. They are saying that Reagan will not stop the stagnation of economic activity, or prevent a further growth in unemployment.

They laugh at the far-out economists in the Reagan camp—like Laffer, author of the "Laffer curve"—who say that the more you cut taxes on the rich, the more total tax collections will increase. The fact is that tax rates on the rich and the corporations have been going down for two decades, and so have their tax payments as a percent of economic activity or government expenditures.

What about cuts in the civilian budget: Well, no Republican would call for cutting interest payment to the bankers. And with a tight money policy and big deficits, interest rates can only go one way—up. The Reaganites regretfully concede that in the first year they have little chance of cutting social security or medicare benefits, the largest and most rapidly growing items in the civilian part of the budget.

Obviously there is no intention of ending the many subsidies to big business, such as the Chrysler bailout, and they are eager to dish out tens of billions under the Synfuel programs—and for whatever else may come along as a feasible way for monopoly capital to feed on the public trough under the slogan of "encouraging private initiative!"

There is a big brouhaha being made about slashing waste and graft in the budget. No question—there is a fantastic amount of both—but almost all of it is in the Reaganites' favorite parts of the budget: in the military, in the subsidies to big business, in the "international" aid to the various puppets of imperialism. That waste and graft are part and parcel of the profit incentive that is the basis of Reaganomics. Far from cutting them, one can only anticipate further amendments to Pentagon and related regulations to permit wider profit margins, leave more loopholes for waste and graft of every kind.

All this will result in flailing away the small existing benefits for the most oppressed, poverty-stricken, suffering sections of the population—food stamps, aid to dependent children, rent subsidies, supplementary payments to workers unemployed because of imports. Only 9% of the total budget is appropriated for civilian needs and social services, and this relatively small amount is the target of the greedy.

However, successful resistance and progressive change have always depended on mass action. Now millions who formerly relied on Carter or on the Democrats in Congress, can realize this. And do not mistake it—victories for labor, for peace, for equality can be won with Reagan in the White House, with a right-wing Republican Senate. And it's to that end that all progressive forces must unite and direct their energies.

• • •

1/31/1985

Economic Outlook for Reagan's Second Term

The main economic program of the first Reagan administration consisted of three parts:
- Record reduction in taxes on corporations and capitalists.
- Record peacetime increase in military spending.
- Record cuts in welfare spending.

These were connected with related policy measures: notably a government-big business offensive against labor and civil rights; encouragement of growth of monopoly power, through deregulation and the virtual abandonment of anti-trust laws; and increased military intervention and economic pressure against developing countries, alongside efforts to achieve aggressive military superiority over the USSR.

This program was carried out almost completely—except that the USSR maintained effective military parity.

The overall economic effects of these measures included:
- Huge federal budget deficits, which doubled the national debt and produced long-term record high interest rates.
- The lowest tax rate on high incomes in 50 years, and on corporations in 40 years; while the overall tax burden—federal, state, and local—on labor increased, becoming to a greater extent than ever the main source of tax revenues.
- Reduction of social income and benefits—especially those needed to relieve poverty, hunger, and homelessness—for working people and retirees.
- Record rate of increase in corporate profits and incomes of the capitalist class, relative to the small overall growth of the economy.
- Real wages at the lowest level in two decades, and 15% below their peak; the highest average level of unemployment in 50 years; and an absolute reduction of jobs in industry.

All of these measures add up to a sharp increase in the rate of exploitation of labor—that is, an increase in the share of income going to capital and the rich, and a reduction in the share going to workers and the poor.

- The worst decline in real farm income on record.

These changes have resulted in an extremely unbalanced economy. When combined with similar distortions in international economic relations, they set the stage for even worse economic and financial crises than those of the first Reagan administration.

For his second term, Reagan, with overwhelming big business support in most respects, intends to move even more decisively in the same disastrous directions. However, he faces stronger potential resistance from labor, farmers, the hungry and homeless, the organized peace forces, and the peoples of developing countries. Moreover, sections of the capitalist class differ with parts of the program; and international conflicts with capitalists of other lands have become more serious.

Centerpieces of the second term program are the Regan-Reagan tax program and the Reaganite spending programs.

Reagan's overall plan is to cut civilian spending by $165 billion in three years—including $50 billion for fiscal 1986, starting in October. A major objective is the proposal to skip a whole year in inflation adjustments in Social Security pensions—meaning a real cut that would probably exceed 5%. Reagan pretends he is waiting for "overwhelming" congressional support before exerting full White House pressure.

Other prime targets are spending for Medicare, Medicaid, education, housing, and the humanities. These cuts would victimize sick workers, poor workers, retired workers, workers' children—all workers. They would downgrade housing and culture for the entire population. If these budget proposals are put over, all workers are bound to suffer—Black and Hispanic workers doubly so.

Big business agrees with the $50 billion in cuts Reagan is seeking for fiscal 1986. They recognize that some token cuts in military authorizations will be needed to put over the main, civilian welfare cuts. But their real intention is merely to cut some of the fat that's in every Pentagon budget proposal. Congress has made that kind of "cut" every year, while doubling military spending in five years and tripling weapons procurement and research in only six years. Senate Republicans have rapidly retreated from talk of a Pentagon budget "freeze" and are planning to dicker over a few billion of the Weinberger-Reagan proposal, so they can come back to the voters claiming they dealt "fairly" with military and civilian programs. House Republican leader Robert H. Michel, after meeting with Weinberger, is offering the Democrats a "deal" whereby, in exchange for a 2% cut in Weinberger's huge budget request, the Democrats will support the MX.

This is a total fraud. What Congress passes is **authorization** bills. The Pentagon spends the funds that have been authorized when it wants to. Over the last five years, it has accumulated $130 billion more spending authority than it actually spent, and it expects to have at least $50 billion of that totally uncommitted by the end of this fiscal year. According to press reports, the Pentagon plans to get around any cuts Congress makes in mere **amounts** by spending up to $20 billion of the excess funds at its disposal, without holding up a single one of its six main destabilizing new nuclear weapon programs, or its all-out preparation for space warfare.

To make real cuts in the Pentagon plan, Congress would have to completely eliminate major items and totally ban space weapons research, in addition to sharply reducing new authorizations and forbidding use of the banked-up surplus funds.

Congressional resistance is stronger than during Reagan's first term; but with the tremendous pressure from big business and military-industrial lobbies—and with the overwhelming majority of members of Congress representing the capitalist class—such resistance cannot prevail without mass support.

• • •

9/19/1992

Recovery? Only for Capitalists

The cover of the August 24 *Fortune* magazine shows a worker facing a parched wasteland; the highlighted caption: "The job drought: Why the shortage of high-wage jobs threatens the U.S. economy." The cover of the following issue shows the smiling faces of eight billionaires. Together, these covers epitomize the contradictions in the U.S. economy today.

The plight of the worker is a source of elation to the super-super-rich. Despite Bush's claim of a recovery—albeit "sluggish"—the economic depression continues and, for the working class, deepens. Unemployment mounts, real wages decline, more people lose homes, and more children go hungry.

The media conveyed a dismal Labor Day message: workers can no longer look forward to the "American Dream" but face further sacrifices, which Bush & Co. are determined to impose. There is a recovery underway, however—in corporate profits and in the incomes of the plutocrats.

Corporate profits, as adjusted by the Commerce Department, rose at an annual rate of 14.5% between the third quarter of 1991 and the second quarter of 1992—an increase of $50 billion—$28 billion above their 1989 level. The number of billionaires on the *Fortune* list went up from 182 in 1990 to 233 in 1992. Americans accounted for 64 of that number, 4 more than a year ago.

Fortune's researchers report that growth in employment, lagging behind growth in the labor force, has been concentrated in low-end jobs. In 1979, 18.9% of full-time workers fell below the poverty line; by 1991 the figure was 25.7%. Thus, during the 1980s there was a rise of 5 million in the number of full-time workers who received poverty wages. Their wretchedness fueled the increasing

fortunes of the billionaires and the salaries of their hired managers. Between 1979 and 1989 the number of those whose salaries were $1,000 or more per week (adjusted for inflation) jumped from 3 to 5.1 million.

More and more of the gross profits of big business are distributed among the top layer of executives, a seeming contradiction when employers are out to "cut costs." But these are the cost-cutting engineers who cut wages and salaries of production workers, reduce their number and squeeze more output from those who remain. It is the job of the high-paid executives to plan and implement the relocation of production facilities to lower-wage, non-union states and countries; to break unions and defeat organizing drives; to ignore safety conditions and environmental regulations. The function of lower-level bosses is to push each subordinate to the limit and to get rid of "troublemakers." In Marxist terms, their aim is to get more surplus value from each worker.

The recent much publicized layoffs affect only a handful in the managerial ranks. As a matter of fact, their number continues to increase; and *Fortune* predicts that will continue.

However, the time when ordinary white-collar workers had relative security is over. "Much of the pain," *Fortune* reports, "will be felt by the 18 million back-office workers." A decade of computerization is finally catching up and being used against them. As their advantages over blue-collar workers dwindle, their objective need for unionization and independent political action, in order to rebuild the organized strength of the greatly enlarged working class, will become clearer.

How does *Fortune*'s job drought "threaten the U.S. economy?"

The fact that the normally over-optimistic journal features the problem is a reflection of the bad state of affairs. In effect, the declining purchasing power of the masses depresses consumer markets; and governments—federal, state and local—aren't doing anything to counteract this. The *Fortune* writer, who examines various proposals, rejects the only really positive one: economist Lester Thurow's call for a higher minimum wage. The writer ends up confused by the contradictions in capitalist recipes, but warns:

"What everybody should agree upon is that the U.S. cannot support a thriving consumer economy—or avoid an eventual increase in political and social unrest—if it continues to force the majority of its population into an ever lower standard of living."

What everybody should agree upon is that the first requirement for changing the gloomy outlook is to oust the Bush-Quayle gang—the hypocritical aggressors against American workers; the perpetrators of conquest and exploitation the world over.

• • •

12/20/1997

Financial Crisis: A Symptom of the Global Crisis of Capitalism

The deepening world financial crisis and crisis of overproduction is currently centered in Asia; but it is already spreading to Africa, Latin America, Europe and yes, even the United States.

The long boom in Thailand, the first of the "Asian Tigers" to collapse, brought wealth and extravagant living to the capitalists who exploited Thai workers and to the compradors who acted as go-betweens and enforcers for the Japanese, American and other foreign investors who reaped the largest part of the plunder from the poverty-level wages and inhuman working conditions of Thai laborers.

Now, as overproduction forces the closing of scores of Thai factories, the first wave of laid-off workers has no place to go: 449 of them from the bankrupt PAR Garment factory are sleeping on straw mats outside the plant gate, with no hope for the future. Thai economists fear an additional 2 million impoverished workers will lose their jobs by the end of 1998. In relation to population, that's equivalent to 8 million U.S. workers.

Throughout Southeast Asia, governments are being forced by the U.S.-controlled International Monetary Fund (IMF) to slash social and public benefits of all kinds, including education and health services.

Asian countries were prevailed upon to get large loans at very high interest rates from U.S., Japanese and European banks. The scale of this international borrowing went far beyond their base in real production. As a consequence, there was a drastic drop in the exchange rate of their currencies. With widespread bankruptcy of Asian companies, U.S. transnationals are quick to buy up properties at bargain prices. With real wages of Asian workers cut in half, the profits of the transnationals are soaring as the movement of U.S. production to Asia accelerates—and will continue to accelerate.

U.S. workers are, of course, losing as a result of these and other measures, with more yet to come. The vicious welfare/workfare law, immigration laws, attacks on affirmative action and persecution of militant trade union leaders are just the start, even as official reports show employment and wage levels are rising. As a London *Financial Times* headline put it, "Asian woes cool U.S. pay pressure," reflecting the upper hand given employers to renew the downturn in real wages that prevailed through most of the past 25 years.

U.S. imperialism is using the financial crisis to further its long sought goal of world domination, a fact underscored by *The New York Times* headline, "Asia's surrender: reeling from blows to their economies, countries agree to financial concessions."

But the concessions were not solely by Asian countries: 102 countries have agreed to remove most controls and restrictions on the intrusion of foreign capital, while there were absolutely no U.S. concessions in return. Although it is true that while Wall Street will be free to invest in Myanmar (Burma) without restrictions, Myanmar is free also to invest in the United States. But with what capital? With what ability to compete with U.S. power?

The world crisis is, in part, a manifestation of capitalist contradictions. But it is mainly part of the process of struggles that, in some respects, precipitated the crisis and have sharpened in the course of the crisis.

One struggle is that between capital and labor, particularly in Asia where the crisis so far is deepest and where the capitalists use the situation to increase the exploitation of labor. But the workers are resisting this and, especially, the IMF dictates directed against workers.

A second struggle is between capitalist and developing countries. Imperialism, be it U.S. or Japanese, uses the crisis to reinstate full neo-colonial subjection on its debtors, cutting short their attempts to develop economic independence and jacking up the scale of plunder available to transnational corporations. It is the workers who most strongly uphold the national integrity of the victim countries, who strike and demonstrate to prevent or delay implementation of IMF prescriptions.

This fightback has been especially noteworthy in South Korea, where the working class has a tradition of Communist-influenced trade unionism that has won significant gains in recent years, including a level of real wages equaling that in some western European countries.

The third struggle is among capitalist powers for redivision of the world—most apparent between the U.S. and Japan. Japan's aim was to achieve parity with—and supremacy over—U.S. capitalism in overall economic strength and control of Asia. These pretensions were partly smashed by the prolonged Japanese crisis and depression starting in 1990. The severity of the present financial crisis has further weakened Japan's influence. The losses involved in the actual and threatened bankruptcies have brought bailout costs to half a trillion dollars—and still rising.

It is far from certain whether Japan's treasury has the reserves to handle that amount, or whether Japan can avoid surrender to the IMF and acceptance of its humiliating terms.

U.S. and European capitalists are using the crisis to increase their global domination. At the same time, they hope to contain the crisis before economic life in the smitten countries collapses absolutely. And, above all, before political opposition becomes sufficiently organized and unified to threaten anti-imperialist revolutions.

• • •

4/11/1998

Super-Merger

The zoom of U.S. capitalism and its stock market has American imperialism and its super-rich outprofiting the robber barons of old many times over. General Electric, the world's most lucrative company, boasts that its $8 billion of annual profits reflect the fact that it leads its competitors in almost all of its many enterprises.

The growth of monopolies and their profits has been speeded by a wave of corporate mergers, which usually result in higher profits: among other ways, by downsizing thousands of workers whose functions are combined in the larger enterprise.

It's not surprising that the stock exchange 9000-day coincided with the announcement of the largest merger yet—between Citicorp and Travelers. Citicorp is the company name of Citibank, the most profitable U.S. bank and by far the largest profiteer from overseas holdings—in Asia, Latin America and Europe. Travelers, a long established insurance company, has in the last several years expanded by taking over Salomon Brothers, one of the top Wall Street investment banks, and Smith Barney, one of the top brokerage houses. It has become a monster of the financial community, disregarding the hoary anti-trust laws supposed to prevent exactly such merging of different types of financial corporations.

This merger is apt to result in higher insurance costs for the American people and in higher costs of doing banking business.

The Travelers-Citicorp merger combines companies with total assets of $700 billion, a stock market value of $83 billion, and combined profits of $7.5 billion, just behind GE. From cutting costs alone, the super-monopoly hopes to add another billion a year to its profits. At least several thousand of their combined labor force of 162,000 workers will lose their jobs.

Concerning this and other features of the negotiations leading to the merger, John S. Reed, CEO of Citicorp, said: "You have to keep these kind of things quiet." While Sanford I. Weill of Travelers commented: "This is not about layoffs. This is really about cross marketing . . ." However they explain it away, the prospect is still there.

The *Wall Street Journal* reported that this was not only ". . . creating the world's largest financial services company . . . it could also trigger the formal end of" the major anti-trust law limiting financial corporation monopolies. Certainly there will be plenty of congressional debate and administrative hearings. However, the way American politics has gone, it's likely that the merger will go through, with perhaps some amendments. Already it has raised the drive for mergers to fever pitch among other financial giants: Chase Manhattan, J.P. Morgan, Merrill Lynch, Lehman. They will have to merge to stay in the same league with the Travelers-Citicorp giant.

The merging of corporations into super-giants dominating whole industries is for the sake of private profits. But it shows that the U.S. economy is ripe for public ownership and management of major industries for the benefit of the majority of Americans, in a socialist United States.

• • •

5/15/1999

Kosovo's Doom: Stock Market's Zoom

The looming war economy promises a bonanza for big business. As the bombing started, the stock market took off—jumped 10% through early May. The Dow-Jones index, which had been stuck below 10,000 for some time, took off and not only reached 10,000 but passed 11,000.

The Clinton-Albright-NATO aggression against Yugoslavia was brewing for the last six months. Anticipating the assault and the war orders to come, corporate sales and profits soared. Profits had been expected to stagnate or decline in the first quarter of 1999; but, in fact, for 100 large corporations they went up 18% over the previous year.

The 300 members of the Business Council, top moguls of monopoly capital, recently met. A press conference was called by the nine-member executive committee—heads of Citigroup, General Electric, Eastman Kodak, etc. Citigroup CEO Sanford Weill, who received over $100 million last year, summarized:

"The sentiment was unanimous: 'This is really the best of times,' Mr. Weill said, flanked by smiles and nodding heads. 'I don't think anyone at this table has seen better times.' He lauded the . . . seemingly unbridled economic expansion." (*Wall Street Journal*, 5/7/99)

Quite a change from six months earlier when, at the Business Council conference, "A number of CEOs fretted that impending profit squeezes would cause them to cut capital spending and hire fewer workers."

Current optimism is attributed to the fast economic growth during the past two quarters; indications that the world capitalist financial crisis is easing; the fact that wage increases have been skimpy, lagging behind rising productivity; and rising retail sales.

But the underlying cause was preparation for the assault that finally exploded in the overwhelming, cowardly bombing in Kosovo. Increasingly non-military areas, including a hospital, have been hit; scores of civilians have been killed; and the President of Yugoslavia and other leaders in Belgrade have been targeted for assassination.

The payoff to U.S. industry in special budgeting for this war, raised to $13 billion for this fiscal year (ending in September), was approved by Clinton and the Republicans. Because of the joint "cap" on military and civilian "discretionary spending," an equal amount will be taken from already underfinanced federal authorizations for education, health, poverty and hunger programs.

For the stockholders and top brass of the mega-corporations, the $13 billion pays big dividends: for every war dollar budgeted, there's $5 of extra business stimulated by the war economy; for every dollar of extra arms spending, $10 of planned destruction of the Yugoslav economy.

So by all means let us be realistic about the motivations behind this and the other "humanitarian" aggressions —e.g. Iraq—U.S. military forces are engaged in!

• • •

10/30/1999

Debt!!!

I have referred several times to the excessive debt burden of individuals and corporations. But I didn't realize how serious the problem is until I read the article in the current issue of *Business Week* (11/1). If the high level of the stock market is comparable to a bubble waiting to burst, an oft mentioned characterization, the debt level is like a mighty river building up pressure behind a deteriorating dam. *Business Week* refers to it as a "debt bomb": "The debt load on the U.S. economy is bigger than it has ever been, and such a burden makes even a thriving economy much more vulnerable to any kind of shock."

In 1985 personal debt was "only" 65% of disposable annual income (DAI). Rising at an accelerating rate, it is now up to 98% of DAI, and the trend threatens to continue, pushed by telemarketers; postal and e-mail come-ons to take credit cards; invitations of deferred payment until the year 2000 or even 2001 for household goods and clothing; offers of supplementary home mortgages; and even bids to low-income families to borrow needed funds. Personal bankruptcy filings have gone way up; and Stuart A. Feldstein, president of a research corporation specializing in debt analysis, predicts a rise of 8-15% in these filings next year over this year. Mortgage delinquencies will rise because of higher interest rates and the recent explosion of high-risk mortgage lending.

"Even more dangerous," according to the article, "is a quadrupling of margin debt—borrowing to fund stock purchases." In the past five years, this margin debt has tripled, to $179 billion. With a major decline in the stock market, that will have to be repaid immediately.

And soaring corporate debt is at least as serious. Corporations are obtaining additional capital mainly by borrowing—and there is much borrowing by high-tech and internet companies, which have little revenue. Many of them borrow in order to buy back their own stock, pushing up the market value but reducing the real equity capital.

Business Week lists prominent corporations whose long-term debt has doubled, tripled or more over the past two years, including ATT, Bell Atlantic, MCI World Communications, Raytheon, Seagram, Monsanto.

Most dangerous is the rising debt of financial corporations—up from 18% to 80% of the gross domestic product (GDP) since 1978. *Business Week* notes: ". . . the U.S. is now using 72% of net global savings. An amazingly high percentage."

The world financial crisis that is still chewing up countries in several parts of the world hasn't yet reached the United States. The debt burden is the main mechanism by which it threatens to cause havoc and suffering here. Under capitalism, sci-tech leadership gives no protection against this menace, nor does the overwhelming military might so boastfully flaunted by U.S. imperialism.

Finance: I

8/26/1961

Playing the Market

What do I think about mutual funds? Readers want to know as a matter of public interest, and some hope to get useful advice—Sylvia Porter and Marxism, too!

Nine out of ten American workers have debts, not savings, and couldn't afford to buy stocks if they wanted to.

In 1959 over 12 million Americans owned stock. Much effort is devoted to persuading workers to buy stock. The promoters hope buyers will bid up prices, and become tied psychologically to capitalism, opposed to strikes and socialism. And not without some success. I recently heard about a print shop where the workers have switched small talk from the races to the stock market—from pari-mutuels to mutuals.

But this swelling of stockholders' ranks is economically unimportant. As I have shown in books and articles, the millions of "people's capitalists" have no influence on American corporations and, with few exceptions, derive no significant economic benefit from their holdings. While 50,000 wealthy families own 70% of all stock, 2,500,000 families of small stockholders have only 1%. And tens of millions have none.

The Rockefeller clan owns four times as much stock as **all** blue collar workers in the United States. The average worker-stockholder (white and blue collar) gets yearly dividends equal to about two days wages—1-2% of the profit the employer gets from his labor.

About 1,250,000 own only "mutual fund" shares—and, it sometimes seems, almost as many sell them! Investment trusts were popular in the 1920s, but were nearly forgotten after the big crash, when some of them became worthless. Now this convenient vehicle for pulling in the small saver has been revived in the form of the mutual fund.

The fund manager buys shares in many corporations. The investor buys shares of the fund, equal in value to a pro rata fraction of all the shares in the fund's "portfolio." The value of his investment goes up or down by the same percentage as the fund's portfolio. And he receives a pro rata portion of the dividends collected by the fund. He may buy his mutual fund shares through regular monthly installments, and cash in his share at full value at any time.

But small investors are likely to buy the wrong stocks at the wrong time, so many of them lose even in a bull market. Brokers, financial columnists, and corporate insiders engage in high-pressure promotion to unload stocks on "the public" at peak prices, and to scare them into selling at bottom prices.

A special danger today is that stock prices are very high by any traditional standard. Typically, they are several times as high as the "book value" of the assets they represent, and dividend yields are generally lower than savings bank interest. Some business economists claim the old standards are obsolete and will never return. Others stress resemblance to the pre-1929 situation, and they **may** be right this time!

I know professionals who successfully study the dynamics of the market, the economic situation of particular companies, keep their ears open for relevant information, and make money on the stock market. I know workers who put savings into American Tel & Tel stock years ago, stood pat, and are far ahead of the game. But for even the most studious and cautious, the market involves a gamble. It is not as safe as crossing the street. The buyer can lose, and plenty.

Stock ownership does tend to give the worker-owner a feeling of identification with the exploiting class, and to weaken his labor solidarity. Stock ownership today usually means participation in war profits or the profits of modern colonialism. American Tel & Tel, for example, is one of the largest armament contractors.

It is tough enough for a worker to obtain any financial security in this cannibalistic society. If he can make himself a better and easier life through successful investments, more power to him. But remember the tension that goes with it, the risk of serious loss, and the political contradictions involved.

Weigh carefully—will it make you less of a partisan of the people's rights? Will it distract you from the fight for peace? These activities can yield your children a more secure life, which all the shares in Wall Street cannot guarantee.

For those who do buy stocks, what about mutual funds? For small investors it has the advantage of not requiring the comprehensive study of securities, of providing a regular form of investment, without brokers' pressures and nerve-wracking in-and-out trading.

But the typical commission is 8%, which means that you immediately give up 8% of every dollar you invest—in some installment schemes, 40% of the first year's investment! And the fund managers take out 10-15% of the dividends to pay themselves fees and expenses.

Heed well the cautious stockholder's truism: "Don't play the market if you can't afford to lose."

• • •

8/31/1963

Why the Wall Street Policy Shift?

Is a real shift taking place in American foreign policy? The top men of Wall Street, who unfortunately still call the tune, are signaling it.

An important signal was the June 24th *Wall Street Journal* ad signed by businessmen calling for a nuclear test ban treaty and looking forward to the possibility that this might pave the way for gradual disarmament. The ad said "our own security" and "world survival" would be aided by the test ban, and that disarmament could foster large investments in education, housing, health, etc. for American as well as for Russian people.

While one of the 21 businessmen had appeared several times before as a signer of pro-peace statements, never in the cold war period had such a representative group of first-rank executives spoken out for peace. Several were from corporations traditionally in the Morgan financial bailiwick—Clayton of Anderson & Clayton, Connor of Merck & Co., Robinson of Coca-Cola. Even though oil interests and Rockefeller financial associates were absent, this ad helped persuade our big business President to finalize the partial test ban treaty.

Then, on August 15th, *The New York Times* carried a two-page ad urging senatorial approval. It was signed by most of the 21 and a number of others, ranking still higher in the financial firmament. There were Sidney Weinberg of Goldman Sachs, Thomas D. Cabot of the Boston Cabots. Most significant of all, the signature of Winthrop Aldrich, elderly dean of the Rockefeller clan, followed Nelson Rockefeller's qualified endorsement. Such impressive top financial support explains why the two-thirds Senate ratification is assured.

The same forces indicate the direction of possible next steps, arising out of the worsening U.S. balance of payments deficit. As of early July, the administration was still tenaciously refusing to curtail foreign bases and intervention, basically the only way to improve the balance of payments.

But then, in another departure, the American Bankers Association came out with its statement on the fresh balance of payments crisis. Regardless of political and military objectives, they assert, "our ability to finance overseas military expenditures without jeopardizing" the position of the dollar in world finance "clearly has declined." Hence "consideration must be given to the near-term redeployment of some of these military forces. In view of technological changes over the past decade, it is not obvious that greater centralization of troops and military installations on United States territory would weaken the nation's military posture."

In short, U.S. imperialism must retrench or default on its sacred financial obligations. Their worry about the world financial leadership isn't mine. But a withdrawal of troops to the United States would certainly lessen the danger of war—which is threatened daily by U.S. forces in South Vietnam.

The statement was prepared by David Rockefeller of Chase Manhattan Bank, Thomas S. Gates of Morgan Guaranty Trust Co., Jesse W. Tapp of Bank of America, and others at the very peak of American high finance.

Thus a mutual reduction of forces in Germany, as proposed by the USSR, could be a logical, achievable, next step. Strauss and von Brentano [West German right-wing political leaders] scream at the thought, and Washington denies any such intentions. But the recognition of contingent necessity by our financial rulers is a weapon to help peace advocates overcome resistance on both sides of the ocean.

The widely supported campaign of the American Ministers Committee— protesting U.S. intervention in South Vietnam—fits in not only with the demands of advocates for peace and national liberation, but also with serious financial pressures felt by Wall Street.

Of course, top U.S. industrialists haven't given up the cold war. They remain dangerous, aggressive and imperialist—ready to start a thermonuclear war against progressive social forces any time they think they can get away with it. But they are increasingly being blocked.

The arrogant big financiers are finally having to recognize the changed balance of forces in the world, to understand that they cannot blow up the world's revolutions without causing their own destruction. Long drugged by munitions profits, they are also reluctantly learning that disarmament and peaceful coexistence may help them maintain some of their positions and save them from economic catastrophes of incalculable consequences.

Dulles [former U.S. Secretary of State] always sought to tie all the knots tighter and never gave up a position except when he was directly knocked out. But now Washington and Wall Street will consider loosening some knots, and recognize they may gain thereby. That is, I believe, a shift in policy.

• • •

2/21/1965

Essence of Johnson's Budget

The *Budget* and the *Economic Report of the President*, issued late each January, are the key economic policy documents of the administration in power. This year we must distinguish carefully between the cover and the content:

The President's Budget Message and Economic Report are reprinted or summarized in the media and discussed by commentators; the 480-page *Budget*, its 1,263-page Appendix, and the 268-page *Annual Report of the Council of Economic Advisers* are the documents studied by economists and corporation financial specialists, but little known to the general public.

The résumé features Johnson's "Great Society" slogans, restates his campaign promises of the right to a job for every worker, to full education for all capable youth, to equal opportunities without discrimination for all citizens, to good housing, attractive cities, and access to the nation's natural wonders for everyone.

During and after the election campaign I commented favorably on Johnson's "Great Society" promises, and noted the need for massive public pressure for their realization. Now Johnson has made it clear that so far as he is concerned, these were typical political propaganda, which he has no intention of carrying out.

In some cases the full report directly contradicts the promises; in others it does so implicitly by omitting the necessary measures of implementation.

In essence it describes and promises to carry out those economic and financial policies most suited to the needs of U.S. big business at this juncture, in the opinion of the administration economists and financial experts. This means:

- Economic stimulation sufficient to guarantee increasing profits but not enough to heighten tension in the labor market and thereby raise labor costs;
- Provision of some additional schooling, health services, jobs and employment; provision of a more than ample supply of people trained for the modern industrial employment requirements—but not enough to reduce markedly the hardships of the rapidly growing youth population;
- Maintenance of the lucrative defense/space billions for the arms contractors, but with a decline in the number of jobs provided;
- Financing these activities with continued reduction in taxes paid by the wealthy, continued increase in interest payments to the bankers—with the working class paying the entire added expenses in the budget.

This program is calculated to keep the heavy burden of unemployment, discrimination, poverty, undereducation, inadequate health service, slum housing, on the masses of workers for the indefinite future—with slow, measured, reduction planned in the scale of some of these evils.

In honesty, we must criticize his duplicity. But we must not overlook the possibilities of the concessions offered. They go considerably beyond the economic and social steps offered by any prior postwar administration.

But reactionary politicians and business groups will try to scuttle or curtail concessions. The AMA has already intensified its crusade against the limited Medicare proposal. Labor, the Negro people, students and teachers, peace supporters, and all others directly interested will have to campaign very hard to obtain enactment of even the limited measures proposed.

The unity of all progressive classes and forces to campaign, in and out of Washington, is necessary to force the Johnson Administration and Congress to move decisively beyond its two-faced program, towards a genuine realization of its "Great Society" promises.

3/21/1965

Reversal on the Military Budget

In 1964 the USSR cut its military budget and the U.S. followed with a lesser cut. Again in 1965 the USSR cut, but this time the U.S. didn't. The Soviet defense budget was cut 4% each year. The U.S. cut was 3% in 1964-65, and nominally 0.5% for 1965-66. But adding other mainly military sections of the U.S. budget leaves a cut of only 1.5% in 1964-65, and a rise of 1% for 1965-66.

The new Soviet defense budget is only 12.8 billion rubles ($14.2 billion), compared with the U.S. "national defense" sum of $52.5 billion and a grand total, including related items, of $61.8 billion. Even allowing for lower Soviet military wages and weapon prices, the real USSR arms budget is far below the American.

On December 9th Kosygin explained to the Supreme Soviet the proposed defense budget cut as follows: "The representatives of the U.S. Government have submitted to us respective statements—that the U.S. Government also intends to reduce the military expenditures in 1965-66 fiscal year. Thus the reduction of the military expenditures of the Soviet Union—and the expected reduction of U.S. military expenditures—represent a certain positive step toward a relaxation of international tension."

The U.S. press discussed supposed informal understandings, and projected long-term substantial military budget cut plans. However, in his January 25th Budget Message, Johnson effectively canceled out the claimed informal agreement. Also, total obligational availability for the Defense Department was increased nearly a billion dollars. This can foreshadow a later rise in actual spending instead of a long-term downtrend. The budget does not refer to long-term cuts, but of further strengthening the armed forces without raising the budget "each year"—which implies raising it some years.

The Defense Budget continues to emphasize "general purpose" and "airlift" and "sealift" forces, those most involved in fighting wars of colonial conquest—as in Vietnam and the Congo. These components go up $1 billion to $20.6 billion; while the "strategic retaliatory" and "continental air and missile defense" forces are cut to $6.3 billion (obligational availability).

•

Besides apparently violating an informal agreement with the USSR, failure to cut the arms budget threatens to violate the pledge to the American people contained in the civilian sections of the budget.

The trend towards higher public sector spending, just getting started, became possible precisely because of the easing of international tensions in 1963-64, plus the subsequent modest cut in arms spending. Further promised gains in welfare outlays, inadequate as they are, are predicated politically on continuation of the easier trend in international affairs and corresponding reduction of the financial burden of the military.

Failure to cut the military budget was just the first link in a sinister chain. Next was expansion of the war in Southeast Asia. If this is carried through to any of the threatened next stages, the military budget will escalate by many billions. The whole character of the budget will change. All talk of raising federal welfare programs will end. Instead increases in taxes on the people will begin.

Apparently anticipating the new trend, big investors started bidding up prices of armament stocks in the second half of 1964. By February 17, 1965, Boeing went up from 36 to 70; Douglas from 21 to 37; General Dynamics from 24 to 39. Other leading arms stocks also rose.

The welfare and safety of the American people depend upon slashing Johnson's military budget—and the profits of the munitions makers.

• • •

2/12/1967

Budget Propaganda and Reality

The President's Budget Message is a propaganda document trying to minimize the cost of the Vietnam War and the resulting inflationary budget deficit. In 1966 Johnson predicted a rise in administrative budget national defense spending of "only" 7%, to $60.5 billion, this fiscal year. The increase is now estimated at 22%, to $70.2 billion. This column was one of the first (in mid-1965) to accuse him of grossly understating the cost of waging the Vietnam War. **Now** he claims he has learned his lesson. **Then**, he says, he expected the war would be over by June 1967. **Now** he doesn't calculate on its ending by June 1968, and concedes it might continue to expand thereafter.

But his statistics are doctored, as ever. This time they show a fiscal 1968 rise of 7.5% in administrative budget defense spending, and only $2.5 billion in Vietnam War spending, as against an admitted (and understated) increase of $13.6 billion for Vietnam in the present fiscal year.

This forecast is ridiculous. By the end of the present fiscal year, military expenditures will already be at an annual rate exceeding the $75.5 billion Johnson now projects for fiscal 1968. His proposed increase in military pay and manpower, other inevitable higher costs, his additional military programs, and even the relatively slow Vietnam buildup the Pentagon admits it intends, will bring the actual cost up many billions over its level at the start of fiscal 1968.

Johnson's budget estimate will prove realistic only if he stops bombing Vietnam, stops sending troops there, de-escalates the ground war, and starts negotiations with North Vietnam and the NLF by the beginning of the fiscal year. But that is not the present program of the administration, which aims to destroy Vietnam or to compel its surrender.

Johnson claims that the 1968 budget, including Vietnam, and the trust funds, "will account for only 1.5 percent more of our gross national product than it did 3 years ago." Here he becomes confused by his own triple bookkeeping. A chart in the budget message, which Johnson prefers, shows the national income sector, including trust funds, rising from 18% of the GNP in fiscal 1965 to 21% in fiscal

1968—despite the continuous price and other statistical inflation of its official statistics beyond actual production increases. That's a rise of 3%, not 1.5%, and brings the percentage up to the Korean War peak.

Johnson claims the national income accounts budget is better than the cash budget or administrative budget. He says the national income accounts budget has been used for three decades by experts to judge the impact of the *Federal Budget* on the economy. In fact, experts have used the cash budget as the most realistic measure, and rightly so.

The national income account records taxes when they become due, the cash budget when they are paid. But the main economic impact is when they are paid. For example, increased federal withholdings from paychecks since last April reduced consumer spending, even though there was no change in taxes due. And the consequent big tax refunds in the spring of 1967 will then lead to a sudden spurt in consumer buying, even though the national income accounts will show nothing.

The national income account excludes lending activities of the federal government, the cash budget includes them. But government lending involves a turnover of tens of billions of dollars yearly, and has a major influence on economic activity. For example, government loans for housing construction are being expanded now with the deliberate purpose of stimulating this depressed industry. Similarly, Export-Import Bank loans aim to increase production and export of the goods covered.

For once I agree with the *Wall Street Journal* (1/26) that the cash budget comes closest to providing a real measure of the impact of the *Federal Budget* on the economy.

Johnson's real motive for stressing the national income accounts budget this year is transparent. This method shows the smallest fiscal 1968 deficit, $2.1 billion, as against $4.3 billion in the cash budget and $8.1 billion in the old-fashioned, administrative budget. By emphasizing the lesser amount, Johnson hopes to allay fears of further price increases, and to head off demands for higher wages and for price control. This year with the estimated deficits, by the three methods, of $3.8 billion, $6.2 billion, and $9.7 billion respectively, living costs are soaring. All three of Johnson's 1968 forecasts are manipulated to reduce the apparent deficit through various devices, in addition to the understatement of prospective military spending.

Next year the deficit will be even larger than in fiscal 1967, no matter how it is measured, if the Vietnam War escalation continues. The pressure for higher prices and higher taxes on workers will mount accordingly.

1/23/1971

Socialized Sin on Wall Street

Poet: When you have time, please explain to me this law the President just signed insuring stock market investors.

Economist: Right now. In just 90 seconds. It's to insure stock market investors and speculators against losses when their brokers go broke.

P: Why does the stockholder care if the broker goes broke?

E: Because the broker has the stockholder's money and his stocks.

P: Aren't the customers' accounts kept separate?

E: Yes, but. The brokerage house partners use their customers' stock as collateral for money they borrow to invest for their own profit.

P: Isn't that unethical?

E: Only if they lose. They're supposed to win. Only the customer is supposed to lose.

P: But I read that 200 brokerage houses went bankrupt or needed financial help last year. What happened?

E: "Bunny" Lasker, chairman of the New York Stock Exchange, went to see his old friend Dick Nixon too often, to get stock market tips. They didn't know what would happen when Dick invaded Cambodia.

P: So the brokers failed because they played hanky panky with Other People's Money?

E: Also, they had back office problems. It all came about because the business was so successful. So many new customers! 14 million share days! 16 million share days! The offices had to stay open overtime every night to catch up with paperwork. But nowadays the back office personnel do not have the right spirit. Too many are long-haired Hippies. Some are even Black or Puerto Rican. They want higher wages. They want extra pay for overtime. They no longer cooperate so that some day they too can become Masters of Capital.

P: Was there no solution?

E: Tom Watson came up with a solution. Computers! All the big houses bought big computers. It sent Overhead zooming, but it was supposed to save on wages. Unfortunately, the programmers didn't know all the ins and outs of the securities business. There were mistakes. The bigger the computer, the bigger the mistake. When a $10,000,000 computer makes a mistake it takes 10,000 clerks 10,000 hours to correct it.

P: How much did investors lose on account of brokerage failures last year?

E: Nothing yet. They were all promised payment out of $99 million put up by solvent members of the New York Stock Exchange. But that money has run out. Now with the government insurance scheme, everybody will be safe. The non-stockholding taxpayers will take care of them.

P: You mean it will become safe for the 20 million American stockholders to play the market?

E: Oh, no! No red-blooded American would want that! You have to be ready to lose if your stocks go down. It's just to insure you against unfair losses when the broker goes bankrupt.

P: How many brokers who lost other people's money were sent to prison?

E: Horrors, what a thought! Would you send Edmund duPont to prison? He was head of the second largest brokerage house. The duPonts took their capital out when it began to lose money. But the company was saved by H. Ross Perot—he got it for $10 million. Cheaper and more profitable than trying to rescue prisoners from North Vietnam.

P: Still, it seems as if there may have been some criminal acts.

E: Don't say that. Perhaps some of the brokers sinned a little.

P: I take it you favor the new law insuring stock market investors.

E: Yes and no. Without it people might stop playing the stock market, and then where would the financial wizards get their money? But there's a dangerous side to it. It's socialized sin. Who knows what that might lead to? Even socialized railroads.

P: Perhaps that may be necessary with even the Penn Central going bankrupt.

E: Nonsense. The industry is really flourishing under private enterprise. Look at Grand Central Station. Nobody goes to the information desk any more. All the crowds are around the Merrill Lynch booth, trying to get a peek at the prices flashing on the board. And soon the ticket booths of the bankrupt New Haven will reopen for Off Track Betting! Who cares if the trains stop running!?

• • •

4/8/1971

How to Balance the State Budget

Legislators in Albany are wrangling over the $7.5 billion New York State budget. They are arguing about how to close a deficit of several hundred million dollars by raising taxes on the working people and cutting public services. New York City and other communities are in deep financial trouble.

The largest single source of local revenue is the real property tax. This falls mainly on workers as home owners or tenants. But in modern capitalist society the main form of property is not bricks and mortar, but pieces of paper. Stocks, bonds, notes, and mortgages are the "intangible" property that enables the multi-millionaires to own and exploit the country.

This "paper" is almost wholly untaxed, and the New York State Communist Party has raised the issue of how much a 1% tax on such property would yield for the state.

The value of such "intangible" property in the United States will reach $3 trillion by the end of this year. Over one-sixth of it, or more than $500 billion, is owned in New York, divided more or less evenly between individuals on the one hand, and giant banks, insurance companies and other corporations.

A 1% tax would yield $5 billion this coming fiscal year. That would provide for over one quarter of all the general expenditures of New York state and local governments combined. It would be enough to meet the most urgent requirements of the people and permit cancellation of the sales tax, instead of its increase.

All such tax receipts should be distributed to the cities and localities, taking into account not only population, but also:

- The amount of industrial production in the area;
- The degree of financial activity, the role of the locale as a business center;
- The percentage of unemployment; of inadequate and/or substandard housing;
- The requirements of Black and Puerto Rican peoples, recognizing their more-than-average need for municipal services, per capita, because of the special oppression to which they are subjected.

With such a formula, New York City would get at least half the $5 billion in the coming fiscal year.

• • •

6/29/1978

Inflation Profiteers

Polls show inflation as the main concern of the public. It is cutting the living standards of the working people, and is a central feature of the crisis in the American way of life.

But it isn't hurting everybody: It brings superprofits to those who cry loudest about it. Monopolists want "moderate," controlled inflation, to be achieved at the expense of **workers**. The people want to end inflation at the expense of the **monopolies**, to restore social services, to end racism.

In his State of the Union message, President Carter called for a deceleration of wages and prices. The monopolies accelerated price increases and are preparing for formal wage control. But meanwhile they hope to have the best of two worlds by effecting wage control through intensive propaganda, lockouts, anti-strike laws, collaboration with right-wing labor officials, and intensified racist discrimination.

While Robert Strauss and Barry Bosworth, Carter's "inflation fighters," applaud Bethlehem Steel for "only" increasing prices 20% in the last year, real wages have been trending downward, with cyclical fluctuations, for 6 years. In the first quarter of 1978 real wages were officially 3.3% below the 1972 level.

The **announced** goal of big business and the administration is to hold wage increases to 5% or less. Since prices are increasing at a rate of 10% per year or more, and this is expected to continue, this is a program to cut real wages by 5% per year.

The **unannounced** goal is to use wage cuts to demoralize the unions and, where opportunity offers, to smash them by using scabs and injunctions, as with the Coors Brewery.

Labor Department figures show a steady deceleration of wage increases over the past 3 years, and the 5% rise formula is being put over in more cases. In January, service workers in New York City were saddled with a 3-year contract at under 5% per year. The same is happening in many new construction contracts; and in some cases union construction workers are pressed into accepting direct wage cuts to avoid losing the work to non-union contractors.

The coal miners, through months of struggle, supported by workers and farmers throughout the country, turned back the mine owner/government offensive. But even their settlement calls for a compound rate of wage increase of 8% per year, signifying a likely 2% per year cut in real wages.

Employers are aiming their main blow at the most vulnerable sector—the public workers in the big cities. These workers are restricted by special laws limiting or denying the right to strike. Here wages are not paid directly by the industrialists, but from taxes paid by the people of the cities themselves—after Washington has taken its slice; after the employers, who profit from city workers' labor, pay their taxes elsewhere; after the bankers have taken "their" interest.

Moreover, the deepest attacks are against big cities with high percentages of minorities. It is part of the reactionaries' racist offensive that is compounding the urban crises, especially in these cities. And New York City, the bailiwick of the most powerful financiers, has been the target of the sharpest assault. The layoffs there were far more severe than anywhere else. And now New York City municipal workers are threatened with a settlement, agreed to by their union officials, that will give them two 4% wage increases spread over 2 years. With the 10% per year rise in living costs, they will end up with an 11% cut in real wages, over and above their loss during the recent wage freeze.

Then there is the real problem: the excess of taxes New York City pays to the federal government over the city's federal aid receipts is more than the entire budget of New York City. The military part of that alone is enough to rehire all workers, pay them all good wages, and provide first-rate services and housing.

In Detroit, the municipal workers and the city government are boxed in by the revenue and spending ceilings imposed by the auto magnates and the Carter administration. They are offered 4.5% per year, real wage cuts of 5% per year. And in California, the passage of Proposition 13 has imposed a one-year wage freeze on all state workers, which means a 10% real wage cut.

The offensive against the working class is justified as necessary to combat inflation. But this turns the facts upside down: workers do not cause inflation, they are its victims.

The monopolies and the government are using both inflation and wage restrictions as twin cutting edges to cut living standards and raise profits.

1/24/1980

Carter's War Budget

Spokesmen for President Carter boasted to *The New York Times* reporter Richard Burt that "Mr. Carter was the first peacetime president in the post-World War II period to increase the Pentagon's budget for three consecutive years." (1/9/80).

One can go much further: never in U.S. history has any president carried out such a rapid, persistent armament buildup in peacetime. In fact, his past and about-to-be-issued new budget, taken together, cannot be called peacetime budgets: they are budgets to prepare for aggressive war. That's the only interpretation possible for the escalation in and the emphasis on major weapons.

Carter deceives the public when he says his past increases in military spending have been "only 3% per year 'real' " and that he now calls for "only" 4.5% per year "real" in the next 5 years. When he talks about "real," he dismisses most of the increase in spending by attributing it to inflation.

It's proper to talk about "real wages" corrected for inflation because $100 of wages today can buy much less than $100 three years ago. But it's wrong to talk about "real missiles" corrected for inflation because $1,000,000,000 of missiles today can kill more people, expertly, than $1,000,000,000 of missiles 5 years ago. The "progress" in destructive power of weapons is much faster than the general increase in prices.

When Carter talks about 3% or 4.5%, he is referring to the total military budget. But part of the military budget, when corrected for inflation, hasn't been going up at all. Before actual fighting begins, the number of men in the services remains virtually unchanged; the use of fuel and other supplies is relatively constant. It is only when actual combat starts that millions are inducted and vast stores of jet fuel, uniforms, medicines and other supplies are purchased.

However, the procurement of weapons is another matter. That is where the arms race is centered: in missiles, planes, bombs, warships. There is clear evidence that this part of the military budget has been accelerating more than 10% per year. And under Carter's new budget, it will go up as much as 20% per year!

The new budget will cover 5 years, fiscal 1981 through 1985. Enough has already been published to give a good idea of what it will show.

The big push, as in the past 2 years, is in procurement of major weapons—from $33.2 billion in 1979, to $55.8 billion in 1984, and to $89.2 billion in 1989 (*Fortune*, 1/14/80). That's an annual rate of increase of 10.9% for the first 5 years, and 10.4% for the entire 10 years.

A large part of the total expenditure for research and development goes to "improving" weapons and their components. Thus, the "quality" of the weapons, their ability to destroy people and property, accelerates more rapidly than their cost. The Pentagon, with its cost overruns and contractors' profiteering, gets "more bang for a buck" each year.

For example: a large and increasing proportion of all munitions expenditures consists of computers, electronic products, advanced communications equipment, etc. Their price/performance ratio is constantly **declining**.

The price index that the U.S. government uses to "correct" budget figures to "real" dollars ignores most of these quality improvements in weapons. It uses a false index of rapidly **rising** prices, as if the Pentagon were getting less materiel per dollar.

The "real" increase in the arms race is not the 5% that Carter says he plans, but the roughly 20% per year in current dollars that will be allocated for procurement. Such an inflated military buildup swells the political power of the military/industrial complex and the rightwing hawks, already heightened during the first 3 years of the Carter administration.

Slowing down and finally defeating the menacing military buildup of Carter and Co. will not by itself guarantee the avoidance of a military catastrophe. But without a major struggle against that budget, the probability of war, already high, will rapidly mount.

• • •

12/1/1983 & 2/9/1984

Reagan's Budget: A $200 billion deficit

This is a consolidation of two related columns that analyze and critique the budget deficit and the 1985 Budget and Economic Report of President Reagan.

Corporation presidents, economic pundits, financial columnists, all express horror over Reagan's $266 billion-plus annual budget deficits. They warn it will be inflationary, drive up interest rates, and cut short the anemic economic recovery.

These deficits will run around 7% of the GNP, a record in this century except during the two world wars. Even during the Great Depression of the 1930s, deficits were a smaller percentage of the GNP.

It's ironic that the arch-Republican, Reagan, mocks generations of Republican propaganda for a balanced budget by setting up these record deficits, which will expand further if he gets a second term. And it's ironic that the Democrats are borrowing the traditional budget-balancing rhetoric.

The present deficit is caused by Reagan's doubling of military spending, plus radical cuts in taxes paid by the corporations and the rich.

This particular deficit is a centerpiece of the capitalist assault on the working class.

But politicians and economists—except for Reagan and a few of his "supply side" ouija-board consultants—**are** worried about the huge shortfall. And for once they're right, although not always for the right reasons. It is estimated that the federal debt will reach over $2,000,000,000,000 ($2 trillion) by 1986, from about $400 billion in 1972—an increase of five times.

In 1972 the federal debt was one-third of the GNP. By 1986 it will be one-half. The **interest** on that debt will multiply 10 times, to more than $166 billion gross.

This is bad for workers, employees, retirees, youth, farmers, and unemployed for the following reasons:

The 10 times multiplied interest on the debt is going to the richest people and to the banks; it is being paid mainly by workers, who now pay most of the taxes— and their share is increasing; it's a huge redistribution of income—in the wrong direction.

Government borrowing competes with private borrowing for the savings that are offered for lending. When government borrowing is so great, demand exceeds supply, and the rate of interest goes up. Partly for this reason, interest has stayed higher longer than any time before in the history of the United States.

Total gross interest payments in 1983 passed the trillion-dollar mark. A large part of that was paid by workers on their mortgages, cars, refrigerators, TVs. A large part was paid by farmers and small businessmen. Those were direct costs. Even more were the indirect costs paid by workers through the higher prices they paid because corporations added their interest payments to the prices of goods. So again, there is a huge redistribution of income—in the wrong direction.

High interest rates hamper home buying, public construction, factory building and machinery purchases. That sets off economic crises and depressions, deepens them, and contributes to mass joblessness, bankruptcies, and foreclosures. Then the powerful monopolies and multi-millionaires pick up the pieces.

Vast amounts of foreign funds are flowing into the United States because of the high interest rates and for protection against revolutionary uprisings. That raises the value of the dollar in relation to other currencies, making it possible for foreign producers to export goods to the U.S. for sale at low dollar prices, holding down our inflation rate at the cost of millions of U.S. jobs.

The huge deficits are used as an excuse to minimize welfare programs, entitlements, hundreds of billons of dollars worth of urgently needed public housing, public works, facilities for health and education, and for job training.

They are contributing to the worsening quality of life, to the loss of jobs for millions of workers who would be employed under the eliminated public programs, to the worsening of discrimination against the oppressed peoples, who bear the main brunt of the cuts in federal civilian outlays.

And establishment economists are going for a deeper cut in all social benefits. Their major targets are where the most social money is—Social Security and Medicare. They want to reduce retired workers' pensions by a wide margin, far more than the limited cuts already imposed. And they want to radically reduce Medicare benefits, without cutting into the profiteering of the hospital corporations, drug companies, and all-too-many doctors.

The Congressional Budget Office has just published updated estimates of "tax expenditures"—loopholes to us—embodied in the present federal tax laws and collection procedures. The totals rise from $296 billion in 1983 to $493 billion in 1988, a small fraction of which are saved by workers. But just cut out the tax loopholes of the corporations and the rich, and the federal deficit would vanish and be replaced with a surplus!

Further, just cut Reagan's military budget—rising from $245 billion in 1983 to $433 billion in 1988—to a reasonable $50 billion a year for the actual defense of the United States, and there would be a 6-year total of $1¾ trillion dollars ($1,750,000,000,000), enough to rebuild America, eliminate poverty, finance equality, and provide full employment at decent wages.

10/4/1984

Figures Don't Lie, But . . .

Reaganites boast that real per capita income has increased 9% since he took office. I know statistics bore most people, but let's analyze the two-tone "magic" behind that figure.

Consider a capitalist with a yearly income of $100,000 and nine workers with combined incomes of $100,000. That makes 10 people with combined incomes of $200,000, for a per capita income of $20,000. Suppose that the next year the capitalist's income goes up 50%, to $150,000. The workers' income goes down 20%, to $80,000. The total income of the 10 people is now $230,000, for a per capita income of $23,000—an increase of 15%!! That's the only kind of real per capita income gain that has taken place under Reagan.

3/21/1985

The Dollar and Gunboat Economics

The dollar seems to have gone for a ride on the space shuttle, and reports of its rise on foreign exchange markets are front page news.

That means real gains for U.S. buyers.

Because of the rise in the exchange rate of the dollar, it is now much cheaper to buy a commodity or a service in many foreign countries than in the United States. Likewise, it costs less to produce an item abroad. Thus, it is profitable to import goods into the United States, and unprofitable to export goods. As a result, foreign imports to the U.S. have risen far above exports. The U.S. Secretary of Commerce estimates that imports will amount to $140 billion more than exports in 1985.

That translates to a loss of 4 million U.S. jobs in industry and agriculture.

Clearly, the dollar is overvalued. With world markets so interconnected, if exchange rates were in line with underlying values, they would balance so that effective prices of goods would be about the same everywhere.

Why doesn't this happen? Because funds for investment and speculation flow

10 times faster than for the purchase of goods and services, and hence determine how exchange rates move. In the modern world of capitalism, it is much easier to move money than goods from one country to another.

World trade in goods now totals $2 trillion each year. But world transfers of funds are in the range of $20-30 trillion a year. (No one knows exactly how much.) That is several times the total world production of goods. It is also more than the total amount of money, in all currencies, in the world.

The incredible scale of these financial transactions, and the absence of any controls over them, greatly increase the anarchy and instability of capitalism and give the giant banks more opportunities to drain huge tributes from the world's peoples.

Even a moderate lack of balance in these vast financial flows has significant effect on exchange rates. Thus the booming net flow of funds into the United States has pushed up the price of the dollar.

Throughout most of this century the U.S. was the world's leading **exporter** of capital. But for the last 3 years it has been a net **importer** of capital. There has been a marked slowdown in the amount of new dollar capital U.S. companies have invested abroad. That does not mean they have stopped moving production facilities abroad to get access to foreign markets, or to take advantage of lower wages. But they can finance these investments by borrowing in other countries, to take advantage of lower interest rates and the cheaper currencies.

Meanwhile, foreign capitalists have rapidly expanded their investments in the U.S. In 1982, the net import of capital was $9 billion; in 1983, $42 billion; and the preliminary figure for 1984 is $103 billion. There are two basic reasons:

1. Exploitation of labor in the U.S. has so increased that the rate of profit is higher than in most developed capitalist countries. As Leonard Silk, the economic columnist of *The New York Times*, put it (3/1/85), foreign capitalists are lured, among other factors, by "higher after-tax real returns on capital." The higher rate of interest in the U.S. is one reflection of that higher rate of gross profit.

2. Again in Silk's words, "the nation's political stability . . . makes it a safe haven in a turbulent world." To be more precise, the capitalists and puppet dictators of many developing countries, fearing national liberation movements and the strengthening mass pressure for socialist transformations, have poured billions of capital into the U.S. for safe-keeping. Even some West European capitalists, fearing powerful labor unions, strong Communist parties, and even mild reforms that might result in tax increases for them, invest their capital in the U.S., with its pro-big business, anti-labor administration.

While the flow of trillions of dollars of capital is not controlled in detail, it is very much influenced by the policies of governments, by the strategy and tactics of state monopoly capitalism. The Reagan administration, along with the financial oligarchs and the military/industrial complex, want this high-flying dollar and, with all the President's talk of deregulation, did much to bring it about.

Federal Reserve chief Paul Volcker frankly told Congress the motives behind Washington's high-interest policy: the U.S. needs the inflow of capital to finance its huge budget deficit. With lower interest rates, the inflow would stop and the dollar would tumble in exchange value. "We should be on our knees thanking God that we have such a strong dollar," he said. Once the dollar starts downward, Volcker warned, foreigners will pull their investments out of the U.S. to benefit from the high exchange rate before it is too late.

To take it one step further than Volcker admitted, without the influx of foreign capital, the soaring Pentagon budget, combined with Reagan's tax giveaways to the rich, would have to be covered by overextending the money supply. That would result in rampant inflation, followed by a drastic financial and industrial crisis.

So Washington does everything it can to continue the inflow, while Volcker manipulates the money supply to try to keep the "real" rate of interest (interest rate less inflation rate) high.

Also, the Treasury stopped withholding income taxes on the foreign purchase of U.S. government securities, making them even more attractive to foreign buyers. The U.S. presses Latin American and other debtor counties to impose "austerity" programs, which would pauperize and starve their workers, in order to pay interest to the U.S. bankers. This invasive policy leads to mass struggle and makes the U.S. even more of a "security" magnet for the ruling circles of developing countries.

In its own interests, U.S. intervention weakens the rest of the capitalist world.
- It drains capital that Western Europe needs for economic recovery and growth, so its industry stagnates and unemployment mounts.
- It is deepening the structural crisis of U.S. basic industry as European, Japanese and South Korean goods flood the American market to take advantage of the higher dollar-dominated prices.
- It is forcing 30% cuts in real wages in many Latin American countries, halting or reversing much needed basic development programs. To meet the super-high interest payments, they are forced to export to the U.S. the goods needed by their own peoples.

Jeffrey E. Garten, a former White House economic staffer, currently a Lehman Brothers Wall Street banker, estimated that the forced import of goods from Latin American debtors costs 400,000 U.S. jobs. He criticizes the complex of policies directed against the other capitalist countries as "gunboat economics," an unusually apt characterization (*Foreign Affairs* Vol. 6, No. 3, 1985).

That policy is part of the gunboat economic warfare against the socialist countries and developing nations seeking to take an independent course; part of the gunboat economic warfare against the U.S. working class, farmers, Black and Hispanic peoples. And it is part of the "covert" military war against Nicaragua, El Salvador, Afghanistan, Ethiopia and—in partnership with China, Israel or South Africa—against Kampuchea, Lebanon, Angola and Mozambique.

Popular support in the U.S. is sought by claiming that the high exchange value of the dollar slows the rise in living costs. That is true, but this is more than offset by negative effects:

- It contributes to high unemployment, which is used to reduce real wages, worsen working conditions and break unions.
- It aims to put over Reagan's anti-people budget, including absolute reductions in many welfare items, and a major cut in Social Security benefits now being plotted in Congress.

These negatives far outweigh any gains resulting from a slightly slower rise in living costs. With a half trillion dollars a week of currency exchanges, shifts in the direction of flow caused by the elemental force of capitalist greed are bound to dominate. And sooner or later "what goes up must come down." Speculation that pushed the dollar far above its value in terms of comparable buying power will pull it back down. The further the overvaluation of the dollar goes, and the longer it lasts, the sharper and more drastic will be its reversal, and the more severe its inflationary impact on the U.S. economy.

• • •

8/8/1985

Gross Profits = Profits of Control

Fortune's cover story for July 22 is on "Executive Perks"—the many ways in which corporation officials get huge benefits over and above their enormous salaries. The author, Felix Kessler, says these perquisites (perks) are under fire because they have become so flagrant as a means of siphoning off profits to avoid taxes.

Reagan's "tax reform" program pretends to impose limits on perks to "reasonable" amounts. For example, a limit of $25 for a "business lunch." "If you're going to have three martinis, you'll have to skip the lunch," quips Kessler.

Kessler points out that these perks have "more than held their own." He cites as examples super-limousines provided by the company; vacations with complete medical checkups at the luxurious Greenbriar Inn in West Virginia; $100,000 [$112,918] a year apartments near corporate headquarters for the top brass when they have to work late; loans of millions of dollars at only 2% interest; country club memberships, legal and financial advice, etc.

The huge salaries, bonuses and perks of the high-level corporate officials are an important part of what I have called the "profits of control" in my book, *The Empire of High Finance*. That's what the key shareholders—who own enough stock to control the corporation, select its directors and top executives, and decide from whom to buy and to sell—are able to take out of the gross profits of the corporation.

Profits of control also include stock options; chipping off highly profitable segments of the corporation for personal ownership through "leveraged buyouts"; putting relatives, close friends and loyal associates in top management positions; and taking advantage of advance knowledge of profit ups and downs.

These profits of control drive such highly publicized corporate takeover operators as T. Boone Pickens, Carl Icahn and Ted Turner to borrow billions in order to gain control of large corporations by offering high prices to stockholders. Along with the principals are wealthy associates and bankers who will participate in the "take" if the takeover succeeds.

In general, profits of control far exceed stockholders' receipts. That can be seen if we examine the distribution of **gross profits**. Exxon reported a gross profit of $32.8 billion in 1983, or 6½ times its **net income** (after taxes) of $5.0 billion. IBM reported a gross profit of $23.8 billion, or 4 times its net income of $5.5 billion.

The gross profit just about equals the **surplus value**—the amount that the workers produce over and above what they are paid. For U.S. manufacturing, the surplus value—or gross profits—equals 2½ to 3 times the wages paid to production workers.

While the Internal Revenue Service does not publish a gross profits figure for all corporations—and only about one out of three corporations actually publishes the gross profits, usually in the back of the annual reports—it can be calculated by subtracting the cost of sales and operations, plus depreciation, from the total of business receipts.

For 1981 gross profits came to $1,538 billion. Of the $1,538 billion gross profit, only $209 billion was reported as net income before taxes, against which only $58 billion was paid in U.S. income taxes and $126 billion paid out in cash to stockholders.

The compensation of corporate officers, together with their pension, profit-sharing, stock bonus and annuity plans, came to $172 billion, **exceeding dividends to stockholders**. Some $555 billion was paid out in interest to bankers and others, partly from gross profits and partly from interest received not included in business receipts.

That leaves companies with a little less than $900 billion for wages and salaries for all production, or nonsupervisory, workers and employees in the entire private nonagricultural economy, including many workers employed by unincorporated bosses.

What's the point of such calculations? Workers face employers' demands for givebacks so they "can meet foreign competition." Youth face Reagan's demands for subminimum wages, which would hit Black and Latino youth especially, to "encourage business."

The only profit figures publicized, or shown to workers and their union representatives, are net profits after taxes, a small fraction of the gross profits. Generally, when losses are claimed, there are still very large gross profits.

Workers and their unions should insist on gross profits figures in their bargaining over wages and benefits.

That is what workers, who produce all the values and gross profits, should look at. The ratio of gross profits to wages and salaries of nonsupervisory employees has been going up very rapidly. It's time to reverse that trend!

12/19/1985

The Profit Orgy

Why is the stock market soaring to new highs? Production is sluggish; plants continue to close; unemployment and poverty remain rampant. Foreign debts, government debts, private debts are way out of bounds. There are predictions of a new recession, of financial calamities. Yet the Reagan bull market has roared into high gear.

The reason is simple: profits. With all the weaknesses, dangers and personal hardships, the capitalists' bottom line—profits—has zoomed under Reagan as never before.

Corporate after-tax profits, as adjusted by the U.S. Department of Commerce, are up 19% through the third quarter of this year over the same period last year. They have more than doubled since 1980, the last year before Reagan. The big jump in this third quarter sparked the latest stage of the bull market.

Where do the zooming profits come from? A small part reflects inflation. Most is from intensified exploitation of workers. It's the bonanza from speedup, layoffs, wage cuts, runaway shops. The squeeze on farmers means more profits for food corporations and banks. More and more comes from fleecing the people in other countries by transnational corporations.

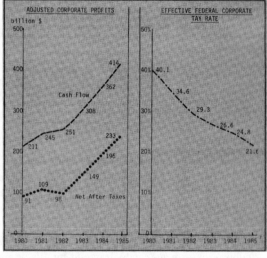

And let us not forget Reagan's reduction of the corporate income tax. Despite soaring profits, federal corporate tax liability this year has actually been less than in 1980. The average federal tax rate, as adjusted by the Commerce Department, has dropped each year, from 40.1% in 1980 to 21.6% in the third quarter of 1985. This makes a mockery of the official 46% rate that corporations are "required" to pay on their profits. Truly a cynical business!

Just a few figures: Adjusted corporate after-tax profits in 1980 were $91 billion; in 1984, $196 billion; in 1985 (third quarter rate), $233 billion. Even more to the point are the figures for adjusted corporate cash flow—the amount the controlling owners, banks and insurance companies have to play around with. In 1980 it was $211 billion; in 1984, $362 billion; and in 1985 (third quarter rate), $414 billion.

These vast sums are stimulating the wave of corporate takeovers, the fierce battles for control, the rush of insiders to buy off lesser stockholders and have it all for themselves by "going private."

These corporate maneuvers directly harm workers. The new control group examines the structure product by product, shop by shop, and tests each segment of the work force—blue and white collar—for profitability. All who fail the test of super-high profits are headed for the scrap heap. All pretense of anti-trust limitations on these manipulations has been abandoned. On the contrary, Reaganites boast of "deregulation."

The working class, through unions and political organizations, through shop actions, through struggle on a corporation-wide scale and political actions nationwide, can reverse the course of these developments.

• • •

7/25/1987

Inflation: What's Happening

A new round of accelerated inflation took off in the spring of 1987, beginning at the wholesale level, but certain to spread to the retail level. Between mid-year 1986 and mid-year 1987, the *Journal of Commerce* index of industrial materials prices rose 21%; the Commodity Research Bureau index, 13.5%; and the price of gold, 30%.

The zooming inflation of the late 1970s and early 1980s slowed in 1983 because of the economic crisis, the collapse of basic commodity prices—especially petroleum—and the temporary rapid rise in the exchange value of the U.S. dollar, which kept down prices of imports.

But the inflationary trend never stopped, and it remained significant. Official boasts that it had been licked were based on the "evidence" of the BLS consumer price index (CPI), which went up only 0.8% between December 1985 and December 1986. This index was used to knock down workers' real wages, senior citizens' real pensions, food stamp allowances, and real living standards. Since the actual increase in the cost of living was much more than the BLS figure, the wages, pensions, etc. that were adjusted according to the CPI were thus actually reduced significantly in real terms.

Irwin K. Kellner, chief economist of the Manufacturers Hanover Trust (MH), and his staff recognized that costs were going up much faster than the official version admitted. In 1984, the MH team began collecting actual prices in New York, and then they checked the same items two years later. They found, for the two-year period from January 1985 to January 1987, a 27.8% weighted average increase, as compared with the 5.3% admitted by the CPI.

Used effectively, these results are potential political dynamite; but the bank economists do not intend to carry these independent studies forward. They will, however, continue to study the trend of the major parts of the CPI, except for transportation and housing. That is significant because these sectors are the ones that are most distorted by BLS. Thus the MH calculations based on the BLS data—excluding housing and transport—increased only 9.4% in the two years ended May 1987, still considerably more than the 5.3% shown for New York by the CPI index.

Why is inflation accelerating? Primary commodity prices turned upward, including petroleum, the most important single basic commodity. The exchange rate of the dollar began to drop in the spring of 1985, but it was only this year that it reached a point where Japanese and other importers began to raise sharply the prices they charge for goods sold in the U.S.

Import quotas negotiated by the Reagan administration on behalf of U.S. monopolies enabled U.S. companies to raise prices domestically. Then the Reagan deregulation policy lifted all restraints on prices, reflected in this year's hikes in airline fares. Huge deficits, caused by the ever rising military budget and the massive tax cuts for corporations and the rich, are motivating a new upturn in U.S. interest rates, which raises prices and costs in many ways.

Business circles expect the latest acceleration of inflation to continue. *Fortune* forecasts "a dangerous climb" in prices for the next 18 months. Morgan Stanley, the prestigious Wall Street house, advises its millionaire clients to put 5-10% of their wealth into gold as an inflation hedge.

• • •

8/17/1989

The $1,000,000,000,000 S&L Swindle

The $169 billion savings and loan (S&L) bailout law marks a new high in financial corruption. The swindles of investment bankers, commodity traders and HUD officials pale in comparison. Also, this time the American people are the direct victims, programmed to pay an estimated $1,500-$3,000 per capita extra in taxes for the final bill—which will exceed $300 billion.

The law is not to protect the modest savings of low and middle income depositors—workers and employees. Of the nearly trillion dollars (million million) on deposit in S&Ls, only about 10% consists of accounts of less than $10,000, owned by some 30 million small depositors. This sum could be covered by the regular federal insurance premiums paid by sound banks.

Much more—the sum isn't revealed—consists of deposits of $100,000 or more. Insurance is supposed to cover only the first $100,000. Capitalists who want higher interest for larger amounts are supposed to take their chances that the banks will not fail.

In practice, the insurance agency has ignored this limitation, paying **all** depositors in full. How come? Take the millionaire who is not satisfied with the 8% interest on U.S. Treasury bonds and wants to get 12% just as safely on $500,000. It's been simple. He divided the $500,000 into five packages of

$100,000 each and deposited them under different account names or, better yet, in different banks. This ploy worked, mainly with the banks that were shaky: the ones that offered extra-high interest in order to keep afloat a little longer. Moreover, with a 5-year certificate of deposit (CD), depositors would be guaranteed the 12% for 5 years.

According to media reports, the first $15 billion will pay off the CDs in 250 banks already taken over by the government. Another $5 billion will be given as fresh capital to banks about to fail. In some cases it will be a giveaway to the present owners. In other instances it will go to banks that bid for the privilege of taking over the insolvent S&Ls.

In either case the owners, old or new, will get "clean" banks, without any bad loans or foreclosed property on their hands.

All of that mess will be taken over by the United States and placed in a new government bank, the Resolution Trust Company (RTC).

So hundreds of billions of dollars will be spent to take over the bad debts, to liquidate the 672 banks listed by the *Wall Street Journal* as almost sure to fail, as well as an equal number not yet named. And the RTC is expected to end up with $400 billion worth of perfectly good homes, office and commercial buildings, factories and other real estate—not for use in the public interest, but for sale to well connected capitalists at bargain basement prices.

The prospects for profit are beyond all normal bounds, a gigantic grab-bag for politically connected landlords, real estate operators, manufacturers and trading companies to get property for expansion at a fraction of its value.

The administration, with all its talk of privatization, will be setting up the world's largest financial institution as a government-owned bank. That's the logic of state monopoly capitalism! Whatever yields the greatest profits, starting with private or public ownership, is fine. Why set up the RTC? Perhaps because its function is to give $400 billion to monopoly capital.

Over the bitter opposition of the Republicans, a slight concession was made to progressive congressional representatives: for every $1,000 given away in the S&L scam, 50¢ will be spent on "moderate income" housing!

As this swindle becomes more evident, calls for redress will become stronger. Labor, consumer organizations, and fighters for integration and equality should raise demands, such as:

- Confiscate all deposits over $100,000, no matter how concealed, and use these funds to provide for people's needs.
- Provide jobs and, where necessary, retraining, for all workers in closed-down or marginal S&Ls.
- Make available all vacant foreclosed housing held by the RTC for low-cost, integrated occupancy, thereby providing hundreds of thousands of families with decent apartments.
- Nationalize the whole savings and loan complex, including the "good" parts as well as the "bad" slated to be turned over to the RTC. Convert the S&Ls to a chain of banks to provide convenient facilities for

workers' savings and as sources for low-interest loans. This would provide a major competitor for the giant monopoly banks, forcing them to provide better, cheaper services to the American people.

• • •

12/11/1993

The Great Deficit Scam

President Clinton's 1993 economic agenda, with its slashes in social services and betrayal of his promise of a jobs program, was put over with a big hue and cry about the deficit. According to the administration, the deficit was soaring to unheard of heights, which even the rigorous proposals of Clinton would take years to bring down to a tolerable level.

But "the deficit" is forgotten when it comes to spending for prisons and police, foreign interventions and the military.

The debate and action on Clinton's economic program took place last spring and summer. According to his *Budget,* published in April, the deficit was scheduled to shoot up from a record $290 billion in fiscal year 1992 to a shocking $322 billion in 1993 (fiscal years end in September). Even if his program were fully adopted, Clinton said, the 1993 deficit would still be $317 billion, and reduction would begin only in the following year.

Those who prepared that document must have known it was a lie, even if the President never bothered to check the figures. By the first quarter of fiscal 1993 (i.e., the fourth quarter of calendar 1992), the deficit had dropped sharply to an annual rate of $264 billion, with a further slight drop in the next quarter. In the spring of 1993, while the Senators were declaiming about the deficit, it fell to an annual rate of $223, and by summer—the final quarter of the fiscal year—to a rate of $211 billion.

That's more than $100 billion below the goal Clinton was aiming at in his deficit- and benefit-cutting propaganda. It is below anything predicted as far out as 1998 even without Clinton's program, and below what he predicted for 1995. The current deficit is 3.3% of the gross domestic product: the average for the ten-year period 1983-1992 was 5.5%.

Is the current deficit a "good thing?" Of course not. A balanced budget would be better, if it were balanced in the right way—implementation of programs to meet people's needs at the expense of the rich and the corporations.

But the present deficit might not be a particularly bad thing, if it were to be used for the benefit of the people and didn't increase the national debt faster then the national income. But that's the rub: it isn't used for people's benefits, but for their detriment.

Modern capitalism needs a deficit as long as exploitation and plunder are so extreme that the majority cannot buy enough out of their incomes to sustain economic activity. The budget deficit injects extra money into people's pockets, as a "fix" needed to stimulate economic activity.

When that fix is removed, economic activity runs down. In Mexico, under pressure of U.S. banks, Salinas has ended deficits and runs a surplus. Bang! The economic boom was replaced with a slump, with poverty and unemployment spreading.

Having used the deficit bogy to put over big business' program, Clinton has shifted his target, focusing on the "committee on entitlement spending and tax reform," headed by two right-of-center Senators who are planning to hire a Bush tax-aide as chief of staff.

All signs point to a new budget with a more stringent round of "entitlement" cutting—at the expense of the hungry, the jobless, senior citizens and the racially oppressed. The savings could be used for the police and prisons program and for "tax reforms"—i.e., new loopholes for the rich and the corporations.

Labor showed it could mobilize against NAFTA. Now is the time to organize labor's struggle against Clinton's forthcoming budget.

• • •

4/23/1994

'Inflation' Hokum Used vs. Workers

"Inflation" is the buzzword of modern capitalist economics—a word misused to be an anti-labor weapon. The old Webster's unabridged dictionary (1964 edition) defines inflation correctly as "an increase in the amount of currency in circulation, resulting in a relatively sharp and sudden fall in its value and rise in prices."

That situation occurred when "continentals" were issued during the U.S. War for Independence and, although somewhat restrained by price controls and rationing, when there was a huge amount of currency issued during World War II. Essentially, there is inflation when money in circulation is far more than the available supply of goods. That is happening now in the former Soviet Union, in victims of capitalist counterrevolution, in Brazil, and in some other countries oppressed by imperialist intervention.

Shortly after World War II, capitalist economists revised the definition of inflation to mean any rise in prices. Catering to these economists, the new editions of standard dictionaries have amended the meaning of inflation. E.g., the 1992 *American Heritage Dictionary* defines an inflationary spiral as "A trend toward ever higher levels of inflation primarily as a result of inter-active increases in wages and prices." The implication, being stressed in all the media, is that workers' wages cause inflation.

Because of monopoly power, consumer prices are always rising, faster or slower—even in a period, like the present, when raw material costs and real wages are falling. That makes an exceptionally palatable spread for the rich, causing their profits and incomes to skyrocket.

Economic activity is expanding after several years of crisis and depression. By savage use of overtime and speedup, industrialists avoid rehiring, and the unemployment rate remains high—critical for African Americans and Latinos. But labor is restive: last year union membership went up for the first time in decades, and many significant strikes took place.

Capitalist policy is to keep unemployment high enough to retain a labor market balance favorable to employers. And Alan Greenspan, Chairman of the Federal Reserve Board, with his appointed—not elected—"open market" committee of regional bankers and officials, is the person chosen to execute this policy by raising interest rates.

Greenspan is known for hiding his intentions with longwinded gobbledygook about "inflation." But Stuart Weiner, a Federal Reserve economist of a Kansas City bank, laid down the line in public. As summarized by the *Wall Street Journal*, he suggested: ". . . the economy may be closer to its 'natural rate of unemployment' than previously thought. If so, qualified job seekers soon will become a precious commodity, and wages will rise. A 5.75 percent unemployment is generally viewed as 'natural'. . ."

But even that may be too low! Mr. Weiner continued: "Nonwhites tend to have a higher unemployment rate . . . than whites . . . [As a result] as the U.S. becomes more ethnically diverse, the natural unemployment rate is likely to rise" (4/5/94).

In other words, everything is proper to keep that "commodity"—the working class—in surplus supply. And to use racism to drive the white unemployment rate up to the high level of Black and Latino workers, just as racism is used to drive down wages of all workers.

Thus, when industrial production spurted late in 1993 and early in 1994, entrepreneurs decided it was time to put on the brakes. Alan Greenspan got out his inflation worry beads. Twice, by manipulating the financial markets, increases were forced in the interest rate. The aim was not to brake hard enough to cause another "recession" but just enough to keep expansion at the pace that provides a feast for capital and famine for labor.

A side effect was turmoil in Wall Street, with bond and stock prices tumbling. That has stabilized for the time being, but financiers are giving Greenspan conflicting advice: some say go all the way to higher interest rates at once, to end uncertainty; others warn him to take it easy lest he plunge the country into a stock market crash and the worst crisis since World War II—such as Japan is now experiencing.

The influence of the "Fed" is not as decisive or inevitable as some think. But it is real. And isn't it an outrage that a small group of unelected officials and bank presidents—the "Open Market Committee" of the Federal Reserve Board—can act as the government regulators of the economy? And that their top man, a devotee of spiritualism and doubletalk, is able to mask the real anti-labor goal by talking about inflation while opposing even modest proposals for government caps on drugs and other monopoly goods and services?

8/5/1995

What Keeps the Balloon Up So High?

One day in July the Dow Jones average fell by more than 100 points. By the end of that day more than half the fall was recovered, and later in the month prices soared to new highs.

Many people thought a financial crisis was beginning. Maybe one will soon, but not then. The "blue chip" stocks are at stratospheric prices, a phenomenon that has foreshadowed significant market breaks in the past. The ratio of prices to profits (P/E ratios) are at peak levels. Dividend yields are exceptionally low; Microsoft and other high-flying high-tech stocks pay **no** dividends.

What keeps pushing stock prices upwards, although with sharp day-to-day instability? It is the law of supply and demand. The demand for shares of common stocks keeps increasing faster than the supply. Demand increases rapidly for these reasons:

- Blows of capital on labor, which increase the rate of exploitation and profits and widen racist differentials, with resulting superprofits; rapid immigration from Latin America, the Caribbean and parts of Asia, making millions of workers available to pull down the overall wage level. While 10 to 20 million people share in the profit feast—bankers, brokers, industrial bosses, professionals, small enterprise owners, government and corporate bureaucracy—few get the fabled multi-million dollar rake-offs. But receipts that accrue to lesser capitalists are considerable.
- In a society where gambling has become big business, it's easier and cheaper to "play" via a phone call to a broker than to fly to Las Vegas; and the potential for winning is much greater.
- Avalanche of investments in the mutual fund business. Pages of financial sections quote prices on thousands of mutual funds, and smaller investors or speculators can buy into a package of multiple stocks.
- Foreign money. The flow of capital into the United States now exceeds new foreign investments by Americans and their corporations. The investors include plunderers fleeing turmoil and mass struggles in Latin America, profiteers from the destruction of the USSR and from global "privatization" campaigns, oil barons and drug racketeers.
- The sharp fall in the exchange rate of the dollar against key foreign currencies, making U.S. stocks cheaper to Japanese, Germans, Swiss, etc., than to Americans.

Meanwhile, the supply of additional stock is small, or non-existent, for two main reasons:

1. There have been relatively few sales of stock to the public by previously privately held companies, or sales of additional stock by established corporations.
2. Corporations are buying back shares in their own companies in order to raise the price of the remaining stock as the profits per share rise. This

enriches top executives from stock options and strengthens the position of the firm in the merger battle wave that is consolidating the monopolization of U.S. industry and finance.

The favorable demand/supply balance is reinforced by tactical successes of the ruling class. The huge Savings and Loan bailout is a recent example. Salvaging the failing Mexican banks by the United States is another.

All those factors result in inevitable periodic downturns in the stock market, become "corrections" rather than major industrial crises and depressions. Even the drastic stock market break of 1987 was made up in a year or two, and prices have multiplied since.

Where will it end? Will there be major financial-industrial crises, more serious than recent "recessions?" Almost certainly, because the successes of capitalism are also excesses, causing widening imbalances.

Whether they will go beyond the point of manageability, of too many economic balls to juggle at the same time, depends on developments in the class struggle, on the fight for national liberation, on battles for socialism, on conflicts among the imperialist powers, on blunders by the power brokers.

• • •

1/9/1999

Stock Market Bubble Will Burst

Watching the stock market has become the national pastime for the middle class as well as for capitalists.

There are tens of millions of "investors," most of them small scale. Stock market gambling rivals race track betting and playing roulette and the slot machines in the mushrooming emporiums.

Stock market operations, unlike other speculations, are affected by the real economic life of the country. "Bull" and "bear" markets influence the lives of most people, including the majority, non-investors.

Historically, stocks brought owners a share of corporate profits, through dividend payments. That's still true of preferred stocks, which, like bonds, pay a fixed rate of return. But the present highly publicized activity is in common stocks. And most common stocks, especially the high-flying "market leaders" like Microsoft and Yahoo!, pay either no dividend or only a nominal dividend of a fraction of a percent.

They are bought for capital gains—to sell for more than the investor paid for them.

1998 was the fourth straight year of stock market gains, as measured by the Dow Jones index of leading New York Stock Exchange (NYSE) issues and the NASDAQ index of stocks traded on the "over-the-counter" market.

Investors whose stocks have gone up fuel much of the increase in consumer spending, which buttresses overall economic activity and employment. Typically, investors with "paper profits" feel free to use their credit cards for purchases exceeding in value the actual money in their pockets.

When the stock market goes down, as it surely will, they'll be pressed to pay their credit card debts, they will have less to spend, and the declining consumer spending will start a cyclical crisis of overproduction—with rapidly rising unemployment of workers who never had anything to do with speculation.

A handful of corporate monopolies dominate the stock exchanges and the economic life of the country. Smaller companies are being squeezed and become ready targets for takeover by the giants.

Large mergers soared in number and value last year, reaching $2.5 trillion, a sum equal to one-third of the gross domestic product, the standard measure of the size of economic activity. The pace of mergers and takeovers is expected to rise further this year.

Anti-trust laws are weakly enforced or ignored, easing the way for the predators to swallow up weaker prey in the capitalist jungle. This is related to, and part of, the process whereby the rich are rapidly getting richer while the poor are getting poorer. Those in the middle are losing ground more slowly.

The soaring stock prices of the corporate behemoths have gone beyond any reasonable relation to their profits, creating an expanding bubble awaiting the shock that will cause it to burst, with disastrous impact on the economic life of the country.

My blanket is shrinking all the time!

Finance II: Dollar Crisis

8/10/1963

Instability of the Dollar

The instability of the dollar has again approached a crisis stage. From a slightly curtailed $2.2 billion in 1962, the deficit in the balance of payments jumped to an annual rate of $3.2 billion in the first quarter of 1963, and still higher in the second. Again financiers, fearing devaluation, are taking money out, aggravating the statistical picture. Foreign central banks hint at impending conversion of their dollar stockpiles into gold, at the expense of the dwindling U.S. reserves.

Thus earlier administration efforts to balance accounts by the end of 1963 are reduced to naught, and the situation is more precarious than ever: there is less gold, and more billions of short term claims against it.

The main cause of the deficit is the U.S. annual outlay of $5-$7 billion to support its worldwide power position. The Eisenhower and Kennedy administrations both tried to eliminate the deficit without removing or really reducing this central cause. They failed.

Now the President has sent Congress a new superficially more vigorous program (7/18.) But this, too, is likely to fail. Treasury Secretary Dillon's statement (7/8) explains the philosophy behind the program. He said any measure taken must continue the policy of non-interference with the freedom of capitalists to do what they want with their capital, and must "continue to meet our special responsibilities as world banker."

That is, Wall Street's 'dictat' must take priority over the welfare of the nation. Hence, says Mr. Dillon, simple and direct means of dealing with a balance of payments deficit are out of the question. These include currency devaluation, exchange and capital controls, and "abandonment of our commitments for the protection of the free world."

But if the U.S. will not abandon any bases or foreign dictators it keeps in power—i.e., "our commitments"—and will not restrict the freedom of giant banks to move funds out of dollars into West German marks and Swiss francs, or of giant corporations to establish runaway shops and mines, it may not be able to avoid currency devaluation. Mr. Dillon has proclaimed a set of mutually inconsistent goals, and Mr. Kennedy's attempt to achieve them all simultaneously must fail.

The new program calls for cutting the cost of government activities abroad by $1 billion per year over a 2½-year period. This is too little and too slow, but that is not the main point. Like the previous program, this one aims to cut costs "without any reduction in the effectiveness of our military posture," a modified foreign base version of "more bang for a buck." Experience should have taught him that this cannot be done.

To "economize" would be to cut the profits of U.S. oil companies selling Arabian oil to the U.S. military in South Vietnam; of grain dealers hijacking U.S. surplus grain sent under "foreign aid" to Austria; of West German munitions makers and brothel keepers supplying U.S. armed forces there and providing a modicum of essential political support for the U.S. bases.

A presidential proposal to tax certain types of capital exports (but not direct corporate investments) ran into a squall of domestic and foreign opposition, and probably will be dropped or watered down to insignificance. Other arrangements announced by the President, involving the International Monetary Fund and European central banks, will further add to Washington's ability to maneuver, and may provide another breathing spell. But these are not substitutes for long-run correctives.

Yet, other events and forces may impose on the administration real steps to curtail the balance of payments deficit. E.g., already Moroccans and Saudi Arabians have forced the closing of U.S. air bases, while Italians and Turks have arranged for withdrawal of U.S. IRBMs. Opposition to U.S. bases and investments is growing everywhere, even in Western Europe. Strengthened world peace forces may lead to international agreements, including reduction of foreign bases.

Influential domestic opposition to unlimited militarism and foreign bases, aside from the customary progressive-oriented peace advocates, is appearing. Major bankers suggest curtailment of overseas outlays. For the first time in cold-war memory, Congress has cut the administration's military requests and threatens to cut military foreign aid.

• • •

1/21/1968

Johnson's Dollar Defense

On New Year's Day Johnson proclaimed emergency measures to save the dollar at its present parity price of $35 for an ounce of gold.

The devaluation of the British pound late in November shifted the weight of international financial pressure to the dollar. There was an international "run on the bank" to exchange dollars for gold, and the U.S. Treasury lost a billion dollars of gold before the end of the year. Thus, the reserves to meet claims of dollar holders were running out, since the law requires that 25% be reserved as backing for currency in circulation.

For 17 of the last 18 years the U.S. has paid out more money than it received in international transactions of all kinds. For 10 years the deficit has averaged about $3 billion per annum; last year it was nearer $4 billion. Johnson aims to reduce the balance of payments deficit by $3 billion this year, which would nearly eliminate it. He hopes thereby to restore international confidence in the dollar and maintain the present parity with gold.

The financial expression of U.S. supremacy in the capitalist world has been the gold exchange system, whereby dollars have been regarded as being "as good as gold," and have been universally accepted as payment.

That system is breaking down. In much of the world, the dollar is no longer regarded as being as good as gold. And Johnson's measures, regardless of their short-run effect, will ultimately reduce confidence in the dollar because they restrict further the free convertibility of the dollar into gold or other kinds of money by imposing stricter controls over the flow of capital.

• • •

3/24/1968

Moving Off Gold Standard: The War on the Consumer

The U.S. has partly gone off the gold standard. The price of gold has gone above the long-fixed rate of $35 per troy ounce on all markets that are open.

The U.S. and six cooperating West European central banks have agreed on a joint plan to reduce the role of gold as a world money, and to form an exclusive financial bloc.

This is a stage of the Johnson administration's financial warfare connected with its Vietnam War escalation. And it signifies escalated economic warfare against the American people, with a climactic drive to raise taxes and cut all welfare spending to the bone, a preliminary step towards devaluation of the dollar.

Two months ago I predicted that devaluation could no longer be avoided. Since then, the race to get out of dollars and into gold or some adequately gold-backed currency became a gold hemorrhage, emptying the coffers of Fort Knox and the Federal Reserve Bank of New York at rates sometimes exceeding a hundred million dollars a day.

Finally, on March 15, the London gold market was closed; and the bankers of the U.S., U.K., West Germany, Switzerland, Italy, Belgium and the Netherlands met in Washington on a rescue operation.

The U.S., to show its "sincerity" to the European bankers, agreed to institute an "austerity" program, raising taxes, cutting civilian government spending, and striving to hold down wages so as to cut imports.

But bankers universally agree that nothing is settled permanently. Within a year—some say within a few months—they think the U.S. will either have to largely balance its international payments or formally devalue the dollar in relation to gold. But the Johnson administration has no intention of balancing its payments. One key sentence is in Edwin L. Dale Jr.'s story from Washington:

"It was reported on excellent authority that the President would not and could not do what some financial men most want—pledge to send no more troops to Vietnam." (*The New York Times,* 3/16).

Thus, the U.S. will tend to run a larger deficit in its balance of payments to finance its pending Vietnam escalation. Cooperating continental powers will take credit for a little while, but will probably also drain substantial quantities of gold from the U.S. Congress has removed the gold cover from the domestic currency; and the gold stock, once over $24 billion, will soon fall below $11 billion.

The "normal" resolution of the crisis would have been an outright devaluation of the dollar, through an increase in the official dollar price of gold. This course was considered logical by the First National City Bank, and by many continental European bankers. It was strongly recommended by France. However, the Johnson administration has adopted the more combative plan advocated by the Chase Manhattan Bank, Bank of America, and others, for a two-price system and the attempted demonetization of gold.

The attack on the dollar has been no mere raid by "speculators" or "the gnomes of Zurich." Virtually all major corporations and rich capitalists, American and other, have been converting dollars into gold or stronger currencies. With the continued deficits in the U.S. balance of payments, the loss of confidence in the dollar will grow, and the movement out of the dollar will become stronger and more universal than ever.

The attempt to demonetize gold and reduce its value will fail, because its cost of production is so high, because its intrinsic utility in industry and consumption is substantial and growing, and because confidence in the value of gold is higher than in decades. The U.S. cannot destroy that confidence by decree.

The effect of the attack on the American people depends on how they respond.

It is likely that Congress will be blitzed into passing Johnson's surtax measure. As even the Washington pundits admit, this is like "hitting a fly with a sledgehammer" so far as the balance of payments is concerned. The idea is to sharply slash people's consumption, but only a fraction of consumption is for imports. Thus, a $10 billion cut in consumption might reduce imports and improve the balance of payments by a few hundred million dollars!

Despite the absurdity of this, the Johnson administration, with the central bankers solemnly applauding, will pull all stops to ram the surtax through. West German Bundesbank chairman Karl Blessing has given his blessing; and officials of Chase Manhattan and some other U.S. banks have demanded a surtax of more than 10%, some even calling for 20%.

In addition, the administration will push for a wage freeze, using the phony argument that it will cut production costs and make it easier for U.S. companies to export.

These arguments, from one viewpoint, show the crazy-quilt character of capitalist government economic regulation. But there is method to this madness: it is the basis for raising profits at labor's expense, for making labor finance U.S. imperialism's foreign adventures.

Ultimately, there will probably be a formal change in the gold parity of the dollar and a general realignment of currencies, with several of them having higher parities relative to the dollar than at present. Opinions expressed in the press are that this is likely to happen within a year.

But meanwhile the commodity price rises associated with devaluation are already beginning, and the tendency will be for them to continue. It is very likely that the cost of living will go up more rapidly than the 3% or 4% per year now officially admitted, and perhaps twice as rapidly.

It is especially important for unions to obtain inflation protection in their contracts, through escalator clauses, wage reopeners, short-term contracts, etc., and to plan for other joint action to protect their members from inflation. It is important to demand anti-inflation rises in social security and welfare payments, pensions of all kinds, and to demand the establishment of freeze and rollbacks of monopoly prices, especially of ghetto prices, rents, and service charges.

• • •

5/26/1971

Devaluation and Employment

Q. Will devaluation of the dollar help increase employment in the United States by substituting domestic goods for imports and by increasing exports?

A. To a small extent at best. Devaluation is rarely a powerful stimulant to employment. The United Kingdom devalued late in 1967, and unemployment has increased most of the time since, recently setting a postwar record high. France devalued in October 1969, and unemployment has increased 50% since.

Many elements influence the foreign trade balance of a country. Devaluation is rarely powerful enough to overcome a combination of factors worsening the trade balance for long. And also, a government devaluing its currency usually levies taxes simultaneously to slow up economic activity, to reduce the demand for imported goods. Employment loss exceeds employment gains as a result of devaluation.

The Federal Reserve Board has already reacted to the dollar crisis by reversing its policy on interest rates: They are now going up, instead of down, and there are fears that this will nip the just beginning upsurge in housing construction before it gets started.

The U.S. foreign trade balance has been worsening steadily for 25 years. For the first time in nearly a century, the United States no longer has a surplus of commercial exports over commercial imports. This is due **fundamentally** to the following factors: (a) The U.S. is losing ground generally in economic competition with rivals—in rate of economic growth, technical advantage, stability; (b) The aggressive U.S. foreign policy and militarization adversely affect foreign trade; (c)

U.S. corporations give priority to building plants overseas as opposed to exporting, so the expansive overseas empires of the multinational corporation make for a constantly worsening foreign trade picture; (d) The overvaluation of the dollar.

Devaluation impacts only (d): it is too little and too late to seriously improve the picture.

The dollar crisis makes the struggle of American workers to reduce unemployment more necessary than ever.

• • •

3/24/1973

No Way Out for the Dollar

In February, the devaluation of the U.S. dollar—for the second time in 14 months—failed to end the international monetary crisis. A further de facto devaluation is taking place as the world's currencies are "floating" without a fixed parity. This crisis is having serious effects on the economies of the capitalist countries.

What is behind the crisis? Where is it leading?

Since its first devaluation in 1971, the U.S. position in the world has deteriorated rapidly, economically and politically:

- Economically, President Nixon promised that the first devaluation would bring monetary stability and enable the United States to right its trade deficit. Instead the deficit multiplied from $2 billion to $6 billion.
- Politically, Nixon's mining and bombing of North Vietnam roused anti-U.S. sentiment everywhere. But the December bombing of Hanoi and Haiphong was the last straw politically: large sections of bourgeois opinion in Europe, which had been pro-U.S. out of class solidarity, finally turned against the U.S.

The economic deterioration undermined confidence in any ready solution to the dollar crisis; the political deterioration negated the willingness of capitalist governments to make further sacrifices on behalf of the dollar.

The current phase of crisis is accompanied by an acceleration of inflation throughout the capitalist world. Countries are flooded by dollars and other paper currencies of dubious value, providing the material base for escalating prices. Inflationary expectations add a powerful psychological boost.

It seems likely that actual living costs, as distinct from the crudely doctored official index, will go up 10% or more this year.

George Meany's (AFL-CIO president) advocacy of 7.5% wage increases in place of the administration's 5.5% ceiling is far short of the mark. To match the actual boost in the cost of living and the higher productivity, workers need wage hikes of 15%. Ha! Ha! So capital's share of the national income will continue to rise at the expense of labor's. Which also means that bitter strike struggles may be in the offing.

Nixon's post-Vietnam economic policy announced higher military spending in the budget and Phase III, ending price controls. High military spending fuels inflationary pressures; Phase III is removing the lid from the boiler; and the existing trivial limitations on capital exports are to be eliminated in 1974, thereby contributing to a further increase in the balance of payments deficit at that time.

These policy moves, plus publication of the disastrous 1972 U.S. balance of payments figures, started the flight from the dollar that brought it down. The capitalist giants all over the world participated: Europeans, the Japanese Zaibatsu—to the tune of billions—and the multimillionaires of all countries, including the U.S.

The differences from the 1971 devaluation reflect the intervening deterioration of the U.S. position. The first devaluation was limited to 8%. The recent devaluation started as a 10% cut; but this level could not be held, and a further devaluation is underway, of uncertain depth. Before new stabilization is obtained, the combined devaluations of 1971 and 1973 may be comparable in depth with the 41% dollar devaluation of 1933.

In 1971, the U.S. was able to exact concessions from its allies; but this time there were no concessions, and the United States had to make a sharper devaluation than in 1971.

Following the first devaluation, there was a period of partial stability, a return of billions of dollars that had fled to other currencies. This time, the crisis continued after the devaluation, with only a few days intermission. There still isn't any confidence, even temporary confidence, in the twice-devalued dollar. The price of gold has doubled in comparison with the "official" price. And, rather than spend more billions to support the devalued dollar, the capitalist central banks have scuttled the entire system of fixed exchange rates.

The capitalists of the world are beginning to understand some of the truths of the situation, to shed some of their favorite shibboleths, to lose faith in accepted remedies. Formerly, they believed that some adjustment or moderate revision of the existing monetary system could bring stability. Now they recognize that no stability is in sight. They understand that the capitalist world monetary system is in a deep and chronic crisis, which will be punctuated by more acute phases in the not-too-distant future. And that expectation contributes to the likelihood of still more serious, still more intractable crisis phases.

The main gainers from devaluation are the top capitalists of countries that revalue upwards, or do not devalue. They get their raw materials cheaper and can buy up properties and labor abroad at lower prices. Thus, from all the evidence, the Japanese Zaibatsu are making and will make huge gains from the U.S. devaluation. The capitalists of devaluing countries try to make it up at the expense of their workers, and that is what is happening in the United States now.

Another truth, long realized, is now being admitted: by accepting dollars to cover the U.S. balance of payments deficit, other countries are financing U.S. foreign military bases and wars. And Europeans have also known for a long time that their properties have been bought up by U.S. corporations with these deficit dollars foisted on their national treasuries.

Now the point has arrived where the major capitalist governments are refusing to finance U.S. military and investment activities in this way any more—at least for the time being. This does not make the U.S. balance of payments deficit go away. But it reveals the full depth of the crisis of the capitalist world international economic relations. The more drastic dollar devaluation now going on may reduce the U.S. balance of payments deficit in the area of capital flows, and perhaps tourism, if not in trade.

But there remains an underlying structural distortion, which the world's capitalists still show no sign of recognizing. And this is crucial. The giant U.S. corporations have been so successful in their overseas investments that they have transferred abroad the bulk of their production destined for competition in foreign markets. And these are exactly those U.S. companies in the strongest overseas competitive situation. They cannot and will not compete by using exports from the United States, as this will undermine their profitable foreign properties' sales.

Moreover, while big business collectively wants to improve the trade balance, the logic of intracorporate economics compels each giant corporation to bring into this country more and more materials, components and finished goods produced in their foreign installations. So long as this situation prevails, U.S. foreign trade will not be balanced, and the deficit will tend to grow.

The structural contradiction resulting from the huge U.S. foreign investments is still unseen by the world's capitalists, nor is there a readily apparent solution.

• • •

4/22/ & 5/4/1978

The Decline of the Dollar

The main cause of the decline in the value of the dollar is the huge deficit in the U.S. balance of payments—the excess of imports over exports, not only of goods but also of various "services" including, for example, income on investments.

The U.S. Commerce Department has published more exact figures, which show a 1977 deficit in the balance of payments of $20 billion. That's double the largest previous deficit, $10 billion in 1972.

Why has the U.S. been running deficits in its balance of payments for almost all of the past 20 years? At first higher U.S. labor costs were blamed. But now it is clear that U.S. labor costs are lower, or no higher, than in some of its most successful competitors, e.g., the Federal Republic of Germany and Japan.

Now the official line is to blame large oil imports. But that explanation doesn't stand up. The rising trend of deficits began before 1974 when oil prices escalated. Japan, which imports virtually all of its oil and coal, has a huge surplus in its payments balance.

It's true that in 1976 OPEC accounted for two-thirds of the U.S. trade deficit. But there were also big deficits with other countries: $10 billion with Japan and $4 billion with low-wage havens such as South Korea, Taiwan and Hong Kong. Moreover, about half the deficit with the OPEC countries was counterbalanced by income on investments in these countries, and charges to them for freight and passenger service, insurance, royalties, and fees for technical and military services, etc.

There are more basic reasons for the deficit, reasons that also explain why the United States, the world's largest oil producer, is also the largest oil importer.

The first reason is the huge military expenditure overseas: the cost in foreign currencies of operating the extensive network of bases and of maintaining the troops, air and naval fleets stationed in or operating out of foreign countries. An incomplete accounting of such costs—"direct defense expenditures"—came to nearly $6 billion last year. However, an approximately equal amount is hidden in other budget items, for a total of $12 billion. That's more than half the deficit in the balance of payments.

Another major item, not entering directly into the calculation of the balance of payments "on current account," is the foreign investments of U.S. corporations. In any given year, the net income to the U.S. from foreign investments is a plus in the balance of payments. But in the long run that is counterbalanced several times over, and results in a net loss, because U.S.-owned multinationals abroad—which have proliferated since the end of World War II—have shifted production from the United States to foreign countries. Consequent diversions from U.S. exports and additions to U.S. imports have mounted into the tens of billions of dollars yearly.

Over the long run, this explains why the United States imports more than it exports, and by a widening margin.

A third element, never measured directly but included in a catch-all that the Commerce Department labels "statistical discrepancy," is the "hot money" that big business, the multimillionaires and the CIA spread around the world in bribes to officials and the military of other governments; in runaway capital that deserts the dollar for gold or for "strong currencies"; in transfer of official residence and banking activities to tax-free havens in the Caribbean, Monaco, etc.

Of course, plenty of "hot money" flows into the United States, especially from capitalists and dictators who feel their political grip slipping. But for the past 20 years, much more currency has flowed out than in. In the last three months of 1977 alone, the net outflow was about $3 billion.

All of these items—the overseas military expenditures, the foreign stakes of the multinational corporations, and the bribes and other "hot money" outflow—are interconnected. They represent the military and economic essence of U.S. foreign policy: the use of bloated military power to open doors so that U.S.-owned big business can make huge profits and plunder the wealth and resources of other countries.

Because U.S. military power was dominant in the capitalist world after World War II, U.S. corporations were able to grab the bulk of the rich oil reserves of Asia, Africa and Latin America. Because this oil was so much more profitable to them than domestic oil, they preferred to import it rather than to develop domestic energy sources.

So long as U.S. imperialism was riding high, the booty paid the costs. But with the changing balance of world forces, with the victories of national liberation movements in many parts of the world, costs increased, and the booty no longer was sufficient to compensate. The declining dollar is the result.

The solution requires unwinding the "interconnected complex" of foreign military expenditure, foreign investment operations, and related matters.

Let the U.S. government accept long-standing socialist country proposals that all countries withdraw from all foreign bases. Let it stop bankrolling and supplying puppet or overextended allied armies, such as those of South Korea and Israel. Let it stop its CIA and related interventionist operations in other countries. These measures will save $12 billion a year in foreign currency, more than half the 1977 deficit.

This will not solve the entire problem. The withdrawal from foreign bases will remove the underpinning from the most exploitative foreign investments, increasing the ability of host governments to control the activities of U.S.-owned transnational corporations and, if they wish, to take them over. Some loss of investment income would occur; but this, in turn, might be offset by the decline in new foreign investments by U.S. corporations.

A related measure would be to remove all tax deductions granted to U.S. corporations operating abroad and to wealthy U.S. citizens living in foreign countries, largely to avoid taxes. Additional billions would accrue to the plus side of the payments balance.

Withdrawal from foreign bases would certainly signify a cut in military spending, and would logically accompany overall agreements to reduce armaments and cut military spending. This would lead to a saving of billions yearly in imports of oil and strategic minerals, now being brought into the country for use by the military and the armaments industry.

The name of the game, then, is peace and disarmament. That's the central theme of the course necessary to ease the balance of payments problem of the United States and to curb the long-time decline of the U.S. dollar.

Every wave of devaluation of the U.S. dollar has been amplified by the massive runaway of U.S.-owned capital to other countries. In the last analysis, to insure stability of a country's currency requires control over the flow of capital in and out of the country. This is very difficult to achieve under capitalism, although it was accomplished to a certain extent during World War II. To do this requires very rigid control over all banking and related financial operations, and, for really reliable controls, nationalization of the banking industry.

Thus the reforms suggested would tend to achieve a balance in our foreign payments, and thereby stabilize the dollar. But no reforms can guarantee stability in currency values so long as capitalism remains the prevailing economic system.

Marxism

09/05/1965

Exploitation of Labor

Labor spokesmen often use this term, "exploitation of labor," in referring to cases of exceptionally low wages. Here it is used in the strict scientific sense, referring to the fact that a substantial part of what all workers produce, even the well paid, is appropriated by the owners of capital. Correspondingly, a worker gets paid less than the value he contributes to the product through his labor. The rate of exploitation is the percentage ratio of the amount taken by capital to the amount going to labor.

Example: In 1963, of $190.4 billion value added by manufacturing, $93.3 billion was paid out in wages and salaries in operating manufacturing establishments. The remainder, or $97.1 billion, went initially to capital. The rate of exploitation of labor was 104%—that is, capital got 4% more than labor.

That is a very crude calculation, with obvious errors in both directions. Whatever the "real" rate of exploitation, it is too high, because it means that part of what some people earn is taken by others who do not earn it. The salaries the owners take for themselves are included with labor's share in this calculation. Everything else they get is a tribute for ownership, not a reward for activity. It represents exploitation of labor, even if part of it ultimately performs a necessary social function, financing capital investment.

•

The most important question is whether the rate is increasing or decreasing. Here there can be no doubt. Exploitation has been rising rapidly for the past 8 years, and especially for the last 5 years. The employers' share has been rising, while labor's share in the fruits of its toil has been falling fast.

A common way of measuring labor's share is to consider the ratio of wages and salaries paid to value added by manufacture. These ratios for the last four Census years—1947, 1954, 1958 and 1963—show that the share of all workers and employees declined only slightly for 11 years, but then rapidly, from 52.2% in 1958 to 48.9% in 1963. The drop in the share of production workers was sharper, from 40.7% in 1947 to 32.6% in 1963.

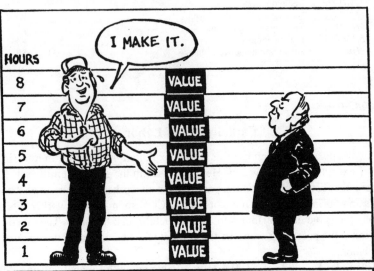

A more realistic statistical measurement compares workers' real wages—how much they can buy—with how much, in quantity, they produce. This comparison of two physical quantities avoids distortion due to differential price movements. Using official indexes, I have calculated index numbers of real wages and salaries paid per unit of manufacturing production for the postwar period. For the first 10 years they do not change much, but thereafter the decline is catastrophic.

Real Wages and Salaries per unit of Production, Manufacturing Index Numbers, 1957-1959 = 100

Year	Index	Year	Index	Year	Index
1956	101.5	1959	97.5	1962	93.3
1957	101.1	1960	96.4	1963	91.2
1958	101.3	1961	94.9	1964	88.9

The index fell without interruption from 101.3 in 1958 to 88.9 in 1964, a drop of 12.2%. There was a further decline of 1.7% in labor's share between the first half of 1964 and the first half of 1965.

• • •

8/23/1975

A Rare Admission

The New York Times carried a revealing column by David Finn, who is chairman of a public relations firm. He starts out with a seeming plea for less hypocrisy on the part of capitalists:

"Business credibility might improve if more executives were willing to admit, even to themselves, that the obligation to pay adequate attention to public needs has not yet become one of the requisites of sound management.

"The problem is inherent in the system. The corporation's success depends on how well it employs capital, not how well it serves society. Although men of conscience do not want their money used for immoral purposes, a good investment does not have to be good for society, it just has to be gainful for the investor."

Finn asserts that the facts of business life are such that "even the most community-minded executive" must "measure his performance by the financial health of the company, not the welfare of the people."

He cites as an example the way capitalism often fails to protect consumers from heavy losses, as when auto companies advertise large cars, but take no responsibility when the price of gasoline doubles, making the cars too expensive to operate. He doesn't go into the most basic contradiction—between the profits of the capitalists and the health, safety and living standards of its workers. Or how the owners of businesses derive extra profits from racism, which is contrary to even the crudest human standards of morality. Or, finally, how business profit-seeking is the root cause of the wars that kill so many millions, and today threaten the entire world.

Having recognized the evil, at least in part, Finn is really at a loss as to a solution. He says the answer **is not** to denounce the critics of business. He says they are making a "vital contribution to the health of our society" by making business "more responsible." Nor is the answer in typical self-serving business propaganda. No, he concludes:

"The reputation of business will improve when the businessman makes it clear that enduring human values are his first concern, and that he, along with his critics, has his eye more sharply focused on the future of mankind than on his company's balance sheet."

This final paragraph is worthy of an exclamation point! It directly contradicts everything Finn says in the body of the article. Perhaps it is meant to advertise the services of his firm, which he believes can do the impossible: putting over an image of business that the public has rejected and which real life, he admits, makes totally false.

Lenin gave a fitting answer to Mr. Finn 60 years ago, when he wrote:

"It goes without saying that if capitalism could develop agriculture . . . if it could raise the living standards of the masses, who in spite of the amazing technical progress are everywhere still half-starved and poverty-stricken, then there could be no question of a surplus of capital. . . . But if capitalism did these things it would not be capitalism—for both uneven development and a semi-starvation level of existence of the masses are fundamental and inevitable conditions and constitute premises of this mode of production. As long as capitalism remains what it is, surplus capital will be utilized not for the purpose of raising the standard of living of the masses in a given country, for this would mean a decline in profits for the capitalists, but for the purposes of increasing profits by exporting capital abroad to the backward countries. In these backward countries profits are usually high, for capital is scarce, the price of land is relatively low, wages are low, raw materials are cheap." (*Imperialism, the Highest Stage of Capitalism, Collected Works of Lenin*, Vol. 22, page 241.)

The capitalists know the score perfectly well, but they will continue to hire public relations experts to give an "image" of "concern" for "enduring human values"—especially somewhere far away—to divert attention from their own smashing of every human value.

The answer has to be given by the people, led by a united working class. It has to be not in improving the image of business, but by abolishing private capitalism, and replacing it with socialism. That was Lenin's solution. It has been applied in 14 countries and is in the process of application in a number of others. It is just as necessary here.

1/31/1976

Lenin on Mellon

When I read that the Mellons kicked out the chairman of Gulf Oil, Bob R. Dorsey, for involvement in the company's massive international bribery, I reached for my Lenin (*Imperialism, Collected Works*). For we have here a truly classic case, bringing out a number of features of the operations of modern imperialism:

"The banks have developed from modest middleman enterprises into the monopolists of finance capital. Some three to five of the biggest banks in each of the foremost capitalist countries have achieved the 'personal linkup' between industrial and bank capital, and have concentrated in their hands the control of thousands upon thousands of millions which form the greater part of the capital and income of entire countries. A financial oligarchy, which throws a close network of dependence relationships over all the economic and political institutions of present-day bourgeois society without exception— such is the most striking manifestation of this monopoly" (*Vol. 22*, p. 299).

The Mellons, along with the Rockefellers and the Morgan group, rank among the "three to five" biggest financial-industrial magnates who dominate the economic and political life of the United States. And Gulf Oil is the most lucrative prize in the Mellon family empire.

"Finance capital, concentrated in a few hands and exercising a virtual monopoly, exacts enormous and ever-increasing profits . . . strengthens the domination of the financial oligarchy and levies tribute upon the whole of society for the benefit of monopolists" (*Ibid.*, p. 232).

And today in the United States, we are paying such tribute in the hundreds of billions of dollars yearly—as exploited labor in the factories, farms, mines and offices; as taxpayers; and as payers of monopoly prices.

"It is characteristic of capitalism in general that the ownership of capital is separated from the application of capital to production, that money capital is separated from industrial or productive capital, and that the rentier who lives entirely on income . . . is separated from all who are directly concerned in the management of capital. Imperialism, or the domination of finance capital, is that highest stage of capitalism in which this separation reaches vast proportions. The supremacy of finance capital over all other forms of capital means the predominance of the rentier and of the financial oligarchy; it means that a small number of financially 'powerful' states stand out among all the rest" (pp. 238-239).

Bourgeois economists conduct endless studies to identify which companies are "controlled" by "outside directors," i.e., by finance capital, and which by "inside directors," that is, by the managers. But they are all controlled by the money men with the controlling block of shares—although in some cases, generally less important, these finance capitalists also engage in direct management of major enterprises.

Thus the Mellon family, with its 20% of Gulf Oil stock, was able to dictate the firing of the chairman of the corporation, of three other top officials, and to grease the skids under the former chairman, E. D. Brockett. And the efforts of Dorsey to save his post with the support of less powerful directors were in vain.

The publicized cause of the firing was the identification of Dorsey's chairmanship with the exposure of tens of millions in political and commercial bribes paid out by Gulf Oil, in this country and abroad.

Lenin writes: **"The rentier state is a state of parasitic, decaying capitalism, and this circumstance cannot fail to influence all the socio-political conditions of the countries concerned"** (p. 278).

This parasitism and decay are associated with the massive export of capital to derive superprofits from colonies and other countries with lower wages, and among its symptoms are systematic corruption and bribery.

Lenin mocks the "amusing petty bourgeois" morality arguments of a German critic, who worries about **"how 'costly' are the millions in bakhshish [bribes-VP] that Krupp has to pay in floating foreign loans, etc. But the facts tell us clearly: the increase in exports is connected with just these swindling tricks of finance capital, which is not concerned with bourgeois morality, but with skinning the ox twice—first, it pockets the profits from the loan; then it pockets other profits from the same loan which the borrower uses to make purchases from Krupp"** (p. 292).

The "monstrous facts concerning the monstrous rule of the financial oligarchy," which had become "glaring . . . in all capitalist countries" (p. 227), have become immeasurably more vile and rotten today. The millions have become billions; and in the area of corruption, it is not merely bribing foreign or domestic buyers to obtain orders, but much more the buying of politicians and generals to sell out their countries. And not only direct purchase by separate financial groups, but their combined use of the U.S. government to conduct such operations on a scale of tens and hundreds of billions, as in Vietnam and Angola.

The profits of the financial oligarchy have multiplied many times, but the opposition to their plunder has multiplied even more—in developing countries, where national liberation movements' battles are supported by the socialist community; in the capitalist countries, where the working class battles for socialism. And in the United States, where broad sections of the population, cutting across social classes, feel the weight of monopoly oppression, and force into the glare of publicity more and more facts about the evil deeds of the financial oligarchy.

Digging into the cesspool of corporate corruption has so far turned up to public view $400 million in bribes, which cannot be more than 1% of the bribes paid out by U.S. corporations in the last several years, and an even smaller segment of the amount spent on their behalf in similar ways by the CIA, the Pentagon, and other agencies of the U.S. government.

In firing Dorsey, the Mellons put on a show of moral righteousness—"A new benchmark for corporate morality," groveled the *Wall St. Journal* (Jan. 15). And in the article headlined a "Morality Play"—it should have been "Morality Farce"—

the writer spread the story that a nun on the board of directors cast the deciding vote on the side of the Mellons and righteousness.

As if the Mellons were oblivious to the bribes paid decades ago, long before the time of Dorsey, to get a 50% share of Kuwait oil! Or to the use of the CIA and its puppets in Bolivia to murder Che Guevara when his guerrilla forces targeted Gulf Oil's properties there! Or to the payoffs to the Portuguese colonialists to get the Gulf Oil concession in Angola, which Kissinger and the CIA are now spending tens and perhaps hundreds of millions to save for the Mellons, including vast bribes to the chief puppets, Mobutu, Roberto, and Savimbi! And who knows what deals there are with the South African racists?

Nor have the Mellons been known to refuse a penny of their share of the billions in profits racked in by Gulf Oil in the past decade, profits that recovered all the bribes paid by the corporation tens of times over.

No. Dorsey is the fall guy, let go to try to quiet domestic resistance to the plunder and decay of the financial oligarchy; to try to clear the way for even more monstrous CIA interventions and corporate bribes on behalf of the Mellons and their fellow oligarchs; to try to make a distinction between "legal" and "illegal" bribery. Dorsey's replacement, Jerry McAfee, is "Mr. Clean" because as president of Gulf's Canadian subsidiary, his "political contributions" to Canadian politicians were "legal" and "tightly controlled"! And with "only" $1.3 million spent in this way, he had the clout to be "the most blunt and vocal" fighter against the Canadian Treasury in avoiding taxes.

In a way, the incident is reminiscent of the Rockefellers' big moral hullabaloo in firing the president of Standard Oil of Indiana, Robert Stewart, when his bribes to U.S. government officials to get oil concessions were exposed a half-century ago. For throughout their five generations, the Rockefellers have been second to none in corruption and in plunder. And they cooperated with the Mellons, with whom they have traditionally had close relations, in this latest operation, striving thereby to clear the skirts of the entire financial oligarchy.

For the person picked to write the report used to sink Dorsey, and to try to whitewash the Mellons, was none other than John J. McCloy, veteran high-ranking lawyer of the Rockefeller group, whose life has been spent commuting between the Rockefeller banks and law firms, and top U.S. government posts, including the War Department, the World Bank, the Disarmament and Arms Control Agency, and the High Commissionership for West Germany, which was responsible for restoring power to the Krupps, Flicks, and other pre-war cartel partners of Standard Oil, General Electric, etc.

6/19/1976

New Jersey Promises Surplus Value

The governors of New York, New Jersey and Connecticut are competing to lure manufacturers into their states, or at least to keep them from moving elsewhere. And they all stress the same theme. Here's the lead from the New Jersey ad in *The New York Times*:

"Only New Jersey widens your profit margin these 8 important ways."

Let's focus on the first claim: "**Profit from the highest worker productivity of any industrialized state in America!** Value added per dollar of wages is a hefty $3.76 vs. the national average of $3.36. That's the only measure of labor cost that matters."

Let's stop right there, while noting for the record that New York is right up there with $3.72.

More than a century ago, Karl Marx developed his theory of capitalist exploitation, in which he proved that the only kind of productivity the capitalist cared about was the production of values over and above what he had to pay his workers who produced the values.

He called the difference surplus value. The New Jersey worker produces $3.76 for every $1.00 he gets in wages. The employer keeps $2.76. That is the surplus value. It is surplus above what the capitalist has to pay the worker so that worker can be fed, clothed, and sheltered enough to keep on working, and to raise children to supply the next generation of workers.

And it is this surplus value that the capitalists keep as profits, except for the dwindling part they have to pay as taxes. How they divide the profits among the stockholders, the bankers, the bribed politicians, etc., doesn't concern us here. Nor are we worried about how much they use for their own extravagant consumption, and how much they reinvest to exploit still more workers and make still more profits.

The apologists for capitalism, including right-wing and social-democratic trade union officials, try to cover up this exploitation of labor, to bury the idea of surplus value. They talk about a fair day's pay for a fair day's work, or, while conceding that labor is exploited elsewhere, say it's surely not so in the "high-wage" factories of the United States.

Well, now the governors of leading states use the idea of surplus value in order to get capitalists into their respective bailiwicks. Contradicting the main propaganda line of their class, they boast of how much "their" workers are exploited.

Marx called the ratio of surplus value to wages the rate of surplus value. In his time, employers usually got twice as much value out of the workers as they paid in wages—$2.00 value added for every $1.00 in wages, leaving $1.00 surplus value for the employers. So Marx spoke of a rate of surplus value of 100%.

But U.S. employers are much more successful in exploiting workers now. In New Jersey they are getting nearly four times as much out of the workers as they pay in wages, for a rate of surplus value of 276%.

Marx worked out his theory in the most basic units—hours of human labor. In New Jersey in 1972, the Census Department figures that Governor Brendan Byrne used show factory employers paid $32.52 in wages for every eight man-hours of labor. During those eight hours each worker created $122.57 of value, over and above the value of the materials and fuel used in the production process. Thus he created $15.32 in each hour worked. So his total pay for an eight-hour day amounted to what he produced in 2.12 hours, or in 2 hours and 7 minutes ($32.52 divided by $15.32 equals 2.12).

On a 7 o'clock to 3 o'clock shift, forgetting about the lunch period, the worker was working for himself until 9:07, and all the remaining 5 hours and 53 minutes until 3 o'clock he was working for the boss.

The New Jersey worker sells 8 hours of strenuous labor, or intense labor, or dangerous and unhealthy labor, or labor with all of those qualities—8 hours of his power to work, of his vital force, of the best hours of his life. And in exchange he gets the market value of his day's labor power, determined by the laws of capitalism as modified by the class struggle. And in New Jersey he gets only 2 hours and 7 minutes worth of the product of his day's labor.

Since the early years of industrial capitalism the workers have struggled to ease that exploitation, to preserve a little of their energy, to prolong their life, by reducing the hours of labor. The capitalists strive by every means to prevent this, and to stretch each hour through speedup, rationalization schemes, making one worker do the jobs of several, etc. And in the United States in recent decades, capitalists have also had great success through directly lengthening the working day via the overtime routes. Recently, Ford workers at Mahwah, N.J., have been on a vicious, exhausting 58-hour week. New Jersey manufacturers, at 1972 wages and prices, and getting 58 hours a week per worker, get an extra $202.60 of surplus value from each worker in a week's time. This means a total of $652.85 surplus value per worker, including the amount exploited during the regular hours.

Yes, $652.85 profit out of each worker per week.

The advertisements of Governors Byrne and Hugh Carey prove what the rank and file have been saying, and what delegations of workers from Western Europe who visit U.S. factories have observed:

The U.S. workers are among the most exploited in the world today. And the fight to eliminate overtime and reduce the basic workweek to 30 hours without reduction in total weekly pay is the most fundamental economic struggle facing the U.S. working class today.

Do not believe capitalist claims that this would drive them out of business. It would simply cut back the rate of exploitation towards a historically normal ratio. If the New Jersey standard workweek were reduced to 30 hours, without reduction in pay, the worker would still be paid only the equivalent of his production in 2 hours and 49 minutes, while the employer would keep the product of 3 hours and 11 minutes. That would leave the employer a rate of surplus value of 113%, even if he didn't succeed in expanding it by getting higher productivity out of workers no longer exhausted towards the end of an eight- or ten-hour day.

So don't pity the poor boss. There's a long struggle ahead before American workers cut down profits and improve their own lives to the extent indicated. And at that it will still leave the boss on top. But the struggle is certainly worth it. Because the employers are not stopping with a 276% rate of surplus value. Every day, in every way, they are striving to further increase the rate of exploitation of their workers. Without a real struggle on basic economic issues, instead of the various sidetracking devices substituted by social-democratic and class collaborationist trade union officials, the situation will go from bad to worse.

• • •

1/22/1981

The Cost of Parasitism

Wages of U.S. workers are now far behind those of workers in a half dozen other capitalist countries, and real wages are falling. Citibank, in its November 1980 *Monthly Economic Letter*, compared the hourly compensation of workers in different countries. Although it uses a very liberal definition of "compensation"—by including generous fringe benefits and employers' payments to Social Security, its estimates run 36% ahead of actual average hourly wages in U.S. manufacturing in 1979—the figures are useful for international comparisons.

In 1970 U.S. workers still had the highest wages in the world, by a substantial margin; by 1975 workers in a number of West European countries had caught up. In 1970 West German compensation was less than half the U.S. level; but by 1979 it was $2.22, or one-fourth, higher than the U.S. hourly rate. Belgian, Dutch and Swedish workers were ahead by the same amount; Swiss and Danish workers by narrower margins.

French workers had nearly caught up and Italian workers were within striking distance—pun intended. The militancy of French and Italian workers, and their strong, often Communist-led unions, have much to do with their gains.

Conditions of British workers, however, deteriorated. By mid-1979, they were making less than half as much as West German workers, considerably less than French and Italian workers, and even a little less than Japanese and Spanish workers.

Old "explanations" about variations in "productivity," "discipline" of workers, variations in supposed national characteristics, etc., are confounded by these changes. What does stand out is that the United States and Britain are the leaders in militarism and foreign investments, in the parasitism of modern imperialism, and that this imposes a heavy penalty on the workers of the two countries.

Much of the cost to workers results from the international runaway shop. Citibank provides figures to explain it. As compared with U.S. "compensation" per hour of $9.09 in 1979, the figures for Brazil were $1.80; Mexico, $2.31; Hong Kong, $1.25; South Korea, $1.14; Taiwan, $1.01; Portugal (1978), $1.63. Citibank explains that as these countries "move up the developmental ladder" and their workers win wage increases, "others will take their place"—such as Malaysia, Indonesia and the Philippines. "Much further down the line, China may someday join the parade."

What is the solution for the United States, Britain, etc.? Citibank explains:

"Faced with such competition in labor-intensive manufacturing and gradually in other lines . . . the more advanced countries have begun to redeploy their industrial strength into more sophisticated and more specialized lines of production. They are pushing the manufacture of high-technology and high-quality products—and of fashion and luxury goods. The push is also on to develop the new 'knowledge-intensive' industries, such as micro-electronics . . . computerized labor-saving systems . . . robots. . . ."

The British economist Hobson described this tendency of modern imperialism nearly 80 years ago, in 1902! He forecast that it would reach its peak with the completion of the partitioning of China:

"The greater part of Western Europe might then assume the appearance and character already exhibited by tracts of country in the south of England, in the Riviera and . . . parts of Italy and Switzerland, little clusters of wealthy aristocrats drawing dividends and pensions from the Far East, with a somewhat larger group of professional retainers and tradesmen and a larger body of personal servants and workers in the transport trade and in the final stages of production of the more perishable goods; all the main arterial industries would have disappeared, the staple foods and manufactures flowing in as tribute from Asia and Africa."

Adjust for the different structure of industry and the advance of technology, you could substitute Western Connecticut, Long Island and various Sunbelt enclaves for the South of England; add oil and cars to other items flowing in from Asia, Africa and Latin America; and add such "arterial" industries as steel and autos to those left to rot—and you get the picture of where U.S. imperialism is moving, to the applause of the capitalists who are luxuriating on the huge profits from foreign investments and domestic racism.

Add a monstrously expanded armament industry, hiring a fraction of the industrial workers displaced by the runaway shop. And add mass unemployment on a scale Hobson could not have imagined.

Lenin, who included the above quoted excerpt from Hobson in his work on imperialism (*Lenin, Collected Works, Vol. 22*, pp. 279-280), made clear that this parasitic process would never be completed—the revolutionary struggles of the workers and oppressed peoples would end the system of imperialism first. That has happened in many countries, beginning with Russia, and is going on in many countries today. The workers and oppressed peoples of the United States will surely enter this struggle as they break free from the influence of the two-party electoral system and of opportunist trade union officials.

5/14/1981

Rate of Profit Up

The latest *Fortune* showed how the rate of profit of large corporations has "gone through the ceiling" in recent years. That is, not only has the total amount of profits multiplied, but the percentage of profits on invested capital, or the rate of profit, has gone to higher levels than ever measured since *Fortune* started making tabulations of large corporate results 26 years ago.

That result gives the lie to many years of capitalist propaganda claiming that the rate of profit has been falling. And it raises an interesting question about Karl Marx' "law of the declining tendency of the rate of profit."

Here's how that goes. The capitalist's profit is derived from the exploitation of labor, by paying in wages less than the value the worker adds to production. Thus, his profit comes directly from only that part of his capital used to pay wages. But a larger part of the capital is tied up in machinery and buildings, and in inventories of raw materials. These values are merely transferred to the finished product without any addition—the materials in full, and the machinery and buildings gradually, through depreciation allowances.

With the progress of technology, there is more and more machinery per worker, and a worker handles more and more raw materials. So the proportion of the capital that doesn't directly contribute to profits becomes larger and larger, while the proportion used to pay wages becomes smaller. So if all other factors remain unchanged, especially the rate at which workers are exploited, the rate of profit on the total capital will decline as the share of machinery, equipment, and inventories in the total capital increases.

Considering this, Marx said there is a **tendency** for the rate of profit to decline. This qualification is important, because some left and radical economists have referred to Marx' law as a basis to accept the capitalists' claim that their profit rate **was** declining. They supported the capitalists' argument, used politically against the workers, in the name of Marxism! They did not critically examine the statistics used by capitalist economists to see how they were rigged. And they didn't study Marx thoroughly enough, or apply his writings to the present-day reality.

Marx devoted much study to the ways in which capitalists counteract that tendency—such as forcing the labor force to work for longer hours; cutting their wages; and investing in colonies, where under conditions of near slavery the rate of profit is very high indeed. So, Marx concluded, the law is only a **tendency**, and its effects become apparent "only under certain circumstances and after long periods."

Marx was writing in the period of competitive capitalism. Now we are living under the domination of monopoly capitalism, of imperialism. The *Fortune* "500" represent industrial monopoly capital; and, with the big banks, they really determine the course of the entire economy.

Monopoly capitalism brings additional economic laws into play, in particular the law of maximum profits, which is based on monopoly, on militarization of the economy, and on superprofits from racism and foreign investments. And above all, maximum profits are obtained by squeezing more out of the U.S. working class, exploiting U.S. workers to an extent never before known in an industrially developed, bourgeois-democratic, capitalist country.

The factors that counteract the tendency of the rate of profit to decline have been working with a vengeance in the United States in recent decades, and especially in the last few years.

Marx analyzed the laws of capitalism not as an academic exercise but to help guide the workers' struggles. These struggles are directed against the harmful effects of the economic laws of capitalism. And gains can be won in these struggles.

During the 1930s and 1940s workers, including Communists, many in leadership, overcame employer and police brutality and established trade unions in basic industry. They won such elementary social reforms as unemployment insurance, Social Security, and minimum wages.

With this foundation, workers won significant gains in real wages and reduced the rate of exploitation of labor, of surplus value. For a while, the law of maximum profits was dealt a setback, and the rate of profit did decline. But with the counteroffensive of big capital, marked by McCarthyism, red-baiting, anti-Sovietism and racism, these gains, and more, were lost.

However, labor, Black and other oppressed people, and peace forces are bound to have the last word.

• • •

3/1991

Adam Smith and Karl Marx

Recently the *Wall Street Journal* carried an ill-informed debate about Adam Smith and Karl Marx. Liberal columnist Hodding Carter attacked the Reagan years as disastrous for most Americans. Assuming that Reagan—with his supplyside, enrich-the-rich policies—was a loyal follower of Adam Smith, Carter wrote: "In the long march of history it is unlikely that the theories of Adam Smith . . . will prove any more enduring than those of Karl Marx" (*The New York Times*, 1/3).

This got under the skin of two *Wall Street Journal* letter writers, whose communications were printed under the head "Aggressive Capitalism Is Nature's Way." That caption aptly characterizes the views of correspondent George W. Schiele, who refers to Charles Darwin and the "natural law" of "all living organisms": to grab what they can ". . . and rearrange to its own advantage the world around it" (1/29).

I assume Schiele never read Karl Marx. I wonder if he ever bothered to read Adam Smith's classic, *The Wealth of Nations*. That pioneer of modern economic science was no social Darwinist. He described and analyzed the working of capitalism. He didn't glamorize "entrepreneurship," "risk-taking," "aggressiveness," and other catchword concepts of bourgeois pseudo-science.

To a man with Schiele's outlook, Smith might seem positively subversive. His cornerstone labor theory of value identified workers as the sole creators of value. He explained, however, that the workers could receive in wages only part of the values they produced, as part had to go to the boss—the capitalist, the merchant, the landlord. Nowadays it's the fashion among apologists for capitalism to claim that the bosses are paid for their "mental labor," their "ideas," "creative vision," etc. Smith explicitly refuted the idea that the capitalist was paid for the labor of "inspection and direction." In fact, he wrote, "In many great works, almost the whole labour of this kind is committed to some principal clerk." The profits of the capitalist, he wrote, are wholly related to the "value of the stock employed," that is, to his capital (pp. 48-49, *Modern Library* Edition).

Smith's work made a significant contribution to that of Karl Marx a century later. Marx developed the labor theory of value, clearly identified the part going to the capitalist as "surplus value," a measure of the exploitation of labor under capitalism. He analyzed the social and economic crises that flowed from its operation, contributing to economic crises and to the sharpening conflicts between capital and labor that must lead the working class to overthrow the rule of capital and create a more effective and equitable society.

Adam Smith, writing in the early stages of the industrial revolution, dealt with the already significant labor conflicts, which then, as now, occurred on a playing field far from level: ". . . the masters, being fewer in number can combine much more easily; and the law, besides, authorizes, or at least does not prohibit their combinations, while it does those of the workmen." (p. 66) Furthermore, he pointed out, the bosses could live off their wealth for a year or two, while many workers would starve after a week's strike. Thus, usually, he thought, the capitalists succeeded in keeping wages down to the lowest level needed to keep the workers going. But sometimes, he wrote, workers succeeded in getting higher wages; and where wages are high, people are happy and the country is prosperous—a far cry from the supply-side theories and government/big business policies and actions deliberately aimed at reducing wages.

As for the outward aggressiveness of European capitalism, of its colonial policy, Smith wrote:

"Folly and injustice seem to have been the principles which presided over and directed the first project of establishing those colonies, the folly of hunting after gold and silver mines, and the injustice of coveting the possession of a country whose harmless natives, far from having ever injured the people of Europe, had received the first adventurers with every mark of kindness and hospitality." (p. 555)

It's interesting that Smith's work was completed on the eve of the American Revolution, and published in 1776. Expressing his opposition to British colonial policy, he urged the liberation of the colonies, which, he considered, brought ". . . more loss instead of profit" to ". . . the great body of the people" (p. 900).

The same could be said of modern U.S. imperialism's aggressions, whether defeated—as in Vietnam—or "successful"—as in Panama and Iraq. They all impose heavy material costs on the American people, mass killings and disastrous wreckage on the victims, and guilt not glory on our country's conscience.

Smith's *Wealth of Nations* is far from out of date. It would make a good text, along with Marx' *Capital* and Lenin's *Imperialism*, in serious economic courses.

"What are you complaining about! I'm saving democracy, ain't I!"

Living Conditions

5/20/1962

Socialized Medicine

President Kennedy's campaign for a medical-care-for-the-aged bill highlights a problem affecting the entire population. We live in a period of corruption, piracy and profiteering. But nothing surpasses the heartless robbery of the people for medical services.

The population's medical costs rose from $6 billion in 1946 to around $23 billion expected in 1962. Per capita costs have gone up almost threefold in 16 years. Nearly all of that represents higher prices, not more service. There are no more doctors per capita than in 1921, and 12% fewer hospital beds per capita than in 1946.

Drug companies have been among the most successful price riggers, setting a norm of 50¢ per pill for many popular lines, and getting away with U.S. prices several times the world level. Hospitals have jacked up rates repeatedly, as have sellers of hospitalization insurance. Many doctors have fallen in with the speculative spirit. Fees for visits have soared, while fee splitting and other abuses abound. Patients are often handled like cartons of produce. Even the BLS concedes a postwar doubling of medical costs, but actually the rise since 1946 has been at least 250%.

The Heller* budget says a worker's family of four must spend $576 per year, or 11% of its after-tax income, for medical costs. But the average family was able to spend only $300 in 1958, when a survey was made. Even if this outlay has gone up $50 since, the survey shows that most American families are falling below required medical services by 40% or more. Families with incomes below $4,000 fall below by 60% or more.

The administration bill for limited social security-financed medical payments for some elderly people is a minimum necessity. It merely scratches the surface of the overall national need. And workers will be paying half the cost of it through their share of social security deductions, adding to burdens they already

89

carry for medical services. Insurance schemes, private or governmental, are diluted by the practices of the sellers of medical services who always strive to raise prices enough to get from patients as much as formerly, over and above what is covered by their prepaid insurance.

Governments—federal, state, and local—have failed to act directly to ease the people's health problems in proportion to growing needs. Considering public and private expenditure for health and medical services, public outlays were 22.8% of the total in 1940, increased to 29.2% in 1945, then fell to 24.7% in 1959.

In the particular conditions of the United States there is a crying need for a universal system of health services, available to the entire population, paid for out of the general revenues. It would cover everything: hospitals, doctors, dentists, nurses, drugs. The government would buy everything at reasonable prices; it would fix fees and salaries. The people would have free access to all medical services and supplies. Of course, many details would have to be studied and negotiated.

Few readers will sympathize with drug companies, which would lose superprofits, or with highly paid boards of trustees, which have made class institutions out of the hospitals while underpaying their staffs.

But is it right to cut doctors' earnings? Certainly a doctor's net of even $50,000 seems reasonable in comparison with a capitalist's $1,000,000 for clipping coupons. But some doctors are taking advantage of working people who cannot afford their high fees. There should be no compunction about fixing fees that would eliminate excesses. The incomes of many doctors, perhaps of most, would not be cut. Wages of nurses and other medical service personnel, and of many resident institutional doctors, would be raised.

It is possible for people to organize and fight for such a program, even while the abuse of capitalism and its million dollar unearned incomes remains.

Socialized medicine? Certainly, if you will. But technically, like the similar British system, it could be a state capitalist system of medicine, leaving the means of production, including drugs, in private hands. It is a reform, realizable under capitalism, that would improve health services for the people—although a socialist society could provide these services better than any reforms under capitalism.

*Walter Heller, JFK's chief economist.

● ● ●

4/5/1964

Why People Are Poor

Herman Miller, in his *Rich Man, Poor Man*, explains poverty wrongly. He tries to fit the poor into special categories, as social workers group their "cases." He describes families without a husband; a million and a half farm families; poor for "reasons . . . about as varied as the poor themselves." Of Negro poverty, Miller correctly says that "racial discrimination is a key cause." But aside from this segment of the truth, he describes rather than explains. Ultimately the case study approach collapses:

"Finally, there is the fifth group, whose poverty has no apparent explanation in census statistics—white families living in or near large cities and headed by a man in his productive years."

In fact, this is the largest of the five groups, with 3 million families, by Miller's inadequate definition. Why, indeed, do one-tenth of all families, bearing none of the crosses that mark the outcasts of American capitalism, suffer poverty during the biggest boom in the richest country in the world?

Mainly, says Miller, they "lack the intelligence to learn a trade or to hold down a responsible job. As a result they are cast into the most menial and lowest paying occupations. Still others get bad 'breaks.' Their employer goes out of business or has a bad year and their incomes suffer as a result." He agrees with an article referring to "unemployables" whose number will "grow rapidly."

Generalizing about all five groups, Miller says: "Perhaps the most distinctive characteristic of the poor is their low productivity."

Where have I read this before? In the textbooks of Marshallian economics*; in the loaded monographs of the Brookings Institution†; in the propaganda blasts of the NAM‡.

Are the iron miners of Michigan's Upper Peninsula poor because of low intelligence, or because their employers turned to more profitable iron deposits in low-wage Venezuela?

Are the Negroes toiling in the steam laundries of New York; driving trucks at poverty wages 40% under those of whites; stringing southern telephone lines as "helpers" to white "linesmen" who stand below and pocket thrice the pay; doing all the housework for idle white wives for as little as $10 for as long as 70 hours a week—are they unemployable?

Are the coal miners of Appalachia living in semi-starvation because of low productivity, or because they have the highest productivity in the world, and "worked themselves out of a job," with the assistance of short-sighted union leaders who connived with employers to introduce super-automated equipment without protection for the men?

And what about the farm laborers who do all the work on the corporation farms of California and Texas for the very lowest wages in America, without houses, without schools, left to starve between seasons—are they not the source of that high productivity of which the Voice of America boasts most in claiming superiority over socialist agriculture?

The common feature of poverty is not low productivity, but often the extra-high productivity that frequently goes along with abysmal poverty. The common feature is capitalist exploitation of labor, its limitless greed, the anarchy of its social system, its fostering of racism as a source of superprofits.

And the same applies to "case poverty." Older workers produced more than enough during their working years to provide a good retirement livelihood. They suffer because capitalist governments refuse them just compensation.

If capitalist power were unchallenged, and each worker bargained only for himself, all workers would still be poor, as they were during the industrial revolution in England.

Many still are in countries dominated by American companies. But there are workers who have won advances in living standards through organized struggles. In Sweden, for example, there is scarcely any poverty as known here because almost all workers have joined in the economic and political battles of labor. American workers can do much better and much more than they have so far to end poverty, even while capitalism remains the dominant system.

The productivity of American labor is sufficient not only to end poverty. It can provide a more than adequate, a good standard of living for all willing to work and their dependents, including the old and handicapped.

The way to provide that plenty, and then raise it steadily, is to reorganize society on socialist lines.

*Marshallian economics: A conservative school of capitalist economics.

†Brookings Institution: A leading establishment social research institute.

‡NAM (National Association of Manufacturers): At the time, a leading voice of American capitalism.

• • •

5/30/1964

Affordable Drugs—'for Animals Only'

For two days our dog curled up in a corner and ate nothing. When I went for a walk he lagged behind and struggled up the last hill. He didn't even bark when somebody approached the house. So I took him to the vet.

The vet treated the big beast with a gentleness and kindness one rarely sees these days on the part of over-busy doctors of humans. Finally the diagnosis: strep throat! He gave Jet a penicillin injection and gave me two packets of antibiotic pills, for morning and evening use respectively. He commented that the medicine and dosage were the same as for a human adult. He gave instructions on the care of the animal; the visit lasted half an hour; the patient recovered speedily; the bill was $5, including all medicines.

A year ago we had taken Jet to him after his eye was practically gone from a fight. He had received the same careful treatment, special medication; the eye was saved, the bill had been the same.

This time, I noticed a large Pfizer & Company bottle on his shelf. It was labeled Terramycin: For Animals Only. I said: "Doctor, last week I cut myself and couldn't find an antiseptic, so I applied some antiseptic ointment we had around from years ago for use on an injured cat."

He said: "For 21 years my wife, children and I have used only animal medicines and have never suffered any ill effects."

Doctor friends to whom I have spoken estimate that costs for treatment and medication for a human's strep throat would be from $25 to $45. Why should we pay five times as much for the same medicine applied to a dog? Or for the same professional treatment?

How long are we Americans going to be the only industrialized nation in the world so unmercifully robbed by the drug-medical-hospital combine? It has long been public knowledge that drugs (for humans) retail for 10 to 50 times any reasonably determined value; and at many times the standard retail price in West European countries, where they are generally state-distributed. In socialist countries they cost next to nothing.

The drug company profiteers divide their take about fifty-fifty with the advertising outfits and the associated newspapers, radio and television networks. This gives them a fantastic propaganda advantage in resisting any attempt at control.

In a recent speech President Johnson said he couldn't for the life of him understand why doctors oppose Medicare. In the first place, not all doctors do. The main noise is made by the ultra-reactionary chiefs of the AMA who are tied in with the drug and insurance company monopolies, the chief profiteers from "free enterprise" medicine. But all too many doctors do oppose even the fragmentary concessions to workers' basic needs embodied in the present Medicare bill.

It is not news that many American doctors have tended to become businessmen and capitalists first, and professional practitioners second. No matter how liberal the provisions for their compensation, every move toward putting medicine on a public service basis—which is what socialized medicine means—undermines the privileges of overcharging, fee splitting, and prescribing brand-name drugs, through which the public's $20 billion medical bill is divided up.

More specifically, any step, such as Medicare, that records more of the doctor's fees, reduces their chances to evade taxes. This was a prominent issue in the Saskatchewan doctors' strike three years ago, and in the recent Belgian doctors' strike.

One can understand their psychology. If the million dollar a year capitalist evades hundreds of thousands of dollars in taxes, why shouldn't the $50,000 a year doctor retain the privilege of evading a few thousand a year?

Imitation of bigger and richer capitalists explains but doesn't excuse those doctors who do it. They are loading added bills and added taxes onto workers who cannot evade a nickel of it. And they are helping deprive millions of Americans of medical care.

Voters can use the election campaign to get candidates to commit themselves to help insure passage of the existing bill, and especially to help enact more far-reaching legislation next year. Some American doctors helped provide medical services to the people of Saskatchewan when doctors there struck against socialized medicine. Many doctors oppose, in whole or in part, the medical monopoly. Ask yours to help Medicare through.

10/2/1971

Questions and Answers on the Freeze

The following interview with Victor Perlo was conducted by Bruce Solowey and Mark Spector over WBAI, Pacifica's New York radio station, the evening after President Nixon announced the wage-price freeze. Mr. Perlo, Marxist economist, is a commentator on the station as well as a writer and lecturer, columnist for "World Magazine," and chairman of the Economics Commission of the Communist Party USA.

Q: How would you say the changes will affect wage earners and consumers in this country; what can we expect to see in the next 90 days during this wage-price freeze?

A: It represents a very sharp attack on the average wage earner by having a real freeze of his wages and a fake freeze of prices. A wage-price freeze was decreed. The wage freeze will be enforced easily because corporations are given the power to refuse to give any wage increases regardless of contracts or escalator clauses or anything else. Presumably there is the threat of government sanctions against any group of workers who insist on wage increases. No machinery whatsoever is set up to enforce price freezes (nominally, the President's Cost of Living Council has enforcement powers, but all its few employees do is listen to telephone complaints), which means prices can be raised in a hundred different ways—from changing the menu in a restaurant to changing the tenant in an apartment building. Furthermore, Mr. Nixon has taken specific measures that will force price increases, like the 10% surcharge an almost all imports. And today 20% of all consumer goods used in this country are either imports or consist of imported components, so this will be transferred onto the retail price regardless of the freeze.

Q: Mr. Nixon said that it wouldn't affect domestic prices at all; that within the country, there was likely to be no change.

A: This is a cop-out. If you study the history of European countries—France, England, and many others—you will see that their devaluations have been followed by accelerated price increases. In addition, domestic manufacturers systematically increase prices whenever prices go up on imported goods. It provides a floor under them, and they feel they can take another notch upwards.

Q: Since you already have painted a picture of gloom, with wages staying as they are and with the chance of prices increasing, and the domestic buying power not getting any better, it seems that the only logical question to ask now is: What was the straw that broke the camel's back? What made the President take the steps he did, these particular steps, opposed to some others that he might have taken at this time?

A: First, the key measures are dollar devaluation, the wage-price freeze, tax giveaways, plus measures to reduce government employment and reduce welfare spending. These are the key operative measures of Mr. Nixon's program. And the driving force behind them is the set of factors that forced dollar devaluation.

Dollar devaluation was fundamentally caused by the war in Vietnam plus all the other factors that caused the huge deficits in the U.S. balance of payments and made the devaluation inevitable. Devaluation is the classical method reactionary conservative governments use.

Devaluations are accompanied by what are known as austerity programs. These are means of making workers pay the cost of devaluation, while carrying it out so that it proves profitable to large corporate interests.

Q: For one minute, I'd like to get back to one point you went over rather quickly. It has to do with welfare. During this 90-day freeze on wages and prices, can welfare payments and allotments be increased?

A: Let me make clear that, in my opinion, this 90-day period is simply a gate-opener, while the administration sets up machinery to impose a permanent freeze on wages.

As far as welfare payments are concerned, I don't know what can or cannot be done, but I think it's fairly clear that the whole trend of government policy is to crack down on welfare payments and reduce their scope. It fits in with the general atmosphere, the talk of government economy, etc., that President Nixon was engaging in.

I realize I slurred over one other question you asked me: "What was the straw that broke the camel's back?" That straw, according to President Nixon, was the international money speculators who attacked the dollar. He neglected to identify them, but I will.

I doubt if there is a single—well there must be one—American worth more than a million dollars who hasn't put part of his money into foreign properties so as to make a profit out of the devaluation of the dollar. I would say there isn't a single important banking institution and big corporation that didn't know that this was coming; that altogether billions and billions of dollars were exchanged for foreign currency; that the main run on the dollar was by American big business, the same cliques that are calling the signals for President Nixon.

Q: President Nixon said that he wanted to attack three economic ills: job shortages, inflation and international imbalance of payments. From what you said it sounds like he was primarily concerned with the balance of payments question, the international status of the dollar. The other two were just riding along as trailers. Is that a correct reading of what you said, that he was more concerned with the international status of the dollar than he was with inflation and jobs?

A: Yes. Fundamentally, yes, with only this qualification: The whole is used as a means for carrying on a class program in favor of big business and against labor in connection with, under the excuse of, meeting the national emergencies around the dollar.

Q: Does big business stand to gain or maintain the status quo?

A: Yes, I would say that big business stands to gain very substantially from this move. First, let's suppose there was a legitimate wage-price freeze, with both prices and wages completely frozen. Then every bit of the gain from the increase in productivity would go into profits and none would go to wages. In the actual situation, where only wages and not prices will be frozen, there is a double gain for business—from higher productivity and from the increase in prices, while wages remain frozen. There is the additional gain: from the proposed tax giveaway—the 10% investment tax credit—which is much larger than the earlier investment tax credit. It is an added tax bonanza on top of a number of other tax giveaways President Nixon has given big business by strictly administrative measures.

Q: President Nixon said that the consumer is going to have more money by virtue of the fact that cars are now going to be much cheaper and that there is going to be a tax decrease, an increase in exemptions, and so forth. Was that a whitewash? In your opinion?

A: A little bit of sugar coating. The tax concessions offered workers were trifles. And the car price business, the excise tax on cars, will probably simply balance the increase that the auto companies just announced a week or so ago. And there is no assurance that the auto companies will pass onto the consumers any reduction in the manufacturers' excise tax.

Let me point out that none of the tax measures, except the 10% import surcharge, is in effect. They require congressional action, and there will undoubtedly be a very sharp struggle over the kind of tax measures to be taken.

Q: I may be reading what you're saying or what the President said wrong, but from what has been discussed here tonight, it seems to me there'll be very little change as far as inflation goes, or in unemployment, and every step he took seems to be defeating itself. What is going to happen as far as unemployment, as far as wages, as far as purchasing power of the dollar goes within the next six months? It's time to get to that point.

A: Well, you see, without attempting to judge what the long term effect on employment will be, the immediate effect, the three-month effect and the six-month effect are not going to reduce unemployment, nor are they intended to do so. There is the intention to pacify the public by promising to reduce unemployment, but not to actually reduce unemployment. As a matter of fact, President Nixon promised a 5% reduction in federal employment, and I would note that this measure, and the attacks on welfare spending, are racist measures, because the main victims will be Blacks and Puerto Ricans in New York City, Chicanos in Los Angeles, etc. That is the situation in respect to employment.

With respect to inflation. For the reasons I mentioned earlier we really cannot anticipate a real easing of inflation. We have to anticipate that the cost of living will continue to increase. Although the index may not increase quite so rapidly for a period, because so many price increases were jammed through just before the nominal freeze was announced and because authorities in a time like this are going to go to special lengths to prevent the index from reporting the increases in prices that really take place.

Q: Suppose all the measures that Nixon said are temporary last for a year or more? Would we then see any change in the direction of more jobs or the reduction of inflation?

A: As for jobs, the immediate effect, I should think, would be to **reduce** employment, simply because many people in many businesses will wait to make their move until they know the situation. Many potential car buyers will wait until they find out if prices go down or not because they have been promised they are going to go down. Many potential investors will wait until they get this tax break before they make an investment. So the initial effect may actually be negative on employment.

The long-range effect, I would say from past experience that a tax giveaway for investment will have a certain but modest stimulating effect, which will be more than offset or equally offset by the negative effect on consumption, because of the reduction in the real income of the population as a result of the measures that are being taken.

Q: This is obviously a political move of some kind on the part of the President: The timing would seem to indicate that. What reaction over the next year, before the elections get into full swing, do you see on the part of the working people in general? Do you see a wave of strikes? Do you see a calming down of the strike cycle? What forecast can you make as far as the working people go?

A: I will not make a forecast. But I'll tell you the factors that are involved in determining what will happen.

On the one hand, George Meany and other top officials of the labor movement have done a serious disservice to their membership by supporting a wage-price freeze, adding the proviso that of course profits should be frozen too and knowing that this would not be done. President Nixon did not even mention the word profits, and the stock market—Wall Street—read the lesson correctly. The Dow Jones Index was up over 30 points, which was an all-time record for a single day. And that is the surest evidence that what I say is correct, that this is a collection of measures to increase the profits of big business at the expense of the living standards of the working people, because that is what the stock market registers.

Q: This might be a good time to take a step backwards, to look at the proposals that Nixon has made. Some of them amount to edicts rather than proposals. Could you explain to us what each of them signifies, what each of them represents, whether they will work the way Nixon planned them and how you think they will work?

A: Well, first, dollar devaluation. This means closing the door to the sale of gold, which in effect destroys the 25-year-old post-war monetary system. I will explain that.

The monetary system is not reciprocal: it's not the same for one country as it is for another. The U.S. dollar has a special role in this monetary system. Namely, its value is determined by the price of gold and guaranteed by the promise of the U.S. government to supply gold on demand to holders of dollars at the price of $35 an ounce. Foreigners hold $40-$50 billion for which, presumably, they had a promise from the U.S. government that on demand they would be given gold. The U.S. government has now said, "We will not give you gold; we default."

Therefore the dollar is worth less than it was before. Just how much less will be determined by the market, and the market value of the dollar will be determined by the trade between dollars and other currencies in the world.

The last time this happened was in 1933. President Franklin D. Roosevelt suspended gold transactions and let the dollar fall. The dollar fell in value so sharply that, measured by the price of gold, the price of gold increased in value by more than 60%. This represented the extent of the fall in the value of the dollar.

Now European bankers are estimating that the dollar will fall between 15% and 20% in value during this period, which may be rather prolonged. And during which international money markets will be in chaos. World trade will be disrupted. That is the dollar devaluation part of the thing. Along with that is the wage-price freeze.

Q: Before we get into that; why did Nixon choose to do that? Why is that a logical response to the situation that pertained?

A. There was only one alternative. First, I am certain that other countries were demanding gold. Second, the inevitable alternative was that all other governments, within days or perhaps this very weekend, would have announced ending support of the dollar.

Now, the other part of the now-destroyed monetary system was that in exchange for the U.S. promise to supply gold, all other governments guaranteed that they would maintain the exchange value of the dollar for other currencies within a 1% range either way of a central parity ratio. Already in May, the West German government and the Dutch government stopped doing that. And the Swiss government accomplished the same thing in a different way. It is certain that all governments would very shortly have taken this step.

Nixon preferred, and from his viewpoint wisely, to take the initiative himself to devalue instead of having it done to him. And, at the same time, to make the demagogic speech to the American public, in which he tried to paint the devaluation as a sign of strength and as a great move toward prosperity, which it is anything but. It is really a tremendous defeat for U.S. capitalism. A tremendous setback for the whole post-war international objectives for American high finance.

Q: Let's go on to the next point then—the wage-price freeze.

A: The wage-price freeze is an edict that is made possible because Congress gave President Nixon, over a year ago, blanket authority to freeze prices and wages, in toto or selectively as he wished.

Q: Does the power of the President to freeze wages and prices have a time limit?

A: It does have a time limit, to April 30, 1972. It is usually extended for several months at a time. This is done because with devaluation, without some sort of restraint, there would be a much more rapid increase in prices and much sharper wage demands than otherwise.

But let me say that influential business circles, and the whole Democratic Party, and all of the liberal economists have been plugging for a wage-price freeze for several years now. There have been differences of opinion about it. The devaluation crisis makes it politically expedient in that it unites big business interests on the desirability and expediency of this move. As I have said, it is a standard capitalist way of dealing with a monetary crisis, an austerity route of slashing mass living standards to pay the cost of the crisis. The way it is done—a real wage freeze and a fake price freeze—is of course deliberate to satisfy the class interests of big business in the country.

Q: This is a point you've mentioned before, so would you explain what exactly a fake price freeze and a real wage freeze mean, because it would seem that it is going to hit the fan eventually, when prices keep going up while the wage-price freeze is on, and wages stay the same. One just keeps moving ahead of the other. It would seem to get worse, and not better at all.

A: Well, you've implied part of the answer, the consequences. You've implied that it will lead to an explosion. Either the workers will force the legislative end to the freeze or its repeal by Nixon or strike against it. It will lead to a much sharper class conflict in the country. Nixon will try to get anti-strike legislation, anti-union legislation, etc., at the first sign of workers' resistance.

But, as to why it's a fake price freeze: In World War II there were tens of thousands of employees, elaborate regulations, price lists, a large enforcement mechanism, which worked, imperfectly but to a certain extent, so that we had a partially effective price freeze.

During the Korean War, when there was a nominal price freeze, there was much less, but still a certain apparatus, and this was a less effective price freeze. Now there is no enforcement and no lists of prices. There is no control whatsoever. It is naive to think that under the circumstances, prices will actually be left the way they are. They will be increased. Not everything and not continually, but prices will be increased by and large just as they have been over the past years.

I want to say one other thing about the wage-price freeze, because it hasn't been discussed yet. I think it's important to understand that none of these measures is going to solve any of the serious problems of the American economy as long as the Vietnam War continues. It was the Vietnam War that sank the dollar, which is the cause of this great inflation that we are having. It is the cause of the recent unemployment. And as long as the war goes on, none of the problems is going to be solved. What Nixon is doing, instead of ending the war, is taking a typical war mobilization measure—a wage freeze. He is trying to do this in order to continue the war, and possibly escalate it, and this means that all of the problems are going to become still more serious, rather than being eased.

• • •

8/1972

The Staff of Life

When Marvin returned from work and was about to sit down to dinner, his wife, Shirley, complained:

S: The price of bread went up again. That delicious, fluffy, Italian bread went up from 50¢ to 58¢ for the round loaf.

M: It's still cheaper than Challah.

S: That's not the point. Will you increase my allowance so I can buy it?

M: It's the Russians' fault. They are going to buy a billion dollars worth of wheat.

S: What's that got to do with it?

M: They forced up the price of wheat 30¢ a bushel. The *Wall Street Journal* and all the other papers say so. And the bakers say they are going to have to raise prices 2 or 3¢ a loaf to make up for the higher cost.

S: I see. How many loaves of bread do you make with a bushel of wheat?

M: I'll look it up. (He digs into the encyclopedia and a cook book and makes calculations.) Sixty one-pound loaves.

S: (She does additional calculating). .... So the 30¢ price increase comes to half a cent a loaf. Why should they increase the price 2 or 3¢?

M: That's sound business practice. The miller has to double the 30¢ increase, and the baker has to double that, and the chain store has to double it once more. That's the American way. It increases profits and profits make the wheels of industry go round, and provide jobs for everybody.

S: Then why blame it on the Russians?

M: Because they won't help the President save freedom in Vietnam.

S: I see. But tell me, does the price of wheat always go up?

M: Of course not. The month before it went down 20¢ a bushel.

S: Then why didn't the price of bread go down?

M: Oh, didn't it?

S: Why don't you try shopping sometime? How naive can you get? The price **never** goes down. It always goes up.

M: It's a ratchet principle. When costs go up a certain amount it triggers a penny increase in the price of bread. But the ratchet has a brake. It can only turn one way. If the price went down, it would demoralize the market and make a depression.

S: Tell me—How much was the price of wheat 15 years ago, when I paid only 22¢ for the round Italian bread?

M: How should I know? Let's see. .... The man upstairs gets *Business Week*. Maybe that will tell. (He goes upstairs, and soon returns, holding open a *Business Week*.) Commodity prices—Wheat—Kansas City—latest week: $1.85; 1957-59 average: $2.11.

S: So there, it just doesn't make sense.

M: But it's all legal. Let me read what it says: "The bakers say they will have to ask the Price Commission for permission to raise bread prices."

S: Why didn't my baker wait until he got permission?

M: That could be for a number of reasons. Maybe he is a small baker, or not in Interstate Commerce. Or maybe his is part of a big conglomerate. Then he can increase bread prices all he wants so long as his average prices for everything from submarines to pencil sharpeners do not go up more than 2.5%.

S: Who's left?

M: Only the Big Three auto companies. President Nixon turned them down, but they can increase prices $125 for quality improvement.

S: It's not fair.

M: Stop complaining. I want to read the paper. . . . Say, listen. Here's some good news. President Nixon and Japanese Premier Tanaka have concluded a history-making agreement. They will increase their purchases of American goods. It'll help employment in this country and the balance of payments.

S: What kind of goods?

M: Let's see . . . Oh, here it is: "These would bring Japanese purchases of agricultural, forestry and fishery products from the U.S. to $2,218,000,000 in Japanese Fiscal Year 1972, the highest such export by the U.S. to any country."

S: Hmmm—more than $2 billion. Won't that raise the price of food and lumber even more than the Russians' billion-dollar purchase?

M: Of course not—officially, anyhow. Japan's our ally. They provide bases for our troops. They repair our equipment to help save freedom and the market for Hondas in Saigon.

S: You can't convince me. The baking company will use any excuse to raise prices—Japanese or Russian, if they can get away with it—that's how it seems to me, anyhow.

M: You're just a cynic.

S: Well, know-it-all, why don't you get a raise so I can afford these higher prices?

M: The Pay Board won't permit it. That would be inflationary,

S: You're just making a lot of double talk. It's just to cover up a lot of profiteering by big business helped by the Nixon administration. I'm going to vote against him in November.

M: You sound like the Communist candidate, Gus Hall. He talks about rolling back monopoly prices and raising wages. It sounds good, but it's not sound economics.

S: It sounds like what the doctor ordered. I'm going to find out more about that candidate. Now, pass the tasteless white bread and let's eat.

• • •

6/1/1990

Inflation: a Shopper's Perspective

The Bureau of Labor Statistics says inflation in the United States was 8.5% at an annual rate in the first quarter of this year. What a joke that figure is! They must have forgotten to print the 1 in front of the 8.5.

Every so often, the BLS falls so far short of reality that knowledgeable observers, such as trade union economists, the chief economist of Manufacturers Hanover Trust, and yours truly, publish calculations—sometimes detailed, sometimes less structured—that give some indication of what is actually happening to living costs.

Consider food prices. Scientists have just established that if rats are kept on a properly balanced hunger diet, they live 50% longer than rats that eat their fill. By that standard, if about half the human population eats only as much as they can afford, they would live to 120. The catch is that they cannot afford the foods necessary for a balanced diet.

To emphasize new understanding of the importance of various dietary requisites, food package labels stress what you are not getting: "only 14 calories per serving," "two-thirds less cholesterol," "no sugar," "low sodium," etc. Then a half dozen chemicals are listed—following the inevitable keynote, "All Natural." Generally, the more you do not get, the higher the price. And that goes for quantity, too.

This time, my informal research involved shopping at a local supermarket.

Take bread. A year ago, my favorite Italian-type bread fluctuated in price between 89¢ and $1.09. A couple of months ago, it took a big jump to $1.35, and just recently climbed to $1.45, where it has remained. All the competition has gone up in tandem. The store's bakery department produces its own small Italian loaves. They used to cost 50¢, now they cost 79¢ each. The Kaiser rolls were six for a dollar two years ago, now they are four for a dollar—up 50%.

As for fresh vegetables and fruit—until the middle of April, I just raced through with my shopping cart, unwilling to pay more than $3 for a bunch of broccoli or a pound of tomatoes. Now that spring is here, broccoli is "only" $1.39 a pound and "bargain" tomatoes "only" 99¢.

With Purdue and Holly Farms dividing the poultry-shelf space, and obviously coordinating prices, chickens, which not so long ago sold at 49¢ a pound, are now regularly $1.19 to $1.29. This week, there was a rare special—69¢ a pound!

Fish prices, for some reason, all seem to end in 99¢—but the first digit is usually from $4 to $7. And other seafood, especially shrimp, is out of sight—$12 to $14 a pound. Fish used to be the cheap source of protein.

I started to buy Savarin coffee because I like the aroma. Now there is another reason: its distributors do not cheat—yet. The two or three food conglomerates that dominate the coffee market have quietly cut the contents of cans from 16 to 13 ounces, and in some cases to 11.5 ounces, without cutting the size of the cans. But coffee from the 13-ounce can costs 23% more, and from the 11.5-ounce can 39% more per pound than the 16-ounce container used to. Why does Savarin still provide 16 ounces? I can only guess it is because the distributor is Tetley, the English tea company, which is apparently not yet a member of the American cartel.

The same ploy has been adopted by the raisin monopolies, I'm certain.

These examples have been confined to a small sampling of food prices. I could fill several columns—as no doubt, could you—with examples of other products we all need for day-to-day living: gasoline, clothing, toiletries, white goods, toys, and especially, medicines. Remember when games used to cost $3 and $4, and dolls and teddy bears were under $5?

I rest my case.

• • •

12/5/1992

NAFTA, Patents & Drugs

An important reason for lower medical costs in Canada than in the U.S. is that Canadian drug prices average 32% less than here. And in Mexico drugs can be purchased for a fraction of the U.S. price. How is that possible when the same drugs are sold in all three countries?

The difference is in the patent laws. U.S. patents permit a company to keep a monopoly on a drug for 17 to 20 years, while these rights are for much shorter periods in Mexico and Canada. When a patent expires, druggists are free to sell, and customers to buy, "generic drugs"—drugs of the same chemical mix as that of the patented drugs, sold under a different name. This allows consumers to buy drugs at half, and sometimes even a quarter, of the price of the patented drug.

Drug makers sold $41 billion worth of patented drugs in the U.S. last year, but only $5 billion worth of generic equivalents. However, taking into consideration the lower prices, the volume and curative power of the generic drugs was much greater than these figures indicate.

Patents today are not fulfilling their original role—rewarding the inventor. Today, while thousands of people work in the research and development (R&D) laboratories of giant drug companies, they have little individual stake in the profits generated by the drugs they develop. The company owns the formula—"intellectual property" in today's terms—and, as owners of that property, do with it what they may. Under this patent structure, prescription drug prices jumped 100% between 1983 and 1991, while overall consumer prices rose 36%.

Drug firms have lobbied hard to maintain their control of prices, claiming the high cost of R&D. But consider the fact that in 1991 combined sales of the three largest drug companies—Bristol Myers-Squibb, Merck, and Pfizer—totaled $28 billion. Costs of production were about $7 billion, leaving an incredible $21 billion in gross profits. And of that $21 billion, only $3 billion was used for R&D.

As a final gift to the most profitable U.S. monopoly, the Bush administration insisted on including a provision in the North American Free Trade Agreement (NAFTA) that requires Canada and Mexico to modify their patent laws to conform with U.S. law. Already, Canadian Prime Minister Mulroney has introduced legislation to do this, and if passed, Canadians will be forced to pay U.S. monopoly prices for drugs. (If it is defeated, however, it would encourage consumers on this side of the border to break the monopoly grip of drug companies in the U.S. and help create conditions for a national health care system no longer controlled by insurance and drug companies.)

Obviously, Mexico will be hit even harder than Canada. If anything reveals the outrageous profiteering of the drug companies, it is their willingness to sell patented drugs on the Mexican side of the border for one-third the U.S. price. Drug companies are not selling drugs more cheaply in Mexico as an act of charity: The poverty of the Mexican masses would prevent drug sales at U.S. prices. And, with their huge profits, drug companies still have enough incentive to encourage these cut-rate sales. Also, unless the Mexican government has effective price controls, U.S. companies may well charge U.S. prices in major Mexican cities.

The U.S. is also trying to impose the same patent limitations on countries involved in GATT negotiations. But the chances of success are dubious since drug prices are under government control in most of those countries.

What is needed is a strong movement to press President-elect Clinton not only to hold down increases in drug prices but to force companies to cut their prices in half.

• • •

1/30/1993

One-Fourth Live in Poverty

In 1937, President Franklin D. Roosevelt said, "I see one-third of a nation ill-housed, ill-clad, ill-nourished."

Since then the productivity of American workers, incorporating the great advances in world science and technology, has multiplied many times. The wealth and might of the "sole superpower," U.S. capitalism, has reached towering heights and looms as a monstrous imperialist threat and plunderer over the people of the world.

These gains have not "trickled down" to the U.S. multitudes.

FDR's statement was made during the world's most prolonged and severe sequence of cyclical economic crises, crises that were much deeper than those of the 1980s and 1990s. Yet if he could view his country today, he would change but one word of that devastating indictment—replacing "one-third" with "one-fourth." But, measured in absolute terms, today's one-fourth is made up of 60 million people, whereas one-third of the population in 1937 represented "only" 40 million.

And again life for millions has become a frantic struggle for existence, despite a bundle of government programs enacted during the New Deal and during Lyndon Johnson's administration. Hunger and homelessness, so prevalent in the 1930s, have reappeared and are spreading.

The magnitude of the situation is underscored by data in the newly released Census Bureau survey, *Poverty in the United States: 1992*. The study puts the "official" count of people living in poverty at 37 million, the largest number in a generation and 14 million more than 1973's postwar low of 23 million.

Not only has the number of poor increased. The impact of racism, an always present factor in the number and composition of the poor, has increased. In 1992, half of the poor were white, numbering about 18.3 million—or nearly one-tenth of the white population. Bad as that is, it pales beside the figures for African Americans and Latinos: one in three African Americans—some 10.6 million—are poor, and the 6.7 million Latinos who live in poverty are nearly a third of all Latinos.

But the official figures in the Census Bureau report, shocking as they are, are barely more than half the number of poor people, a fact admitted by the government itself.

A very simple, straightforward method of counting the number of poor people would be the number of people who receive "means-tested" government assistance, aid given in accordance with strict government tests showing a lack of sufficient income to pay for minimal food, housing or medical care.

In 1992 there were 61 million of these recipients—about 24% of the population, and another 10 million who, while being officially counted as living in poverty, received no means-related assistance. This adds up to 71 million people whom the government admits to be poor, some 29% of the population.

The number of people who qualified for means-tested assistance increased by 3 million in 1992—and this at a time of brutal campaigns at all levels of government to tighten the eligibility screws and throw needy people off the programs!

There is another way of calculating the number of people living in poverty, and this, too, substantiates the undercount of the Census Bureau. Because the official measure of poverty is far too low, government agencies often use a higher figure as a cut-off for aid—generally 185% of the official poverty level ($13,000-plus for a family of four).

Analysts now typically regard 150% or 175% of the official thresholds as realistic for determining poverty. Those levels, for 1992, cover 61 million and 73 million people, respectively. If we were to use the 150% figure, then 46-47% of all African Americans and Hispanics—and nearly 60% of Black and Latino children and youth—would be counted as "poor."

As an aside, and as an example of how the social safety net is being cut to ribbons, the recently adopted Clinton-Rostenkowski Economic Program uses 50% of the official level as its criterion for establishing need, the same standard used in the Clinton health care proposal for determining whether people will be eligible for assistance in securing coverage.

It will take socialism to wipe out the scourge of poverty. The tremendous progress toward that end made by the USSR, Cuba, the DPRK, GDR and other socialist countries in the face of constant war, threats of war and economic warfare by the powerful imperialist bloc, proves that American socialism will surely be able to end poverty—and speedily, too.

12/4/1993

Figures Don't Lie—Liars Figure

The Labor Department has admitted undercounting the unemployed and will add 400,000, one half of 1%, to its official figures.

That's small change: the department admits that these official numbers are off by 50%—some 4.5 million—if underemployed and "discouraged workers" are taken into account. But even this undercounting does not take into account the growing number of young people who never find a job, or the rising population of the nation's jails and prisons. And the statistical methodology used by the Labor Department that excludes large numbers of African American males from the labor force and the unemployed—and from the population as a whole, for that matter—needs major overhaul.

There is another gross distortion, one in which the Labor Department and the Census Bureau collude, that impacts on the public as a whole. I refer to the Consumer Price Index (CPI-U). The index is published monthly by the Bureau of Labor Statistics to measure changes in the price of goods and services bought by urban consumers. It is widely referred to as a cost-of-living index, but it is less than that, since it leaves out increases in taxes and several other components that are part of the cost of living.

The CPI is used to measure changes in real wages, consumer income, the number living in poverty, etc. It's used to calculate the annual increase in Social Security benefits and, in a slightly modified form, cost-of-living allowances (COLA) in union contracts. The CPI shows a 20% decline in real wages since 1973, along with an increase of 14 million people living in poverty during the same period.

Since 1990, these agencies have promoted an alternative index (CPI-U-X1), with the "X" standing for "experimental."

For the past two years the Census Bureau has used only this experimental index in its annual reports on incomes, etc. and in making historical comparisons of these data. The disparities between it and calculations made using CPI-U are stark: in 1968-1992, the experimental index lagged behind CPI-U, the "real" index.

As the Census Bureau puts it, "Based on the CPI-U-X1, median family income increased by 8.1% between 1973 and 1989 in real terms compared with 1.7% using the CPI-U." This chicanery cuts decline in real wages since 1973 in half.

This statistical gimmick is used to prettify capitalism. But its designers have bigger plans and hope to use it for propaganda in direct attacks on the working class. For example, the government sets poverty thresholds, more commonly called the "poverty level." If a family's income is less than 150 to 185% of the threshold, that family is eligible for food stamps, Medicaid, etc.

By using the CPI-U-X1 index, the poverty threshold is increased by $1,000; and the number of people counted as living in poverty is reduced to 32 million, some 4 million below the official count of 36 million. If the experimental index becomes the standard index, millions of people, even tens of millions, will be denied food stamps or become ineligible for Aid to Families with Dependent Children.

I hope that trade unions and organizations of oppressed people will vigorously expose and defeat this sneak attack on the working class.

One need not get bogged down in matters of methodology in order to prevent this from happening. The bottom line is that the CPI-U has always lagged behind actual increases in the cost of living—and any index that lags even further behind is worse.

• • •

8/13/1994

Economics of the Health Ripoff

As President Clinton and Congress lurch toward passage of a "health reform" bill, Wall Street finally seems freed of earlier fears that the most profitable industry on earth might be watered down. A recent example of this new confidence is American Home Products' record-breaking $8.5 billion offer to take over drug manufacturer American Cyanamid.

Annual health expenditures in the United States, expanding by 11% per year, are approaching the trillion-dollar mark—15% of the total gross domestic product. Of this trillion-dollar industry, 45% is generated by facilities such as hospitals and nursing homes. Twenty-five percent goes to doctors and dentists, and 10% goes to drug and medical supply corporations.

Drug companies are merging out of the same motivation that gave us the Big Three auto makers and the oil and steel trusts of a century ago. Fourteen of these pharmaceutical conglomerates are worth a combined total of $200 billion on the stock market, three times the worth of their invested capital.

The average gross profit margin of 73% means that their sales (to middlemen, not to you) are nearly four times the cost of production. We, the retail consumers, pay double that.

Where do the gross profits go? The largest chunk, in some cases more than half, goes to "selling, general and administrative expenses." In plain English, that's what's taken by the corporate brass and their various bureaucracies. There's still plenty left over for stockholders, with hefty annual dividend increases.

Wall Street is rushing to seize a share of this new health care booty. Currently, the fastest growth in profits is from health maintenance organizations (HMOs)—physician-hospital networks that are rapidly transforming doctors into capitalists, some as owners, others as salaried employees. The largest such corporation, Columbia/HCA Health Care, owns 197 hospitals, gobbling up another 20 each year.

Such rapid acquisition suggests that the process of monopolization in the health care industry is still in its early stages. Corporations behave in this manner because they know they have a long way to go to squeeze maximum profits from the public.

Other industrialized nations have established controls over drug and medical service prices. As a result, their health expenditures are less than half those of the U.S. Instead of enacting such controls here, the administration and Congress are working to reduce Medicare and Medicaid benefits. Meanwhile, the drive to privatize public health care facilities threatens to further increase costs.

The single-payer system of health reform is the only proposal that reduces costs while improving service. It eliminates the bureaucratic weight of insurance companies, HMOs and other intermediaries. It would facilitate sharp price reductions by putting a lid on the rising costs of health commodities and services.

The prolonged squabbling over health legislation is exposing both the profiteering of health monopolies and the demagogy of politicians under their sway. At the same time, the success of California's single-payer reform referendum in making the ballot is evidence of increasing popular recognition of the need for real health care reform. California's step toward real reform heralds eventual victory over the monopolies of health care.

• • •

6/26/1999

Drug Prices/Drug Profits

The Clinton administration is again chattering about the high cost of prescription drugs. Proposals revolve around how much the government "can afford" to spend to subsidize the high prices, giving rise to endless and inconclusive debate within the administration—and with the Republicans.

Of course, all health care, including medication, should be as free as elementary education. But with all the discussion, there's no official consideration of how much the companies should be required to reduce their outrageous prices.

The drug companies defend the extortion by claiming the high cost of research and development (R&D) leads to the discovery of new life-saving drugs. That argument is effective propaganda, but it's bunk: the hidden profits contained in the companies' gross profits are many times the expenditures for R&D.

Take Bristol-Myers Squibb (BMY). It spent $1.6 billion for R&D in 1998. But it spent $7.5 billion for advertising, bonuses of top executives and other mainly parasitic purposes. Obviously, BMY could "afford" to slash prices of its drugs without taking anything from R&D.

Or take Pfizer Corporation, noted for its high R&D outlays—$2.3 billion, or one-sixth of its sales. But it spent $6.8 billion, or nearly three times as much, on mainly parasitic items. It could cut its U.S. prices in half, or by $4.1 billion, and still leave $2.7 billion to use as the bosses see fit: for advertising, their pay, etc. And that would leave intact its reported $3.4 billion after taxes, 51% more than in 1997—and a return of 40% on capital.

No wonder the price of Pfizer stock has gone through the roof! Its foreign prices are lower than here because of various government restrictions and national health care systems.

Senators Kennedy and Rockefeller are sponsors of the Senate version of a Democratic Party bill to partly cover prescription drugs under Medicare. The plan calls for a $200 deductible and a 20% co-payment for prescriptions. Complete coverage would be provided for costs beyond $3,000 per year. The average senior citizen takes more than four prescription drugs daily and fills 18 prescriptions a year.

There are obvious shortcomings in the bill. The deductible and co-payments can easily run up to the $3,000 limit, considering the exorbitant prices of most prescription drugs; 100% coverage on all prescriptions would be desirable.

The bill requires the federal government to hire private insurers or pharmacy benefit managers to run the program. That, of course, ensures that the provisions will be interpreted as narrowly as possible, to give the least benefit to Medicare recipients and most profit to the private managers.

According to the publication, *Seniority*, "the pharmaceutical industry is expected to fight the addition of prescription drug coverage to Medicare because of its fear that it could lead to 'price controls.'"

On the contrary, one of the main weaknesses of the bill is that it forestalls such an outcome. And what is necessary is just that: a fight for price controls and reductions.

What's more, the federal government would have to pay for the drugs—that is taxpayers, which means mainly workers. For Medicare recipients to benefit, it is the **drug companies** that should pay, by having to charge realistic, controlled prices.

Many of the beneficiaries would be retired union members. Active support by the trade union movement, as well as by senior citizen organizations, is essential to achieve that goal.

Labor and Industry (1961-1979)

5/7/1961

Kennedy and the Workweek

I first did research on the shorter workweek in 1934. I was asked to calculate the effect on industrial costs of a labor proposal to adopt the 35-hour week at 40 hours pay. My study showed that industry could afford it. But my boss, who came from an upper-crust family, ignored the study.

The workweek is a class issue. An employer who gets an extra hour's labor out of a worker increases his profit by more than one-fortieth. That is why employers often pay time-and-one-half for overtime instead of hiring extra workers.

Because of chronic mass unemployment, major industrial unions are finally campaigning for a shorter workweek without reduction in pay.

President Kennedy, asked about the shorter workweek, answered:

"I prefer it for myself, but . . . I am opposed to a shorter workweek. I am hopeful that we can have employment high five days a week, and forty hours, which is traditional in this country, and which is necessary if we are going to continue economic growth, and maintain our commitments at home and abroad."

The 40-hour week is not "traditional." The tradition in agriculture was from sun-up to sundown; and in industry, the 10 or 12-hour day, the 60 or 70-hour week. The struggle for the 8-hour day was a major theme in American labor history, including the nation-wide strike struggles of 1886, when May Day began.

Thousands of strikes by millions of workers gradually brought the industrial workweek down from an average of 66 hours in 1860 to 50 in 1900, 51 in 1920, and 40 in 1940. The New Deal Fair Labor Standards Act of 1938 made the 5-day week and 8-hour day legal for a minority, generally the best organized sections of the working class.

What was traditional was American workingclass pioneering in fighting to reduce the workweek. Most countries are still behind where we got during the 1930s. There has been no further cut here since, and little serious fight for a cut. That is the break with a century-old tradition.

The 40-hour week is not needed for economic growth. National economic growth was faster during the time when the workweek was cut by several hours per decade, than it has been recently. By increasing employment and the purchasing power of the masses, a shorter workweek without reduction in pay would help get us out of economic stagnation.

The reference to "our commitments at home and abroad" is a prettified version of the old chestnut that the shorter workweek would interfere with the "need" to increase defense production. We need less armaments, not more. Anyhow, there is plenty of unemployment in the munitions industries, especially aircraft. And with full employment at 30 hours per week, the country could produce far more necessary goods and services than now.

The Soviet Union, which has been gaining on the U.S. economically, politically, scientifically and militarily, has been cutting the workweek more rapidly than any capitalist country ever did. The reduction to a 7 and 6-hour day (with a partial 6th day per week) has just been completed. Now the average workweek in the USSR stands at 39.4 hours, the lowest in the world.

The U.S. does **not** have a general 40-hour week. The legal maximum excludes the majority of wage earners, including agriculture, forestry, many trade and service lines, small establishments, etc. The "traditional" 60-70 hour week is still the fate of 3,000,000 wage workers. The average workweek for those who were not part-time workers in the U.S. in February 1961 was 43.8 hours among non-farm wage and salary workers, and 45.5 hours for all gainfully employed. (U.S. Labor Dept. statistics).

The new administration minimum wage bill before Congress does **not** add the 40-hour protection for any workers not now covered.

American labor is vitally interested in closing the workweek gap, and in reestablishing its traditional pioneering role in setting new lows in working time and new highs in workers' leisure.

That is why the economic and legislative fight for a shorter workweek without reduction in pay is second to no other labor economic demand. And labor's organizing efforts should strive to extend equal maximum hours protection to all wage and salary workers without exception.

● ● ●

7/1/1962

Sick Transit

Airlines workers called a strike to save jobs of jet crew members. Maritime strikes erupt continuously, and mergers threaten all workers and passengers. It is timely to study the President's transportation program, largely dormant in congressional committee since April.

According to Kennedy, "pressing problems are burdening our national transportation system," including a "chaotic patchwork of inconsistent and often obsolete legislation and regulation". . . the "traveling public . . . paying higher rates to subsidize weak segments of the transportation industry," "chronic over-capacity and deficits," "increasing highway congestion."

He makes some good proposals, including:

- Repeal of the 10% passenger tax (partial repeal for airlines).
- $500 million aid to improve mass transit facilities.
- Moving expenses for families displaced by federal highway construction.
- Ending government fixing of minimum fares.

It looks as if the first will pass, and something may be done on the second. However, these measures, and others not mentioned, are trifles in relation to the situation.

The President's main concern is with the owners, their supposedly unsatisfactory profits and claimed inequities in profit distribution. He expresses less concern for passengers, and none for transport workers.

By March 1962, with the consumer price index at 130 on the 1947-49 base, the public transportation index reached 215, higher than any other group.

Between 1951 and 1961 transport employment fell 15%, from 2,821,000 to 2,485,000. The 10-year job loss in railroads and merchant shipping approached 50%; in local transit, 40%.

Kennedy says improved transportation "must be achieved by continued reliance on unsubsidized privately owned facilities." Since when? The federal government pays to or spends literally billions in subsidies and aids of one kind or another for the transport companies.

The peak of absurdity is in the shipping industry, where 75% of workers' wages are refunded to the companies and 55% of the selling price of American flag vessels paid to shipyards. Most of the President's program aims to redivide these subsidies "more equitably."

The transportation industry is an extreme example of the mortal illness of capitalism. Permanent subsidies paid to influential monopolies under the plea of "national security" have led to inefficient operation, bloated bureaucracies, and book losses covering up secret payouts to insiders. Regulation, supposedly to protect the public, actually raises and reinforces monopoly prices. Uneven development has led to rapid and disorderly substitution of some types of transportation for others. All these vices are compounded by the overall stagnation in the U.S. economy.

The sufferers are the transport workers, users—and taxpayers. The cure must serve their interests and attack the troubles at their root.

Kennedy says that "the transport system must be built and operated as a whole" rather than as "an uncoordinated set of independent entities." His proposals contradict that correct principle. Ours conform to it.

The only practical way to disentangle the mess is by nationalization and unified government operation. Of course, this would not guarantee a decisive improvement. The government, after all, is the mirror of the society it represents. But it would give people a much better setup in which to fight for:

a) Full maintenance of employment in all transportation industries, including universal application of the 35-hour week; manning according to maximum safety requirements instead of maximum profit requirements.

b) Rapid and complete ending of anti-Negro discrimination, especially rife in transportation employment, and equal access to facilities.

c) A sharp reduction in public transportation costs to the population and improvement in quality, with the present chaotic subsidies replaced by overall government financing, at the expense of corporate shippers and wealthy taxpayers.

This is not socialism. Full solution of transportation industry problems, as of all other economic ills, cannot be achieved without socialism. But public ownership, even within capitalism, can be a framework for limited progress.

• • •

4/27/1963

FDR's Economic Bill of Rights Still Lives

The perspective of American labor has broadened considerably since the first May Day. While more recently adopted traditions have dimmed in the fog of the cold war, they retain general acceptance by the people.

At my suggestion, three students in my class took a poll and they carefully recorded the responses to the following:

"A famous person said: 'Every man has the right to a useful and remunerative job in the industries, or shops, or farms, or mines of the nation'."

1. Do you agree with it?
2. What was the political party of the man who said it?
3. What was his nationality?

A poll was tallied of 114 students at a college in upstate New York. Of these, 77 agreed with the quote; 36 didn't agree; and 1 was uncertain. To the second question, 39 said Democrat, 23 Socialist, 12 Republican, followed by a scattering of other answers, including 6 Communists, 3 Federalists (!) and one who thought it was from Karl Marx. To the third question, 77 said American, 16 Russian, 12 European, and 9 specified European countries.

A printing trades worker asked five people in his shop. All agreed to question one; on two, 4 said Democrat, 1 said Communist; all said American to the third question.

A Harlem worker asked about 75 people in his neighborhood. All agreed with the quote. About 55 associated it with the Democratic Party; about 20, mainly younger people, said Communist; several older people attributed it to the Democrats but said that today it would be called Communism.

None of the upstate college students had any idea of the author of the statement; all five printing workers said they didn't know; only a few of the Harlem residents correctly identified Franklin D. Roosevelt.

The quote was taken from the Economic Bill of Rights, contained in his message to Congress of January 1944. It said, in more detail:

"In our day these economic truths have become accepted as self-evident. We have accepted, so to speak, a second Bill of Rights under which a new basis of security and prosperity may be established for all—regardless of station, race or creed.

"Among these are:

"The right to a useful and remunerative job. . . .

"The right to earn enough to provide adequate food and clothing and recreation . . .

"The right of every farmer to . . . a return which will give him and his family a decent living.

"The right of every business man . . . to . . . freedom from unfair competition and domination by monopolies. . . .

"The right of every family to a decent home;

"The right of adequate medical care and the opportunity to achieve and enjoy good health;

"The right to a good education."

This eloquent programmatic statement of the New Deal president arose out of the struggle of the workers and farmers, summed up the fighting demands of the American people, crystallized after a decade of struggle. And they were Roosevelt's promise to the people of the way they would be awarded for wartime sacrifices in the fight against fascism.

The American people elected Roosevelt to a fourth term. Labor provided the main force in a hard fought campaign, with the pledge of the Economic Bill of Rights as its beacon.

But the promise was betrayed by Roosevelt's successors. Tens of millions of Americans are wholly deprived of those rights; none enjoys them securely as **rights**, rather than "good breaks" of uncertain duration. Domination by monopolies is more complete than ever, over all social classes and every aspect of life. We have never fully gained peace, which was and remains the major promise of the Economic Bill of Rights.

But such setbacks are never permanent. The valid struggles of the people are in tune with history and will certainly be rewarded. The tradition of the Economic Bill of Rights will become fully alive again, in a new wave of popular activity. When it does, it will be further enriched and will aim for still loftier goals.

• • •

10/13/1963

Labor Is Here to Stay

Robert Theobald, in his special *Nation* issue on abundance, writes that the scientific-technical revolution must radically curtail the need for labor, and proposes a universal dole as a constitutional right for an anticipated general condition of unemployment.

The common idea of the rapid absolute replacement of human labor by machines is not valid. Despite publicity given dramatic examples of automation, the overall rise in labor productivity continues to proceed unevenly. Long periods of technical stagnation in some areas accompany radical advances in others.

The officially estimated average annual growth in productivity is 2.5%. Every workingman's family I know could easily and gladly absorb a 2.5% per annum rise in real income for as far in the future as one can foresee. So if that productivity rise were proportionately allotted to higher real wages, there would never be a shortage of demand for the rising consumers goods output, and the need for labor would continue to rise with the population.

Even in America, already having the world's highest productivity, continued progress of automation could be a source of nothing but benefit and would require more and more labor for generations to come.

Moreover, automation opens up better-than-ever opportunities for a shorter workweek.

Under capitalism it is not automation that produces unemployment, but the use of automation to increase profits. The USSR is still behind the United States in average technology, but it is introducing new technique at least twice as fast as America; and its average annual rise in labor productivity is 6%. But this rapid rise, doubling productivity every 12 years, doesn't cause a single case of unemployment.

In a planned economy publicly owned and run for the satisfaction of people's needs instead of capitalists' profits, technical advance is wholly converted into higher production and shorter working hours, combined with a rising demand for labor, which always keeps up with supply.

Finally, Mr. Theobald is suggesting a hopeless future for Americans by depriving them of the opportunity to work. Mankind has evolved as a species for whom productive labor is a characteristic mode of life. Deprive man of this, and you take away one of his key special characteristics.

I know there are tens of millions now doomed to dangerous, or strenuous, or over-long, or monotonous, or dirty work. Still, the misery in America's depressed areas today is more from lack of creative activity than from hunger. One of Marx's greatest contributions was the concept of labor as inseparable from humanity, the perspective of a society in which labor would become man's prime need and source of joy and expression.

Man wants to get rid of underpaid stoop labor on the factory farms not so he can mope in idleness, but so he can build, maintain and operate the control panels of automated factory shops; build and fly interstellar rockets; find a cure for cancer; provide ample first-rate cultural services—in short, do work that gives satisfaction to the supplier as to the user.

8/16/1964

The Democrats and Full Employment

Will the Democratic platform pledge full employment? Will it offer adequate proposals to implement it? Will Johnson center his campaign on it? Positive answers to these questions can win with the biggest landslide of the century.

Neither major party has favored full employment for 20 years. Roosevelt promised it in 1944; but after he died, the reactionaries who gained power broke his promise. Now Johnson is trying to revive the Roosevelt tradition. This spring he told labor leaders:

"As a Congressman I voted for the Employment Act of 1946. It was originally called the Full Employment Bill, but the word 'Full' was dropped from the title. Unfortunately, it has also been dropped from the thinking of too many people. As a result, 4 to 5 million people are out of work in this country all the time, while across the Atlantic such levels of unemployment are a matter of ancient history. We, too, must catch up to modern history. The time has come for labor and government and business to agree that we are going to achieve, and keep, full employment."

The Senate subcommittee on Employment and Manpower, headed by Sen. Joseph Clark of Pennsylvania, indicated the trend of administration thinking on the subject. Unfortunately, it limits its goal to reducing unemployment to 3% by 1968, claiming, "A certain level of unemployment is inevitable and necessary in a free, dynamic economy." Now that is an advance over the position of previous administrations, which equated 4% unemployment with "full" employment. But it isn't very much of an advance.

The justification for either of these figures is the old big business argument about the inevitability of "fractional" unemployment. But most "fractional" unemployment isn't even counted in the official figures. West European experience shows that even under capitalism, unemployment can be cut below 1%.

To be consistent, a full employment pledge must be unqualified; it must call for zero unemployment—a job for every person of working age, not incapacitated, who seeks work. To be effective, it must include a government commitment to provide work to those not employed by private industry.

The Senate report proposes a significant step towards this second requirement: Following the scheme of the Murray Full Employment Bill of 1945, the President should estimate for the coming year the level of gross national product (GNP) required for full employment, and the forecast of GNP to be expected under existing policies. When the forecast falls below the amount required for full employment, the President should recommend measures to close the gap, with higher government spending heading the list. The government should employ these workers to increase urgently needed public sector activities. Further:

"The present underutilization of manpower offers an excellent opportunity to attack festering problems of classroom and teacher shortage, urban blight, substandard housing, air and water pollution, transportation deficiencies, depressed areas, soil erosion, flood control, and recreation needs."

The senators estimate that to cut unemployment to 3% by 1968, federal spending for non-military goods and services must increase by $5 billion yearly—from $10.6 billion in 1963 to over $35 billion in 1968, a rise of three and one-half times. With cuts in military spending, they recommend offsetting additional increases in civilian outlays.

The public sector program is only half of what is needed. The demands of labor and Negro peoples for raising mass purchasing power and ending poverty are the other half. These include the $2 minimum wage and 35-hour week for all workers; radical improvements in social security; some form of minimum income guarantee; shifting taxes from the poor to the rich; full enforcement of the letter and spirit of the fair employment section of the Civil Rights Act.

Also, the public sector proposal should be beefed up to include an unconditional government commitment to go beyond mere estimating, and actually to provide employment for all needing it, regardless of earlier estimates.

Labor and civil rights organizations can make the Democratic Convention a significant opening arena of struggle for an all-out campaign for full employment.

• • •

5/15/1966

Labor's Share of the Loot?

A reader writes: "I have a friend who understands how imperialism benefits the U.S. capitalist and deforms the economies of the colonial countries . . . but he cannot understand that the U.S. worker also benefits from this. He thinks the U.S. worker has a comparatively high standard of living because the U.S. is highly industrialized and has an abundance of natural resources. . . . Could you give me more specific data to convince my friend that the super-profits of the imperialists filter down to raise the workers' standard of living?"

Your friend is substantially right, and you are wrong.

The American workers achieved the world's highest wages before the U.S. was an imperialist power, and before it led in world industrialization. Fundamentally, it happened because of the chronic relative shortage of labor during the period of industrialization, so that workers' bargaining power was stronger here than in Europe. Special political factors and natural conditions also played a part.

But for decades now there has been a chronic surplus of labor. Gains increasingly result from organized struggles, from collective action that sometimes overcomes unfavorable supply-demand conditions resulting from a mass reserve of unemployed workers.

Lenin emphasized the bribery of a segment of labor out of colonial super-profits before World War I, especially in Western Europe, and the connections between that and the opportunism and pro-imperialist policies of many labor leaders. Certainly there are analogies in the U.S. Never before has a group of imperialists robbed the world so much as American monopolies do. Never did so many relatively well paid workers consider themselves part of the "middle class." Never was there such a servile, pro-imperialist top labor leadership as that of the AFL-CIO today [1966].

But progressive Americans should be wary of interpreting this too schematically. The payoff to the pre-World War I English labor aristocracy was always a relative affair. The employers continued to exploit them, but granted them modest gains at a time when labor conditions in most countries were stagnant, or worse. The participation of some British workers in the loot of Africa and India, in the final analysis, was an illusion, but a politically effective illusion in that global framework.

The dynamics of events are different now. Even while American companies are taking over more and more of the capitalist world economy, U.S. workers' relative conditions are declining. Their share of the national income is falling, as exploitation of labor is increasing at home. And their comparative standard of living on a world scale is falling as workers elsewhere catch up to them. In Western Europe and Japan, whose capitalists profit much less from imperialist holdings, labor is making faster gains than in the United States. Workers in socialist countries, who are neither exploited nor exploiters of others, are closing the gap even more rapidly.

Fundamentally this is because of the enhanced political power of labor. Labor dominates governments of the socialist third of the world. It has large trade unions, labor parties, and strong militant Communist parties in many industrialized capitalist countries. Struggling from this power base, workers abroad gain much more than the niggling concessions won from Meany-style "partnership" with employers.

Another element has changed. The oppressed victims of imperialism resist it a hundred times more effectively than a half century ago. The U.S., acting as world policeman and collection agent for giant corporations, spends more money in the process than the corporations make out of it. American labor pays most of the cost through taxes and price inflation.

The "world's highest" living standards of a section of American labor is a residue of historical advantage, temporarily increased by U.S. exclusion from world war damage; and it is now dwindling. It is not a benefit paid by big business for labor support in world conquest.

The holocausts of World War I and II did much to liquidate, at least temporarily, the illusions built up by imperialist bribery in Europe. The working class of some imperialist countries became revolutionary, took power in Russia, and would have done so in a number of other countries if not for direct and indirect U.S. intervention.

American labor cannot afford to wait for another world war to learn its lesson. There might then be no living standards left to preserve. The Korean War and now, especially, the Vietnam War, with its mounting cost in money and lives, have given fair warning. Progressives must convince workers of the illusory character of their gains from war production and foreign investments, of their vital interests, material as well as moral, in breaking with the Meany-Johnson alliance of imperialist aggression.

• • •

7/23/1967

Modern Capitalism and Unemployment

Joseph Califano, Jr., Johnson's top aide on domestic matters, recently pronounced administration policy on massive unemployment, especially among Negroes.

Califano, a product of Tom Dewey's Rockefeller-oriented law firm and of the Pentagon brain trust, has applied McNamara's much touted "systems" method to the problem of unemployment. This method was developed by McNamara for munitions procurement. His followers claim it can be applied to major social problems. In this method electronic computers and high-powered mathematics give an appearance of efficiency and scientific objectivity, which hides the reactionary essence of big business policies—more profiteering for arms merchants and deeper subjection for workers.

Califano asserts we must get rid of the notion that "many millions" on welfare are capable of working. On the contrary, he claims, only 50,000 of the 7,300,000 on the rolls are "capable of being given job skills and training that will make them self-sufficient." (*The New York Times*, 4/20.)

Employer talk about "unemployables" to evade easing unemployment is old stuff. Never has it been given such sweeping official sanction, and so disguised with a veneer of sociological benevolence. The Califanos and their bosses are not satisfied with erasing these people from the statistics of unemployment; they want to erase them from the life of the country. Unfortunately, some progressives and liberals, bemused by the covering sociological chatter and by the potential of the scientific-technical revolution, play into their hands by predicting the early end of human labor for the majority of men, and proclaim the struggle for jobs futile.

The underlying cause of massive "hard core" unemployment was explained a century ago. Smug apologists belittle Karl Marx as applicable to mid-19th century England, but not to modern, efficient, affluent America. However, the following words of Marx were never truer than right now in the U.S.:

"The greater the social wealth, the functioning capital, the extent and energy of its growth, and, therefore, also the absolute mass of the proletariat and the productiveness of its labour, the greater is the industrial reserve-army . . . the greater is the mass of a consolidated surplus-population, whose misery is in inverse ratio to its torment of labour. The more extensive, finally, the lazarus-layers of the working-class, and the industrial reserve-army, the greater is official pauperism." (Marx, *Capital*, Modern Library Ed. Vol.1, p. 707.)

There are new features in the United States, not present in 19th century England. Major, concentrated sections of the industrial reserve army are Negroes, supplemented by other minorities. American capitalism uses racism as a device for splitting the industrial reserve army from the rest of the working class. Of course, not all Negroes are in this reserve army, and plenty of whites are also in it, especially in Appalachia, parts of New England, etc. A century ago the industrial reserve army arose spontaneously as a result of the contradictions of capitalism. Now the spontaneous process is aided by conscious efforts of the capitalists and the government to expand the reserve army, to degrade its conditions of life, to utilize it as a weapon of economic pressure against all labor and as an incitation to racism.

But there is another, vital, new feature. Now it has become clear that unemployment and pauperism can be abolished along with capitalism. Socialist countries have proved this through accomplishment. And in capitalist countries workers, through united struggles, have shown that these evils can be reduced markedly.

Capitalist experts calculate the "desirable" level of unemployment—high enough to provide an industrial reserve army, low enough to keep the white unemployed scattered among the population, and to make unlikely the emergence of a powerful united Negro-white struggle against joblessness.

These conditions were overset during the 1930s, when the masses of the unemployed formed a powerful organized sector of labor that contributed greatly to the reduction of pauperism and starvation, and advanced the cause of all labor. The unemployed and pauperized are now sufficiently numerous among the Negro people that theirs is the cause of all working people, the basis for mass organization and action.

• • •

3/3/1968

The Real Picture of Steel Imports

Steel imports reached a record 11,455,000 tons last year, up 10 times in 10 years. Subtracting the 1,685,000 tons of exports resulted in a net import of 9,770,000 tons, a little over 10% of the domestic supply.

Some qualifications are in order. Exports consist largely of high-price specialty steels. Much more steel is contained in finished products exported from this country than in finished products imported into the U.S.

According to calculations made by the staff of the Senate Finance Committee in its recent study of steel imports, the overall steel import balance, adjusted for these factors, was not very large in 1966. Still, the increasing trend of steel imports undermines employment in the U.S. industry, and is a source of legitimate concern to steel workers.

The steel companies are pressing for enactment of the Hartke bill, which would limit steel imports to the 1964-66 proportion of total supply, or nearly 11%. The United Steel Workers of America supports this measure. It is opposed by major steel importers and leading bankers, who favor the official free trade policy.

Steel manufacturers try to place all the blame for soaring imports on relatively high wages in the United States. However, wage differentials between the United States and other countries are no wider in the steel industry than in industry generally, and much less than they were a decade ago. Nor are steel labor costs out of line. The 1965 *Annual Survey of Manufacturers* shows wages and salaries in iron and steel at 47.3% of value added by manufacture, virtually the same as the 46.8% of all industries.

Between 1960 and 1964, U.S. steel workers' wages increased 2.64% per year, while in competing countries the annual increases ranged from 5.09% in Luxembourg to 12.68% in Italy. In Japan, the largest steel exporter to the U.S., wages went up 9.10% per year. Senate economists calculated that if these rates of change continue, Italian and Dutch steel workers will reach the wage level of American steel workers by 1975 (Senate Finance Committee Staff Study, *Steel Imports*, table 100, p. 180).

U.S. labor costs per unit of production have been stable or trending downwards for the past decade. Between 1960 and 1966 they decreased 5.2% (*Ibid.*, table 89, p. 166). Meanwhile, unit labor costs increased in all major competing countries.

Steel importers must pay $15 for ocean shipping and $7 in tariffs per ton. According to company figures carried in the Senate report, only the Japanese come close to covering that through primary cost advantages. Their net advantage in labor and material costs is given at $17 per ton, or $5 less than the tariff transport handicap they have to overcome.

The basic reasons for the adverse steel trade balance are:

1. The technical advantage of the U.S. steel industry has been dissipated. Japanese, not American, steel producers were the first to equip the bulk of their steel capacity with the most advanced basic oxygen and electric furnaces. Man-hour productivity in Japan advanced from 33% of the U.S. level in 1957 to 74% in 1966; in the Common Market countries, from 61% to 77% in the same period (*Ibid.*, p. 182). Foreign companies were able to pay the big wage increases that their well organized, often left-led workers won, and still keep costs within competitive bounds.

2. Overcapacity, in relation to domestic demand, developed throughout the capitalist world steel industry, including in the U.S. The capitalists of other countries fought hard for export markets, even at the cost of narrowing their profit margins. But American steel manufacturers concentrated on maintaining their monopoly price structure, and essentially gave up the export market except for high-profit, high-price shipments resulting from foreign aid and other "tied" orders.

3. The armament-induced inflation of the Vietnam War has apparently made the American dollar overvalued in relation to other currencies,

and foreign goods therefore are displacing U.S. goods faster than ever both here and abroad.

4. U.S. big business generally has shifted from export of goods to export of capital. American manufacturers are more interested in exploiting foreign workers directly, at lower-than-U.S. wages, than in selling goods made here to foreign countries. They now make abroad three times as much goods as they export. And, increasingly, they are importing goods from foreign factories that they own themselves.

Steel companies, starting later than many others, are now joining the parade. *Iron Age* correspondent G. J. McManus writes:

"American steelmakers could become their own worst enemies. If they keep investing abroad, U.S. mills could reach the point where they are attacking themselves if they attack foreign steel. . . . Despite their attempts to isolate the American market, domestic steel people seem to be involving themselves more and more in the international scene" (*Iron Age*, 1/18).

He lists 16 plants in 11 foreign countries owned by Armco, U.S. Steel, Allegheny Ludlum and Pittsburgh Steel.

U.S. companies are also active in selling process know-how and raw materials to their foreign competitors. Kaiser Steel recently signed a $706 million contract to deliver 50 million tons of high-grade coking coal to Mitsubishi, representing seven major Japanese steel manufacturers. Kaiser is investing $51 million in the Crowsnest, British Columbia, mining area for the purpose. Kaiser also supplies large quantities of iron ore to Japan from Eagle Mountain, CA., and to Australia.

Quotas on steel imports would slow, but not stop, the displacement of domestic by imported steel. Experience with import quotas on oil, watches, and other items shows that there are always built-in loopholes, and government administrators always grant exceptions, so that the proportion of imports continues to rise.

The loss of domestic steel production to direct imports is paralleled by indirect losses on account of rising imports and declining exports of machine tools, automobiles, and many other iron and steel-containing products. Steel quotas would speed up this process as manufacturers, unable to import all the foreign steel they want, would turn to buying and processing the steel abroad, then importing the finished product.

Following industry dictates, the quota bill says nothing about imports of iron ore, which have played havoc with employment in the U.S. iron mining industry. The reason, of course, is that U.S. steel companies own the rich iron mines of Canada, Venezuela, and other countries. Record imports of 45.3 million tons in 1966 amounted to over a third of the domestic supply, and net of exports, to about 30% of the supply.

United Steelworkers' spokesman Joseph P. Molony, supporting the steel import quota bill in testimony before the Senate Finance Committee, recommended an amendment to include iron ore, but chances of such a change are minimal.

American unions have collaborated with employers in seeking protectionist solutions to declining employment in shipbuilding, watchmaking, textiles, and many other industries. But this has never saved the workers. Nor did American labor receive its promised protection for support of the Kennedy Round tariff reductions.

• • •

6/27/1970

Autos' Hidden Profits

The decisive upcoming capital-labor battle is between a million auto workers and their three largest employers. The main issue is wages. The Nixon administration and the employers will use every kind of pressure to try to force the workers to settle cheap. They will claim auto workers are very highly paid, that they have made big gains, that company profits are declining, that excessive wage increases will fuel inflation.

These claims are all the very opposite of the truth.

Real wages of auto workers have gone down $1,100 per year during the 18 months Nixon has been in office. Their ballyhooed "high wages" leave them $3,000 below the government-defined "moderate" living standard. Ever since World War II the companies' share of the production pie has gone up while that of the workers has gone down. General Motors makes more profits from its workers' labor than any other industrial corporation. The workers of the Big Three create more value than the workers of any three other industrial corporations.

Just to restore real wages to where they were in 1968, before Nixon, the auto workers require a wage increase of 59 cents an hour, or 14.3% for the coming year.

To reach the Labor Department's "moderate" income standard they would need an immediate raise of $1.50 per hour, or 36%.

To restore the share of production they received in 1946, they would need an immediate raise of $2.30 per hour, or 55%.

There is no danger of "breaking the companies" by winning "too much." Even if their wages were doubled, the companies would still be getting a surplus value of over $8,000 per worker.

Analysis of the data in the General Motors 1968 *Annual Report* shows that the total surplus value produced by its workers in 1968 was $9,831,000,000. There were approximately 626,000 GM production workers in 1968, with total wages of $5,095 million. Thus, the surplus value was nearly double the total wages. It equaled $15,705 for each GM production worker.

Actually, no conceivable set of workers' gains will eliminate or really narrow the huge surplus value generated by their labor and taken by employers and the government. The reality is that only by successfully fighting for extremely far-reaching demands can the workers restore the same "share of the pie" they had a quarter of a century ago.

7/18/1970

Gravy Trains

The Penn Central is the largest transportation company in the country. And the worst. It follows a public-be-damned policy when it comes to service but a public-pay-up policy when it gets in trouble. The railroad really is bankrupt. Following a $122 million loss in 1969, it lacks cash to pay its bills, banks refuse additional loans, buyers turned down a new bond offering despite an 11.5% interest rate.

The Penn Central is to an exceptional degree, even for a big corporation, the property of the Wall Street financial establishment. There are 13 interlocking directors with big banks. Morgan Guaranty holds 7.2% of the stock, Chase Manhattan, 5.6%. The Morgans traditionally controlled the New York Central Railroad; Nelson Rockefeller married into the Pennsylvania Railroad. That marriage went on the rocks. Now the Morgans and the Rockefellers are married in the Penn Central—and that marriage has likewise gone on the rocks.

The bank owners acted urgently to save their investment. They fired their high-priced front-man managers and took personal charge. And then they went into a huddle with their pals in the Pentagon and the White House. The solution: a Nixon-backed Pentagon offer to guarantee $200 million in bank loans to the railroad.

Meanwhile, the administration prepared legislation giving the Transportation Department authority to lend $750 million to the Penn Central and at least another half dozen lines on the brink of bankruptcy. Airlines would also like to get in on it. This effort backfired. Under exceptional congressional attack from Representative Patman and Senator Proxmire, the administration had to cancel the obviously illegal plan for a Pentagon bailout lest Congress slash Pentagon appropriations even more deeply.

Within 48 hours the railroad filed a certificate of bankruptcy, an event bound to deepen the already serious economic crisis. But even then the administration didn't stop trying to bail out the railroad. Transportation Secretary John A. Volpe pressed harder than ever for the $750 million giveaway. And the Association of American Railroads demanded a giveaway program of no less than a billion dollars a year—minimum!

The aim is to maintain the railroads as a source of gravy for executives, of lush orders for connected equipment and materials suppliers, and of high interest payments to bankers and millionaires, all at the expense of the taxpayers. Workers will be fired for "economy." But bondholders' interest payments won't stop, and fares will be raised to passengers. Volpe blurted out the most important reason of all—to avoid nationalization of the country's railroad system, the only reasonable, modern way to provide transportation service, even in a capitalist country.

Immediately after going into bankruptcy the railroad demanded a 20% rise in Philadelphia-area commutation fares and threatened to fire thousands of workers, while banks refused to cash their paychecks.

The railroads, all of them, should be nationalized, converted into a single transportation system. The bankers should not be paid off for their watered securities. The system should be democratically operated, with maximum participation in management of representatives of railroad workers, commuters and other passengers—of those who have a stake in smoothly run, serviceable railroads, and not in profits.

Government ownership, when that government is capitalist controlled, isn't necessarily good. But, generally, government ownership creates more favorable conditions for democratic struggles, for real gains for working people. Thus, the government-owned railroads of Western Europe give better and cheaper service than the privately owned railroads of the United States. American monopolies, stronger than those of Europe and with less of a radicalized working class to contend with, have especially resisted government ownership in any form. They are trying to eliminate what little bits of it do exist . . . as in the post office system and, potentially, even the school system.

But today there is deeper and broader political opposition to monopoly capitalism than hitherto—more resistance to the military-industrial complex—a general radicalization affecting millions of people. Hence it is possible to campaign seriously for an alternative to the giveaway program. The railroads must not be permitted to stop functioning. They must be stopped from functioning as sources of private loot, and made to function as providers of public service. Much the same applies to the aerospace companies, in addition to the need to change them from war to peace purposes.

• •

Why are so many corporations going bankrupt? This is the consequence of the accumulated financial excesses of the long wartime boom. More and more of the profits of industry were siphoned off into lush expense accounts, salaries and bonuses for executives, payouts to corporation lawyers and advertising agencies. As every company raced to expand, and to borrow to finance that expansion, the bankers increasingly skimmed off the cream of the profits in interest, which has now reached $150 billion per year.

The boom ended and less money came in to corporate treasuries, just as bills for interest, advertising, expense accounts, etc., reached an all-time peak. That, in substance, is the basis for the financial panic.

• • •

7/13/1974

Over-Reacting Over Reactors: What About Nuclear Weapons?

For the past year I have been puzzled and disturbed by the intense activity, and substantial influence among progressive people, of groups in the United States concerned with a very specific ecological issue: they want to close down all nuclear power plants and ban any future construction of such facilities. They claim these plants pose a mortal danger to millions of people and that their waste products might threaten all life at some future time. They favor priority spending to develop solar energy, which they claim is the only pure kind of energy.

I've met with many anti-nuclear plant activists in different parts of the country. They exhibit a singular contrariness: most fail to oppose nuclear weapons, although the danger involved is obviously incomparably greater than that involved in peaceful uses of atomic energy, or to support any measures, such as nationalization of the industry, that would curb monopoly misuse of atomic energy.

I have spoken to active propagandists against nuclear power plants who disclaim any scientific know-how, yet they insist that those scientists who claim nuclear power plants are mortally dangerous are correct; that scientists who claim otherwise are wrong.

They distribute literature and seem to have won over the majority of people active in ecological causes.

At the recent World Peace Council session in Paris, I discussed this problem at length with Academician Evgeny Fyodorov, head of the Soviet Hydrometeorological Service, vice chairman of the Soviet Peace Committee, and formerly co-chairman of the USSR-USA joint committee on questions of the environment. Fyodorov, a veteran of the first (1937) Soviet floating polar ice station, is especially concerned with the interaction of human society and nature, and he has contributed serious articles and speeches on this subject.

Having visited this country, and being well acquainted with U.S. scientists, Fyodorov was well aware of the anti-nuclear power positions. This is his fundamental approach:

Atomic power is less dangerous to the environment than earlier conventional forms of power generation. Coal- and oil-fired power plants were developed during an earlier period, without thought to their effect on the environment. Only now are people paying attention to pollution and trying to correct the environmental damage. But in the case of atomic energy, it was necessary to devote much attention to this problem before beginning to build large-scale plants.

Certainly there can be an accident in an atomic power plant, he said, as in most other kinds of productive establishments. But, with reasonable care, such an accident would happen in an atomic power plant only under the most extraordinary conditions.

There are real problems that the people should be concerned with. For example, the very frequent breakdowns of the Consolidated Edison's Indian Point nuclear facility suggest either that they were "sold a lemon" by the manufacturer of the reactors and the installers of the plant, or that the company's notoriously bad management extends to irresponsibility in handling the plant, or both. Certainly strict remedial measures, approved by really independent scientists and engineers, are in order here.

The real issue is that the danger to humanity arises not from nuclear power plants, but from atomic and hydrogen bombs and other weapons of mass destruction, which already exist in tens or hundreds of thousands, which are built to kill tens of millions of people, which are in the hands of imperialist militarists who have no concern for human life.

Which brings me to the main points. While the fight to protect the environment must go on in any case, the only way to make certain, decisive progress is through nationalization of the fuel and power industries, under democratic control.

There is a contradiction between private profits and environmental costs, since the latter do not contribute directly to the value of commodities produced. The crisis of the environment is one factor in the monopoly-created energy crisis, and part of the reason why nationalization has become essential for the welfare of the people and the future of the country.

Fyodorov said he could not understand the refusal of environmental opponents of nuclear power to combat nuclear weapons. Well, in general, neither can I. But at one meeting I attended, the explanation was clear enough. A supporter of the anti-nuclear-power plant line turned out to be a staff member of the Hudson Institute, which is a "think tank" servicing the Air Force and other military agencies in the promotion of new weapons, and of more outrageous ways of mass destruction of civilians. It has been the most brazen publicizer of proposals to make atomic warfare "respectable." For the militarists, a crusade against atomic power plants may seem to be a diversion from the struggle against atomic weapons.

I do not put all the opponents of nuclear power plants in this camp, by any means. But the need to revive a campaign against nuclear weapons has acquired new urgency, with the drive of the Pentagon and Defense Secretary James A. Schlesinger for "first strike" capability. No other issue should be permitted to divert people from this problem, which is the real threat to human survival.

• • •

8/2/1979

Productivity Up, Wages Down

Finally, in July, President Jimmy Carter conceded the reality of the recession that began in April. This crisis was unusual in that almost all of the major business economists saw it coming, but it came sooner than most of them expected. I know of only one accurate prediction as to timing—by James O'Leary, vice president and economist of the United States Trust Company. But he wrongly, I think, predicted that it would be mild.

President Carter and other politically motivated people try to make OPEC the scapegoat. But Citibank correctly headlines its July *Monthly Economic Letter*, "The recession OPEC didn't start," and in its text states: "The problem is the steady decline in real personal income since late 1978." Irwin Kellner of Manufacturers Hanover Trust writes: "The average worker . . . has seen his real spendable earnings contract for most of the past year," and he points out that a similar decline preceded the 1973-75 crisis.

Because of the decline in working people's real incomes, real retail sales fell 6.5% during the first half of 1979, the sharpest drop in such a short period since the end of World War II. The stage for every real crisis is set by production running ahead of purchasing power of workers. Workers' productivity increases more rapidly than their real wages, so their share in production goes down. What was special about the 1973-75 crisis was that real wages declined significantly, while productivity continued to move upward. The same thing is happening this time, but with a faster rise in productivity and a faster decrease in real wages.

The Carter administration has been trying to obscure this reality by continuing to issue false statistics of stagnant or declining productivity. This is being used to blame labor for inflation and to justify the wage-cutting guidelines. Industrial employers eagerly harp on the "low productivity" theme, but they know better from the results obtained in their own companies.

I have exposed the phony Bureau of Labor Statistics (BLS) method of computing productivity and established that productivity in manufacturing steadily increased through the end of 1978.

The rate of productivity gains, and the rate of decline in real wages, accelerated during the first half of 1979. As a result, the gap between workers' production and their real earnings increased more and more rapidly. Here are the figures (always compared with the same period a year earlier):

- Last quarter of 1978—productivity up 3.5% (revised); real hourly wages down 0.6%; increase in gap, 4.1%.
- First quarter of 1979—productivity up 3.7%; real wages down 1.5%; increase in gap, 5.2%.
- Second quarter of 1979—productivity up 6.5% (an exceptionally fast rise!); real hourly wages down 2.0% (preliminary); increase in gap, 8.5%.

These calculations do not take into account the impact of taxation, which aggravated the loss of workers' real purchasing power, nor of cuts in the average workweek in the second quarter of 1979. Thus, real spendable earnings of factory workers, in the second quarter of 1979, were 3.6% below the same period of 1978.

The unusually fast rise in productivity, combined with the reduction in real wages, made it possible for the majority of corporations to report continued profit gains and, in many cases, big profit gains in the second quarter despite the decline in the volume of production and sales.

The significance of the widening productivity-real wages gap, then, is a rapid increase in the rate of exploitation of labor by capital or, in the most elementary terms, a new high in profits at the expense of the people.

That's why "top executives attending the Business Council meeting reacted calmly to the prediction of a recession. 'The consensus was that this (a slight recession) is what we need, and it isn't all that bad,' said Clifton Garvin, chairman of Exxon Corp." (*Wall Street Journal*, 5/14/79.)

Now economists are speculating on how long and how deep the crisis will be. Many facts, and developments in domestic and international economics and politics, will influence this. But the rapid widening of the productivity-real earnings gap tends to bring about a particularly severe and prolonged crisis and depression, one very difficult to check through typical government contracyclical measures.

As mentioned, the second quarter of 1979 (ended June 30) was the first quarter of the cyclical decline in production, and productivity increased 6.5%. An exceptionally sharp increase in productivity in the first quarter of a cyclical decline is most unusual. I suggest these reasons:

1. Usually crises take employers by surprise; and they do not reduce employment for a while, expecting the boom to resume. This crisis was well advertised in advance, so at the first sign of weakness, employers slashed overtime and laid off some workers. Employment of production workers in manufacturing, seasonally adjusted, began to decline in April, the month in which the industrial production index began to go down.

2. The false administration charges of low productivity gave employers a handle to press workers to speed up, aided by workers' fears of layoffs in the looming recession.

3. Unlike most boom periods, there were no relative shortages of workers in particular industries, occupations, and areas. Such shortages help workers resist speedup and unsafe working conditions. This time unemployment remained at a historically high level at the peak, making resistance to speedup difficult.

The Carter administration announces that it will do nothing to counter a recession this year. It uses the energy crisis as an excuse to justify the sacrifices imposed on the working class by the economic crisis and out-of-bounds inflation. There's general expectation that Carter will offer something next year to try to improve the situation before the election. By the time Congress acts on the anticipated mild tax cuts, the crisis will be a year old; and neither the White House nor Capitol Hill intends any major concessions to the people.

Workers—including the unemployed, those threatened with foreclosures and repossessions, those feeling the real cuts in living standards—should not be required to wait for relief, nor will they be satisfied with minor palliatives to a still worsening situation.

Only an anti-crisis fightback, on a scale not seen since World War II, will surely prevent the overall situation of the working people from reaching a postwar low in real earnings and a new postwar high in unemployment—the actual perspectives if the initiative is left in the hands of the capitalists, the administration and Congress.

Labor and Industry (1980-1999)

2/9/1980

Carter's Threat to Our Youth

Suddenly the youth of America are faced with the threat of being dragooned to fight in the Middle East, for the Seven Sisters—which include Exxon, Texaco, Mobil, Socal, and Gulf. President Carter's official spokesman admits there is no reason to expect a Soviet invasion of oil producing countries, which Carter has been screaming about. The projected U.S. invasion, he indicated, will be to combat the liberation forces of the peoples of oil producing countries.

The U.S. war against Vietnam was brutal. Now U.S. imperialism is planning to carry out another war of conquest against peoples of the Middle East. And the cost to American youth—in corruption, in participation in government-ordered mass crime, in suffering and death—will be as bad or worse than it was in Southeast Asia. And youth, along with everyone else, will be incinerated if such aggression escalates into nuclear war.

Meanwhile, the sharp turn to the right in foreign affairs harms youth economically. Despite the record rise in profits in 1979, youth unemployment remained at its crisis level, and their real wages declined sharply, along with those of the working class as a whole. The 1980 increase of 6.9% in the minimum wage, which many young workers are paid, is barely half the expected rise in living costs.

Most victimized are the urban youth, especially Black, Puerto Rican, Chicano, Native American and Asian-Pacific. It's "logical" that as Carter declaimed his cold war message, New York's Mayor Koch imposed the most brutal cut yet in services, while Chicago teachers went without salaries. The skyrocketing military budget leaves less and less for the needs of the cities.

Carter tried to win some youth support by talking about a $2 billion program for youth training and jobs. That's only half this year's meager budget provision, much of which is frittered away in bureaucratic empire building.

The estimate is that in the war-boom year of 1980, New York City will lose 90,000 jobs. And even on the West Coast, where there is a great deal of armament business, much military work will be at the expense of civilian work as scarce materials and components are appropriated by the Pentagon.

The racist assault against affirmative action, for preserving the "last to be hired, first to be fired" rule, gains momentum along with the racist war hysteria. And youth, with the least seniority, are the first victims.

The large-scale resistance to Carter's program among young workers, students, Blacks and other nationally oppressed youths is important. The future of American youth—and the world—requires a united, organized, militant, mass peace movement in the United States.

• • •

4/1/1982

Youth Unemployment

A new government report finds:

"The labor market experience of youths has worsened in comparison with that of adults over the last 20 years, and most of the worsening, especially since the 1960s, has taken place among non-white youths."(Congressional Budget Office, *Improving Youth Employment Prospects: Issues and Options*, 2/82)

The report notes that in 1981, the white youth unemployment rate was double, and the "non-white" youth unemployment rate more than quadruple, the overall average unemployment rate. Of 24 million youth aged 16–24 in 1981, 3.6 million were officially counted as unemployed. The actual number is much higher. The official unemployment percentage for all youth increased from 9.0% in 1957 to 11.5% in 1964, 12.2% in 1978, and more than 15% in early 1982.

Since 1957, the rate of unemployment among white youths went up about 60%, while that for Black youths increased 225%.

The data for young women are similar, but a little worse for Black women than for Black men.

Alarming as the official figures are, the real situation for Black youth is far worse. Increasing millions, especially of Blacks and Hispanics, are dropped from the official count. This appalling situation is brought out more sharply when it is seen how few Black youths have jobs.

In 1957, 48% of Black male teenagers had jobs, almost as many as the 52% of white male teenagers. But by 1981 only 25% of Black male teenagers had jobs, compared with 51% of white male teenagers. The decline in employment was shattering for Black youth.

In 1957, among males aged 20–24, 78% of Blacks, compared with 80% of whites, had jobs. Again not a wide differential. But by 1981 only 58% of Blacks, compared with 77% of whites, had jobs.

Among young females there is a rising demand for office workers, for which employers favor women, compared to blue collar jobs, for which employers favor men. Thus, among white female teenagers, 46.4% had jobs in 1981, up from 38.3% in 1957. But among Black female teenagers, the proportion with jobs dropped sharply, from 26.5% in 1957 to 19.6% in 1981. Among white women aged 20–24, employment rose over the same period from 43.0% to 44.8%.

To arrive at a minimum estimate of the actual rate of unemployment among Black and Hispanic youth, we may assume that at least as high a proportion of nationally oppressed youth as white youth should be counted in the labor force. As compared with a white unemployment rate (under-reported) of 18.3%, Black unemployment is reported at 45.0% and adjusted to 66.5%. That is, two-thirds of all Black teenagers are unemployed. For Hispanic teenagers, the reported rate is 23.5%; the adjusted rate, 43.8%

Realistically measured, roughly one-third of all youth unemployment is among Black, Hispanic and other nationally oppressed youth. Such massive unemployment is unprecedented in the history of an industrialized capitalist country.

What can be done about youth unemployment? The Congressional Budget Office (CBO) report focuses on the programs that have been in effect, and under which the situation has worsened. Essentially, these programs consist of training programs and incentives to employers. The incentives are either at the expense of the youth themselves, in the form of substandard wages, or at the expense of taxpayers, in the form of direct cash subsidies.

Much attention is devoted to proposals to reduce minimum wages, either by not adjusting the existing minimum for inflation or by cutting the minimum wage specifically for youth. Both are part of the current all-out employer anti-labor offensive. Without pressure on Congress, the minimum wage will not be adjusted upward at the beginning of 1983. If it is held at the $3.35 level until 1985, the CBO estimates the real minimum wages will be cut by 25%.

For years, retail, service and educational institution employers have been able to pay sub-minimum wages to youths enrolled in certain Labor Department programs. The CBO admits that this has not led to a significant increase in youth employment, and that it has tended to provide employment, such as it is, to relatively "more affluent" youth rather than to nationally oppressed youth.

There is a real danger that this session of Congress will pass legislation cutting the minimum wage for young workers generally. Even official studies admit that the result would be, at most, a small increase in youth employment. An optimistically projected 5% gain in jobs, with a 25% cut in wages, would mean a slash of 20% in overall youth income, accompanied by a loss of jobs and income for older workers displaced by the youths hired at the lower wages.

The real objective of legislation to cut youth minimum wages is to increase profits at the expense of workers. This fraud against the country's youth must be defeated.

The CBO admits in its report that the various cash incentive programs have just put money in employers' pockets, without leading to any increase in jobs for youth and without reducing discrimination against Black youth.

It doesn't refer to the general deterioration of the economy, with the resulting rise in unemployment. Nor does it mention the militarization of the economy, with its low employment per dollar spent. And it merely lists in passing "racial and ethnic discrimination."

Racism on the part of employers, in the education system and in all aspects of U.S. life, is the decisive cause of the cruel and rapidly disproportionate growth in unemployment among Black youth.

Only a radical program, including a shorter workweek and creation of jobs with affirmative action, can bring significant relief to youth. Central features of such a program should include:

1. Employment or income for everyone, with the government providing millions of jobs through a program of public services and public construction, which are required in order to meet the tremendous unfilled social needs of the country. Assuring an adequate income for all would substantially increase the overall market for consumer goods. That would result in soaring employment in order to produce and distribute these goods. Such a program could be financed by reducing the military budget.

2. A 30-hour work week with 40 hours pay, which would create 10-15 million new jobs.

3. Affirmative action programs for Black, Chicano, Puerto Rican, Native American and other nationally oppressed youth and women. This means that all employers, private and public, would have to give priority to hiring minority workers, proportionally to the number wanting jobs, until equality in relative employment levels is achieved.

4. Special jobs creation and job training programs for youth to end their extra-high unemployment rates.

• • •

3/3/1983

Women and the Income Gap

Economic suffering among American working women has soared during this prolonged crisis-depression, with discrimination in many ways intensified. Black and Hispanic women, and their children, have been especially affected.

The *Census* report for 1981 showed the median income of **all** women at only 41% that of men. However, these figures included non-working housewives. Among earners, the median for women was 48% that of men, less than half. That included the millions of women who, because of child-caring responsibilities, had only part-time jobs. Among those with full-time year-round employment, women's median income was 60% that of men's. That ratio has hovered at about the same percentage ever since 1960.

Thus women have been victims, proportionately with men, of the sharp decline in real wages during the past decade—and with more suffering, since the losses have started from a lower level. It's well known that employers set up "women's jobs" at lower wages and salaries than jobs that require corresponding skill and training, for which they employ mainly men. The *Census* study showed that the differentials against women were comparable in each major occupational group as against women as a whole.

For example, among professionals, the median income for women was 64% that of men; among managers, 58%; among clerical workers—with the largest concentration of women—62%; among factory operatives, 61%; and among service workers, excluding private household workers, 59%. All these data apply to full-time year-round workers.

Illustrating the discriminatory character of the differentials, the median earnings of women workers in every major category, including professionals and managers, were lower than those for men in **all** groups, including jobs requiring relatively little skill or training. Only male laborers and service workers had lower median earnings than women professionals; and the median earnings of men were far higher, at that, than received by women clerical and skilled craft workers, and by factory operatives.

In a recent U.S. Bureau of Labor Statistics (BLS) study, Nancy F. Rytina showed how this discriminatory pattern persisted in particular occupations. Thus the number of men and women factory assemblers was about equal in 1981, but the median earnings of the full-time women assemblers were only 69% those of full-time male assemblers. As for mastering a new occupation, 63% of the computer operators were women, but they earned only 68% of what male computer operators earned. Over a range of about 100 occupations for which comparisons were given, the ratio of female to male wages centered around 75%.

The official poverty rate jumped sharply during this crisis, from 24 million people in 1978 to 32 million in 1981—and that was before the worst year of the crisis so far, 1982. One out of every 5 children, 12 million, lived in poverty. And fully half of these children were either Black or Hispanic. The most acute poverty was concentrated in the rising number of families headed by a woman without a resident husband. Two out of every five poverty-stricken white families, and two out of every three poverty-stricken Black families, are headed by women without a resident husband. More than half the children in such families, 6.3 million, are living in poverty, including 3 million Black children, or two-thirds of those living in single-woman-headed families.

The median income of families headed by a female with no resident husband was under $11,000 in 1981, less than half the median for all families. Moreover, the decline in their real income, adjusted for soaring living costs, was 4.6% as compared with 1980, somewhat more than the loss for all families. Even where the woman worker had a full-time year-round job, the decline was just as severe and the median family income 41% below the average for all families.

Without any doubt, Black women and their children suffer most. The median income of such families, without resident husbands, was only $7,506—a decline of 8.4%, adjusted for inflation. There was a comparable decrease in cases where Black women had a full-time, year-round job.

Allyson Sherman Grossman and Howard Hayghe showed, in a BLS study, that only one-third of divorced or separated women received financial support; and that, on the average, was a miserable $1,800. The discrimination against Black women was extreme in this respect. While two-thirds of employed white women without husbands received some support, only 18% of employed Black women and 32% of Hispanic women did. Those not receiving support suffered most from unemployment, the rate being 11.9% for white women, 17.8% for Black women, and 17.4% for Hispanics. This was in 1978, when the overall unemployment rate was "only" 6%, roughly half the present rate.

The disastrous prejudice against women workers has been organized by capital and used by capital to increase profits at the expense of workers of both sexes.

Rising living costs, the struggle to maintain the living standards won after World War II, and growing unemployment among men have compelled more and more women to enter the labor force. Employers use this development to substitute women for men in many jobs, radically reducing the real wage level in the process. As unemployment of both men and women rises, wages of men are pulled down in proportion to those of women, and the wide differentials are maintained at the expense of all workers. And all of the wage loss turns into profits for the owners of corporate America.

• •

3/27/86

The differentials against Black workers in wages and employment, however, were much sharper among men than among women. The number of Black women full-time workers—3,020,000—was nearly equal to the number of Black male full-time workers—3,284,000. Among white workers, the number of women with full-time jobs was only 58% of the number of male full-time workers. Among measures required nationally to overcome the gross discrimination against working women is for women's wages or salaries to be raised to the level paid for "men's jobs" requiring similar skill and education. It requires united struggle by the entire labor movement, with male workers playing a full part.

The fight for comparable worth encompasses the struggle against wage discrimination on the basis of race or nationality as well as on the basis of gender. When they are joined, as they were in the historic Yale strike last year, these struggles have the potential both to raise the overall wage level in the U.S. and to build the unity the labor movement needs to win.

11/15/1984

U.S. Labor in Crisis

The latest official monthly report on personal income dramatizes the rapidly worsening situation of labor in the U.S., especially that of the workingclass core that creates America's industrial wealth. The crucial data show the **accelerating** decline in the share of wages and salaries in personal income, the concentration of that decline in the commodity-producing industries, and the decrease, for the first time, in the share of transfer payments in total personal income.

These trends result from the increasing exploitation of labor by capital, from the structural crisis that is crippling the country's industrial heart, and from Reagan's attack on elementary protective provisions for senior citizens, the unemployed, the disabled and the poor.

When this column appears, the election will be over. But the serious situation will have to be faced and struggled against by all working people, regardless of who is in the White House.

Here are the facts. In 1940, 64.1% of all personal income was for wages and salaries. By the decade 1960-1970, wages and salaries accounted for 67.6% of the total, partly due to the decline in self-employed farmers, merchants, etc., and partly because of workingclass victories as the trade union movement reached its peak. After 1970, the share of wages and salaries fell rapidly—to 62.7% in 1980, 60.5% in 1983, and to 59.5% in September 1984.

The decline in labor's share during these 14 years has been faster than statistics indicate, because wages and salaries include the exorbitant salaries of corporate executives and supervisors, which have been taking a larger and larger share of the total.

Wages and salaries paid in commodity-production industries increased from 25.2% of total personal income in 1940 to 28.5% in 1950 and then dropped steadily until, in September 1984, it was 18.7%—almost 10 percentage points from the 1950 peak. And the process is accelerating, as only 7.9% of the April-September income rise went to workers in commodity-producing industries.

Through most of the postwar period, transfer payments—Social Security, Medicare, unemployment insurance, various welfare payments and subsidies—have been a growing share of personal income. This has been mainly because the proportion of senior citizens in the population steadily increased and, more recently, because of mounting poverty and unemployment.

But between 1983 and September 1984, transfer payments fell from 14.7% of personal income to 13.7%, a record decline. That is the payoff of Reagan's prolonged, savage campaign against the hard earned rights of senior citizens, unemployed workers and the poor.

The substantive reduction in workers' income share seriously undermines mass purchasing power. It is an important cause of a new economic crisis, which may already be underway. In any event, crisis conditions are even now being experienced by the most important, producing section of the population.

8/29/1985

The Truth About Productivity and Wages

Do you remember the hullabaloo about "declining productivity" and "excessive wages" of U.S. workers? This campaign was aimed at softening up workers for an assault on their conditions. The attacks hurt labor during the 1970s and have had devastating effects under Reagan. Labor Day is a good time to review the facts.

The Federal Reserve Board (FRB) has just updated, revised, and put on a 1977 = 100 base its indexes of industrial production. The Bureau of Labor Statistics (BLS) uses the same base year for its indexes of "man-hours" of production workers. Putting these reports together shows what has really happened to productivity in manufacturing—the basic area of the economy, and the main area for which we have good production indexes.

In the first 7 months of 1985 the FRB index of manufacturing production was 126.6, which means that production was 26.6% higher than in 1977. For the same 7 months the BLS manufacturing man-hours index was 93.9. That is, workers' man-hours were 6.1% less than in 1977.

Putting these indexes together shows that output per man-hour—in other words, productivity—was 34.82% higher in the first 7 months of 1985 than in the same period in 1977. That comes out to a compound growth rate of productivity of 3.98% per year—4% per year, for all practical purposes. These facts expose the propaganda about "lagging" or even "declining" U.S. labor productivity. The U.S. has actually experienced a high rate of productivity increase, especially in light of the fact that U.S. employers have been less active modernizing plants in this country than exporting capital to low-wage areas.

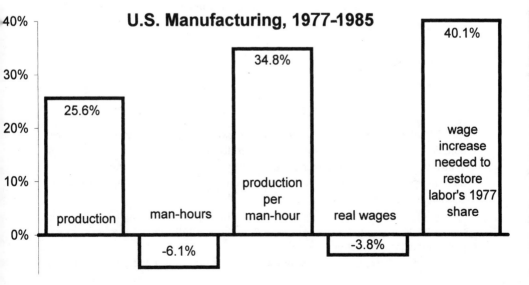

U.S. Manufacturing, 1977-1985

Over the same period the BLS index of real hourly wages of U.S. factory workers has declined 3.8%. Put these two numbers together—the 3.8% decline in real wages per hour and the 34.8% rise in production per hour. If a typical worker was getting $100 for 100 units of production in 1977, he is now getting $96.20 for 134.8 units of production. A little arithmetic shows that this means the worker now gets only $71.40 for every 100 units produced, and must therefore produce 140 units to get the same $100 in real money as in 1977.

Thus, U.S. industrial workers are entitled to a 40% rise in wages merely to restore their none-too-liberal 1977 share of the values their labor created. Similar whopping increases are called for throughout the economy. Even if the 30-hour week with no cut in weekly pay were won, it still would not compensate for workers' losses since 1977.

Official publicity goes to great lengths to conceal this basic truth. The BLS systematically puts out statistics of productivity "decline" or "slow growth," which are not based on any measurement of the physical volumes produced. They are calculated from government figures of real income distribution.

These figures are supposed to add up to the total values produced, but they do not—because they leave out most of the profits, among other distortions. Thus the BLS index of manufacturing productivity is dominated by the bureau's index of sluggish or declining real wages.

That's the trick—use the decline in real wages to calculate a distorted productivity index, and then use that falsified index to justify more cuts in real wages!

Where is the combination of rising productivity and declining real wages going? Into soaring profits—especially soaring gross profits. A major part of gross profits is left out of the published "net income" figures.

The U.S. trade unions have the resources, research and publicity facilities to counter this employer-government propaganda campaign. By doing so, labor can build up the mass sentiment needed to inspire a winning counteroffensive by the working class.

• • •

10/26/1985

Convert to Peace and Create Jobs

Members of Congress often support extravagant, war-inciting Pentagon budgets to keep arms-producing jobs in their districts, and to guarantee campaign contributions from arms makers. The military contractors' drive for more business and profits is a powerful behind-the-scenes factor in Reagan's stubborn resistance to real disarmament agreements.

Job blackmail—the choice between continuing to build weapons and standing in the unemployment line—is used to maintain public and congressional support for weapons systems.

The UAW writes: "It is really a challenge to the U.S. peace movement and labor movement to establish an effective conversion program." (*Ammo*, Vol. 24, No. 4).

Pressure from labor and peace forces is growing. If the battle for conversion to peace production is won, what can be done to save the jobs of workers employed by Pentagon contractors? They numbered 1,560,000 as of June 1985, according to government figures. That's only 14% more workers than in 1980, when Reagan took office, although the military budget has more than doubled. Most people think the number is higher—which is understandable, considering the $300 billion Pentagon budget. Rarely have so few jobs been created with so much extra spending.

How could these workers be employed if weapons production were cut drastically? First, most military production facilities—aircraft, shipbuilding, the military part of the computer and semiconductor industries—could be converted directly to civilian production. For example, plants that make bombers could be converted to manufacturing railroad cars or housing modules. Plants that make sensitive military electronic systems could be converted to manufacturing home and business computers.

Markets for this new production could be ensured by government programs to open up sales to socialist countries, provide easy terms and low prices for sales to developing countries, and require U.S. oil companies and others using ocean shipping to buy replacement and expansion vessels from U.S. shipyards, instead of the shipyards of the South Korean dictatorship.

State and local governments also have a role to play in encouraging civilian-oriented production. Connecticut has passed a "Defense Readjustment Act" to provide incentives to non-military businesses to move into the state.

Conversion to civilian production would make available the skills of the many professional workers and technicians now engaged in research and development (R&D) of increasingly lethal weapons. The Labor Department reports that the majority of the 1,560,000 employees of Pentagon contractors are not production workers, but salaried employees. Their know-how and energy are needed for R&D to improve civilian production.

One reason Japan and West Germany have won such a large share of international markets is that they devote a much larger share of R&D to civilian production than the U.S. With a similar shift here, the quality of U.S.-made goods would improve—along with the foreign trade balance. More civilian R&D would improve health care and the quality of everyday goods.

The changeover from military to civilian production would have the important side effect of creating more jobs. Dollar for dollar, military procurement creates fewer jobs than civilian investment. The percentage of production workers in capital-intensive arms production is far lower than in other industries. In U.S. industry as a whole, the average ratio of production to total employees is 90%. For the auto industry it is 74%. But for ordnance and accessories it is 47%, and for guided missiles only 28%.

Some factories might have to be closed down because they cannot make anything useful for peaceful purposes—perhaps those making guided missiles and parts, and atomic warheads for the Pentagon. Such plants, at a rough estimate, employ 300,000 workers. For the production and salaried employees who may not be able to switch easily to other jobs, the government should guarantee employment at comparable wages and conditions.

Steps in that direction are provided by conversion bills that have been introduced by Congressmen Ted Weiss (NY) and Nick Mavroules (MA). The Weiss bill would set new standards for federal responsibility toward dislocated workers. It includes generous income maintenance provisions, and would create new federal organizations to participate in joint worker-management-community planning.

But much more is needed. An effective conversion program must be part of a broad jobs program with affirmative action, to guarantee jobs for all. This requires a program such as the one proposed by the Communist Party, USA, which includes:

- A 30-hour week with no cut in pay.
- A major public works program to repair and improve the deteriorating infrastructure.
- A massive public housing program for low- and moderate-income families.
- Measures to balance foreign trade, as proposed by Gus Hall in his *World Magazine* article of August 29, 1985.

• • •

9/18/1987

Nine Million Mothers Need Help

Nearly 9 million single mothers—about 30% of all mothers—suffer severe hardships and deserve assistance from society, and the proportion grows yearly with the disintegration of family life.

In 1985, according to a Census Bureau study, some 8.8 million women needed help. Only 5.4 million were awarded some form of child support from the fathers; and of these, only 3.2 million actually received any money, and only 2.1 million got all that was coming to them.

Thus, fewer than one out of four mothers received the full amount they were entitled to. The average receipt, $2,215 [$3,542], was certainly insufficient, when youngsters are involved, to cover even elementary childcare while mothers work. That sum was 12.4% less, in real terms, than the average amount received in 1983. In most other respects also, the situation deteriorated in those 2 years.

The average total income of mothers getting child support in 1985, including those payments, came to $14,776 [$23,625]. That's at best a barely-get-by level under present-day conditions. The mothers without assistance fared worse: consider the 2.8 million mothers below the official poverty level, which is set far below where it ought to be. Only one-third of them received any child support, an average of $1,383 [$2,211], for a total average income of $5,130 [$8,202].

That means there were 8 million women and children living in extreme poverty. It means hunger. It means lack of clothing, medical care and decent housing.

Of these 8.8 million needy women, 6.3 million were white. Thus, a majority of those living in poverty were white. And a majority of those who applied for aid and could not get it were white. This fact is important: it means that the sufferings of women are a problem for the entire working class, of all races.

At the same time, in every respect, the situation of Black and Hispanic women was worse than that of white women. Racism added a special dimension to this serious problem. Up to half of all Black mothers were poor. And of these, three-fifths were refused any child care assistance. Only one-fifth of the Black women who applied actually received aid in 1985. The average amount, and average total income that they got, was considerably less than that of whites. Only 9% of the awards to Black women (27% to all women) included health insurance. More than half the Black and Hispanic women were living in abject poverty; but few received awards, and the amounts were small.

This disgraceful situation is bound to get worse, so long as the approach is limited to pinning responsibility on the father, finding him (if possible), and collecting from him. Certainly fathers should contribute much more; but the increasing millions of women forced to bring up children on their own, with their limited financial resources, cannot manage solely with the irregular help of their one-time mates. Their grave condition results from the decay of society, economic instability, plant shutdowns, and the gross discrimination against Black and Hispanic men that is at the root of their abandonment of women with children.

Social support is required. Every woman bringing up children without the economic assistance of a male partner should be provided with the necessary funds, as well as child care and health facilities, by the federal government.

A realistic starting goal might be an average of $5,000 [$7,994] to each woman with an income under $25,000 [$39,972] who is bringing up children without a mate present. The additional cost to the federal government, in addition to the $10 billion [$15.989 billion] now coming from fathers, would be $30 billion [$47.967 billion]—one-tenth of the direct military budget.

The solution to the special problems of mothers requires revolutionary changes in the political, economic and cultural structure of society. .

• • •

2/17/1988

Roger Smith's Car Imports

Roger B. Smith, GM chairman, boasts that its new models will hold their own against Japanese imports. He neglects to tell where the GM cars will be made.

This year GM plans to increase imports of cars from its 50%-owned South Korean plant by 85%, to 150,000 vehicles, while Ford plans to raise imports from its partly-owned South Korean plant by 13%, to 79,000 units.

The trade bill pending in Congress, even with the union-backed Gephardt Amendment, is much too general to deal with such realities. To restore the foreign trade balance we must prohibit imports by transnational corporations from foreign plants of goods they can make at home.

Production in South Korea is so profitable because of the military dictatorship, which enforces a 56-hour workweek—the world's longest—and low hourly wages, and which brutally attacks strikes and people's demonstrations for real democracy.

The South Korean dictatorship is kept in power by 45,000 U.S. troops and extensive military bases. Bring the troops home and let the Koreans manage their own affairs, and produce for their own people.

These changes could end the Rust Bowl Blues, and put a million skilled workers back into creative jobs they can do as well as anybody in the world.

• • •

4/11/1992

Shorter Workweek = 22 Million More Jobs

The struggle for a shorter workweek has been one of labor's central themes from the beginning of capitalism, a system built by the millions slaving 12 hours a day, 7 days a week. This struggle was established in workers' history by the 1886 inauguration in the United States of May Day rallies, to highlight demands for an 8-hour day.

American workers were among the first in the capitalist world to reach that goal. As early as 1917, the Adamson Act mandated an 8-hour day for railroad workers, though violations of its provisions were common. It was 1938 before industrial workers won the 8-hour day, 5-day week—with a minimum wage.

What most people don't know, however, is that despite the fact that the scope of that law has been widened as union strength grew, a large number of U.S. workers have never been covered.

The struggle for a shorter workweek continued after World War II, especially in Western Europe, where workers finally won a 40-hour week and, during the 1980s, a 35-hour workweek in a number of countries. That goal is being achieved in stages in others.

But with reactionary anti-Communists driving out militants in the U.S. unions in the '50s, complaisant officials in major unions abandoned the issue.

Meanwhile, employers have gone on the offensive to increase the workweek. Their main weapon has been compulsory overtime, even in shops where the 40-hour week is still officially in force. With wages not keeping up with living costs, many workers need the overtime to make ends meet. By 1991, the average workweek for 90 million workers on full-time schedules was officially 43.7 hours;

but when allowance is made for time lost to illness, temporary shutdowns, etc., at least a further 2 hours must be added.

As "evidence" of the country's economic recovery, Wall Street and White House soothsayers are touting a Labor Department report of a rise in non-farm employment, seasonally adjusted, of 164,000 workers in February—neglecting to mention that this simply recovers the January loss! But, they are even more enthusiastic about the exceptional increase of 0.4 hours—24 minutes—in the average workweek.

It's easy to see why. Although that increase works out to "only" five minutes a day per worker, without it the companies would have to hire an additional 1 million workers to get the same number of extra hours of labor!

What are the implications of a 35-hour week without overtime? **In reducing the workweek from the present average of 43.7 hours to 35 hours for 90 million full-time workers, employers would have to hire an additional 22 million workers.**

Of course, labor would have to demand that the shorter workweek be achieved without reducing weekly pay. More than that, however, this shorter workweek would radically change the demand-supply balance in the labor market—in favor of job seekers. Wages would increase, the unemployed would be hired, including the African American and Latino youth in the inner cities who suffer such horrendous unemployment rates. The conditions for winning economic equality for the racially oppressed would be greatly improved. And the life span of millions now worn out by grueling overwork would be lengthened.

It's clear that the fight for a shorter workweek has to become once again a central feature of labor's struggle to protect their members' living standards.

• • •

5/23/1992

Fortune Magazine: U.S. Workers More Exploited

That European workers have been gaining and U.S. workers losing is a widely publicized issue. A provocative version of this theme is featured in the May 4 *Fortune* article that praises U.S. workers in order to derail them ideologically. It promises them "empowerment" to prettify the assaults on labor's organized power base. The cover story claims: "The Truth About the American Worker: Lazy? Dumb? Don't Bet On It."

The article praises American workers' hard work, long hours, skill and high quality output—and even criticizes management's failure to assign workers sensibly, to give them scope, etc. Charts show that today's U.S. worker is more skilled, better educated, less unionized—and less rewarded—than formerly. In comparison with workers in other industrialized countries, Americans are more productive, younger, harder working—and less secure:

"The shock waves in manufacturing—the givebacks and two-tier wage scales of the past decade, the decline in union strength" led to wages that stagnated in the 1970s for 25-34 year-old male workers and fell 11% in the 80s. "The opposite of lazy, Americans responded to the wage slowdown by working more . . . they also toil longer hours" [than in other countries]. Moreover ". . . those unruffled Germans luxuriate in an average 30 paid vacation days a year . . . the American workers make do with a frugal dozen . . . American workers—more skilled and putting in longer hours than ever—perform impressively. Their productivity, the industrial world's highest, is growing faster than Germany's and as fast as Japan's."

In effect, American workers are being forced to give more for less. And in return they suffer more unemployment, more racism and less power as their unions are weakened or smashed. It is, of course, just that combination that *Fortune* applauds, claiming that "good management" generates these veritable Utopian conditions for workers.

In effect, through *Fortune*, the ruling class is saying: now it can be told. We beat them with scabs, right-to-work laws, goons, racism, and a propaganda campaign about how dumb, lazy and unproductive they were. Now it's time to take a new propaganda tack. So *Fortune* claims:

"Under the old union dispensation . . . workers were isolated units, cut off from one another, and as cut off from their supervisors as if they were in solitary confinement. All that has changed"—where the bosses broke the union.

Fortune selects, as a prime example, Phelps Dodge at Morenci, where productivity per worker tripled (and obviously jobs declined in proportion, although that was not mentioned). But the article admits, quoting pipefitter Larry Kerrigan: "My wages aren't really keeping pace. I don't feel like I'm getting ahead."

At unionized General Motors' plants, *Fortune* cites workers who say the bosses won't listen to them, that extra units are squeezed out of them at the expense of quality. Whereas at non-union Honda, ". . . you feel as if you're talking to workers who've truly lost their chains, as content and optimistic as their GM counterparts are resentful and demoralized." Why, at Honda the bosses even eat at the workers' cafeteria!

The 400 workers at Nucor's Indiana mill had to pass competitive tests that were practically equivalent to college graduate level in order to get jobs:

"At Nucor you can see a new labor elite in action—an elite that is a pure meritocracy, not the old privileged class based on union power in oligopolistic industries." The workers and their bosses are pictured as fraternal teams of supermen.

These are isolated examples of companies currently riding high in the battle of monopolies for markets. IBM used to be the darling of such propaganda, but no longer, as the company loses ground to rivals, slashes 100,000 jobs, contracts out work, and ends the fiction of being practically a "country club" for employees.

All this anti-union flummery covers up the main point: **unorganized workers are paid 25% less than union members.** This is true for every occupation level and industry; but in manufacturing the unorganized get 39% less. Every time an employer smashes a union, it contributes to the downward trend in wages, the worsening of conditions all along the line—and soaring profits for the capitalist class.

The admission that U.S. workers have inferior conditions teaches us a lesson directly the opposite of *Fortune*'s propaganda ploy: American workers need more and stronger organizations, both trade union and political; there must be an ideological struggle against the fictionalized propaganda that touts the "benefits" of labor-management "teamwork."

• • •

6/13/1992

Double the Minimum Wage!

Hy Clymber summarized salient features of the new Census Bureau report on "Workers with Low Earnings, 1964-1990" in a recent issue. "Low earnings," as defined by statisticians, are earnings so low—$12,195 in 1990—that a worker with a spouse and two children to support, earning that amount, would be counted as "poor." Thus, a more accurate term: "poverty wages."

The main conclusion publicized in the press was that the number of full-time workers receiving poverty wages doubled between 1974 and 1990, reaching a total of 24 million—not counting the 33 million part-time workers living on poverty wages. Nor was there mention of the pronounced racist bias among those working for poverty wages: 14.7% of white, 21.2% of Black, and 27.6% of Hispanic workers.

Press commentary ignored another important feature: the number of workers getting poverty wages declined by half between 1964 and 1974. Therefore the question: what accounted for that reversal—rapid progress toward decent wages, then a lengthy retreat beginning in 1974?

Changing tides in the class struggle was one factor. But, more concretely, labor won a significant political victory in 1960. Between 1964 and 1969 the minimum wage rose 28%, exceeding cost of living increases, and an additional 20 million workers won minimum wage coverage. While the higher minimum left many in poverty, it helped all workers at all levels get raises, pulling many of them above the poverty line.

Compare that with the years 1974-1990 when increases in the minimum wage, frozen under Reagan and scarcely improved under Bush, were half the rise in living costs. In that period, purchasing power of the minimum wage declined by one-third, helping employers cut real wages at all levels and shoving millions into poverty.

In terms of purchasing power, the minimum wage peaked in 1968. To regain that level today, the minimum wage, now $4.25/hr. [$5.22], would have to climb to $6.75/hr. [$8.29]. However, minimum wages should be raised beyond that to compensate for the 30% rise in productivity that even the Bureau of Labor Statistics admits has taken place since 1968.

This combination—regained purchasing power and increases commensurate with productivity—justifies the demand for an $8.50/hr. [$10.44] minimum wage, double the present level. In manufacturing industry, where productivity has increased 80%, the minimum wage, calculated on the same basis, should rise to $12.25/hr. [$15.05].

• • •

10/24/1992

Do Big 3 Manipulate Statistics? Do They Ever!

A headline in the *Wall Street Journal* caught my eye: "GM Employee Level Creates $795-Per-Car Gap With Ford."

According to figures in the Harbour Report, compiled with the cooperation of the Big Three, Ford's labor cost per car is $1,563; Chrysler's, $1,872 and General Motors', $2,358. GM uses these figures to justify its planned firing of 74,000 blue and white collar workers.

What struck me is something quite different: how much auto workers are exploited! These labor cost figures are not just for final assembly—they also cover metal stamping, as well as engine and transmission manufacture.

Last year's median retail price of cars sold in the United States was $16,150. Let's figure this year's, conservatively, at $16,500. So Ford's labor cost is less than 10%, and GM's less than 15%, of the selling price of a car. Of course a large part of a car's value—about 63%—consists of the steel, plastic and other materials used. The other 37% is the value added by manufacture: that is, by the workers in the auto plants.

With average car worth $16,500, the value added comes out to $6,100. Thus Ford's labor costs equal about 25%, and GM's 40%, of the value added by the auto workers. Which means that for every dollar the workers receive, Ford keeps $3, and GM $1.50, in gross profits. Part of the difference between GM and its two main rivals may be due to the fact that GM makes more of its parts "in house."

Poor General Motors! Its gross profits in the first half of 1992 were $8.9–$15.5 billion, depending upon which accounting system GM chooses to use!

In any case, for all three companies, that's more than enough to keep plants open, reduce working hours, and lighten production per worker from the present killing overtime pace—and still leave a good profit.

A GM spokesman praised the Harbour Report. But I called and questioned Mr. Harbour, who told me the labor costs cover everybody who enters the plant doors—from the plant manager down to the secretaries and floor bosses, as well as the workers. Industry statistics show that production workers account for less than 80% of plant payrolls. Moreover, Mr. Harbour said the data are calculated on the basis of labor compensation of $39.50 per hour: $20.50 direct wages and $19.00 fringe benefits.

Actually the $20.50 isn't that much higher than the latest actual hourly earnings of auto production workers, $18.40, considering that the higher paid managers, etc., are included in Harbour's calculation. But the $19 fringe figure is far out. It's a public relations figure—the one used in labor contract negotiations.

According to the Census Bureau, the 1990 (the latest year for which data are available) cash payroll in the industry was $10 billion and supplementary benefits were $4 billion, or 40% of cash payroll. Moreover, of the $4 billion, $1.1 billion was the employers' share of social security—and Harbour doesn't take that into account.

• • •

1/9/1993

The Productivity Hoax—Again!

Capitalist economists and journalists call for higher labor productivity. They argue that U.S. productivity has slowed dangerously: that is why American goods cannot compete; why wages cannot rise.

In a *New York Times* article, Peter Passell says that wages are determined by productivity. He says that productivity rose rapidly between 1948 and 1973, as did wages. According to Passell, if productivity growth had continued at the former rate, wages would be 50% higher than they are. But his data are wrong on two counts.

First, they show real wages rising since 1973, when, in fact, there has actually been a substantial decline in real hourly and weekly wages of production and non-supervisory workers in the private economy.

Second, and more important, Passell's productivity figures are nonsense even if he uses the official productivity figures of the U.S. Department of Labor's Bureau of Labor Statistics (BLS).

To understand what's going on, let's start with "What is productivity?" That's easy. To the average person, productivity is measured in things—how many widgets are produced per worker during a specific time. And productivity increases, or decreases, depending upon whether output per worker goes up or down. If the same number of workers produces more widgets, say 10% more, then productivity increases by 10%. If fewer workers, say 10% fewer, produce the same number of widgets, productivity increases by about 11%.

So, let us calculate what has really happened to labor productivity. And we'll use government statistics, too! Let's take manufacturing, the core of the economy, where the values created support the economic structure. (The same applies to agriculture, mining, construction and other areas of material production; but the results for manufacturing are consistent with the productivity growth in other sectors of material production.)

There is a good, standard index of manufacturing production published monthly by the Federal Reserve Board. This index, divided by an index of man-hours of manufacturing labor, published by the BLS, gives a realistic index of labor productivity. That index of productivity and an index of manufacturing wages are shown in the chart.

The productivity line shows a very fast increase between 1948 and 1973, and even a little faster in the period since 1973. The real wages line shows an increase

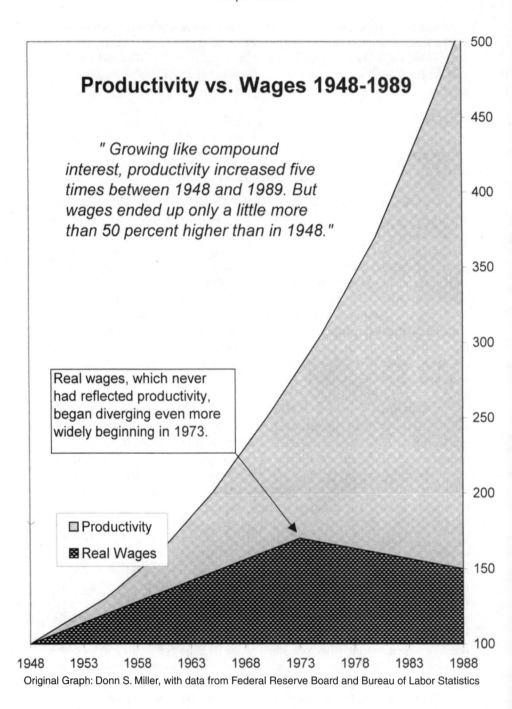

Productivity vs. Wages 1948-1989

" Growing like compound interest, productivity increased five times between 1948 and 1989. But wages ended up only a little more than 50 percent higher than in 1948."

Real wages, which never had reflected productivity, began diverging even more widely beginning in 1973.

☐ Productivity

▨ Real Wages

Original Graph: Donn S. Miller, with data from Federal Reserve Board and Bureau of Labor Statistics about half as fast as productivity in the earlier period and an actual decrease since 1973. Productivity went up at a rate of 4% per year in the first period, and 4.1% in the second period. Growing like compound interest, productivity increased five times between 1948 and 1989. But wages ended up only a little more than 50% higher than in 1948.

If productivity really determined wages, which it should, workers' wages would be much higher now than they actually are; or part of the higher productivity could have been used to reduce the workweek, or to provide social benefits and useful public jobs for all who have been left unemployed.

The historic truth is that the trend of wages is determined—within a wide range of possibilities—by the relative organization and bargaining strength of capital and labor, influenced to a considerable degree by government intervention, which today is decisively on the side of employers. During the last two decades employers have launched a determined offensive against labor with the conspicuous participation of the Reagan-Bush administration, the judiciary and the police.

Labor's concern is not to fulfill the employers' demands to raise productivity even faster. It is to organize and change the balance of forces to win back the ground lost in the last 45 years.

• • •

1/16/1993

More on Productivity

U.S. productivity is higher than in any other industrialized country. That position is reinforced by a 1992 report on "The State of U.S. Economic Performance," comparing productivity in industrialized countries. The authors, NYU professors William J. Baumol and Edward N. Wolff, say:

"[The U.S.] productivity level remains far higher than that of its rivals for the world's manufacturing export market . . . the German growth rate . . . has for some time fallen well behind ours. . . . The Japanese growth rate . . . is now almost neck and neck with ours. . . ."

At the same time, the authors use the flawed BLS productivity figures and accept the assumption that the U.S. productivity growth rate fell 65% since 1973. The authors note that the BLS has revised its method since 1973 to make its productivity rates grow more slowly: ". . . some observers believe it has been overdone, and suspect that the true U.S. figures are higher than shown in the graph."

Of course the revision was "overdone." Without it, employers would not have been able to use the "declining productivity" argument to fight labor.

As I pointed out in last week's PWW column, the productivity of U.S. manufacturing workers has increased at a 4% annual rate since 1948.

Marxists call the gap between the values that workers produce and the wages they get "surplus value." Capitalists call it "gross profits." The widening gap between soaring productivity and wages has brought about a notable rise in surplus value.

Part of the surplus value created by labor goes into services: services bought by capitalists with part of their profits; services provided by government; and, with the commercialization of most service industries, their purchase by workers.

Any attempt to lump productivity in the service sector with productivity in the sectors that create material values is misleading.

With the growth of monopolies, small independent producers and capitalists are squeezed out. Between 1934 and 1970, while the labor force increased by 60%, the number of self-employed declined 30%—from 10 to 7 million. But since 1970 there has been a significant turnaround: the number of self-employed rose steadily, exceeding 10 million by 1991; and the number of self-employed in the service sectors doubled.

Does that mean that there has been a reversal of monopolization? Or that productivity had gone down in the service industries? Not at all. What it means is that the trend is a result of the decay of capitalism. The increasing number of people who lose decent-paying, productive jobs or who can never get a job seek to survive by "going into business for themselves."

In my small home town there is an absurd number of bars, pizza parlors, delis, Chinese food takeouts. There is a constant turnover as shops go broke after a couple of years. According to the BLS method of calculation, the low incomes of these service establishments reflects "low productivity."

The business done by such small suppliers of services has nothing to do with the actual productivity in the economy. But the declining profits and rising losses of 10 million small businesses are counted as part of "production" in determining productivity. This goes far to explain "slowed growth rate of productivity" that employers, government representatives and academics fret about.

Clinton's idea of tax incentives for new businesses, with an emphasis on high-tech, has a dubious relation to productivity—but it does have a tendency to evolve as another tax giveaway to capital.

Workers' objective interests are different. They want/need a reduction in the workweek to 35 or 30 hours with no overtime and no cut in weekly pay. That would have no predictable negative impact on productivity per man-hour but would, if carried out effectively and extensively, create many millions of additional well paying jobs. It would raise the bargaining power and overall incomes of the working class, and it would help to reverse the ever widening gap between extreme wealth and the poor.

9/4/1993

Youth on a Toboggan

Sociologists and media commentators report that youth feel they are not doing as well as their parents, and that their children face a still gloomier future. It is clear that the capitalists' Holy Grail—a secure and rising middle-income living standard—has become an unattainable mirage for most young people.

A recent Bureau of Labor Statistics (BLS) report shows just how bad the situation really is. The report tracks the hourly earnings of groups of young workers for the period of their first 5 years out of school, during the 1970s, and for similar cohorts 12-13 years later, during the 1980s. The comparisons are for groups with the same level of education in each decade. All the figures are in dollars of constant purchasing power. The report concludes:

"Hourly wage rates fell dramatically for young men in their first five years out of school between the 1970s and 80s. This decline was particularly severe for young men with 12 years of education or less."

According to the report, the earlier male high school graduates averaged $10.95 an hour in 1969, the first year after leaving school. Their counterparts who first worked in 1982 made only $7.06—down $3.89, or more than one-third! Although both groups gradually increased their earnings, a young man who completed his fifth year of work in 1986 was earning $4.25/hr. less—almost one-third less—than those who completed their fifth year of work in 1973.

For male college graduates, losses were somewhat less extreme. Still, in their fifth year of work, male college grads of the 1980s received $3/hr. less than those who graduated in the 1970s. And, most shocking of all, male college graduates in the 1980s averaged no better than male high school graduates in the 1970s.

All in all, never before in U.S. history has there been such a drastic deterioration in workers' wage levels.

The result for young women surveyed was quite different. Among high school graduates, the wages of the 1980s group ran "only" about 10 percentage points less than the 1970s contingent in the first year of work, and a little more in the fourth and fifth year.

Women college graduates made a little less in the 1980s than in the 1970s, their first few years at work, and a little more in their fourth and fifth years.

Thus, there was a marked reduction—by more than one-half—in the sex differential. But, as the report puts it, "most of the reduction in the differential appears to be a consequence of the fall in male wage rates," with no overall gain for women. Their wages and salaries are still intolerably low.

The report points out that workers lost more in the 1980s than the losses in hourly wages. Figures for different races were not shown. However, other sources indicate that, unlike the narrowing sex differentials, there has been no narrowing of the unjustifiable Black/white and Latino/white differentials.

Of course, the labor movement cannot accept this situation. A vital, specific demand should move to the top of the common agenda of the labor and civil rights movement: **Double the minimum wage**.

That and demands for anti-scab legislation, for defeat of the North American Free Trade Agreement (NAFTA), for affirmative action with quotas and timetables, constitute a powerful foursome for softening some of the worst blows of the economic crisis.

[See 12/04/1993, **Figures Don't Lie**, p. 106.]

• • •

10/14/1995

Big Lies Making the Rounds Again!

"Productivity to the rescue," brays *Business Week*. "Thanks to a remarkable upsurge in productivity, corporate America has risen from the ashes—and U.S. companies have regained the edge over their global rivals. . . . This tide will lift all boats. . . . For U.S. workers, the productivity payoff is on the horizon."

So is pie in the sky! Look at the record: between 1973 and 1994, corporate profits jumped 389% while real wages fell 21%!

Even the phony indexes of the Labor Department show big increases in productivity. A direct calculation of manufacturing productivity, based on the Federal Reserve Board Index of Manufacturing Production, shows production up 74% with 15%—2.2 million—fewer production workers. That amounts to an increase of 103% in productivity per worker, meaning that each remaining worker is producing twice as much as before.

Or, put another way, real wages per unit of production declined 62%, meaning that workers are now getting only 38% as much per unit of production as a worker got in 1973. Even working a 10-hour day, with two hours of forced overtime, **the average factory worker produces enough in the first two hours to pay his wages for the entire day.** The value produced in the remaining eight hours accounts for the nearly five-times increase in corporate profits.

That's what Marxists mean when we talk about exploitation.

3/9/1996

Beware Corporate Hit Men

The cover of the Feb. 26 issue of *Newsweek* features the mug shots of four CEOs responsible for the slaughter of thousands of jobs. Above this rogue's gallery a banner headline, set large in red type against a black background, screams "Corporate killers." Below the photos a subhead reads: "Wall Street loves layoffs. But the public is scared as hell. Is there a better way?"

Inside, a feature article gives the gory details: Robert Allen, CEO of AT&T, salary $3,362,000; January 1996—40,000 layoffs.

Louis Gerstner, CEO of IBM, salary $2,625,000; July 1993—60,000 layoffs. And like data is given for 11 other corporate chiefs.

The article continues: "You can practically smell the fear and anger in white-collar America, because nobody seems to care. Where will I find another job if I get downsized? . . . Will my boss ruin my life to make another cent on her stock options?"

And big business economists answer in the same article: "Cheer up, you're serving the greater good by being blown away by . . . the gale of creative destruction." *Newsweek* says that except for "oddballs" like Stephen Roach, the chief economist at Morgan Stanley who keeps warning of a workers' backlash, "Wall Street and Big Business have been in perfect harmony about how in-your-face capitalism is making America great."

Editors of *USA Today* got into the act on Feb. 19 with their headline article, "Restructuring and layoffs, here to stay." An accompanying chart shows that real earnings of the bottom two-thirds of workers have fallen 5.5% since 1979 with mass layoffs, formerly concentrated among blue-collar workers, now hitting white-collar workers, including professionals and managers, nearly as hard.

And then the admission in the same article: "Particularly hard hit: women and minorities, Hispanic, Asian, and African American workers, tend to have less seniority. . . . With companies operating under a last-hired, first-fired policy, they find themselves at risk."

USA Today asks, "When will it all end?" and answers, "It won't, experts say. . . . Few doubt the 21st century corporation will be far faster to hire and fire than its 20th century counterpart." The article then quotes Labor Secretary Robert Reich who admits ". . . the job security many workers experienced after World War II probably is gone forever."

Newsweek makes several excuses and rationalizations for the corporate hit men:

1. U.S. companies need to compete in the "global market."

False. Output per person in manufacturing is higher in the U.S. than in 7 of the 10 other industrialized countries. In Western Europe and Japan working hours have been slashed 27% since 1960; in the U.S., they have increased by 1.5%. So workers in other industrialized countries are less exploited, have more leisure and have made gains, while U.S. workers have lost. Further, the highest profits of U.S. transnational corporations are made abroad, not in the United States.

2. Productivity increase in the U.S. has slowed.

False. The Bureau of Labor Statistics now claims, falsely, that productivity rose only 1.6% per year in the 1990s vs. 1.9% in the 1980s and 1.5% in the 1970s. But even with those figures, a real wage increase of 48% since 1970 would be in order to match the compounded productivity rise.

But the productivity indexes are biased. They are not based on measures of production, but largely on workers' wages, especially where no value is created—as in advertising and gambling.

However, indexes compiled by the Federal Reserve Board do show that physical production in manufacturing—where the basic profits, or surplus value, are created—went up 3.4% per year since 1970 and up 3.6% per year since 1990. To remain even with their productivity during the past five years, workers would need wage increases of 6.6% per year (3.6% plus 3% for rising living costs). Instead they got less than the hike in living costs. Workers' share of production fell from 40% in 1970 to 20% in 1995.

A question: With workers getting a smaller share of what they produce, how can they buy back enough to keep the economy afloat? The answer: They can't. The lower two-thirds of the population are forced to cut consumption. But the upper third, especially the top 10%, buy more than ever, from $50,000 Mercedes to multi-million dollar homes.

Mass retailers—outfits like Macy's and K-Mart—are going bankrupt or closing stores. A large share of the gross profits—the amount exploited from workers—goes to pay the multi-million dollar salaries and perks of the top corporate brass.

As *Newsweek* says: "When AT&T . . . announced . . . it would fire 40,000 people, the stock market went nuts. AT&T shares roared upward. Bob Allen said he felt bad about firing people but saw no point in giving up some of his pay or perks as a shared sacrifice with the workers. And, he said, he saw no reason to apologize. Allen made more than $5 million when the value of his stock and options soared after the layoffs were announced."

More of the gross profits than ever are spent on advertising, on bribes to domestic and foreign politicians. But record amounts are still left for the "bottom line." Corporate profits after taxes rose from $209 billion in 1990 to $380 billion in 1995, a gain of 82%—while real hourly earnings declined 2.3%! This unbalanced situation cannot continue long. Our country is on the verge of a real recession, which newly reappointed Federal Reserve Chair Alan Greenspan may want to hasten to help his Republican friends in November.

Poverty is becoming the permanent fate of the victims of downsizing. *Business Week* shows that from 25% to 44% of those thrown into poverty in European countries were able to escape within a year. In the United States, only 17% of whites and 9% of Blacks suffering a similar fate were able to recoup.

Allan Sloan, author of the *Newsweek* article, sees the "solution" as a handful of corporations that treat their workers with consideration. But what is really needed, of course, is the overthrow of the killer—capitalism. And millions of workers are coming to agree.

Labor and community groups fighting for higher minimum wages, supporting the Martinez public works jobs bill, focusing on defeating Gingrich and the 73 ultra-right Republican congressional first-termers, all are acting to improve the balance on our side of the class struggle. But such efforts have to be united and multiplied to win.

• •

7/25/98: General Motors: Let's Look at the Books!

John F. Smith Jr., the CEO of GM, got $7,228,000 total compensation in 1997. . . . And Smith got less than the CEOs of Chrysler ($11 million) and Ford ($20 million), which helps the media create an image of a GM just bumbling along, having to export jobs and outsource parts production in order to maintain its standing in the industry.

• • •

8/14/1999

Prison Labor in the U.S.

What country leads the world in the number of prisoners? Yes, the United States, with about two million incarcerated—and the number doubles every 10 years. Inmates are overcrowded, abused by guards, terrorized by other, violent prisoners.

We have a half-million more prisoners than China, which has nearly five times our population. We have twice the rate of South Africa or Cuba; five times the rate of China, Canada or Mexico; six times the rate of Germany or France. Our Black population of 35 million approximates the Black population of South Africa. But there are 900,000 Blacks in U.S. prisons compared with 140,000 in South Africa.

U.S. imperialism uses cries of "prison labor" to attack China and other socialist countries. Unfortunately, the UAW leadership, in its magazine *Solidarity*, puts China "on probation" for various sins, notably "human rights violations" like prison labor. These statements help General Motors instead of union members. Those concerned with human rights should look homeward.

Many states use prison labor for making license plates and other government items. Driving through the South 40 years ago I saw chain gangs, that cruel relic of slavery. Now that barbarous practice has been revived. And what's new is the growing use of prison labor directly for corporate profits; e.g., in California prison laborers book flights for TWA. Elsewhere, Microsoft uses prison labor to ship Windows software to save money for the world's first $100 billionaire, Bill Gates. Toys-R-Us uses prisoners to clean and stock store shelves.

According to Gordon Lafer in *The American Prospect*, "Corporate America can't imagine a better work force than prison inmates: sub minimum wages, no health benefits, no union, no vacations, no absenteeism, no overtime. They have no means of filing a grievance or voicing a complaint."

During the past 20 years, more than 30 states have legalized the use of prison labor by private companies. In Ohio, Honda pays $2-per-hour for prison laborers who do the jobs that UAW workers did for $20-per-hour. Of course, such prospects have fueled a boom in privatizing prisons—owned and run by private companies.

Lafer names Allstate, Merrill Lynch, and Shearson Lehman as investors in shell companies that buy prisons. These companies are profitable because the cost of their operations are less than what the states pay them for running the prisons, and for contracting out the prisoners to other companies for practically no wages. The difference is pocketed as profits.

In Georgia, a recycling plant laid off 50 sorters, replacing them with prisoners. Of those laid off, 35 had taken the job to get off welfare. Now they have neither work nor welfare.

Oregon is one of the worst offenders. A 1994 law requires the state to actively market prison labor to private employers. Thousands of public service jobs have been filled by convicts, private sector employees replaced by inmates. The prison legislation was enacted in response to a campaign by the Oregon Roundtable, a right-wing group headed by the union-hating Shilo Inn chain. Each member of the Roundtable contributes $100,000 yearly for anti-labor campaigns.

The campaign against prison labor in Oregon is picking up steam. The fightback is headed by the Teamsters, the Building Trades unions and the American Federation of State, County and Municipal Employees, whose members include correction officers. The unions provide the strength needed by the coalition of prison activists, progressive policy organizations, and Black and Latino community groups that are fighting against the use of prison labor and for the repeal of the laws authorizing it.

Income Differential

3/20/1986

Bosses Up, Workers Down

While real wages continue to drop, executives' salaries and bonuses are rising faster than ever. According to the *Wall Street Journal* (Feb. 28), executive salaries, bonuses and incentives combined increased four and a half times from 1967 until 1985.

In 1967, the chief executive's salary was 38 times the average worker's wage of $5,296. By 1985, it was 58 times the average worker's wage of $15,660. Of course, inflation entered into that. Based on the consumer price index, real salaries and bonuses of executives increased 40%—while workers' real wages declined 7%. And these summary figures do not take into account:

1. Executive expense accounts, which cover an increasing share, sometimes all, of their luxurious lifestyle;
2. The growing use of stock options. By now, according to the *Wall Street Journal*, more than 90% of executives get them. In today's stock market boom, these add up to literally hundreds of billions in extra profits, without real investment, for the major market manipulators;
3. Reagan's drastic tax cuts for the wealthy.

Workers, on the other hand, have lost much more than 7%. The downturn in real wages began in 1972. By January 1976, official figures showed a fall of 14.2%. But the government stopped publishing the increases in income and Social Security taxes on workers—which raise the loss in real take-home pay to at least 20%. In relation to the January 1986 average wage of $303 per week, that means a loss of $61 a week, or $3,172 per year. To all this must be added the losses from the growing unemployment, which have pushed millions of working people below the poverty line.

When companies sit across the bargaining table from unions, they use their "net income after taxes" as a measure of what they can afford to pay the workers. They bemoan the fact that their net income after taxes is too low. What they don't say is that their total gross profits—figured before they have paid exorbitant executives' salaries, bonuses, stock options and expense accounts—are usually from five to seven times the amount of their "net income after taxes," by their own published figures.

Most of the rise in "real" executive pay charted by the *Wall Street Journal* has taken place during the Reagan years. In all respects—executives' pay, dividends, interest and rents, capital gains, lower taxes—the Reagan years have provided a profit orgy to the corporate elite.

The bosses' take is part of the **profits of control**, which is a major portion of the rapidly increasing gross profits of the capitalist class. The profits of control also includes payments made to corporate lawyers and advertisers, strikebreakers and politicians—and the additional billions in stock market profits resulting from options, and access to information before it is public.

The frenzied corporate takeovers and mergers—the struggles for domination—are aimed at those profits of control. The takeover tycoons are willing to pay tens of millions in "golden parachutes" to displaced bosses because they expect to get hundreds of millions or billions out of their victories.

Soaring profits, gross and net, are the "objective" basis for the speculative stock market boom, which isn't all speculation by any means. The Reagan bull market in stocks hasn't gone farther than the Reagan bull market in profits.

Of course, the economy is heading for a fall: it is on course for a cyclical crisis. The boom can't go on indefinitely because the economy is so unbalanced. Sooner or later it will collapse from the weight of domestic and international debt, lack of mass purchasing power, too much national income being taxed away for the Pentagon and the bankers.

Meanwhile there is no boom, but continuing depression, for the working class. The rising rate of surplus value and falling real wages do not just happen because of "economic laws." They result concretely from the big business anti-labor offensive, headed by Ronald Reagan and the instruments of state power he wields. It continues today in the widening corporate union-busting drive for 20% wage cuts and all-around attacks on working and living standards.

• • •

10/14/1987

Billionaires vs. the Rest of Us

I'm turned off by the media celebration of the super-rich, but I finally picked up the *Fortune* issue with details about more than 100 billionaires. Among them they own, net of debts, $255 billion—$30 billion more than all the U.S. currency in circulation. About 50, with a total of $125 billion, are Americans.

I wanted to see how this compares with the much touted "average middle class" American family—actually, a slightly better off workingclass family. Government statistics report that the median family owns a total of about $25,000. That includes everything: car (if paid off), equity in a home, furniture and savings account.

This "median" family is right in the middle. Half of all families are richer; half are poorer. Typically, this might be the family of a reasonably well paid office worker, an elementary school teacher, or a highly skilled union construction worker employed year-round.

It would take the combined wealth of 5 million of these families to equal that of the 50 American billionaires, or 100,000 of them to match a single billionaire. And as the average blue-collar worker's family owns, net of debts, $8,300, it would take 15 million of them to match the 50 billionaires, 300,000 to match a single billionaire.

At a higher point in the economic scale, the average "self-employed" manager is worth $87,000. It would take 1,400,000 of these small capitalists to equal the wealth of the 50 billionaires, or 28,000 to match a single billionaire. That's a long way to go to make it against monopoly!

Who are the billionaires?

Among them are listed the notorious old families of exploiters: the Rockefellers, Fords and Hearsts. But they rank below names we never heard of 50 years ago.

The second richest American today is Lester Crown, with $5.7 billion. The Chicagoan owns a controlling 23% of General Dynamics, one of the Big Six armament firms.

The richest person in the Federal Republic of Germany is Friedrich Flick, son of the Nazi war criminal, top sponsor of Hitler. The father was let off with 3 years in prison and permitted by U.S. and British authorities to pass on his fortune, generated by slave labor in Hitler's arms factories, to the current Flick family.

These names carry heavy weight with politicians like Reagan and Kohl.

• • •

9/2/1995

Inequality: Real and Growing

Right-wing propagandists have taken on the task of "proving" that the studies about growing inequality—about the rich getting richer and the poor poorer—are so much hokum. They would have us believe that the "middle class" is growing, and the poor are almost flourishing because of "excessive" government spending on Medicare, Medicaid, Social Security; and that too much money is going to provide food stamps for hungry children and prenatal care for unwed mothers.

I've been asked about all this. My answer is this column. My calculations are all in constant 1993 dollars; and my sources are government publications, primarily reports published by the U.S. Census Bureau.

The downtrends I describe began when the Republicans were in control of the White House. They stayed there for 20 of the last 25 years and made sure that all government agencies were run by right-wing administrators. So if there is bias, it is their bias—a bias meant to make things look better than they are. But even with that, the truth can't be hidden.

Consider family income. Each year the Census Bureau calculates the percentage of families making over $100,000 a year which, broadly defined, is "rich."

In the late 1960s, about 2.3% of all families had incomes equal to $100,000 or more. By the 1990s the number was 6.9%. That means the proportion of rich families tripled in 25 years. If we go up a couple more rungs on the income ladder, IRS figures reveal that the number of people making more than a million dollars a year multiplied more than 12 times over the same period.

But what about the other end of the income scale—poor families, with annual incomes under $5,000? They also increased—from 2.8% of all families in the late 1960s to 3.4% in the early 1990s.

True, the categories of families measured by family income have changed. But the increases have been in two categories—families with yearly incomes at or above $75,000 and those at or below $15,000. On the other hand, there have been sharp decreases in the proportion of families with incomes in the $25,000 to $50,000 range. These are the middle-income group of working families who are being squeezed out of their "middle class" standard of living by big business cuts in decent-paying jobs.

These trends apply to all racial groups, with one important difference: in 1993 some 8.5% of white families were making over $100,000, and 2.1% were at $5,000 and under. Among Black families, 2.4% were in that upper group, and 10.7% at the bottom. For Latino families, 2.4% were in the richest and 5.8% in the poorest.

One more statistic, one that measures the impact the anti-labor offensive of the last 25 years has had on real incomes. Since the 1973 peak in real wages, the median income of all males has declined 19.5%; for white males 17%. On the whole, the losses of minority males were sharper. The hardest hit were what the Census Bureau calls "Hispanic" males, whose median wages declined by a disastrous 32.2%.

My question: if the decline in the income of white males is the result of "reverse discrimination," why are the wages of minority males falling even faster? My answer: because affirmative action programs have not been enough to prevent, or even seriously reduce, racial disparities in incomes.

The losses of white males, as with all other workers, are due to increased exploitation by the rich—mostly white and mostly male—who own and control the means of producing the nation's wealth and who use that control to enhance their fortunes and their political power.

3/13/1999

Of Riches and Rags

Monopoly rides high . . .

The ten largest corporations have a combined market value equal to one-fifth of the GDP (gross domestic product); the 30 largest, a combined value equal to one-half of GDP and one-third of the market value of all stocks. Historically, the combined market value of all stocks was about 65% of GDP. By 1995 it exceeded GDP, and reached 170% of GDP—$14 trillion—by the end of 1997.

. . . While children go hungry

Recent Census Bureau figures show an ominous rise in poverty, especially among children, in New York City suburbs.

In Westchester County, the number of poor went up 60%; poor children, 92.5%. In Putnam County, the figures were 73 and 113%; and in Rockland, 58 and 95%. **These are counties with average incomes well above the state's average—** not that the rest of the state did so well: poverty up 30%, 40% for children.

Statewide poverty rose from 2.2 million to 2.8 million—16% of the population. As a result of cuts in federal and state welfare programs, the burden on private aid programs has intensified. The Westchester Coalition for the Hungry and Homeless (WCHH) served 4.7 million meals to 240,000 people in 1997, meaning that one-fourth of Westchesterites needed aid to allay hunger.

Referring to the children fed in the pantries of Westchester's largest cities, Rosa Boone, WCHH executive director, said: "These are the children of the working poor . . . people who can't afford to pay rent and buy food."

• • •

10/2/1999

The Rich and the Poor

It is a truism that the rich are getting richer and the poor are getting poorer. But a new study (Report by the Committee on Budget and Policy Priorities, based on Congressional Budget Office data), reported in *The New York Times* 9/5/99, reveals that this process has picked up speed in the last 22 years—and it's not only the poor who are losing ground, but also most of the working class. The usual presentation of these data minimizes the reality of the impact. In fact, the average family in the lowest 20% of the population, who received $10,000 a year in 1977, got $8,800 in 1999, whereas the average income of the top 20% rose from $74,000 in 1977 to $102,300 in 1999—from 7.4 times more to 11.6 times more than the low-wage workers.

However, what's most significant is that the average income of the top 1% of the population, which rose from $235,000 in 1977 to $516,000 in 1999, went up by 120%. That $516,000 per average rich family is 58 times the $8,800 of the lowest fifth; and the combined income of the top 1% families is accordingly three times the combined income of all the families in the lowest 20% of the population.

The report also shows that the widening of the income differential has accelerated as never before. Roughly speaking, during the last 6 years the gap has accounted for 60-70% of the widening spread over the past 22 years.

But the report doesn't deal with a central factor: the social content of the income differential—the gap between the capitalist class and the working class. The income of the average capitalist class household is 25 times that of the average workingclass household. The number of workers is 60 times the number of capitalists. But the total income of the capitalist class now nearly matches the total income of the 60 times larger working class. In 1977 the income of the average capitalist class household was 11 times larger. What accounts for this development?

1. The incredible rise in exploitation, the result of the higher productivity of labor combined with declining real wages during most of the 22 years. This development makes mockery of the 2-3% wage increases that workers have been able to win, even in these boom times. Especially notable is the praise by UAW president, Yokich, of the 3% wage rise that he has accepted, along with only partial COLA or improvement in working conditions and benefits, and no significant protection against outsourcing to unorganized subcontractors.

2. The accelerated scale of superexploitation by U.S. large-scale capital of workers in neo-colonial countries with wages one-tenth or less the U.S. level. This practice has been heightened by the world financial crisis of the past several years, which afflicted mainly the neo-colonial countries.

3. Reduction of taxes on the rich and corporations, accompanied by tax increases on workers.

• • •

10/16/1999

How Rich Is Rich?

Forbes magazine recently published a list of the 400 richest Americans, headed, of course, by Bill Gates of Microsoft, with a net worth of $85 billion. The list has several interesting features.

One is the escalation in the wealth of the richest Americans, which went up from $125 billion in 1984 to $1 trillion (1,000 billion) in 1999—eight times more.

Yes, a small part of that can be ascribed to the rise in prices that has taken place; but even adjusting for that, the gain was five times in the 15 years.

Meanwhile, what happened to the real income of workers, whose labor provided that bonanza to the rich? Zilch!

The official data of real hourly earnings show no significant change over the 15 years. The big drop in real hourly earnings occurred during the decade after

1973, the peak year of real hourly earnings. The recent "rejiggering" of the consumer price index, under pressure from Greenspan and others, has made the decline in real wages appear less sharp—but that is illusion.

The rate of increase in the wealth of the 400 has accelerated. During the last three years alone—1996–1999—their wealth rose from $548 billion to $1 trillion, a compound rate of 22.2% per year, compared with the 14.9% per year of the entire 15-year period.

Two-thirds of the 400 are billionaires, and even among these moguls there is a wide variation in the rate of accumulation of wealth. The worth of the richest, Gates, zoomed 360%, whereas that of the lowest listed of the 400 went up "only" 20%, from $520 million to $625 million. But the growth rate of Gates' income was nearly matched by those just below him on the list.

The "old money" families are all represented, including Wrigley, Rockefeller, duPont and Mellon. Mellon heir Richard Mellon Scaife is prominent in ultra-right politics. Of course, most of them support and finance right-wing forces in politics.

Needless to say, there are no workers on the list. Nor are the 400 representative of the ethnic diversity among the American people. There is a handful of women and at least one Black—Oprah Winfrey, the TV star.

Judging by name—recognizably not a wholly reliable indicator—there are a few apparently of Jewish origin and no obvious Latinos, although two Cuban émigrés are among those who narrowly missed inclusion on the list.

Histories of the originators of the "great American fortunes" show them as unscrupulous pirates in relation to business rivals and the U.S. government, as well as to employees and workers.

The present generation of billionaire heirs gets considerable publicity for donations to charities, their support of environmental and conservation societies, and financial bequests to "culture." But there is little recognition of the fact that they are the decisive force behind the global aggressions of U.S. imperialism, anti-labor practices and politics, and the intensified racism polluting our lives.

Social Security

9/2/1982

The Blitz Against Social Security

Social Security is at the top of big business' anti-labor agenda for 1983. The campaign, started by Carter in 1979, picks up steam in odd years. Since politicians fear the votes of senior citizens, they are reluctant to act in an election year. Striking right after an election, however, they hope voters will forget their guilt by next time around.

Reagan, using divide-and-rule tactics, made other social service programs, especially those benefiting the poor, priority targets. With the concurrence of Congress, he slashed them mercilessly, and the process continues. He was even successful in chipping away at Social Security. Now, with poverty programs nearly extinct, workers' pensions have been set up for legislative massacre.

The entire Establishment—conservative and liberal, Republican and Democratic, *The New York Times* and *Wall Street Journal*—is clamoring for Social Security cuts, hoping to create a momentum that will put them over in the early months of the next Congress.

Readers! Get your organizations to warn candidates that failure to resist cuts will doom them in 1984. Exact their pledge to maintain, and increase, Social Security.

Preparing to ram through the legislation, the Reagan gang fired Murray Weidenbaum as chairman of the Council of Economic Advisers and replaced him with Martin S. Feldstein. *Business Week* says: ". . . the White House is getting ready to focus on the tough steps needed to bring the runaway budget deficit under control. . . .

"Feldstein is the ideal man to spearhead that effort. White House aides have characterized 1983 as 'the year of entitlements'—a period between elections that will finally allow the Administration to seek budget relief by cutting down . . . such automatic benefit programs as Social Security, federal pensions, and unemployment insurance. Feldstein . . . is one of the nation's leading authorities on all of these programs and has long called for reining in their expansion" (8/23).

A cruel and aggressive reactionary, Feldstein has through the years provided arguments used by Congress to cut expenditures for people's needs to balance cuts

"This bench is o.k. on a sunny day, but we may be sleeping here if Washington doesn't shift gears."

in big business' taxes. Social Security is his special target: in March 1982 he urged Congress to reduce Social Security benefits 15% by 1987.

The aim of the campaign to reduce Social Security benefits is to use workers' social insurance tax deductions to increase the military budget faster, and to lower capitalists' taxes even more. The aim is also to further impoverish the working class and to weaken its ability to resist wage cuts.

The arguments for cutting Social Security benefits are fraudulent.

One argument is that actuaries calculate the fund will run into a deficit by the year 2020. What a joke! Capitalist "experts" cannot predict accurately even a year ahead, no less 40 years.

The argument that Social Security is a major factor in the federal deficit is an outright lie: it is already being used to reduce the deficit. Budgeted collections of Social Security taxes for fiscal 1983 total $199.5 billion, $23.9 billion more than the anticipated outlays of $175.6 billion. At the end of 1981 the reserves of the four main social insurance funds were $49.2 billion, up $4.5 billion from a year earlier.

But there is one sure way of providing funds to prevent any future deficits that might result from depression cuts in revenues and from sorely needed increases in real benefits: end the exemption high-paid executives and capitalists are entitled to on that share of their salaries over $32,400. That is, in 1982 an executive with $100,000 salary in effect pays only one-third the regular Social Security tax rate. If Social Security taxes were collected on all of their reported salaries and self-employment income, along with matching payments by their employers, the social insurance funds would add $40 billion, or 20%, to their 1983 collections.

And there is still far more Social Security income available for collection if salaries and other income hidden in expense accounts and other loopholes were taxed.

One formula proposed for cutting Social Security benefits is for these entitlements to be raised by less than the rise in consumer prices (CPI). When the CPI goes up 10%, benefits would go up only 7%. And another, particularly vicious proposal is for no adjustment at all to be made for one year. It is argued that since active workers' wages are being cut, retired workers should not get "special privileges," should not escape the "sacrifices" in living standards all workers are being called upon to make on the altar of the Pentagon and big business supply-side tax cuts. It is also argued (by the *Wall Street Journal*, among others) that the CPI exaggerates the rise in living costs. Untrue. The cost of living goes up faster than the CPI, not slower.

Lately there has been much emphasis on linking Social Security benefits to wages instead of to living costs. They say Social Security benefits should be raised 1.5% less than wages on the grounds that workers' wage increases reward them that much for greater productivity, and retired workers aren't producing.

What an argument! So long as real wages are declining, capitalists are getting all the profit from higher productivity while workers lose. Also, retired workers, who contributed decisively to high productivity in their active years, should share in the benefits of current advances, along with all presently employed people. The capitalists calculate that if they can cut real wages 3.5% and pensions another 1.5%, or 5% altogether, benefits will soon be so low that senior citizens and disabled workers will be forced to continue competing on the job market, helping employers to lower the general wage level further.

The present Social Security provisions are far too low and must be increased. But the capitalists plan instead to raise their own pensions and lower their taxes by cutting workers' pensions.

While plotting a major amputation of Social Security, the bosses have been busy padding their luxury level retirement pensions. What they get from Social Security upon retirement, even though double what the average retiree gets, is just chicken feed to them. Corporate executives' pensions plans, financed by the gross profits amassed from workers' labor, are not only extremely liberal but also have been the most rapidly rising component of the spiraling executive compensation sector. Meanwhile, Congress has been passing tax-free funds for executives' retirement, and the currently pending tax bill includes a further liberalization of some of these devices.

The more Social Security benefits are cut, the less Social Security taxes the corporations and their executives will have to pay, and the more they will have for their own expense accounts, tax-sheltered retirement funds, and dividend checks.

Finally, the surest road to adequate, decent Social Security benefits is through reducing the military budget $150 billion per year, as well as by raising taxes on the rich and the corporations at least enough to reverse the hundreds of billions in tax cuts and loopholes put over during the last two decades.

• • •

4/7/1983

Attacking Social Security

Peter G. Peterson, chairman of the board of Lehman Brothers and former Secretary of Commerce, is the leading organizer of Wall Street's campaign against the Social Security system, part of which Congress is now enacting into law under the guise of "rescuing" the system. Not satisfied with the pending reduction in real pensions and addition of charges for Medicare, Peterson campaigns for much more drastic attacks against the retirement and health benefits of workers (*New York Review of Books,* 3/17).

The argument is that under expected Social Security tax laws and levels of employment and wages, the trust funds will run huge deficits and be unable to pay benefits.

The hypocrisy of capitalist executives calling for workers' pension cuts must be exposed. Men like Peterson do not depend on Social Security. The company will pay them more in a year than the average worker will get during all his years of retirement—in addition to a six-figure life insurance policy. Their post-retirement benefits aren't being slashed to save financial resources; rather, they're rising rapidly, along with their salaries, bonuses, and tax-avoiding fringe benefits.

Peterson argues that the country has limited resources and simply cannot afford to maintain the present real level of workers' pensions. What blatant nonsense! With industry operating at two-thirds of capacity, half the crop land being idled and 20 million workers fully or largely unemployed, the unused potential of this country, valued in money terms, is several times the total of Social Security benefits.

Peterson claims that rising spending for Social Security benefits takes away savings from investments. The benefits, he claims, exceed total investments plus research and development outlays by U.S. companies. His facts are wrong. Gross private business fixed domestic investment in 1981 equaled $346 billion, exceeding by 55% the $223 billion spent for all social insurance benefits, including Medicare, and the percentage margin widened over the previous 5 years. The main limitations to domestic business investment have not been financial, but declining ultimate markets and the preference of corporations to invest in lower-wage areas abroad.

In predicting enormous deficits in the Social Security trust fund, Peterson assumes that real wages will stagnate until 1995 and that unemployment will remain close to its present crisis level, thus holding down the growth of Social Security revenues. This is not really a prediction. It is an expression of the aims of big business to continue the downward trend of real wages in order to increase the rate of exploitation of labor and corporate profits. Big business wants to keep unemployment high because it is proving very useful in squeezing drastic concessions out of millions of workers.

Peterson argues that it is not right to separate the old age and disability insurance fund from the health insurance fund. He points out that health costs are rising twice as fast as the general cost of living and will soon cause the deficit in the combined old age, and disability and health insurance systems to rise into the hundreds of billions of dollars if present Medicare benefits and taxes are maintained.

Yes, health and medical costs are soaring. In 1981 total health expenditures of individuals, governments, corporations and non-profit agencies reached an incredible $330 billion—14% of the national income—and nearly $200 billion of that was paid by individuals. The lack of control over prices and fees has permitted outrageous profiteering by doctors, drug companies, and the burgeoning corporation-owned hospitals, from which Wall Street is making such a killing. Imagine, Medicare pays these hospitals a 19% profit on their investment, multiplied by watered stock—over and above the grossly padded cost bills they submit.

Peterson makes it clear that an all-out offensive against Medicare and Medicaid is high on Wall Street's anti-working class agenda. Every even moderately civilized capitalist country provides more health care than the United States and exerts some degree of restraint on profiteering in this area. And the Soviet Union, along with other socialist countries, provides free medical care to all.

6/1/1996

Swindling Senior Citizens

Lester C. Thurow, MIT professor and TV personality, launched the latest ideological attack on Social Security with an article entitled "The Birth of a Revolutionary Class," in the May 19 issue of *The New York Times Magazine*. His overall theme: Older people are taking everything, ripping off the rest of the population.

His most outrageous statement is: "The elderly have a median per capita income a whopping 67% above that of the population as a whole." He portrays elderly people as veritable Rockefellers, with an average net worth of $222,000—another of his inventions. Sure, there are retired capitalists with incomes in the millions. But workers?

What are his sources? Here are mine: according to the latest consumer income report (1994) of the Census Bureau, the median income of males under 65 was $23,000; for those over 65 it was $15,000. Median incomes peak at $35,000 for 35- to 44-year-olds before dropping to $17,000 for those age 65-74 and to $14,000 for those 75 and over. The figures for females have a similar pattern but are lower all along the line.

Because of inadequate pensions, 3.7 million—2% of all senior citizens—fall below the poverty line. More to the point, 10.6 million—33% of all seniors—fall below 175% of the official poverty line when they have to rely solely on Social Security pensions.

Another Thurow whopper: He claims that if ways aren't found to cut Social Security and Medicare, the government deficit will multiply eightfold by the year 2030. He errs twice here: he couples Social Security, which has its own funding, with Medicare, which does not. Then he implies that the Social Security Trust Fund (SSTF) will contribute to the huge deficits he projects.

Actually, the accumulated surplus in the SSTF soared from $23 billion in 1980 to $414 billion in 1994. The Social Security Administration expects the surplus to reach $1,272 billion by 2004, when it will continue to grow by $120 billion annually.

Thurow also claims that spending on the elderly squeezes government investment for infrastructure, education, research and development. Nonsense! What is squeezing needed federal government investment? Well, in 1995 federal military expenditures came to $345.7 billion, including $43.3 billion of investment—more than double federal spending for non-defense investment. Also, interest payments to the wealthy and, above all, tax cuts to rich individuals and corporations robbed federal spending for civilian purposes.

The attack on Social Security is part of the plan to gut the SSTF, to get access to these billions of dollars, and to force Social Security to compete with other claimants for federal money under a so called "unified budget." This ploy must be rebuffed; and the trust fund, half of which is paid for directly by workers, must be reserved for its dedicated purpose—to provide pensions for retirees.

2/15/97

A Program to Save Social Security and Medicare

Wall Street is out to wreck Social Security and Medicare. They are in a hurry to do it while they think they have a chance. They have on hand the same trained seals—Senator Daniel Patrick Moynihan and Michael J. Boskin, George Bush's chief economic advisor—who provided ammunition that significantly weakened the Social Security system in the 1980s. And, in his Jan. 26 news conference, Bill Clinton joined the clamor.

Social Security was won by labor and other militants in a campaign led by Communists during the 1930s. The U.S. system is much weaker than those in other industrial countries where unions are stronger and Communist parties are larger.

So far, opposition to the wrecking attack is weak and defensive, offering concessions to the pirates and making no demands for improvements—a strategy much like bargaining against yourself.

When Social Security became law in 1935, President Franklin D. Roosevelt envisioned a system that would provide a minimum level of comfort to workers in their old age. But that is not the case today: The Social Security Administration (SSA) says that the system only provides the average worker with 42% of previous earnings—and this while admitting that the average retired worker needs at least 70% of his previous income in order to live with a modicum of dignity.

In an attempt to rationalize these low benefits, the SSA claims that Social Security is only one leg of a three-legged stool, a leg that is splintered and in danger of collapse. The other two legs are private pension plans—which 82 million workers do not have—and savings and investment income, which even fewer workers have, so that the average worker doesn't have a stool to sit on. Or a chance for a decent retirement.

Those puppet statisticians who warn that the system is about to go bust present elaborate tables to "prove" that the SS Trust Fund will run out of money 30 years from now. Such long-range forecasting is just statistical game-playing, and their 75-year projection is pure snake oil. Think about it—these experts can't even project a 5-year budget!

But even by their calculations, enough money will pour into the system so that the present $500 billion in the trust fund will multiply six times to nearly $3 trillion by 2019. Wouldn't it be sensible to assume that with such a prospect we should wait and see if problems develop after 20 years? And further, they have an alternate set of calculations that shows that the fund will never decline but will soar to $82 trillion—that's 166 times the present level—by 2070.

The assault on Social Security has two principle aims: 1. To reduce benefits and raise taxes on workers, freeing the surplus for tax cuts to the rich. 2. To invest at least 40% of the trust fund in the stock market instead of in Treasury securities, as the present law dictates. This is fraught with danger: the long bull market is bound to be followed by a major bear market. Wall Street wants to use the workers' Social Security fund to prop up the over-priced stocks a little longer before the market collapses—and the money is lost.

The Communist Party recommends the following program, which is designed to put Social Security on a firm financial base for meeting workers' needs:

1. Make the Social Security Trust Fund the minimum guaranteed source of benefits, with whatever else is needed to provide benefits to come from general tax revenues, as is the case in other industrialized countries.
2. Double Social Security benefits.
3. Restore retirement to full pension at age 65 instead of 67, with workers in heavy or dangerous jobs eligible at 55.
4. Full Social Security retirement benefits for women workers at age 60.
5. Recalculate the Consumer Price Index upwards to more accurately reflect the real growth in the cost of living.
6. Limit investment of the Social Security and Disability Trust Fund surplus to U.S. Treasury securities, as provided by present law.

There are several ways to finance improved benefits, beginning with the provision that total wages and salaries be taxed for the Social Security fund instead of limiting Social Security deductions to the first $63,000 as is presently the case. Tax all income of the rich—capital gains, interest, etc—at the full Social Security rate, as proposed by the National Council of Senior Citizens. Other solutions include doubling the employers' contribution to Social Security, slashing 90% of the military and all of the CIA budgets, and use as much of those funds as needed for the SSA.

The immediate target of those who would destroy Social Security and other entitlements is Medicare. This program was enacted in the 1960s, along with the civil rights laws, in an effort to ward off mass struggles against the Vietnam War.

But Medicare has been shot as full of holes as a victim of machine gun fire. In 1960, before Medicare, the elderly spent 11% of their income on health care. Now they spend 18% of their income on health care—and this over and above Medicare.

There's a special trust fund for hospital charges in the Medicare program, and that fund will run out soon. Because hospitals raise prices so rapidly, 65% of all Medicare outlays go to hospitals, with their rich profit margins. Since Medicare payments for hospital service are limited to what's in the trust fund, the proposal is to "save it" by increasing taxes on workers and retirees and by sharply curbing benefits by making medical care more and more like an assembly line: in and out of the hospital in half the time necessary for proper care; in and out of doctors' offices in 15-minute time slots.

Then there's an additional aim: to force people to buy "Medigap insurance" to cover expenses not paid by Medicare. Prudential, which has one-third of this business, raised its fees 23% in the last two years, as did Blue Cross-Blue Shield and others.

Another objective is to herd people into health maintenance organizations (HMOs), which are rapidly taking over more and more doctors' practices. The HMOs are favored in Medicare payments, so people are left with little option but to join. But through HMOs, patients are limited to part-time doctors, second-rate drugs, and have to pay profit margins of 15-25% to the HMOs.

The Communist Party program for health care:

1. Make Medicare obligations absolute, over and above trust funds.
2. Extend Medicare to include dental and eye care and the cost of medicines.
3. Strictly regulate and reduce prices paid to all providers of medical services.
4. And further, nationalize the entire health care industry. Coordinate it with a national health insurance act, which Bill Clinton promised but never delivered.

• • •

12/12/1998

Social Security: A New Round of Sabotage

President Clinton has made Social Security the main domestic issue for his remaining time in office. He called a special conference on the subject earlier this week and intends to ask Congress for legislation next year. The issue is being publicized as an attempt to "save" Social Security; the aim is actually to dismember—thus wreck—Social Security.

Social Security benefits are paid out of two trust funds: one for old age and survivors insurance; the other for disability insurance. The system is funded by the 6.2% deductions from employees wages and salaries plus equal contributions from employers. These funds are not part of the regular budget of the United States; they are legally designated solely for payment of the specified pensions and benefits.

However, President Clinton has incorporated these and other off-budget items with the regular budget to claim a surplus of $70 billion this fiscal year. In fact, "borrowing" $105 billion from the turst funds means there's a real deficit of $35 billion.

The objective of this brouhaha about Social Security going broke is to take the "trust" out of the trust funds, to use the income for other purposes than for Social Security—which in effect is happening.

Those who tell us that major surgery is needed to "save" Social Security offer a number of unsatisfactory "solutions." Details of the latest proposal, a most dangerous one, are still vague; but, in essence, only two-thirds of Social Security taxes would be used to finance benefits while the other one-third would be privatized—that is, will be available for purchase of stocks, bonds or some other forms of investment or to pay bills.

This campaign fits in with Washington's determination to reduce taxes on the wealthy and corporations. Equally important is the anticipation of a vast flow of funds into the financial markets that should accompany privatization of part of the Social Security payments—the infusion of billions to the banks, brokerage houses, investment advisers and managers, mutual funds.

2/6/1999

More on Social Security

I, among other nationally recognized economists and financial experts, have publicly exposed the Social Security hoax that is being foisted on the American people.

Detailed analyses have proven that under any reasonable, even conservative, set of statistics, the Social Security Trust Funds (SSTF) will never go broke. In fact, even using the Trust Fund trustees' data, the funds could reach $51 trillion by the year 2075.

We say, "Don't let the Establishment appropriate the SSTF to enrich Wall Street. Let's use those trillions to improve the inadequate benefits presently paid to this generation's senior and disabled recipients and double Social Security benefits!"

Social Security retirement benefits do not provide an adequate retirement income unless buttressed by other, more generous, private or government pension systems. But only 42% of all workers are covered by private pension plans, and that number is being cut by employers trying to "reduce costs"—i.e., raise profits.

For the most part, labor and other organizations resisting the attacks on Social Security are not challenging the major fraud—that the trust funds face a financial crisis of major dimensions. Their proposals are defensive, aiming to prevent, or minimize, losses imposed by the executive and legislative branches on workers and retirees. But they should go on the offensive.

Use the trillions of surplus funds, which the trustees admit will accrue in the next 10-15 years, to raise benefits an average of 25%.

Eliminate the "cap" on income taxable for Social Security; tax all higher income at the same rate. That will finance an additional 50% improvement in benefits.

Under most government and private pension plans, employers pay twice as much, or even more, than workers into the pension funds. But the U.S. Social Security System is unique in requiring equal payments by workers and their bosses. Increase the employer tax by 50% and that will provide for another 25% increase in Social Security benefits.

An important method of raising Social Security funding is by increasing the minimum wage. Sen. Kennedy's proposal for $6.65 an hour would multiply the number of workers benefited. But better yet, the minimum wage should go up enough to compensate for the 40% loss in its purchasing power since 1968. At $7.50 an hour, that would exert leverage to raise wages of all low-wage workers—and the Social Security Fund would then rocket upward.

President Clinton, in his State of the Union Address, made the campaign to "save" Social Security his leading domestic issue. Starting with the problem raised by the Trustees' calculation that payroll taxes will no longer balance benefits by 2013, Clinton urged that there be no "drastic" cuts in benefits, no increase in payroll tax rates and no drain on resources from the SSTF.

However, in order to "insure" Social Security until then, he accepts and promotes Wall Street's manipulated calculations that require a 25% cut in benefits now in order to "save" the system.

He is guided by the biased statistics supplied by the Trust Funds' trustees, headed by Robert Rubin, Wall Street's Secretary of the Treasury. Their approach is like that of insurance companies, which charge property owners insurance on the basis of damage forecasts double those that can reasonably be expected.

Wall Street's most powerful guru, Federal Reserve Chief Alan Greenspan, has entered the fray, and more and more congressional Republicans and Democrats are adding to the chorus. But all of those involved, including Rubin and Greenspan, agree that the SSTF will pile up trillions of added reserves during the next 10-15 years.

Yet the financial and political establishment wants to cut benefits now—even more drastically than the President proposes, on the basis of what they say may happen 30 to 50 years hence.

Just think about it! It really takes chutzpah to launch the vast propaganda campaign on a fraudulent issue that affects masses of the population who cannot be expected to understand the skullduggery involved, or its effect on the future.

Greenspan led a commission in the early 1980s that pushed through both tax increases on workers and benefits cuts. Now he is pushing a "long menu" of cuts.

A two-year rise in the retirement age, enacted in 1983, means a 13% cut in total benefits for men and 11% for women—and of 14% and 12% for African American men and women. And now Republicans are pushing for a rise in the retirement age to 70—this at a time when corporations are disposing of more and more employees when they reach 40!

A long-standing problem has been the budgetary robbery of the SSTF. By law these funds are to be used solely for old age, survivors and disability benefits. Other sources can be tapped for those ends, but no funds should be taken from the Trust Funds for other purposes.

However, the increasing practice has been to merge Social Security funds with the regular budget and to publish a combined budget showing either surplus or deficit. Now that gimmick has become crucial: the much touted balancing of the federal budget has been accomplished mainly by using surpluses in the SSTF.

Much worse than accounting trickery, the government is preparing to use Social Security funds to reduce the federal debt. President Clinton says that these funds will just be "on loan" and will be returned to Social Security 30, 50 or 75 years from now when the funds may run out of money. (Of course, Clinton will not be around to keep the promise. And he can't "will" the responsibility to future administrations.)

Racism

1/7/1962

Discrimination by Government Contractors

Ten million workers are employed by the 100 largest arms contractors. Tens of millions more work for employers profiting from government orders, credits and subsidies. All ships and most houses are built with federal credits or guarantees. Food processors receive price support subsidies.

The federal government is legally responsible for stopping employment discrimination in all these activities. This would be decisive in winning equal job opportunities everywhere. The Civil Rights Commission report on employment shows that in this respect, as in its own direct hiring, the government has failed almost 100%.

Since the termination of FEPC (Fair Employment Practices Commission) in 1946, executive orders have forbidden discrimination by government contractors and recipients of government aid. But no administration has enforced its decrees. A Truman-appointed committee found in 1952 that the non-discrimination clause in government contracts was "almost forgotten, dead and buried under thousands of words of standard legal and technical language."

President Eisenhower set up a new committee, under Nixon, amidst great fanfare. Nixon tried to climb into the White House with calls for "firmer methods" by the Pentagon. But not a single contract was canceled or denied because of discrimination. Public utilities selling services to the government refused even to go through the motions of signing non-discrimination clauses, and got exemptions.

A Commission study of three cities—Detroit, Atlanta, and Birmingham—in 1961 showed that war contractors generally conformed to local patterns of discrimination.

In March 1961, President Kennedy set up his new committee under the oil-steeped Texan, Lyndon Johnson. Kennedy, Johnson, and Goldberg gave it a big send-off, and many people hoped for real progress. The NAACP has submitted hundreds of documented complaints.

A week after Kennedy's Executive Order, the Air Force awarded a billion dollar contract to Lockheed, which has a chronic record of Dixiecrat discrimination in its Georgia aircraft plant. A fresh complaint compelled the new committee to intervene, and it announced a settlement. Lockheed signed a generally worded "Plan for Progress," with the Air Force left to check up on progress. The Negro workers won a minor concession in desegregation of some plant facilities. Twenty-one major contractors signed such "Plans for Progress" and will file annual "compliance reports."

Previous committees also started out with brave statements and a flurry of surface activity, but accomplished little. The Commission on Civil Rights hopes for improvement now, because of supposed indications of contractor and Pentagon cooperation and "strong" presidential support.

I remain skeptical. McNamara's disgusting act of crossing a Negro people's picket line to rattle the saber before a gang of militarists in a Jim Crow southern hotel is the key to what we can expect from Pentagon "cooperation."

Other contracting agencies have records as bad: the Health, Education and Welfare Department under Ribicoff, as under his predecessors, has not even attempted to insist on non-discrimination in hospital and school construction.

The Federal Aviation Agency fails to post its formal non-discrimination clause at government-aided airport construction jobs on the cynical grounds that it lacks funds for the posters!

The Bureau of Public Roads is the largest source of federal government-financed employment outside the Pentagon. East of the Rockies it doesn't even require a standard non-discrimination clause in its contracts, and makes no attempt to post or enforce its short-form substitute clause.

Kennedy's order ignores federal grant and aid programs, and federally financed recruitment and training programs. The Report shows that this last area is one of the worst examples of Washington-sponsored segregation and discrimination, and says: "It is questionable" whether the new committee "can effectively implement an equal employment opportunity program unless its authority extends to these areas as well."

There may well be more significant gains in Negro employment opportunities in the next few years than heretofore—but if so, all the credit must go to the heroic Negro people, and to the white people who cooperate. So far no credit is due the AFL-CIO nor the Kennedy administration, despite the fine words.

6/2/1962

Michigan's Negroes and Unemployment

Last summer I wrote on Michigan's special depression resulting from the stagnation and dispersal of its one-crop auto economy. This year's boom provides only temporary and partial relief, with 9% officially unemployed in March.

Newly published census data dramatize how the Negro people have borne the brunt of Michigan's depression. Ford and other auto magnates long ago began to include substantial numbers of Negroes in their labor force, especially in the foundries and other heavy jobs. In 1950 some 43% of all Negro male workers in Michigan were in autos, an unusual concentration: the figure for white males was 22%.

This concentration in a high-wage industry had its advantages so long as auto employment grew. Per capita income of Negroes was higher and closer to that of whites than in any other state. Naturally more Negroes moved in; and by 1960 they constituted 29% of Detroit's population, the largest proportion for any northern city.

But with Michigan auto employment declining, that concentration has become a disadvantage. Between 1949 and 1959—the census interval—the median income of Negroes having income went up 10%, while that of whites went up 43%. The official consumer price index for Detroit rose 23% in the decade, signifying a rise of 16% in white real incomes, but a decline of 11% for Negroes. In 1949 the median income of Negroes was $500 higher in Michigan than in New York, but in 1959 it was $200 lower. The difference between whites and Negroes was especially wide in the Detroit area, where the per capita income of Negroes was only about half that of whites in 1959.

The worsening of the Negroes' economic situation in Michigan is associated with extra heavy unemployment. Between 1950 and 1960, joblessness among Negro males jumped from 11.5% to 16.9%, as compared with a rise from 4.9% to 5.9% among white males. The census takers, in 1960 especially, counted out of the labor force substantial numbers of Negroes in Michigan—a standard device when there is much long-term unemployment. Adjusting for this statistically, it appears that in 1960 the real unemployment among Michigan Negro males was 23.2%, as against 13.6% in 1950. And the spring of 1960, when the census was taken, was a boom period in autos!

Of those Negroes retaining jobs, many were forced out of high-paying industrial jobs into low-paying service jobs. Or, more often, Negro male workers who had earned $4,000 per year in industry were replaced by Negro women workers earning $1,300 in household drudgery.

Between 1950 and 1960 the proportion of Negro workers employed in industry, construction, transport and utilities fell from 57% to 43%, while the proportion employed in services or in unidentified lines increased from 30% to 44%. There is much propaganda about the growth of services representing an advance in living standards. But in present-day capitalist society, it is a two-sided proposition. One side is the increased luxury living of the wealthy and upper middle classes. The other side is the super-exploitation of a growing section of the working class, made surplus to industry by the decay of capitalist economy, and forced into these service-rendering jobs at shamefully low pay and poor working conditions. An especially large proportion of the Negro people are placed in this situation, economically resembling the semi-slave South.

Discrimination against Negroes in Michigan industry has been more complex than the first-to-be-fired formula, although that has figured. Statewide, over the decade, losses in automobile employment were more than offset by gains in other industries, e.g., machinery, aircraft-missiles, food, printing, chemicals. But while Negroes absorbed their full share of job losses in the automobile industry, they have been kept out of the expanding industries, other than in the traditional janitorial jobs and the like.

Negroes constituted 22% of the rise in population of working age, so should have gotten that proportion, at least, of new industrial jobs opening up in the state. But in fabricated metals they got only 3%, in machinery 3%, in electrical machinery 2%, in aircraft 0%, in printing and publishing 7%, in food 5%, in chemicals 3% of the additional jobs.

The state Fair Employment Practices Commission and the unions should initiate a vigorous struggle to open up Jim Crow industries to Negro workers. And Jim Crow communities too: one cannot expect to open the chemical industry to Negroes when the city of Midland, the Dow Chemical stronghold, has only three Negro women, presumably live-in maids, among its 27,779 inhabitants:

• • •

10/27/1963

Anatomy of Jim Crow

The Census Bureau has published the most comprehensive statistics ever comparing earnings of white and non-white males according to age, education, occupation and region. The compilers, headed by Howard Brunsman, deserve credit for the volume, *Occupation by Earnings and Education*, of the 1960 Census.

Here we can examine the anatomy of economic discrimination in detail. We find it deeply embedded everywhere, at all age levels, stages of education, and occupations. Summary results on mean (average) 1959 earnings of male experienced workers show:

Whites	$6,112
Non-whites	3,260
difference	2,852
Percent non-white of white	53%

Altogether, there were 10% as many non-whites as whites. But at the top, with earnings above $10,000, were only 1% as many; and at the bottom, below $1,000, there were 35% as many.

A common saying is that lower Negro earnings reflect less education. Of course, less education is also a result of discrimination, and lower earnings can partly be traced to this cause, but not mainly. Non-whites with 8 years schooling earned 69% of equally educated whites; high school graduates, 64%; and college graduates, 55%.

The more the education, the more the discrimination! Why? Because the Negro who gets more education gains economic advantages over other Negroes, but not nearly as much as the educated white gains over other whites. And the Negro college graduate averages about as much as the white high school drop-out.

At 21, the non-white earns 67% of the white; at 30, 59%; at 40, 54%; and at 50 and 60, only 49%. Why? Because the Negro has much less chance for promotion as he reaches the prime of life, and is discarded sooner as he approaches retirement age.

Apologists say lower Negro earnings reflect less skill. But the differentials prevailed in each occupation group and separate occupation:

Earnings (dollars)

Occupation	White	non-White	pct.
Doctors	$19,908	$9,393	47%
Schoolteachers	6,148	4,742	77
Mail carriers	5,298	4,996	94
Shipping clerks	4,654	3,616	78
Carpenters	4,618	2,928	63
Bus drivers	4,468	3,708	83
Truck drivers	4,943	3,018	61
Factory operatives	4,855	3,618	75
Farm laborers	2,118	1,255	59
Laborers, other	3,895	2,802	72

By properly combining the percentages for each occupation group we find that the Negro averages 68% as much as the white at the same skill level.

Of course, much of the alleged differences in skill are not real differences. They are simply invented by discriminating employers and union leaders. Many Negroes called laborers have more skill than many whites called craftsmen. But even as defined, skill, like education, is a secondary factor. The figures show that most economic discrimination is unadorned, simple racism. It is just less pay for the same work.

Half of all Negro workers are in the South, and discrimination is much worse there, as shown by these regional figures:

Average Earnings (dollars)

Region	White	non-White	pct.
North & West	$6,356	$4,123	65%
South	5,407	2,427	45

In the North, the white averaged half again more than the Negro. In the South, the white averaged two-and-one-quarter times as much as the Negro.

What about trends? Differences in what was measured prevent exact comparison with the 1950 Census. Allowing approximately for these differences, it seems that in the whole country the average differential is a little less than 10 years ago (perhaps 2-3 percentage points). But in the South, and in the North, it is a little more than 10 years ago.

How is that possible? In 1950 just 39% of Negro male workers were in the North and West; but by 1960, 48% were in those regions where the differential is less extreme. So the northern differential counted more and the southern differential counted less than in 1950, in the national average.

Does this mean all the struggles were useless? No. Even the possibility of so many Negroes migrating from the South to higher earnings was a gain. And the really big mass struggles for economic equality began after 1959.

• • •

5/23/1964

Harlem and Maspeth: Vivid Contrast

In Harlem, 300,000 Negroes are packed into three square miles; four times the average population density of the whole city of New York. Statistics palely mirror the exploitation, rent-gouging, discrimination and segregation in every area of life. We compare one Harlem Census Tract, M222 (122-126 St., Lenox to 8th Ave.), with a tract in Maspeth, Queens, Q527, also within NYC. All but 67 of the 6,629 people in M222 are Negroes. None of the 2,714 people in Q527 is (all statistics from *1960 Census*).

Both are solid working class sections, far below borough or city averages for white families in all social and economic indicators. Many residents in each are underpaid and poor. But comparing Harlem to Maspeth is like comparing Hell to Purgatory.

The Negroes of M222 average 8.6 years of school completed, close to the 8.3 years of the Q527 whites; both are 2 years under the city-wide averages. Actually there are fewer illiterates and more college graduates, proportionately, in M222 than in Q527. So the Harlemites have as good a general background for work.

And more of them do work. Among Harlemites 18 and over, 70% are in the labor force, as compared with 63% of the Q527 residents. Among women it is 58% in M222, 38% in Q527. But what a difference in job experience: 8.2% of male Harlem Negroes, 2.0% of male Maspeth whites, are unemployed.

Now take three groups of jobs: 1) **better:** white collar and skilled; 2) **medium:** semi-skilled; 3) **worst:** unskilled and service

Here is the pattern:

	M222	Q527
Better	19%	47%
Medium	23	33
Worst	58	20
Total	100	100

Three-fifths of the Harlem Negroes, one-fifth of the Maspeth whites, are in the worst jobs. One-fifth of the Harlem Negroes, almost one-half of the Maspeth whites, have better jobs. One out of every three Harlem women workers is a domestic servant—none of the Maspeth women is.

For dirtier, harder jobs, Negroes get still meaner pay. The median income for all M222 families and single individuals is $2,583, under half the $5,943 for Q527, and much further under the city median for mainland whites. For families only the median is $3,519 in Harlem, $6,434 in Maspeth.

The official poverty line is $3,000 [$16,718], but actually it takes $5,000 [$27,864] to meet minimum big city standards today. Thus 71% of the M222 families fall below this realistic poverty line, compared to 27% of the Q527 families.

It takes $10,000 to be part of the "affluent society." Only 4% of the Harlem Negroes, and 17% of the Maspeth whites, make it. Another sign of the "American way of life" is the automobile. Only 12% of the M222 Negroes, but 54% of the Q527 white households, have them.

The housing picture is most outrageous. Only 9% of the M222 housing units are structurally sound and have all plumbing facilities. The rest are in various stages of slum deterioration. 18% are "dilapidated," i.e. falling to pieces. Only 32% have bathrooms. In Q527, some 82% are structurally sound with all plumbing, 94% have bathrooms, 3% are dilapidated. And that's in an old, run-down area. For these statistics to make Maspeth look good emphasizes how bad the Harlem ghetto must really be!

Slum rents in M222 average $28 per room compared with the $12 per room average in Q527. Harlem residents—more crowded, in worse quarters, having less income—pay $30 per capita rent as compared with $18 in Maspeth.

The school system handicaps workers trying to get ahead in the modern world, and Negroes most of all. For every 100 M222 kids in grammar school, only 5 are in college; for Q527, 6 are in college. For the whole city, Negro and white, the ratio is 17 per 100. Since one needs four years of college to qualify for a good job today, these figures mean that only one out of eight in Maspeth—and many fewer in Harlem—have a fair chance to make it.

The President allotted $1 million dollars for Harlem. There is talk of $110 million. Merely to bring Harlem incomes up to the inadequate Maspeth level would cost $500 million each year. To do the same for all Negroes, Indians, Puerto Ricans, Mexicans, in America would cost $50 billion yearly.

Yes, whatever is needed should be spent to provide the best in schools and housing for the Negro (and white) working people of America, to provide public jobs where there are no private jobs. But money can't do everything, or even the main thing. That is the complete ending of discrimination and segregation, which will impose a cost only on the exploiters of underpaid and overcharged Negroes. And will not require anything of the nation except the enforcement of its own Constitution.

• • •

2/12/1966

Gould, Arkansas: The Time Has Come to Ask 'Why?'

A SNCC (Student Non-violent Coordinating Committee) worker at a northern meeting described conditions in Gould, a rural village near the center of Arkansas.

The highway and railroad tracks run together through the village. On one side are the paved streets and private houses of the whites—nothing special, about on the level of a "lower middle class" northern suburb. On the other side is the Negro quarter, where 80% of the population lives. There the roads are all dirt—seas of mud in the rainy periods, otherwise dust bowls. "You just never get the dust out of your clothes, face, and eyes." Open sewers. Rickety shacks of scraps, tarpaper and weatherbeaten boards.

One white man, with his family, rules the village and surrounding township. He owns the dominant plantation, the cotton gin, and four stores in the village. He appoints and gives orders to the "mayor" and the "sheriff." Census statistics show the 1959 median income for Negroes in the county: families, $990; males with an income, $663; and females with an income, $374.

Of 1,097 Negro workers, 731 work in agriculture and 167 in personal service. Male workers in agriculture get $3 per day. But there is work for most of them only during the cotton chopping and picking seasons. The rest of the time there is just no money in the Negro community.

Contrast in the two schools is sharpest of all. The whites have a modern, roomy school with all new equipment. The Negroes have an ancient barn plus a few of its outbuildings, all with big holes in them. The interiors are cold in winter, classrooms leak when it rains. There are no lunches at the Negro school. Its only books are those discarded as obsolete and/or in poor condition by the white school.

The federal government provides school lunch funds to Gould, based on total pupils in the township, but it all goes to the white school that has a minority of the pupils.

The sheriff beats up or arrests Negroes at will and on any whim. When he needs money, which is often, he makes an arrest on any pretext. Being illiterate, he sometimes asks his victim to write up the arrest warrant.

A note of bitter irony: Gould is in Lincoln County!

Most SNCC workers have been arrested and beaten up. They have set up freedom centers in several Arkansas towns, conducted classes, and helped the Negro people to organize and fight for their basic rights. The struggle currently centers around the schools—for integration, equal facilities, for a proper share of government funds, and for an end to child labor.

The SNCC workers are young men and women from the North and the South, white and Negro students, some with exceptional academic records. They are the young heroes of America. They put out publications, largely written by the local people, in the towns where they work.

The following are extracts from a poem by M.S.D. of Forrest City, in *The Arkansas Voice*. No apologies are needed for the poor grammar. The median education of adult Negroes in Lincoln County is 5.9 years. Of 7,000 Negroes, exactly four are in college.

WHY?
Why is the black man in the back row?
Why can't we sit and go where we want to go?
Why do we have to go to war when we have nothing to fight for?
Why do the peoples that stand back get benefit for what we do?
Why do our children pay so many fees at school?
Why can't there be Negro on the school board?
Why do white man try to run everything?
Why do white man look upon the Negro woman in desire?
Why do they kill or take a Negro man away from his family just cause a white woman
said he looked at me?
Why can't all peoples see that God made man in his own image?
Why do the white man try to make it a lie?
Why can't a Negro be a man when they have all way did hard work?
Why is the white call man when they do woman work?
Why do Negro work right beside white man when the white are getting more money and doing less work?
God help the man that help himself!
Wake up, fight for your rights!
Don't believe that if you wait it will come.
I mean **Freedom**.
Believe in **Freedom**, and want to live in **Freedom**.

• • •

5/24/1969

What Discrimination Costs White Workers

Twenty years ago I calculated that American employers made $4 billion extra profits per year by paying black workers less than white workers for equivalent work. This was a cautious, minimum calculation. But it was the first time, to my knowledge, that anybody published such a figure, and called it by its right name— racism for profits. Since then, prices have doubled, and many more black workers are employed in industry. The added profit from discrimination now runs into tens of billions of dollars.

When officials made similar calculations, they turned them around. They estimated $15-$30 billion per year of business lost, because black people have less money to spend than whites.

Both ways of looking at the difference are correct. From the viewpoint of national economic well-being, and especially from the point of view of the deprived black people, the loss of purchasing power is most important. But from the point of view of employers, it is the extra profit that counts. This provides the motive for discrimination.

What about the profits lost by merchants on account of lower sales to black people? Only part of the lower sales represents profits lost, and much of that is made up by the higher prices charged black people. Moreover, most profits are not made by merchants and manufacturers of consumer goods. Much more are made by manufacturers of producers' goods and of armaments, by bankers, etc.

Another side of the story: What is the effect on white workers of job wage discrimination against black workers? That is a crucial question. Many white workers have been led to believe that they gain by getting more money than their black brothers. Many fear that any gains of black workers would be at their expense.

The fact is just the other way around. Discrimination against black workers costs white workers: they would gain greatly from the end of discrimination. Wide understanding and publicity of the proof of this would go far to freeing white workers from the influence of racist employers, union leaders, and real estate-banking interests. Here is one of many pieces of evidence:

Discrimination against black workers is much more severe in the South than in the North. More southern white people, comparatively, feel they are gaining from their "privileged position."

According to Commerce Department figures for 1967, in the South, black families' earnings averaged 54% of white families' earnings. But in the North, black families' earnings were 72% of white families' earnings. Black families in the South averaged $2,265 less than black families in the North. Black workers are kept out of good jobs much more completely in the South than in the North.

If the southern white workers were really privileged by discrimination, they would come out far ahead of northern white workers. On the contrary, white families in the South averaged $1,212 less than white families in the North. Applied to 12,300,000 southern white families, this means a loss of about $15,000,000,000 per year of income for all southern white people.

Whether they realize it or not, the southern white workers have to compete against the lower paid black workers. The employers, despite their prejudices, reserve the weapon of hiring black workers at lower wages if the white workers ask for "too much." That proved the main factor. It counted for more than the "privileges" granted the white workers.

But what about the North? If the reasoning about the South is correct, then northern white workers are also losing because of discrimination against black workers, although less severely than southern white workers. But we have no area with no discrimination against which to compare the situation of northern white workers, so a direct statistical calculation is impossible.

It is my opinion that white workers over the whole country are worse off by several billions of dollars per year because of discrimination against black workers. And I am convinced that, when discrimination is completely ended, white workers will enjoy corresponding money gains, as well as vast material, social and moral gains that cannot be expressed in dollars.

• • •

7/25/1970

On a Note of Challenge

This spring a small group of black musicians picketed the New York Philharmonic Symphony Orchestra at Lincoln Center in New York. Today they await a decision by the Human Rights Commission on the complaints of Earl Madison and Arthur Davis charging the New York Philharmonic with discrimination against them and black musicians generally.

There are just five black musicians among the 550 permanent members of the five major symphonies. The first was bassist Ortiz Walton, hired by Charles Munch of the Boston Symphony in 1957.

Davis, along with Walton and Fred King, who now plays with Pablo Casals' orchestra in Puerto Rico, sparked the struggle to integrate the symphonies in 1957-58. At that time they won adoption of non-discrimination by-laws by N.Y. Local 802 of the Musicians' Union, and insertion of non-discrimination clauses in its contracts. Unfortunately, it is little observed in practice.

Responding to this early struggle, in 1959 the Urban League investigated the employment of black musicians and reported that discrimination existed. The Philharmonic then hired Elayne Jones to substitute on tympani. This took the heat off. But they called her back only once, for publicity purposes, when the issue heated up again in the summer of 1969.

Miss Jones, tympanist with Leopold Stokowski's American Symphony, is one of the country's outstanding artists on the drums. She was a pupil of Sol Goodman, tympanist of the New York Philharmonic, who gave her his highest recommendations. But that wasn't good enough for the personnel directors of the top orchestras.

Earl Madison started on the cello at the age of 3. His father was music director of schools in Chicago. After several years as a leading cellist with the Pittsburgh Symphony, Madison called to apply for an advertised opening in the New York Philharmonic. He was told to come in. Because of his reputation, he did not have to take a preliminary audition. But the Philharmonic brass turned him down on the final audition. And on two later applications, he was not even admitted to the final audition.

Davis won a scholarship at the Eastman School of Music, but didn't go because the only housing they offered him was in a bedbug-ridden slum dwelling. He also ran into racist difficulties at Juilliard, and so he went to the Manhattan School of Music.

His teacher there was Anselmi Fortier, for 33 years principal bass of the Philharmonic. Fortier sent a letter to all of the principal symphony conductors recommending Davis—then 18. He got two answers: Fritz Reiner of the Chicago Symphony said he would like to see him when he was older and mellowed like old wine. William Steinberg of the Pittsburgh Symphony said there was a dual union in Pittsburgh, and he could only hire musicians from the white local!

Following the 1959 publicity, the Philharmonic promoted one black substitute to a regular post, violinist Sanford Allen. He is still the only one, and sits in the back of the second violin section, although people hired later have moved in front of him. How familiar to black workers in industry!

Following the latest round of struggle over cellist Madison and bassist Davis, which began over a year ago, two more major orchestras have hired their token black musicians. The Chicago Symphony still has none, the Philadelphia has two, and Cleveland—the current saying goes—has as many black symphony musicians as it has black mayors.

Mrs. Lucille Dixon, president of Concerned Musicians, which conducted the Philharmonic picket line, contends that the demand for black soloists such as Leontyne Price and Andre Watts does not contradict the charge of discrimination. "These soloists are big drawing cards," she told me, "and their success is used by the wealthy sponsors of orchestras and opera to give an impression of non-discrimination. But this is a cover-up of the gross discrimination in the whole wide world of music."

Mrs. Dixon, a bassist, was one of the two black musicians on the National Youth Administration orchestra disbanded in 1942 because of the war. All of the white musicians on that orchestra got jobs with major symphonies. Neither of the black musicians did. She was one of the founders, in 1965, of the Symphony of the New World, the first truly integrated symphony orchestra in the United States; 38 of its 90 musicians are black. Conducted by Benjamin Steinberg, the orchestra gives three concerts a year at Philharmonic Hall, and it also plays in black communities. Small ensembles play at black colleges.

But the Symphony of the New World is a part-time orchestra because it cannot support its musicians. While the nearly lily-white Philharmonic gets top contributions from the super-rich, the integrated New World can't get any big money.

The super-rich are directly responsible for the racist policies of the major orchestras. The Rockefellers virtually own the Philharmonic like everything else at

Lincoln Center. They and their placemen in the front offices of the symphonies have provided the rationale. It's the old saw, heard in every occupational line: "Not Qualified"!

Whitney Young Jr., of the Urban League, commented in the *Peekskill Star* (10/15/69):

"If there is anything Negroes have been known for in this country, it is musical skill. White Americans sing and dance to music written, played, or inspired by black writers and performers. . . . How strange it is, then, to hear the Philharmonic's music director explain that his 99 percent white orchestra's audition standards take into account the 'warmth that emanates' from a player, and his 'rhythmic understanding.' The stereotype is used against Blacks, and then discarded when it comes to evaluating black musicians for jobs that supposedly value the very same qualities."

At Human Rights Commission hearings several months ago, John Hammond, the commission's expert witness, testified that there were qualified black musicians when Philharmonic officials claimed there were none.

Mrs. Dixon emphasized that the black people continue to follow their musical aspirations despite economic difficulties:

"The poorest family will start their children on the piano. My family was poor, but they had a piano and I started at the age of 7. If you went through Harlem and saw all the music teachers, this would give you an idea of how many kids are studying. Violin comes next to piano. Instruments like the bass viol come when they get to school."

About 15-20% of the 33,000 musicians in Local 802 in New York are black. They are discriminated against both in the classical and in the jazz fields. They get hardly any of the club dates, weddings, and other lucrative one-night stands. In addition, since filing suit with the Human Rights Commission, Davis has been "blacklisted"—the term has an ironic ring here—from many of the jobs he formerly got.

The Commission is expected to rule soon on the Madison-Davis case. Regardless of its decision, the issue must be fought out. The union has been of no help. Many white musicians have been influenced by racist propaganda to fear that they will lose secure positions if black musicians get their fair share.

But, of course, it is apt to work the opposite way, just as the breakthrough of black ballplayers helped the game and the position of all professional baseball players. Since black musician Henry Lewis has been appointed conductor of the New Jersey Symphony, it has gotten excellent notices and enlarged attendance.

If the Human Rights Commission does not hand down a decision in time, or if their decision is unfavorable, look for more picket lines at Lincoln Center this fall. And the Concerned Musicians hope that more of their black brothers and sisters and white supporters will turn out than did last spring.

3/1/1975

Council of Economic Racists

The 1,959 page *1975 Economic Report of the President* is more lacking in useful content than usual, except for some handy statistical tables at the back. But it is full of vicious propaganda.

Previous reports have denied the existence of discrimination against Blacks, or have attempted to justify it by a technique that in essence blamed it on the Black people themselves. My forthcoming book, the *Economics of Racism*, exposes the *1974 Economic Report* on this score.

In the new report the presidential economists examine why Black unemployment is double that of whites. Using a favorite trick of academic apologists, they "factor out" unemployment differentials according to various alleged causes, but still find a significant residue due to racism, to discrimination. Like the damned spot on Lady Macbeth's hand, they couldn't get rid of all the differential by this method. In fact, they admit the "spot" is spreading, that discrimination is an increasing factor. So they evolved a new argument—racism is the result of equal employment legislation! So help me! Here is the tortuous reasoning:

"Even if discrimination in the labor market were widespread, it could result in lower wages instead of higher unemployment for Blacks relative to whites with the same skill and other relevant characteristics. If there were no equal opportunity legislation or other restrictions on wages, and if employers discriminated against Blacks, Blacks might work for less pay than similarly qualified whites; this would provide an incentive for employers to hire them, although the incentive might not always be sufficient . . . discrimination could take the form of reduced compensation, inferior jobs, or segregation, rather than higher unemployment."

The report continues: "Discrimination is more likely to lead to unemployment differentials when employers are prevented from paying different wages for equal work because of legal, union, or social pressure." Employers may prefer to discriminate in employment "because it is sometimes more difficult to prove overt discrimination in hiring than in overt pay differences. . . . Moreover, the prospect of equal pay may encourage Blacks to quit jobs with low pay and search longer for more promising positions" (pp. 112-114).

This racist mish-mash has no logical or factual justification. Equal opportunities legislation is supposed to apply to employment and wages equally. However, existing legislation has not resulted in equal wages for equal work, as the report implies. There remains a vast gap between whites and Blacks in pay for equal work. And discrimination in employment is plenty overt since the 1972 law, which places the burden on employers to achieve job equality for Blacks, hence making differentials in employment and in wages for like work illegal.

The intent of the report's "reasoning" is to convince employers and white workers that Blacks should be forced to work for substandard wages, regardless of the level of their work, "in their own interest," and that Blacks are to blame for trying to get decent-paying jobs with prospects of advancement.

In "factoring out" discrimination in employment, the presidential economists emphasize the fact that the proportion of youth among Blacks is higher than among whites. Since unemployment is higher among youth than among older people, this "accounts for" part of the differential. Of course, this whole line of argument collapses when one sees that unemployment among Black youth is more than double unemployment among white youth.

And President Ford's men combine their racist assault on Blacks with an attack on youth in general, and Black youth in particular. They consider why youth unemployment rates have increased faster than any others:

"Part of this relative rise in teenage unemployment may stem from the extension of minimum wage coverage and from the growth of social legislation that raises the cost to the firm of teenage compared to adult labor. The minimum wage may also have a more insidious long-run effect on the careers of youths, particularly teenagers out of school."

These youths, they say, need training on the job, and it is "unprofitable" to employers if they have to pay the minimum wage. So "The youths who suffer the most would be precisely those who need the most help—youths with little schooling and greater learning difficulties and those subject to discrimination." (p. 107)

Nixon tried to get legislation ensuring substandard wages for all youth, but was only partly successful. Evidently Ford is out to complete the job. The whole approach is to offer Blacks in general, youth in general, and Black youth most particularly a fake "choice" of how they want to be discriminated against—in jobs or in wages. The real objective is to increase discrimination in both areas and thereby to undermine the wage and job levels for all workers, young and old, Black and white.

The members of the Council of Economic Advisors—Alan Greenspan, chairman, William J. Fellner, and Gary L. Seevers—should be called to account for this brazen racism.

• • •

2/21/1980

A Racist Budget

President Carter's budget is racist; it is a preparation-for-war, guns-instead-of-butter budget.

Blacks and other minorities are hurt most by slashes in all kinds of social services and civilian government activities that accompany the extravagant arms buildup. They are hurt by the shift in jobs from civilian to military industries, where discrimination is stronger. They are hurt most by the accelerated inflation that comes with a militarized economy, as they have least ownership of property to offset inflation. They are hurt most by the rise in effective tax rates on workers, as they include the highest percentage of workers.

They will be the prime victims of Carter's proposed draft, and the first to be killed in the aggressions being hatched in the Pentagon.

The crudest racist feature of Carter's 1980 economic program is his announced intention to violate the Humphrey-Hawkins Act. This law, passed in 1978 after prolonged struggle by labor and the Black liberation movement, requires the government to reduce unemployment to 4% and inflation to 3% by 1983.

Cutting unemployment is the top priority economic requirement of Black people. In his 1980 economic report to Congress, Carter "postpones" the 4% unemployment goal to 1985 and the 3% inflation goal to 1988. Since, even if re-elected, he will be out of office in 1985, this amounts to a flat refusal to carry out the law's provisions.

Really, he never intended to. In last year's economic report, he went on at length about how difficult, nearly impossible, and in fact undesirable, it would be. Carter adheres to the big business line that 4% unemployment, as officially measured, is too low, and that anything below 6% is "dangerous." Indeed, he projects 6% for 1983, just about the recent level.

The most significant omission from the budget is any mention of affirmative action programs except in relation to government employment. The Carter administration has systematically sabotaged efforts to enact decisive programs that use quotas and other means to effect real equality in jobs and promotions, real access to housing everywhere, etc.

Carter calls for legislation to slash social services and real wages of government workers all along the line. The total "savings" from his legislative proposals mount from $5.6 billion in 1981 to $8.8 billion in 1983. The cuts in health programs, which especially affect Blacks, amount to $1.3 billion in 1981, rising to $3.2 billion in 1983. Additional billions are cut from income security programs.

Consider Aid for Dependent Children (AFDC), the most common form of public cash assistance. Carter proposes a real reduction of 8% between 1979 and 1981, despite his anticipation of markedly higher unemployment, and in the number of people requiring aid. Taking into account the increased number of families expected to be covered, the real reduction per family will be something like 25%.

And he calls for legislation to cut the school lunch program by 10% in 1981 alone, and considerably more per child. The expected expenditure of $3.6 billion comes out to about 70¢ per meal, and one can imagine what kind of swill will be dished out to the ghetto children with that kind of money—after allowing for administration and profiteering on food and service contracts, and after another year of raging inflation. And that's "generous" compared with the allowance for subsidized meals for the elderly, at 48¢ per meal!

Anticipating sharply rising unemployment, the budget calls for a 7% drop in real benefit payments—again, of course, with Blacks most victimized. Plus, there are also real cuts in education programs, especially in student assistance for higher education, critically important for Black youth.

I've emphasized the blow to Blacks. But it's obvious that the budget and economic program of Carter is a severe blow against the entire working class and especially harsh against women and all oppressed peoples.

• • •

1/12/1991

A Tale of Two Banks

There is an important lesson in class bias in the saga of failure of two banking concerns, one African-American, one white.

The Freedom National Bank was the third largest African-American owned bank. It sustained losses in real estate and other loans, and its capital fell below rigid federal standards. Without warning, federal authorities ordered the bank's closing. Depositors were forced to stand in long lines to collect their funds; and many African-American organizations, including the National Urban League, lost a large part of their deposits.

The Bank of New England is a white-owned bank, a merger of big money in Massachusetts and Connecticut. The bank has huge losses: one-sixth of its loans were "non-performing," and equity capital was virtually wiped out. But the U.S. Treasury kept it afloat by depositing $2,000,000,000 while bankers in New York and Tokyo maneuvered for terms to take over its deposits and sound loans, leaving taxpayers to pick up the tab on the bad loans.

What this contrast reveals is a combination of two dominant features of government/big business financial policy:

1. The traditional procedure of government assistance to the strong, allowing the weak to be eliminated in the financial arena, so that the surviving giants can plunder the public without effective competition.
2. Institutionalized racism, now being followed on a national scale with the cynical cruelty of the erstwhile system of slavery.

The Bank of New England "rescue" operation began in mid-1990 while Freedom National was forced to close in November. The shocking loss of funds by Black organizations was announced days later.

It works like this: protection of deposits is legally guaranteed by government insurance only up to $100,000 a deposit. But in practice, the Federal Deposit Insurance Corporation (FDIC) winks at larger deposits when it suits them. For example, they repaid "jumbo" deposits, running into millions of dollars, at high rates of interest by following instructions of the big money center banks to divide deposits into numerous accounts of $100,000 each, in the name of different family members, joint accounts, etc. That was the procedure followed for the bailout of the Silverado Bank, in which Neil Bush is heavily involved. And now that is the policy being followed in the case of the Bank of New England. In fact, 50% of the billions that taxpayers are being forced to underwrite is due to this policy of compensating "jumbo" depositors 100%.

But for the depositors in the African-American-owned Freedom National Bank, the $100,000 limit was strictly enforced. Thus the Fort Greene (Brooklyn) Senior Citizens Council got back only $100,000 of the $350,000 it had on deposit. Other losses were even larger, and totaled 15% of the deposits in the Harlem bank. The United Negro College Fund, National Urban League, a number of churches, and Rep. Charles Rangel's campaign fund were among the depositors ripped off.

Further: depositors in a white-owned bank, the National Bank of Washington—with deposits of just over a billion dollars, 10 times Freedom National's—were paid off in full. FDIC Chairman William Seidman called the contrast "a graphic illustration of unfairness."

How generous of him to admit his guilt, knowing that he won't have to make restitution. The rationale for this crude discrimination is that the large banks are "too big to fail" because their failure would "damage the public interest." The losses incurred by the small investors in the failed smaller savings and loan institutions do not count as "public interest" to the millionaires involved with the giant banks.

The closing of Freedom National Bank and discriminatory theft of its depositors' funds is not an isolated example. Black people are also subject to obvious discrimination at most white-owned banks. Hence, ownership of banking facilities is important in the attempt of Black business people to survive, for consumers to get credit and access to mortgages for home purchases.

The combined assets of the 37 Black-owned commercial banks at the end of 1990 came to $1.9 billion. This is less than the amount provided by the U.S. Treasury for the Bank of New England bailout and one-thousandth of the assets of white-owned banks. Trends show that Black banks continue to fall further behind their white-owned counterparts. Two Black-owned banks were forced into receivership over the past year, and 9 of the 33 Black savings and loan associations failed.

The financial front is but one of many arenas in which struggle for equality must be waged. It must be part of the struggle for equality in employment, housing, education and civil rights, which directly affect Black workers.

The perspective for Black ownership of a reasonable share of U.S. banks is not bright, which makes even more relevant the struggle for nationalization of the entire banking system, under workingclass control—white, Black and Hispanic—to be run under policies of affirmative action with respect to employment, credit availability and other financial services.

• • •

2/29/1992

The "Welfare Loafer" Lie

The number of people living in poverty in the United States is shocking. Even before the full fury of the economic crisis hit, 2 million more were added to the official rolls in 1990. But the actual number of poor people is roughly double the 34 million the government counts. Though far from all the needy receive any help, 53 million people receive some form of government assistance because they are poor.

Because of the key role that racism played in the development of U.S. capitalism, oppressed peoples bear a special burden as the crisis deepens. Ten million, or 32% of all African Americans, a modern record, and 6 million, some 28% of all Hispanics, another record, are designated as poor. Also, 17 million, 9% of all non-Hispanic whites, fall into that category. (Because almost all Hispanics are also counted as white in official documents, they have to be removed from the white totals to get a realistic figure. That has been done throughout this column.)

The slander brazened by KKK leader David Duke and his ilk, and implied by "more respectable" politicians, is that poor Blacks and Hispanics are "welfare loafers," draining government funds and causing deficits. Facts show this to be false.

In 1990, 56 million people received government "transfer payments"—social security, unemployment insurance, pensions, etc. Black recipients got 25% and Hispanic recipients 53% less, on average, than white recipients. Oppressed peoples were not overdrawing on the Treasury, they were short-changed by the Bush administration.

Unemployed Black workers received only a little more than half, and Hispanic workers little more than a third, on average, of what unemployed white workers get for unemployment insurance. Similarly, the amount of "means-related" assistance to poor whites was more than the amount received by needy African Americans and Hispanics.

Which doesn't mean that white workers got more government benefits than they deserved: they got far less—in social security, unemployment benefits and poverty relief.

Who does get too much government money? Well, government payments to corporations and other contractors, plus government interest payments, came to about $700 billion in 1990, exceeding the total of all transfer payments to individuals. Big business, the Pentagon and the banks are the ones fattening at the government trough.

Now, what about the claim that African Americans are loafers, that they don't work? Here are facts. In 1990, whites got 72% of their incomes from wages and salaries; Blacks, 80%, and Hispanics, 81%. Even in the fourth quarter of 1991, with the heavy unemployment, a substantial majority of the much maligned single Black mothers were working for their living, overcoming the handicaps of getting jobs and caring for children.

Of course, the fact that whites get a smaller share of their income from wages and salaries does not mean that white workers do not work hard. It reflects the fact that the capitalist class and their flunkies, collecting property income and exploiting workers, are overwhelmingly white, bringing down the average.

It is important to expose the racist frauds, but it is more important to end the blatant discrimination against poverty-stricken African American and Hispanic people. Affirmative action is needed to make well paying jobs accessible to them, to double and triple the assistance they receive to alleviate their poverty, for their old age pensions, their unemployment compensation.

But such recompense must be at the expense of corporations, the Pentagon and the banks, not, as the David Dukes would have it, at the expense of white workers. That is the capitalist's game. To keep us fighting each other instead of them.

• • •

1/29/1994

Racism = Profit for Banks

An Associated Press release reveals that President Clinton will call for a $2 billion slash in the already shamefully inadequate funds for public housing in his forthcoming budget. And public housing, with all its shortcomings, has provided homes for some African American and Latino people, as well as for low-income white families and seniors of all races—albeit a woefully small number.

The cut of $2 billion will be used to increase the giveaways to corporations for "research in new technologies," and to "put an additional 100,000 police on the streets," according to *Business Week*.

The capitalist class makes huge profits from racism. I have calculated the additional profits of more than $100 billion a year just from the wage differential against Blacks, Latinos, etc. In addition there are the vast profits from segregated housing, the barrios and ghettos created by the giant banks and their satellite financial institutions.

A study by the Federal Reserve Board revealed the extreme discrimination against African Americans in granting home mortgage loans by virtually every significant bank in the country. This practice hikes profits for landlords of Black tenants, who have to crowd into the insufficient supply available—as well as from the high rents charged white tenants for the "privilege" of living in nearly all-white communities.

Even more outrageous is the plunder extorted through usurious interest rates charged African Americans who are granted mortgages.

Recently Fleet Financial, a $47 billion "super regional" banking and mortgage network, was sued by African American homeowners in Atlanta for charging interest rates ". . . that sometimes exceeded 30%." In settling the suit, Fleet agreed—in addition to cash payments to the homeowners—not to charge more than 18% on future mortgages and to hold prepaid finance charges to 5%. That meant Fleet would still charge double the prevailing interest rate, 8% at the time, and triple the prevailing advance charges of 1.5%.

Similar ripoffs are involved in usurious lending to minority small business owners. The giant New York City banks have been notorious for collecting deposits from ghetto residents, and then refusing loans to the area merchants, even though both the Small Business Administration and a special New York City fund guarantee these loans against significant defaults.

In response to public outrage, the banks are going through the motions of effecting a ghetto small business loan program. In the fall of 1993, Chase Manhattan Bank held "Small Business Days" at five Bronx branches. Although many applicants showed up, the bank wasn't about to put much of its $100 billion in assets to work there. A Chase official explained: ". . . you may go through 60 applications to make one loan," adding that the applications involved extraordinary paperwork.

Pedro Baz, a small grocery owner, applied for a mere $5,000 loan to pay suppliers following a robbery where he lost a week's cash. Months later, Chase had not approved the loan. Meanwhile Paz operates with a $100,000 loan, at 24.5% annual interest—paid in weekly installments to the Sea Crest Linen Supply Corporation. Sea Crest is one of several "specialists" in ghetto financing, the only outfits that Black and Latino borrowers have access to.

Although Sea Crest, and others like it, probably borrow their capital from major banks—and possibly at a premium over normal lending rates—their interest payments would still be a fraction of what they charge their victims.

At least two basic steps are needed to end financial superexploitation of African Americans and Latinos and other nationally oppressed peoples:

- Effect real housing integration through a massive public housing program of 2 million units a year. These should be built throughout metropolitan areas, especially near areas of sizable job opportunities. Integrated occupancy, with low rents charged African American, Latino, Native American families, as well as poor white workingclass families, should be guaranteed; and the units should be located to preclude formation of another ghetto.
- Nationalize the banking industry, under workers' supervision of management, in order to strengthen and enforce rules, with criminal penalties against usury.

• • •

7/26/1997

How Much Are Latino Workers Exploited?

Because of the overall strength of the economy, the demand for labor, especially for service jobs, is strong. And for these lowest-wage jobs, employers prefer Latino workers, many of whom are immigrants.

Latino workers accounted for 45% of the rise in employment between June 1996 and June 1997, and the proportion of Latinos with jobs rose from 60.3 to

63.2%. But even so, the average wages of Latino workers are markedly lower than those of any other oppressed national minority, and the extent of discrimination against them has been rising.

A recent article in *The New York Times* dealing with the crisis facing New Britain, Conn., points out that Puerto Ricans make up 25% of the city's population—a city once the home of Stanley Tool Works and other industrial establishments. Today fewer than 19,000 employees are still on the Stanley payroll, with fewer than 2,000 in Connecticut. And now Stanley's chief executive, John R. Trani, has announced another 4,700 cuts. (The price of Stanley stock rose 70% since Trani, who sharpened his job-cutting skills at General Electric, took over.)

As has long been the case with African Americans, Latino workers are frequently blamed for a company's financial problems. According to *The Times*, a report prepared for New Britain "business leaders" blamed the "bad work habits" and "poor family values" of its Puerto Rican community for the city's plight.

The Times said that employers were encouraged to "tell a researcher their most intimate, racist thoughts." The researcher, William W. Hansen, found their remarks so reprehensible that he eventually revealed the identity—and the slanders—of those who made them.

Enraged by the revelations, the Puerto Rican community held demonstrations and formed the Puerto Rican Organization for Unity and Dignity (PROUD). They made a series of demands, including membership on all public finance boards and commissions and a voice in economic planning. Preparations are underway to run candidates for public office.

City Councilman Edgardo Saavedra said the report woke up "a sleeping giant. There is an awareness now of the size, potential and power of the Hispanic community."

• • •

11/7/1998

'That's Where My Dad Lives'

A recent feature article in the *Wall Street Journal* began by saying, "America has the largest system of incarceration in the world, with 1.7 million people behind bars. The number of people in state and federal prisons has quadrupled over the past quarter century. States' spending on prison systems has more than doubled over the last 10 years."

From time to time, the *Journal*—despite its editorial policy devoted to the goals and aspirations of the business community and the capitalist system—publishes articles of outstanding social significance. Such was its harrowing report on Oct. 27 describing the effects a prison complex has on the nearby African American community of Baltimore.

In it, the author tells of 10-year-old Sabrina Branch who "points to a modern brick building encircled by barbed wire. 'That's where my Uncle Tony was.' She cranes her neck and points across the street to a soot-gray building . . . the city jail. 'That's where my dad lives.'"

Although Sabrina lives only 10 minutes away from Johns Hopkins University, it is the nearby complex of four prisons and jails that looms largest in her life.

Sabrina and her siblings now live with their 48-year-old grandmother who, the article says, "wakes up at 5 a.m. to get the children off to school, then leaves for her job as a home health aide for elderly patients." She arranges her schedule so she can be home by 4 p.m. to help the kids with their homework and make sure they do their chores.

"Despite her strong will, the burden is so great that she sometimes breaks down in tears. 'I feel overwhelmed. I've struggled so hard to keep this family intact. But when the sadness comes in Sabrina's face, I can't change that.'"

Jail and prison conditions throughout the country continue to worsen. In the last two years, there was an increase of 35,000 in the number of U.S. prison beds, but an increase of 70,000 inmates.

The article explains why—and inadvertently, exposes the racist nature of the justice system: "Even more important [than highly publicized crimes] has been the crackdown on drugs. Today, about one-fourth of state and federal prisoners are serving time for drug crimes."

Use of narcotics is commonly accepted among rich whites as much as among poor African Americans. But the laws, police and court practices and system insure that Blacks are sentenced to prison many more times and given stiffer sentences than whites. For example, federal guidelines decree a five-year term for possession of 500 grams of powdered cocaine, the form sold mostly to whites; but the same sentence for possession of only 5 grams of crack, the form more often supplied to Blacks.

That's in part why 28.5% of Black males go to prison during their lifetime, and 16% of Hispanic males. But only 4.4% of white males—and even that is a very high figure. But for Black communities:

"The stigma against going into the criminal justice system is almost gone. In New York City's Harlem neighborhood, according to social worker Geoffrey Candada: 'It's like going to war. Everyone gets called. You go, you do your time. It's no big thing.'"

But it is a big thing. A recent AP release reports that 13% of Black males in the United States are, for their lifetime, deprived of their right to vote because they have a prison record. But wealthy white cocaine users can indulge in their illegal practices with impunity—and immunity. And vote!

1/16/1999

Racism in Disenfranchisement of Prisoners

The unreconstructed southern slaveowners and their descendants have never given up their efforts to prevent African Americans from exercising their citizenship rights, especially their right to vote. For a century the bigots' main weapon was outright terror, the "lynch law." Then the civil rights struggles of the 1950s and 1960s forced enactment of federal legislation granting the right to vote, among other concessions. So the southern racists were forced to shift tactics.

A recent study by a civil rights organization, the Sentencing Project, describes one important tactic: criminalizing African Americans—and other minorities.

Legislation by all but four states has disenfranchised all prisoners, and in most states even parolees can't vote. And since Blacks are the majority of those in jail, this deprivation of a basic civil right is directed mainly against them. The percentage of Black males barred from voting in Florida is 31.2%; in Mississippi, 28.6%; in Virginia, 25.0%. In ten of the southern states, those convicted of a crime can never vote again—even after release from prison and no longer on parole.

In New York State, 85% of those in jail are minorities. In 1996, New York State prisoners brought a lawsuit demanding the right to vote. But they dropped their suit after then attorney general Dennis Vacco went to federal court to block prisoner voting. So now it is up to Spitzer, who just defeated Vacco, to support the suit of New York prisoners. Excessive criminalization of African Americans throughout our country is a racist crime. All prisoners and probationers should retain their voting rights, a move that would help overcome pervading biases in the U.S. electoral system.

Of course southern racists also use other methods to minimize Black voting effectiveness: the gerrymandering of districts; intimidation of voters; the campaign against a full census count of the population through the use of sampling.

The far-right southern politicians control the Republicans in the present Congress. They are a neo-fascist group running wild over Washington, over the issue of impeachment. They are leading supporters of militarism—the South has the largest share of military contracts, major military bases, pro-confederate generals and admirals, prominent promoters of a super-imperialist U.S. foreign policy, including armed invasions and bombings.

Restoration of full voting rights to all of the Black population would lead to the electoral defeat of many, if not most, of the influential right-wing elements in American politics.

A comparable situation, involving Hispanic peoples more than African Americans, is the imposition of more stringent barriers against citizenship by the Immigration and Naturalization Service, including a doubling of exorbitant fees and delays of two years or more in processing citizenship applications.

Education

5/27/1962

Education vs. Thought Control

Seven men prepared a report telling how economics should be taught in high schools. Leading businessmen complained that it "emphasizes possible inadequacies of the private economy," that it doesn't stress "personal freedom," and is against "people who work hard" and get wealthy. The *Wall Street Journal* attacked it editorially several times as biased in favor of socialism. The Committee for Economic Development (CED) urged that it be kept out of the hands of students.

Who are these "Communists" trying to smuggle "subversion" into the schools? To my best knowledge, none of them ever wrote for the *Worker*; and all could pass FBI "loyalty" tests. Indeed, they are completely respectable professors. Five are top officials of the American Economic Association (AEA), including one prominent economic advisor to President Kennedy.

Here are the facts behind the hullabaloo.

The CED has interlocking membership with the National Association of Manufacturers (NAM) among corporate giants, but is somewhat less hidebound. It became concerned that most high school students are taught no economics. The 5% who get some usually are given purely descriptive material by teachers without specialized economics background. The businessmen want students to get a "minimum understanding"—that is, an elementary indoctrination in capitalist economic thinking, which might insulate them against radical doctrines.

So the CED appointed a task force to recommend how economics should be taught in the schools. But to show objectivity it arranged for the AEA to name the members, and stipulated that they would have complete freedom in preparing their report.

Certainly the AEA could be relied upon to appoint "sound men," and it did. But the CED failed to reckon with some points. The better academic men were brought up in the Roosevelt era, when the liberal tradition of examining both sides of an argument was in vogue. They are defenders of capitalism but have not become shoe-shine boys for the millionaire trustees.

The task force report was completed in September 1961. Most of it is a simplified syllabus, and much of its contents is the usual liberal apologia for capitalism—which I will delight in arguing against on another occasion. But included is a rather honest discussion of income inequality and poverty, including: "It is im-

portant to remember that many people receive incomes from the productive services of accumulated (and also inherited) wealth which they own, not from human services which they themselves provide." This stuck in the throat of A.L. Williams, the president of IBM and a CED official. He would prefer that the students forget that!

Still "worse," in teaching about socialism the professors point out positive features as well as negative distortions. They find that Communist societies have achieved more economic stability than capitalist, and "have worked more effectively than many observers originally thought possible." They would let the students know that "underdeveloped countries view communism and capitalism as 'active alternatives.'"

A number of countries have gone in for varying decrees of socialism, but "this does not mean that these countries are any the less democratic or any less friendly toward the United States . . . there needs to be recognition that different peoples . . . choose to organize the economies in different ways."

This, of course, is nothing less than teaching the concept of peaceful coexistence. But that is anathema to the State Department and the Pentagon as well as a cause of "concern" to T.O. Yntema of Ford Motors. It really upset the *Wall Street Journal.*

Finally, the professors urge that one-sided views not be rammed down the students' throats. Students should do their own research and express their conclusions without fear or reprisal. Controversial issues should be examined. School authorities should encourage classroom debate:

"It is not expected that such searching analysis will be universally welcomed. But to deprive students of the opportunity to think through controversial issues for themselves is to deprive them of fundamental training for good citizenship and to deny the fundamental tenets of a free and democratic society. To insist upon and defend this right of the teacher and of the students is the duty of every citizen, as well as of teachers, administrators, and school boards, even when particular groups criticize the teacher involved. Ours is a strong society which need not fear open discussion of its economic institutions and processes."

Only the last sentence is inaccurate. Ours is a morally weak, corrupt society, whose rulers fear open discussion like the plague. After six months of stalling, the CED embarrassedly gave its approval to this report, with the stipulation that it be given only to teachers, not to students. The *Wall Street Journal* recommended instead that students and teachers be given a thing specially prepared by the National Education Association that recommends fulsome chatter about "freedom" [to profiteer . . . VP] in place of serious economic study.

A toast to the task force for sticking to its guns and refusing to revise the report under pressure. Its last mentioned proposals are eminently correct. But they can only be realized if students, teachers and parents unite to fight for them, against John Birchers, American Legionnaires, compliant school boards, and the tycoons behind the efforts to stifle all freedom of thought and discussion in the U.S.

9/8/1963

Why Not High School Stipends?

In Brooklyn, in neighborhoods where family incomes average below $4,000 [$22,436], only 79 youths attend high school for every 100 aged 14-17. But in neighborhoods with incomes over $9,000 [$50,482], for every 100 in that range, 108 attend high school (evidently some older or younger went also). A rich youth has 38% more chance of going than a poor youth. In Chicago the ratio is 80 of 100 for the poor, 100 of 100 for the rich.

Labor Department reports, based on 1960 Census figures, show a similar situation in Detroit, Houston, and Birmingham.

Why? Lower-income children have less opportunity to learn outside school. Curricula are pitched to advantaged kids with higher-income backgrounds, and schools in wealthier areas are better. Segregation means less training for Negro children, usually among the poor. Equally important, many of the poor must quit when they reach working age to help their families financially.

In all these cities, a big majority of lower-income youth are Negro or Spanish speaking, while hardly any in the top bracket are. So there is anti-labor, anti-Negro, and anti-Puerto Rican discrimination in high school education. The report shows that at the same income levels, more Negroes than whites attend high schools. This answers those who claim Negroes can't learn or do not want to. It reflects the special struggle the Negro people are making for education today.

Los Angeles differs strikingly from the other cities. At all income levels, there are about 100 high school youths for every 100 aged 14-17. Perhaps there are special reasons for this seemingly outstanding performance: I hope California readers will explain it to me.

Officials stress the need for educated manpower in the age of cybernetics. A youth without a college degree can get few good jobs, and one without a high school diploma is usually doomed to prolonged unemployment, with occasional jobs at the lowest pay.

If 80 out of 100 lower-income youth are in high school, it means that only 60 out of 100 finish high school. What can be done to enable the other 40 to have a chance, and to lighten the burden on the parents of the 60 who do make it?

Obviously it will help considerably to desegregate the schools, provide more and better teachers, and orient teaching more to the needs and backgrounds of workingclass youth. But it is also important to ease the economic problem.

I suggest that every city government should provide a scholarship of $200 [$1,122] per year for each high school student whose family's income is below $1,250 [$7,011] per capita, so long as he or she maintains reasonably good marks— say an average of 75 or better.

This would provide a real incentive to the student to study, and to parents to be supportive and to cooperate with the teachers. It would give a chance to hundreds of thousands of outstanding young people whose talents are now doomed to lifetime wastage because economic stringency does not even permit them to finish high school.

I can just hear the reactionaries try to howl this proposal down. They will insist it will pamper the poor, bankrupt the city, and Communize the country.

N.Y. City people pay taxes of $600 per year to the state and the city for every public school student enrolled at all levels. If a youth receives $800 in four years through this scholarship, it will be less than what a family pays, directly and indirectly, in taxes to support education during these years, and a fraction of what a family pays during an entire childhood.

Again in N.Y. City, the scholarship might go to 100,000 high school students, including tens of thousands who otherwise wouldn't be able to attend. The cost would be $20 million yearly. That is less than 3% of the education budget, and less than half the average annual increase in that budget.

Suppose the federal government finances it nationally—which is the best way to do it. That would benefit 2.5 million youth, and cost $500 million per year, which is 0.5% of the budget, and one-tenth of what the government now spends on missiles.

• • •

9/21/1963

Support New York Teachers

The New York teachers' winning of higher salaries, smaller classes and other concessions was a result of their unity and determination. Why did thousands of teachers vote enthusiastically to strike despite threats against their jobs, pension rights and teaching licenses?

Workers struggling along on $60-$70 weekly may find it difficult to sympathize with teachers starting at $5,300 and averaging $8,000 yearly. But the greater deprivation of the former doesn't change the fact that New York teachers are underpaid—in relation to living costs, to other professional salaries, and to their past position.

The latest Heller budget, updated by living cost indexes, comes to nearly $7,000 for a wage earner. Professional workers' budgets run several thousand higher. Right now 12,000 of the city's 36,000 regular teachers make less than the Heller budget, not to speak of up to 15,000 substitutes. At the top of the 14-step salary ladder are 14,000 veteran teachers making between $9,170 and $10,445 per year. That is more like a professional salary nowadays, but still far less than veteran professionals get in most other private or government offices.

Labor Department statistics show that New York City teachers' salaries increased 110-120% between 1941 and 1961, equaling the 110% consumer price index rise. But taxes went up much faster; and the official index understates living cost increases in other ways. Thus New York City teachers receive lower real salaries than before World War II. In Chicago and Los Angeles, and in all cities as a group outside of New York, the raises ranged between 180% and 200%. No city of over 250,000 population has so small a rise as New York. In the same 20 years, salaries of federal employees went up 186%; railway office workers, 165%; and factory production workers, 252%.

Traditionally, New York schools led the country in salary levels—appropriately, considering the exacting educational standards, crowding and other difficulties, and high living costs. But by 1961 New York salaries were in the range of other large cities, and lower than in many suburbs. In 29 of 45 Westchester districts, starting salaries for teachers with master degrees run $100 to $400 more than in New York City.

Meanwhile, the difficulties of teaching in New York have escalated. Educational and salary standards have deteriorated together. No wonder teachers leave the city school system in droves. In nine years the number of resignations went up threefold. By September 1962, out of 43,000 teaching positions, there were 7,000 vacancies and close to 6,000 leaves of absence. Only 30,000 jobs were actually filled by licensed teachers, 70% of the authorized number and half the 60,000 really needed to teach a million pupils properly.

These 30,000 deserve credit for sticking with the New York City system and fighting for improved teaching conditions. Their victory is a victory for the working people of New York, especially Negro and Puerto Rican children getting an inferior and often merely token education. But the gains are not enough to bring about a decisive improvement.

Sooner or later the city will have to raise salaries very substantially and make other radical improvements to prevent the complete collapse of public education. If it continues to grant improvements too little and too late, the decay of a once great school system may be aggravated.

But if all working people support the teachers, it will be easier to connect their battle for decent salaries and conditions with the people's struggle for desegregation, for more schools and teachers, smaller classes, the end of part time and special schedule schools, real teaching for all pupils instead of a small "advanced" elite.

The principal thrust of the city parents today, mainly but not exclusively the embattled Negro parents, is the fight for school integration. Indeed, this is the key that can unlock the door to a generally better school system. By and large, it must be said, the teachers have given little more than token support to this struggle.

The situation cries out for full-fledged cooperation among teachers, unions and civil rights organizations, among teachers and parents and pupils, for a joint fight for better conditions for teachers, a bigger and better school system, and a complete and immediate end of de facto segregation. Such a uniting of forces could lead to major victories in many American cities.

2/24/1970

The Education of a Bronx Teacher

A Review of:

The Year Without An Autumn:
Portrait of a School in Crisis
By Robert Rossner

Not the least interesting feature of "The Year Without an Autumn" is the author's development. Robert Rossner matured during the New York school struggles of 1968, which culminated in the racist teachers' strike/lockout called by Albert Shanker.

"I'd been teaching for eleven years. I'd been completely apolitical during most of my life. Since my college days, I had been observing the scoundrels of the left and right. And three years earlier, I'd moved my family off to the country."

He stood on the sidelines when 30 teachers and hundreds of students at Bronx High School of Science demonstrated April 26 to protest the Vietnam War and the assassination of Dr. King. Cynical about politics, he was not above red-baiting. He tended to be impressed with the Shanker arguments of "academic freedom" and "teacher's tenure" used to defend racist teachers at Ocean Hill-Brownsville.

But cumulative experience and events changed him.

"And yet, I'd taught in ghetto schools. I'd seen kids graduate from high schools without being able to answer a classified ad in *The Times*."

He saw teachers show utter contempt for the ghetto youngsters; participated with Westchester neighbors, white and black, in a parade to honor the murdered Dr. King; was influenced by the propaganda of progressive teachers and militant students—the erstwhile "scoundrels of the left"; and he was finally moved to action by observing the vicious attacks on demonstrating students by cops and right-wing thugs, tacitly supported by school authorities.

By September, when Shanker declared a strike/lockout against the students of New York City and against community control by ghetto people, Rossner was one of the first of the growing group of Bronx Science teachers who carried out a persistent, partially successful struggle, together with white and black students, to open the school.

There is apt appreciation of the issues:

"Well, it's going to be a funny strike. From Taffel's (the principal's) actions, it's obvious that, for the first time in history, Labor and Management will walk the picket line together. . . . Against whom, then, is this strike directed?"

Rossner exposes the collaboration of cops, principals, supervisors, the city bureaucracy and political machines, the Board of Education—with Shanker against the students and black people. He shows how the Mayor's formal support for keeping schools open meant little in practice, because of his failure to fight for a position and to exercise firm authority over cops and other city personnel, who actually took their orders from elsewhere—just where, Rossner obviously didn't know.

He shows contempt for the deceitful school authorities, the slimy social-democratic type principal ("My mother was a union organizer"), and for the renegade ex-leftist teacher who has become a virtual Goldwaterite. He creates sympathy for the militant student leaders, especially the impressive black leaders who developed during the struggle.

Two black student leaders from Bronx Science and nearby DeWitt Clinton, Harold Young and Guy Oliver, by brilliantly combining legal research and organizational skill, played the key role in getting the school open. Oliver's wisdom in winning the black Clinton students over to support the predominantly white Bronx Science students who fought to keep the school open was particularly marked.

After it was all over: "Change comes, no matter how furiously it is resisted. The future, after all, is Dana Driskell and Reggie Lucas [student leaders] and the kids who attended that meeting."

Change, yes, but at a price. An exorbitant price: On Sunday evening, May 25, Guy Oliver was murdered shortly after leaving a Black Panther meeting. "He would have been seventeen years old on June 27."

Rossner, a Jew himself, deals well with the phony charge of anti-Semitism used by the racist union leaders. He brings out the important and serious fact that the continued support of Shanker by the majority of white middle class parents, including Jewish parents, was decisive in preventing the outright defeat of the lockout. He describes the inner struggles of individual teachers, between their traditional loyalty to the union and their desire to fight for justice in this particular struggle.

Lou Heitner was an old-time progressive, one of the group who supported the students. But at first he couldn't cross a picket line, no matter how anti-labor its essence. Finally, at one meeting, Rossner asked him: 'Lou, you know you're going to end up coming in with us. When is it going to be?' He looked at me for a moment. Then he blurted out, 'Wednesday.' And as he did so, he broke into a tremendous grin, and ten years dropped off his face."

The book's worst weakness concerns red-baiting and the role of Communists. Rossner, towards the end, does show the use of red-baiting by racists, and notes its sharp edge directed against none other than the sympathetically drawn Heitner.

He realizes that many of the teachers who stuck with the students and fought racism were old-timers from the Teachers Union, but he gives a completely distorted stereotype of that organization as a group "under Communist Party domination" that "lost the bulk of its membership at the time of the Nazi-Soviet Pact in 1939" but which "hung on . . . a small and impotent force . . . until 1962."

But one cannot understand the real story of 1968 without knowing the history of the Teachers Union. In the 1930s and 1940s this was the teachers' union that fought for decades for union recognition, for the needs of the students, especially the poor and minority pupils.

It was Teachers Union members, like Alice Citron, who were loved by the ghetto kids. After World War II, the Teachers Union led the fight for adequate school budgets, smaller classes, special aid to poor pupils, and for real school integration.

The decisive weakening of the Teachers Union was not the result of Soviet diplomacy in 1939. It was the mass purge of Communist and Communist-sympathizer teachers carried out in the first wave of McCarthyism that swept this country after World War II. If those hundreds of teachers had remained in the system throughout the past two decades, it would have been impossible to organize a racist teachers' strike/lockout in New York City.

As the union began to recover from that blow, the trade union consciousness of teachers grew. It was then that the ruling political group in the city selected Shanker and the group of red-baiting social democrats around him to be their chosen instrument in "collective bargaining"—in order to avoid successful militant unionism. They knew that Shanker could be relied on to limit himself to "bread and butter" trade unionism; that he would collaborate with the key political objectives of the city's power structure, and fight against the Teachers Union emphasis on the needs of the schools and the children.

Rossner has left Bronx Science and now teaches in Northern Westchester. Has he left the struggle and returned to his earlier indifferent cynicism? I hope not. For at the place he teaches now, the issue is every bit as acute as in New York. There have been militant struggles conducted by the black students, and the ruling clique of the town follows ruthless racist policies.

Regardless of Rossner's personal future, "The Year Without an Autumn" is a worthwhile contribution.

" Rush that top-secret government job...The
Navy is scheduled to scrap it next week! "

Bureaucracy, Corruption, Decadence

10/8/1971

4,000 for 1

Dairy capitalists reaped $4,000 for every $1 they contributed to Nixon's 1972 campaign fund. The story is told by Jerry Lanauer, *Wall Street Journal* reporter, who described how Nixon personally made a deal with the dairymen "that's still paying off both for the nation's dairy farmers and for President Nixon's political financiers." (9/27)

The Department of Agriculture regularly supports prices of dairy products. This amounts, in effect, to a government enforced dairy cartel system. The government guarantees to buy all milk not privately sold at the support prices. It is worse than a simple subsidy because it raises prices all along the line, with the ultimate consumer paying the entire bill twice: once in higher prices, and once in higher taxes to cover losses on the Government purchases.

Early in March this year, Agriculture Secretary Hardin decided that the milk support price for 1971 should be at the same level as that for 1970. This action was approved by the Council of Economic Advisers and by budget officials.

But all this bureaucratic caution was smashed to smithereens when a dozen leading dairymen went to see Nixon. Immediately dairy capitalist organizations began to make contributions to Nixon's 1972 campaign funds. Two weeks later Hardin, obviously on Nixon's orders, reversed himself and raised the milk support price. Thereupon the farm organizations formed scores of dummy "charitable organizations" in order to secretly contribute large sums to Nixon. So far they have contributed $255,000, and Lanauer speculates that the total may reach a million dollars.

And now for the payoff. Hardin increased the support price from $4.66 per 100 pounds to $4.93 per 100 pounds of milk. That's an increase of 5.79%. Such increases normally are passed on to the consumers, with proportionate markup at all distributive levels.

Examples this writer has noticed: since March the chain store price of evaporated milk went up from 19 to 20 cents a can; standard brands of cottage cheese now sell from 42-45 cents a pound, up 6-8 cents.

How much does this 5.79% increase cost consumers, most of them workers? Last year the American people spent $18,475,000,000 on dairy products, including those eaten in restaurants. A 5.79% increase amounts to $1,070,000,000—that is, more than a billion dollars.

The people are paying that billion extra, and the dairymen, the dairy product processors and the retail chains are pocketing it. The payoff by the people amounts to 4,000 times the $255,000 Nixon has gotten from the dairymen. Dairy farmers, according to government figures, now get 48% of the consumers' dairy product dollar. So, their share of the take is $514,000,000 or "only" 2,000 times as much as their "sure bet."

The dairy contribution is only a tiny fraction of the scores of millions Nixon will collect from big business for 1972. And to each group—bankers and oil barons, multinational auto tycoons and armament profiteers—Nixon will pay off just as generously, whenever he can get away with it. And each time the American working people are forced to pick up the tab. The total cost to the electorate is simply staggering.

Meanwhile most Democratic hopefuls are making similar deals for their probably smaller campaign funds, since all they can pay now is with promissory notes. However, these notes will be presented for payment, again at the people's expense, if the Democrats win.

That's the dismal economics of American two-party politics today.

It's a basic bread and butter reason for forming a new kind of political coalition—based on workers, Black people, etc.—really independent of big business.

● ● ●

9/16/1972

The Whites of Georgia Law

The *Wall Street Journal* has a feature story about Lamar B. Hill, a small-town banker from Cartersville, Georgia, who is under indictment for allegedly embezzling $4.7 million from the First National Bank of Cartersville.

According to the article, the case against him is solid. Townspeople "universally assume that Mr. Hill is in fact guilty," but "they don't much hold it against him."

Hill comes from a wealthy Georgia family, was a former bank examiner who became president of this local bank in 1965. It seems that he was a high rolling gambler, and, it has been charged, he freely dipped into the bank's till to pay for his continuous losses. However, "good friends" have taken care of Hill. He is free on bond, continues to live in a hilltop mansion. His friends have supplied him with a brand new Lincoln Continental to replace the one the government impounded. He has a job at a friend's credit company. He transferred all his personal property to his wife and friends, so he still has the use of it.

Insurance covers most of the bank's losses. And the holding company that controls the bank has used the occasion to increase its grip by buying up shares from scared owners.

Georgia, says the article—that is, the Establishment white upper- and upper middle-class Georgians—still thinks Hill is a pretty good guy. And his future isn't so bleak: in 19 convictions for embezzlement in northern Georgia since 1968, sentences have totaled 21 months in jail and 45 years of probation. The maximum penalty for embezzlement is 5 years, but that isn't regarded as much of a deterrent. That is why, says the *Wall Street Journal*, "it is becoming an increasingly popular crime," with 5,500 cases involving $113.5 million investigated last year.

This is Georgia, mind you, where there are still prison labor gangs working on the road, where police brutality, especially against Black working people, is not far removed from lynch justice.

The moral once again, of course, is that the whole system of law, of crime prevention and punishment, is a class weapon in the hands of the rich and the capitalists, used against those they exploit, used as a weapon of racist repression. It is meant to protect their own kind, no matter how much they violate the letter of the law, so long as they remain within the bounds of the system, politically and socially.

• • •

7/12/1975

State Monopoly Corruption

Exposés of the bribery, thievery and general corruption of U.S. multimillionaires and multinational corporations have become a daily occurrence. And the scale of corruption exposed keeps expanding. The Pentagon has revealed, in a yet unpublished Senate subcommittee report, that U.S. arms manufacturers paid "sales agents" $200 million over a 2½-year period in connection with export orders.

Of course this is bribe money. And there is nothing new in principle. More than 60 years ago the Armenian, Gulbenkian, acted as go-between to get the oil concession from the Turkish Empire in what is now Iraq. He was paid off with 5% of all Iraqi oil production through all the wars and changes of concession owners until, at his death, he was one of the richest men in Europe.

Today the corruption of U.S. capitalism has become so universal, so massive, that it has become a factor with significant economic impact. Political and economic motives are intertwined. Bribes aim simultaneously to open up new corporate profit possibilities and to achieve imperialist military/political objectives.

On the universality of bribery, a U.S. government investigator said: "I wouldn't say the whole *Fortune* 500 [largest industrial corporations . . . V.P.] made illegal payments, but maybe the *Fortune* 250 did." (*The New York Times*, 6/9).

Recent publicity has focused on overseas bribery. Its scale and brazenness may be greater because of the chauvinistic contempt of U.S. capitalists for other peoples, because the stakes in superprofits are so high, and because the U.S. government will often pick up the tab through various kinds of government contracts, "foreign aid" programs and the like.

The American capitalists make out as if bribery is a crime domestically, but not when they make payoffs abroad. Thus Gulf Oil Chairman Bob R. Dorsey, admitting his $5 million in political bribes overseas, regretted only the "inept way" they were handled. He concluded with Nixon's famous last words: "I'm not a crook." (*The Times*, 6/7.)

Capitalist domestic bribery may be more discreet and at lower percentages, but its costs to American workers are enormous. Thus the payoffs to racketeers, themselves corporate executives, of several cents a pound on all beef delivered to the New York metropolitan area costs residents of that area something like $75 million per annum in higher prices. And nobody has figured out yet how much it cost residents of New York and New England when New York Congressman—now Governor—Hugh Carey allegedly helped put over a huge improper price hike for fuel oil sold by his brother's company, which supplies much of the oil for regional power companies.

Recently, for the first time, the government published statistics estimating the total of just one major form of business payoffs and bribes, the so called T & E expenditures—travel, entertainment and gifts. The latest figure published, for 1967, was over $11.2 billion (*Survey of Current Business*, Feb. 1974). If the amount increased only in proportion to the gross national product—and there is evidence it increased faster—it reached about $20 billion in 1974.

This figure—$20 billion—is a minimal estimate of business bribery, essentially within the United States. Published corporate accounts include this within a broader category of "general, selling and administrative expenses," which include, in addition, the take of the corporate insiders and their bureaucratic associates out of the surplus value created by the workers.

These quantities reach incredible levels, especially for multinational corporations. General Electric reported $2.1 billion in 1973; Exxon $2.4 billion in 1974; IBM beat them all with $4.8 billion in 1974, a little more than the cost of producing the goods and services it sold!

The Commerce Department reported that, in 1970, expenses in this broad category by 298 multinational corporations came to $46.2 billion, or 15% of net sales. This indicates a total of at least $66.1 billion in 1974, assuming an increase proportional to that of gross national product (*Statistical Abstract*, 1974, p. 487).

Besides bribes paid by corporations, there are those paid by the U.S. Government on behalf of specific corporations and U.S. monopoly capital as a whole. A significant portion of the $8 billion spent for the CIA and other intelligence agencies goes for bribery, payment to provocateurs, spies, puppet politicians and armies, opium smugglers. The same applies to a large part of the $6.3 billion spent under the "international affairs" label, as well as the "military aid" section, of the "national defense" budget. Billions contained within the "commerce and transportation" and other sections of the budget go for direct subsidies to corporations, allocation of juicy contracts to preferred capitalists—such as the just exposed racketeer, Rep. Sikes of Florida. And he was paid off in return for his congressional leadership of Pentagon budget drives, adding up to thousands of times what he made out of it personally.

The whole of this payoff money, domestic and foreign, amounting to tens of billions yearly at the most conservative estimate, is borne by the people of this country, through higher taxes and prices. And as the bribery and corruption factor increases, so does the cost. This is part of the cause of chronic inflation and declining real wages.

None of the big capitalists who are the main bribers is ever punished, except for trivial wrist-slap fines in connection with illegal political contributions. The only people punished are petty politicians and some minor capitalists and gangsters.

It's time for an outcry to imprison the chief bribers.

• • •

5/27/1982

Corruption Is Anti-Labor

Not since Harding's Teapot Dome has an administration been so deeply steeped in corruption as this one. The CIA director, the Attorney General and the Secretary of Labor have already been tarred with broad brushes.

Fortune, a big business magazine, investigated the affairs of Secretary of Labor Raymond J. Donovan. The *Fortune* investigation showed how capitalist payoffs to gangsters are used to slash wages and bring the bribers multimillion superprofits through superexploitation of workers.

FBI concealment of evidence prevented verification of charges against Donovan at his confirmation hearings before the Senate Labor and Human Resources Committee in 1981. But pressure by Senators Orrin Hatch (R-UT) and Edward Kennedy (D-MA) forced the FBI to reveal some incriminating tapes and the Attorney General to appoint a special prosecutor, who is now conducting a grand jury investigation of the charges.

Donovan, then an insurance salesman, became a major partner in the small Schiavone Construction Company in 1959 with an investment of $5,600. The explosion of this company to a major one with hundreds of millions in annual business is hardly a Horatio Alger story, although perhaps typical of capitalist success in the United States.

Donovan's company, *Fortune* revealed, obtained huge contracts, mainly for turnpikes, tunnels and bridges, in New Jersey and New York: "All this has made Donovan extremely wealthy. Besides his $30 million stake in Schiavone, he has extensive oil and gas holdings and Florida real-estate investments." There are details of alleged relations between the Schiavone partners, including Donovan, with gangsters—including high-spending affairs with hints of sex orgies. According to some tapes referred to by *Fortune*, Donovan may have been the main payoff man for the firm.

What did Schiavone buy from the thugs and corrupt union officials who worked with them?—a promise to keep union-scale workers off the jobs, substituting non-union workers or members of low-wage locals of rival unions.

A $2,000 payment in Donovan's presence, described in considerable detail by blaster Mario Montuoro, was made to Louis Sanzo, president of Local 29 of the Blasters Union, to keep members of Tunnel Workers Union Local 147 from getting jobs on the 63rd Street subway in New York. If we're talking about 400 jobs (the membership of Sanzo's local) at, say, $5 per hour below the regular scale, Donovan's company stood to make an extra $2,000 per hour, $80,000 per week, and more than $4,000,000 per year extra profits on the tunnel job. Of course, these are hypothetical figures, the actual ones might be higher or lower. But whatever the exact facts, the capitalists got back in superprofits hundreds or thousands of times what they paid to the pipsqueak gangsters.

The *Fortune* article also disclosed unsavory details about Donovan's connections with corrupt Teamsters Union officials, contacts that enabled him to submit the low bid for 73 big New Jersey contracts with the inside information they sold to him for $50,000—a small fraction of the millions his firm reaped.

The *Fortune* article does not go into the historical background of corrupt unionism—the murder of honest militants, the use of anti-Communism to turn many locals and national unions over to corporate agents—but of course, without this history the corruption described by *Fortune* could not have taken place.

Capitalist corruption occurs at the expense of the working class. *Fortune* gives examples of the most direct form of anti-labor corruption. But the huge tax swindles and "cost overruns" of "defense" contractors are all paid for, finally, by workers, through added taxes and reduced public services. And how can one rely on Attorney General William French Smith—who just pocketed $99,000 in tax refund for his investment of $33,000 on which he has not yet lost a nickel—to prosecute financial swindlers any more than he enforces civil rights laws?

The ramified connections of Reagan with the crudest crooks are completely consistent with his rabid racism, his labor hating, his anti-Communism, and his anti-Soviet warmongering. The fight for peace, for labor rights, for the freedom of Afro-Americans and other oppressed peoples is at the same time a fight for elementary honesty in government and for purging the huge swindles going on today in the United States.

• • •

3/21/1985

Ohio Banks and B-C-D

The closing of 71 Ohio savings banks has tied up $5.5 billion belonging to 500,000 workers, farmers and small businessmen, including money needed to pay taxes, loan installments and doctor bills. It's tough in Ohio—part of the central industrial region that is feeling 6 months of declining industrial output and employment—after only partial recovery from the Reagan crisis of 1982.

Why? The answer can be found in my overflowing B-C-D file: Bureaucracy, Corruption, Decadence. All are flourishing under Reagan's "deregulation" and "free enterprise":

Bureaucracy: "Regulators" who let the financial magnates manipulate without restraint.

Corruption: The $100 billion *Fortune* estimates is now "laundered" yearly through the big banks; the huge loans to bank "insiders" at below-market interest rates; the hundreds of millions of insiders' takes and bribes by General Dynamics, the largest Pentagon contractor; the record number of high Reagan officials exposed.

Decadence: The drugs, prostitution, casinos and crime from which the $100 billion flow; from which the bankers take their cut, and then gamble with the rest of other people's money.

Washington found it in the "national interest" to salvage the giant Continental Illinois Bank, but considers failures of farms, small banks and businesses "healthy" application of the law of "survival of the fittest" under capitalism. The Ohio victims are the half-million depositors, who join the 4 million U.S. homeless, 12 million jobless, and 20 million hungry.

The Ohio drama started in Florida when big-time financial manipulators set up ESM Government Securities Corp. With high interest rates, they lured over $1.5 billion from reckless or poorly advised bankers and city administrations. They and their friends garnered tens of millions in giveaway loans; and to cover the giveaways and pay the high interest, they had to gamble in government securities. The losses they piled up were concealed for years by a "respectable" accounting firm until finally a Florida bank failure uncovered the ESM insolvency.

Home Savings Bank of Cincinnati, having poured an incredible $150 million into ESM, was the largest loser. The loss, exceeding the entire state insurance fund, had to be revealed. Depositors started a "run" on the bank, and it had to close. Depositors at the other state-chartered savings banks—those without federal deposit insurance—rushed to get their money out. So Governor Celeste ordered all state-chartered banks to close.

An attempt is underway to reopen some, gradually, through "qualifying" for federal insurance. The Reaganites may unbend and salvage most of these small banks for fear of the rapidly spreading consequences otherwise.

The Ohio crisis, coming along with the Boston bank laundering exposé, the financial collapse of Texas oil barons and New York financiers, and publication of the $102 billion balance of payments deficit, has made the U.S. public, and the world, conscious of the financial instability of U.S. capitalism. In Los Angeles hundreds of millions are being withdrawn from a major savings bank complex, the Financial Corporation of America. The world's capitalists, who were attracted by high interest rates and Reagan's promise to safeguard their money, are beginning to see the truth: Reagan and the Pentagon are military-political gamblers on a global scale, along with the transnational corporations and banks. Foreigners are having second thoughts about entrusting their savings to U.S. banks and over-valued dollars. They are wary of Reagan's initial sabotage of Geneva, his intense pro-Pentagon lobbying. In a single day the dollar lost 3-5% against other curren-cies, and the price of gold increased more than 10% as the White House rammed the deficit-building MX through the Senate.

The danger of a deep financial/industrial crisis is growing. It may be tem-porarily contained, but not for long without a major change in direction. The way out in the interest of the people and the country is to reverse budget priorities from war to peace, for detente and disarmament, for social needs and jobs instead of bankers' profits.

• • •

4/21/1987

Corruption and Decay

In a CBS television interview concerning the major financial crimes rocking Wall Street, prosecutor Rudolph Giuliani said: "There's nothing illegal about be-coming a millionaire in your thirties—in fact it isn't a bad idea. You have to do it legally."

That brings out one element of the structural decay of the system—glorifi-cation of greed. Rapid accumulation of wealth is quite acceptable, even praise-worthy, no matter how parasitic the method, no matter how much exploitation, cruelty, immorality are involved, so long as they stay within certain special legal bounds unrelated to any social or moral criteria.

Robert Lamb, a professor of "Business and Ethics" at New York University, was asked what his students think of these financial crimes:

> Up to 50% of the class have said either they know someone who's doing it or that they would do it themselves . . . 'everyone else is doing it, if I don't do it and other people are doing it I will be worse off . . .'

He expressed the opinion that "a lot of people have felt during the Reagan Administration that they are playing with the net down"—in effect anything goes, if I can get away with it, and I probably can.

Since the late 1960s, when Lamb started teaching, there has been an ideo-logical deterioration among students in "not just ethics, but a sense of selfishness, just 'I'm in it for me. . . I have to in effect look out for number one.'"

Formerly, then, it was possible to convince students aspiring to be capitalists that they could combine ethics and exploitation, greed and good behavior. They could enter the business world with the illusion that their actions, while benefiting themselves, would be socially desirable. In real life, of course, they would soon be disabused of such illusions, but would continue to pronounce them as truths to justify their own actions and those of their class.

But now, the masks are off. Hundreds of thousands of youths are ready to learn how best to strive for maximum accumulation of wealth, by whatever means might be required.

The interviewer, Lesley Stahl, asked: "Are you agonized by this? What is your feeling? You are in the middle of watching these young people come up, you teach ethics. . .".

Mr. Lamb:

> A lot of us talked about this and worried about this. We have a case . . . where students take the part of members of the board of directors of the Upjohn Company, marketing a drug called Penalba that has killed people, over twenty-two people. And the students decide, almost universally, to keep the drug on the market and fight the FDA [Federal Drug Administration—VP]. We have been doing this case for a number of years; it's done in a number of other business schools. And the students not only decide to keep it on the market here, but after it's been banned here and illegal here, they decide to keep it on the market abroad and to sell off as much of it as they can elsewhere. So, it's not simply Wall Street."

Ms. Stahl: "That's a shocking story."
Mr. Lamb:

> It's shocking to us, too. This is not something that we wanted to find out . . . It's not something that is that easy to deal with when you have 80 or 90 percent of a class taking this attitude so that you realize you have a long way to go to try to get them to come to grips with ethical problems. (*Face the Nation*, Transcript, 2/22.)

The feral drive of capitalists for money, riding over every obstacle, killing their prey with no compunction, is not part of human nature. It is the nature of a system in its extreme decay. It explains why its rulers are so unwilling to ban the most destructive "drug" of all times, the atomic bomb.

Fortunately, the masses who demonstrated April 25th, who voted against Reaganism in recent elections, the big majorities for peace and decency in recent polls, reject the ideology of unlimited greed, corruption and decay that permeates the centers of capitalist wealth. They can and must curb it, restore elementary standards of ethics to American life at all levels.

3/15/1989

The Ethics of Bush's 'Untouchables'

President Bush's closest friends and associates, mainly multi-millionaire Ivy Leaguers from Texas, are known as the "untouchables." But already they are very much touched by corruption scandals. Evidently they consider it normal to use government posts bought with their political contributions to multiply their personal wealth, enhancing that of their social class.

James A. Baker III, Reagan's Treasury secretary from 1984 to 1988, is now Secretary of State, the leading post in the cabinet of his long-time friend, George Bush. As Treasury Secretary, he had a voice in the decision to bail out, without punishment, the financial thieves who gutted the Texas S&Ls and gave away billions of these banks' good assets to takeover plutocrats, including his fellow Texan, financier Robert Bass, at an ultimate cost to taxpayers officially estimated at $230 billion.

The main source of Baker's wealth was the Texas Commerce Bank, founded by his grandfather. In 1980 Baker III, as an insider, reported owning more than $7 million worth of its shares, to which should be added those of his family. Along with the other major Texas banks, by 1987 it was sustaining heavy losses from the collapse of the Texas oil drilling and real estate booms. Chemical Bank came to the rescue with an over-generous billion dollar takeover, the Washington connections helping to make the price worth paying. Baker's stake is now in Chemical stock, presumably worth several times the $7 million of 1980. He "was both financially and emotionally attached to the stock." (*The New York Times*, 2/15.)

The Chemical-Texas Commerce combine merges Wall Street and Texas high finance, protected and promoted by direct representation in Washington. Among Chemical's current directors is Ben F. Love, old associate of the Bakers and chief executive of Texas Commerce, still the Texas part of the operation for Chemical. No less important is director Emil Mosbacher Jr., relative and business partner of Robert A. Mosbacher Sr., chief fundraiser for Bush in 1988, now his Secretary of Commerce and one of his "untouchables."

Chemical Bank is stuck with $6 billion of uncollectable Third World debt, including $600 million taken over from Texas Commerce. Traditional rules would have barred Baker, as Treasury Secretary, from dealing with this problem in which he has so big a personal interest. But Reagan's ethics adviser gave Baker a green light. Nor did his own conscience deter him.

Escaping publicity about his holdings, Baker took the lead as policy maker for the capitalist world's banker-lenders. He pushed the Baker Plan, essentially a variation of the ongoing policy of squeezing maximum interest for the banks, at a terrible cost to the living standards of hundreds of millions of people in Latin America, Africa and Asia. The new angle was a scheme for American corporations to take over the national industries of the debtor countries in exchange for part of the debts.

The Baker Plan failed. The debt crisis deepens. But the debtor countries, as yet unable to unite in resistance, continue to pay out billions in interest. The average market value of Latin American debt, as of mid-February, was down to 33.9 cents on the dollar. Several major banks, Chemical included, would be insolvent if forced to mark down the loans to their real value. Federal regulators, however, are most considerate. There are already hints that when finally necessary to salvage the banks' owners, our tax money will be used to take the bad debts off the banks' hands.

And now a new twist: Bush's White House counsel, "untouchable" C. Boyden Gray, his own corruption exposed, turned around and made public Baker's larger violation, enraging Baker and impelling him to announce his intention to sell his Chemical stock.

Today Baker is playing for larger stakes. He loses no opportunity to proclaim "American leadership" and the dominant role for its "vital interests" in all corners of the globe. He is wholly negative with respect to the most crucial aspect of foreign relations, those with the USSR. He has already expressed opposition to developing economic ties and has pressed European allies not to trade with the Soviets. He is hostile to the START strategic weapons plan, which offers the most promising prospect for disarmament. And he opposes cooperation as an equal with the USSR in resolving the dangerous Middle East crisis. Arrogantly he refers to the USSR as a minor factor in world affairs.

The Bush-Baker foreign policy will also fail. It is based on an unrealistic estimate of the balance of world forces. The worldwide movement against economic domination and nuclear blackmail is growing and cannot be overcome.

Fallout

Big Business and Profiteering

6/10/1961

Froth or Substance in Anti-Trust Flurry?

In a historic first, electrical equipment company officials were briefly imprisoned last year for price rigging and dividing markets. The Supreme Court has finally ordered duPont to sell its General Motors stock, while AT&T is under fresh anti-trust investigation. The Federal Reserve Board has vetoed important Wall Street bank mergers. New York state and city authorities request federal action against monopolies for gouging on public purchases. Following Senator Kefauver's recent hearings exposing electrical equipment trusts, there is strong support for his proposals to make the anti-trust laws stronger.

Is the tide really turning against monopolies? Unfortunately, not in any practical sense. In Los Angeles, *The People's World* reports, big company gasoline dealers uniformly raised prices 5 cents a gallon. The steel companies have announced that next October they will simultaneously decide to raise their prices. Monopoly-dictated living costs continue to inch upward.

Monopoly gets stronger and extends its control still further. It robs the public increasingly with rising price margins and taxes to pay for rigged charges to the government. Oil-proration, fair-trade laws, one-sided public utility regulation, multi-billion dollar subsidies are examples of the additional favors they acquired. But the most effective monopoly builder is the $25 billion awarded this year to giant corporations for munitions. Monopoly capitalism has graduated to state monopoly capitalism.

The anti-trust approach cannot accomplish much because it is based on the petty utopian notion of restoring small private enterprise. The only possible direction is forward, from government-monopoly partnership to a government by the working people controlling production in the interest of all.

The U.S. has a unique legal and traditional framework. Thanks to the anti-monopoly struggles of the 19th century, monopolies are illegal, regarded as bad in official statements and conventional morality. Other capitalist governments aid monopolies openly. Ours does so secretly and hypocritically.

Continuous anti-trust suits and congressional exposés fail to stop the inexorable march of monopoly power and wealth. The first major anti-trust case was concluded exactly 50 years ago with the "breakup" of the $660 million Standard Oil Trust. Now, formally divided into a number of giants, it has $22 billion in assets, or 33 times as much.

The limited methods of the old party politicians have failed and are bound to fail. To weaken and ultimately destroy the economic grip of monopoly we require a powerful people's anti-monopoly movement that makes the entire monopoly structure its number one economic target. Trade unions, farmers organizations, and other people's groups should lead millions in coordinated actions: voting for anti-monopoly candidates, sending mass delegations to Congress and regulatory commissions, conducting demonstrations and strikes with anti-monopoly demands.

An anti-monopoly political party is needed most of all. It should build on and modernize the traditions of the Non-Partisan League and the La Follette progressives. It should obtain real power through the leadership of 17 million organized workers and the millions of Negro people already combating monopoly-inspired and protected segregation practices.

Such a movement would emphasize demands directly affecting relations between the trusts and the people. It would call for government regulations lowering monopoly-rigged prices of important goods, such as drugs, packaged foods and cars. It would press for sharp cuts in utility and transport rates everywhere. It would urge the government to force price reductions on needed procurement and construction, including exercise of the right of eminent domain to seize stocks of goods and to seize and operate productive property, where necessary, to supply public needs at reasonable prices.

It would demand the ending of the arms race, the root source of the big business political and economic offensive of the past 15 years.

• • •

11/17/1962

War Contractor-Pentagon Profiteering

The 936-page volume, *Sole Source Procurement*, is one of many issued by Rep. Hebert's subcommittee of the House Armed Services Committee exposing various aspects of war contractor-Pentagon racketeering.

This report adds another dimension to one's understanding of arms profiteering. About 86% of all military hardware is obtained by direct negotiation with a single supplier, rather than by competitive bidding. The Pentagon uses the excuse that only one company is able to handle a job. In 1960 the Pentagon bought $3.3 billion of spare parts this way, almost all of them simple, standard items that many companies could make at a realistic price.

The Comptroller General studied cases where the services for one reason or another were shifted from "sole source" to competitive bidding. E.g., first they got a certain bolt from Boeing @ $1.83. Then, under bidding, it came from the Valley Bolt Co. @ 35¢. The average saving in 12 such cases was 72%.

For two-thirds of the items bought from the supposed "sole source," this "exclusive specialist" didn't even make them, but farmed out work to another, or several other, smaller companies. Westinghouse got the contract for a certain bolt, farmed it out to Chandler Products @ 90¢, then turned around and charged the government $6.83. On 42 items studied, the government paid $4,166,000 to prime contractors, who paid only $1,904,000, or less than half as much, to the producers.

Conclusions from this and other recent hearings:

Munitions profits are far higher than any outsider suspected. What had been considered exceptional outrages are the rule.

Profits before taxes on munitions may absorb over half of the $30 billion yearly the government now spends.

Because of the large proportion of munitions expenditures siphoned off into profits, the employment provided is far less than from other types of government spending, perhaps as much as 50% less. That is, a billion spent for munitions may provide only half as many jobs as a billion spent for education or housing. Thus, the growth of the garrison state is contributing to, not offsetting, the uptrend in unemployment.

It is the largest, most "respectable" corporations that engage in the most unrestrained thievery—a crooked and racketeering business even by the corrupt standards of monopoly capitalism—to a depth and on a scale overwhelming in its enormity.

It is to preserve and increase these profits that the tycoons are so rabidly prowar. For this reason they urge a tougher anti-Soviet foreign policy, invasions of weaker countries. On behalf of these looters of the public purse, President Kennedy resists negotiations for peace, raises the arms budget continuously, plots and executes successive crises, and orders the U.S. Navy to engage in piracy on the high seas.

War profiteering figures mighty large in the total picture. For these tainted billions the recipients and their political representatives are ready to doom hundreds of millions of people.

Most Americans would fight to prevent the robbery and assault of an innocent neighbor. The fight for peace is comparable on a global scale. It is urgent, and is the most noble cause that history has ever placed before Americans.

• • •

3/17/1963

The Stockpile Barter Racket

Senator Symington's Strategic Stockpile hearing revealed that the government holds five separate inventories of 98 commodities gathered over 23 years at a cost of $8,711,579,200. The stockpiles already exceed the maximum goals by $3,400,000,000. And that amount was for an all-out nuclear war lasting an impossible 3 years! Large segments are in inventories admittedly unrelated to military emergencies, designed just to get the product out of circulation. One, the billion-dollar "supplemental stockpile" of minerals, was acquired by the Agriculture Department under Public Law 480, which provides for dumping farm surpluses abroad.

This brings up the most fascinating aspect of the stockpile racket—the barter program.

Fifteen years ago U.S. capitalists sneered at socialist and other countries for using barter to help overcome wartime devastation. Now the U.S. has reconsidered and provides its trading partners with commodities they need, while helping capitalists of all countries get rid of the commodities nobody wants—at the expense of U.S. taxpayers.

The State Department boasted of our "multilateral" trading system. Some of the barter deals are multilateral, all right, if scarcely believable.

In 1961 the lead mining companies asked the U.S. government to barter away surplus lead so they could raise prices. State and Agriculture Departments obliged, concluding deals with Australian and Canadian companies, the latter involving 55,000 tons of lead priced at $8 million. One transaction was as follows:

Canada sent surplus lead to the U.S., which sent surplus tobacco to Portugal, which sent surplus iron and manganese ore to West Germany, which sent surplus glass to Canada. Since we can't have government bureaucrats messing things up, the arrangements were made by private enterprise, in this case the Minerals & Chemicals, Philipp Corp., the leading stockpile barter operator.

Minerals & Chemicals has made the big time, with a N.Y. Stock Exchange listing, a turnover of $300 million, and after-tax profits of $10 million. Its directors include Richard H. Mansfield, former Rockefeller financial aide, now a partner in the Paris-Wall St. outfit Lazard Freres, and David E. Lilienthal, who became a big business bigshot in reward for services as chairman of the Atomic Energy Commission. It has Lehman Bros. as investment banker, Morgan Guaranty Trust as fiduciary, and Treasury Secretary Dillon's law firm as counsel.

Everybody makes money out of the deal: Canadian and U.S. metal companies, American tobacco companies, Salazar [dictator of Portugal], West German glass manufacturers—and Minerals & Chemicals, Philipp takes its cut from all. Everybody makes money except the taxpayers, who pay the $8 million cash outlay, and higher prices for the products propped up by this scheme.

Of course, "politics" enter into it. Take aluminum. The stockpile of this metal and its raw materials (bauxite and alumina) is larger than any other in cost ($1.1 billion) and in physical volume. If you piled up the 14 million tons of bauxite on a square city block, it would reach a half mile up. But we still buy it, at the rate of a million tons a year, from the Caribbean holdings of the big three U.S. companies. When the Democrats came into office, the share of Alcoa, whose Mellons contribute to the Republicans, was reduced and then eliminated. Kaiser and Reynolds, whose owners contribute to the Democrats, got bigger contracts.

The stockpile barter racket has essential characteristics in common with the entire $62 billion national defense and related budget. Besides subjecting the country and the world to unprecedented dangers, this budget is the most gigantic profiteering grab-bag in all history.

Witnesses explained the shifting legal basis of the stockpile transactions. But I know better. It was all done under one rule: *Catch 22*. Which means anything goes that you can get away with at the people's expense.

• • •

12/20/1969

Napalm—from Dow to Dowling

Dow Chemical has lost the contract for napalm. However, Herbert Dow Doan, the company president, continues to defend its manufacture as a "matter of principle," although he does not say what the principle is. He says he now opposes the war in Vietnam. Yet he bid for the napalm business again this year and plans to do so in the future.

Doan's father married the boss' daughter in 1917, and since then Dows and Doans have run Dow Chemical and become ultra-rich as their company became a billionaire corporation.

As usual, Doan denied making money on war, claiming "the profits on the napalm business did not even match civilian profit ratios . . . and it was carried at a loss if the time that Dow executives spent on the problem was included" (*The New York Times*, 11/22).

But figures give him the lie. Dow spokesmen admitted that it took only 10-12 workers to make $5 million worth of napalm, the amount of a year's contract. That is $400,000-$500,000 worth of napalm per worker, or 60 to 80 times the average worker's wage. Assuming that raw materials equal half the value of product, normal for this line of chemicals, total cost of materials and labor come to less than $2.6 million, leaving nearly half of the $5 million contract for profit and overhead, an unusually high percentage.

The actual amount of napalm business is a secret. But in 1966 the trade press reported volumes in the $50-$100 million worth per year.

During the Vietnam War years, Dow Chemical has done better than any of its rivals among the chemical giants. Its sales shot up from under $1 billion in 1963 to $1.8 billion in 1969, and its profits from $80 million to $150 million in the same period.

In 1968 Dow Chemical turned down a firm offer for its napalm facilities and claimed it wasn't bothered by public opposition. But now Dow admits that it lost out in one important respect: resistance to its recruiters cost it an unknown number of outstanding graduates for research and development work. This is of crucial importance for a chemical company. *The New York Times* article reported: "Dow is taking advantage of its exit to try to rebuild its position on campus."

But Dow should not be let off the hook. It still makes its major military product, triggers for hydrogen bombs, designed to annihilate more people more speedily and more indiscriminately than napalm.

• •

This year's napalm contract was won by American Electric Co. of Long Beach, California. It is a subsidiary of an old New York company, City Investing, long engaged in the real estate business, especially office buildings, hotels and theaters.

American Electric, exclusively a munitions maker, formerly manufactured the bombs into which Dow's napalm was loaded. In order to prepare for this year's bid, it built a polystyrene factory to assure raw materials. Then it underbid Dow, or overinfluenced the Pentagon, and got the napalm contract. Now it runs a "fully integrated" operation, from chemical kettle to bomb bay.

The people of Long Beach, in an unusually broad front, are opposing the genocidal weapons maker, but as yet have been unable to reverse the courts and governmental support for the company. Already a serious explosion in the company's plant has damaged many homes, and a truck spilled napalm all over the highway. Fear of community damage merges with peace sentiment in opposing the napalm maker, who got the permit for manufacture by pretending to plan "plastics" manufacture.

R.W. Dowling, City Investing's chairman, a one-time athlete and theatrical promoter, is on various cultural boards and rich people's do-gooder organizations.

In 1966, G.T. Scharffenberger, then executive vice president of Litton Industries, was brought in as president and chief executive officer of City Investing. Litton, under Scharffenberger, had mushroomed as a war-based conglomerate. The owners of City Investing decided to follow the same course and, in the first half of 1967, began to take over other companies, starting with three munitions firms: Hayes International, American Electric, and ZD Products.

It also obtained a score of civilian companies making everything from steel containers to mobile homes, operating motels and steamship lines, owning big insurance firms and real estate developments. It is now about to buy an airline, with the approval of a Civil Aeronautics Board examiner. Indeed, the government looks with favor on applications of napalm makers!

By 1968 City Investing became one of the top 100 Defense Department contractors, ranking 63rd, with a total of $88 million. In 1969 it moved up, with $109 million, and made the top 500 industrials list of *Fortune* for the first time.

Since it went into munitions, City Investing stock multiplied five times in price. Chairman Dowling has a paper profit of $18 million on his 730,000 shares, and all directors and officers, a profit of $50 million. The company's profits multiplied four times in the last three years, and increased another 44% in the first half of this fiscal year.

To aid in getting munitions business, City Investing has on its board physicist John R. Dunning, a well known Pentagon science administrator, and a leading developer of nuclear weapons in World War II.

Company officials have repeatedly answered that they are willing to stand judgment for their decision to make napalm if history proves them wrong. But humanity has already judged the goals and methods of the U.S. in Vietnam. The Nuremberg Judgment, the United Nations Convention against genocide, the most elementary moral criteria judge as criminal the use of napalm and other weapons of chemical warfare, as well as the many means of mass annihilation of civilians practiced by the Pentagon in Vietnam.

Today the directors of City Investing have taken on themselves the same burden of guilt. And their position could not be taken without the approval of the top Wall Street bankers who are their fellow-directors.

• • •

2/26/1981

Oranges, Milk and Oil

Oranges

Do you know it's a crime to sell half this year's western orange crop in the United States?! Under federal law, a committee of 11 of the largest orange plantation owners and shippers decrees each year the permissible sale percentage. Anyone who sells oranges beyond that percentage "can face civil and criminal prosecution by the Department of Justice" (*The New York Times*, 2/15/81).

The unsold half of the current crop is fed to cattle, given away to juicing plants, or dumped in a special plot in Tulare County, California.

The percentage of oranges withheld from the market has increased from 20% in the 1950s to 30% in the 1960s, 40% in the late 1970s, until now it is 50%. As a result of this Catch 22 imbroglio, there is a huge and rising volume of production. Fresh oranges in the supermarkets are priced beyond the reach of a large percentage of the population, so that consumers can afford to eat fewer fresh oranges and are being forced to buy frozen juice. And despite their receipt of free fruit, processors are able to raise the price of the inferior frozen juice to record levels, as long as they stay below the price of fresh oranges.

Another factor: because of the reduced volume of oranges shipped, railroads have an excuse to raise freight rates, adding further to retail prices.

Also, similar compulsory quota destruction keeps down the supply and raises the prices of peaches and other types of fruit.

Growers are permitted to sell the "surplus" abroad, but protective tariffs limit sales to Western Europe, and economic warfare against the USSR prevents sales there.

The orange-destruction committee is dominated by subsidiaries of monopoly conglomerates, for which orange growing is but one part of a complex of operations.

These companies join with the U.S. government to enforce inflation-accelerating monopoly profiteering—state monopoly capitalism in action.

Dairy Products

The Federal government has a fast-growing stockpile of over a billion pounds of milk products—four pounds per capita—for which storage space will soon be exhausted. This hoard was accumulated under a law requiring price supports at 80% of parity, with parity soaring along with inflation.

As a result, lower income people cannot afford fresh milk, butter, and cheese. The big milk producers, often part of corporate conglomerates, make superprofits out of the floor price, jacked up twice yearly. Half the subsidy of $2 billion this year will go to 12,000 large farmers, an average bonanza of $83,000 each. The small dairy farmers, who need price support to avoid bankruptcy, will get $3,300 each.

If the government paid the necessary subsidy to keep the small farmers in the market, without putting a floor under prices, monopoly pricing by the dairy giants would be restrained, the cost to the government would be small, and consumers would save billions of dollars. The vast surplus could be given away to hungry people in the United States and in developing countries. But that isn't why U.S. imperialism engages in "foreign aid"!

Gasoline and Fuel Oil

Gasoline stocks are at such record high levels that oil industry publisher Dan Lundberg says:

> What refineries are going to do with it, I don't know. The industry may have to drink it (*The Times*, 2/16/81).

With stocks at record levels and government regulations removed, shouldn't prices come down? On the contrary, they jumped 10-12 cents per gallon, instead of the 3 cents predicted by Energy Secretary Edwards. And in a television interview, John E. Swearingen, chairman of Standard Oil Company (Indiana), predicted that prices would go up another 7-10 cents in the next few months. Home heating oil in some areas will go above $1.50 per gallon, with gasoline prices obviously still higher.

The oil monopoly is the oldest and most powerful in the world. Even so, last year, with price controls, it was not able to charge the maximum allowable price because of the surplus stocks. Why, then, with the ceiling removed and a bigger surplus, is it now able to collect far more?

Because of the other part of the deregulation. Formerly, "entitlement" regulations gave some protection to the smaller independents, who offered some mild competition. But the deregulation decreed by President Reagan ended this provision and restored full monopoly power to the giants.

Will the Justice Department prosecute under anti-trust laws? Hardly, when it is busy threatening to prosecute orange growers who might violate monopoly edicts!

• • •

11/19/1981

Mergers and Madmen

News item: Justice Department drops nine-year-old anti-trust suit against General Electric.

News item: Congress passes law permitting supertrust AT&T to spread out further, setting stage for Justice Department to drop its decade-long suit against the communications monopoly.

News item: The anti-trust suit against IBM will drag on for many more years, with the company leisurely presenting its "defense" while dickering for abandonment of the suit.

Washington has dropped all pretense of enforcing the anti-trust laws. Carter's final budget did not even mention anti-trust, except for its listing as a statistic in a tabulation. The "deregulation of business" started under Carter has become a prime, highly touted objective of Reagan. Publicized as a means for permitting business to compete freely, "deregulation" actually removes all barriers against big business activities "in restraint of trade," i.e., raising prices, conspiring to hold down supplies, combating unions, wrecking social legislation, discriminating against minorities and women, driving independents to the wall—all without interference. In the past, the possibility of anti-trust suits, with all their limitations, served to slow up the increase in industrial and financial concentration. Now, with that inhibition gone, Wall Street is swept with the most gigantic merger mania in history. Only during the period around the turn of the century has the process of trustification proceeded so rapidly.

And that supercartel of the banks and the government—the Federal Reserve Board—acts as Wall Street's enforcer of super-high interest rates, depriving millions of housing, raising all living costs, driving scores of thousands of farmers and smaller businesses into bankruptcy, wrecking municipal finances, increasing unemployment for the expressed purpose of weakening the working class, forcing down real wages and increasing corporate profits.

Both the Democrats and Republicans are totally involved in expediting the process whereby it will be possible for monopoly to strengthen its deadly grip on the life of the country. The need for a people's anti-monopoly party that will take vigorous action to break this stranglehold, including but by no means limited to enforcement of the anti-trust laws, is greater than ever.

Budgeted outlays for anti-trust activities this fiscal year (1982) stand at $47.7 million—not allowing for the 12% across-the-board civilian cuts that Reagan is trying to put over. The 1982 amount barely exceeds the $46.1 million in fiscal 1979. Adjusting by officially estimated price increases, this amounts to a reduction in real outlays of 26%. And that anti-trust appropriation accounts for just under 1% of total budgeted outlays under the caption "administration of justice," and 1.8% of the Justice Department budget. (Some "administration of justice" outlays are in other agencies.)

The amount provided for anti-trust is 6% of that for the FBI and 12% of that for the repressive Immigration and Naturalization Service, which is also in the Justice Department. The anti-trust sum, together with similar expenditures by the Federal Trade Commission and the Securities and Exchange Commission, are a drop in the bucket compared with the hundreds of billions of federal monies being shelled out to big business through military orders, loans, subsidies and tax "expenditures."

• • •

2/14/1985

Reagan's Record

President Reagan is boasting that real gross product increased 6.8% in 1984, the largest percentage increase since 1951. To get a realistic picture of whether the economy has improved under Reagan, however, we must compare the figures for his entire first term with those of the seven post-World War II presidents who preceded him.

The increase from 1980 to 1984 was 11.1%, or 2.66% per year compounded. It was exceeded in six of the preceding eight presidential terms. In only two terms was the increase less, and that was not by much: in the **second** terms of Presidents Eisenhower and Nixon-Ford. If there is a comparable deterioration in Reagan's second term, it will be the worst 4 years since Herbert Hoover.

Much more important than the production rise, weak as it was, is the question: **who gained from it, and who lost?** The facts are eloquent and, for working people, dismal.

The average rate of unemployment in Reagan's first term was the highest of the nine post-World War II presidential terms. In 1984, a recovery year, unemployment was officially 7.5%, higher than the average rate over any previous 4-year presidential term.

The rate of real hourly wages declined 4%, averaged over Reagan's first 4 years, and was 6.1% below the index base year of 1977. It was the sharpest decline of any presidential term since Hoover. Moreover, the index of real hourly earnings in 1984, a year for which Reagan boasts of economic growth, was actually lower than in 1983.

Meantime, capitalists and corporations gained—at workers' expense—faster than ever. Between 1980 and 1984, executives' pay rose 51%. In 1984, when workers' money wages increased 3.4%, executive pay jumped 12.6%. It is scheduled to rise another 12.5% in 1985, so that executives' pay will have more than doubled since 1978.

Corporate profits, as adjusted by the Department of Commerce, and eliminating price increases, averaged far higher during Reagan's 4 years than in any previous term. Profits in 1984 were 82% higher than in Carter's last year and 28% above the previous record.

Soaring profits were matched by war spending. Defense Department military prime contract awards increased 2¼ times between 1979 and 1984, while the physical output of armaments in 1984 was 25% above the Vietnam War peak. And the correlation isn't accidental: anti-Soviet war propaganda was essential in putting over the continuing Reaganite/big business offensive against U.S. workers.

It all adds up to a sharp increase in the rate of exploitation of labor. Reagan's first term was "Heaven" for the capitalist elite and the Pentagon; "Hell" for the working class, farmers, and the Black and other oppressed peoples.

Let the second Reagan term be marked by a united labor and people's fightback for jobs, improved wages, peace, disarmament and an end to discrimination—no matter what happens to the gross national product statistics.

• • •

Early 1993

Why Runaway Health Care Costs?

The price of drugs manufactured by Merck, the nation's third largest pharmaceutical company, is 4.7 times the cost of production. Bristol-Myers Squibb's prices are nearly 4 times production costs; and at Pfizer, one of the fastest growing pharmaceuticals, prices are more than 3.5 times the cost of production. In other words, more than 75% of drug company sales is "gross profits," or, better put, is "gross profiteering" at the expense of people.

We are told that President Clinton's "managed competition" will end this disgrace—but will it? And the answer is "no."

When sales representatives of drug companies visit a doctor's office to explain the merits of their respective cardiac medicines, they never argue that theirs is more economical. Insurance companies and health maintenance organizations (HMOs) add another big chunk to the already extortionate prices charged by providers of medical goods and services. United Health Care Corporation, one of the largest private HMOs, marked up its medical charges 59% in 1991.

In every case the largest part of the gross profit does not go to stockholders—who get plenty—or to the government as taxes. And it doesn't go to research and development (R&D) despite the claims. Instead, it goes to a nebulous catch-all called "selling, general and administrative expenses" (SGA).

To call SGA "bureaucratic waste" misses the point. It's the "profits of control,"* ripped off by the owners of the decisive blocks of company stock. From this control come the multi-million dollar salaries, the bonuses and stock options and the fleets of jet planes, free apartments and vacations for the executive elite. And don't forget the substantial amounts filtering down to relatives and friends, to directors and managers, special funds for lawyers and slush funds for politicians—and, when needed, strikebreakers.

Consider, for a moment, Pfizer: In 1982 its gross profits were $1.9 billion—2.2 times production costs. By 1992, profits had climbed to $5.2 billion—3.6 times production cost. Wages and salaries declined from 40% of gross profits in 1982 to 25% of gross profits 10 years later. And Pfizer spent 3.4 times as much on SGA as on R&D.

Drug companies' standard excuse for high prices is their large outlay for R&D—and R&D does cost money. But the major cost items were those that go to enhance the fortune of the corporate elite, not for research for new or better drugs.

Bristol-Myers Squibb also admits that it spends more on "marketing" than on R&D, claiming this is "necessary" to "educate" physicians and pharmacists on how to use the drugs.

To head off price controls, Pfizer has offered to increase prices no faster than increases in the cost-of-living. But that's wholly unsatisfactory: prices should be cut in half in order to wipe out much of the superprofits of the industry. Similar restrictions should be put on charges of doctors, dentists, hospitals and nursing homes. The best and simplest course would be to put doctors and dentists on excellent, but not outrageous, salaries.

As for the insurance companies and HMOs, who needs them? Under a single-payer government system, financed by taxes on the rich, they would be out of the picture. With elimination of multiple bureaucratic stages, the cost of universal coverage would be far less than the cost of partial coverage today. Of course, there would be the danger of an overwhelming government bureaucracy. To prevent it, control should be exercised by labor and community based people's committees.

* See Finance section column 8/8/85: Gross Profits = Profits of Control, p. 50.

• • •

9/5/1998

The Economy in Crisis: Mergers

A record wave of mergers and takeovers of already huge corporate giants is sweeping the land. It's spurred by the virtual lack of any anti-trust enforcement, by desire to maximize corporate strength against the deepening world financial crises, and, mostly, by the drive for ever higher profits.

Most mergers result in job loss, even in industries where overall employment is increasing. The savings in wages is the principal initial source of higher profits—for the stockholders, corporate executives, investment bankers and lawyers who negotiate the terms and pin them down.

The U.S. boom in bank mergers is moving toward the situation in Germany and Japan, where a few giants control almost all finance. By merging, the Wall Street banks gain the muscle to extend their global reach, their main source of profit growth.

Chase Manhattan is largest in terms of assets, nearly $400 billion. But Citicorp, the leading global bank of U.S. imperialism, leads in profits: 55,000 of its 94,000 employees are scattered over 98 countries. The labor of workers and peasants of "emerging nations"—the neo-colonial empire of the U.S.—provides 60% of Citicorp's profits. And its operations intensify the financial crisis facing these countries.

Citicorp's pending merger with Travelers will create a super-monster, ranking first in commercial and consumer banking, insurance, investment banking and brokerage, with initial annual profits of $9 billion, highest of all corporations.

The most dynamic mergers are headed by "super-regionals," banks based outside the main financial centers but still dominant in smaller cities across the nation. The largest is Nations Bank, based in Charlotte, North Carolina. Through multiple takeovers, it has grown in size by 11 times in the past 10 years. Now it is taking over California-based Bank of America, once the country's largest.

Thousands of employees will lose their jobs, and the merged bank, which will be called Bank of America, will reap additional yearly profits of $1.2 billion.

Bank One, another super-regional headquartered in Columbus, Ohio, is taking over First Chicago-NBO, itself a merger of the top Chicago and Detroit banks. Again, thousands of employees are slated to lose their jobs, thereby providing an additional $930 million of yearly profits to the merged bank.

In both of these bank mergers, "institutions"—pension funds, trust funds, mutual fund conglomerates—controlled by Wall Street hold the majority of the banks' stocks.

The projected $40 billion takeover of Chrysler Corp. by Daimler Benz, Germany's largest industrial corporation, is formally a merger of equals. But the detailed terms make it clear that Daimler Benz will be calling the shots. Chrysler shareholders will receive a premium of nearly 40% for agreeing to give up control of the company. And billionaire Kirk Krekorian, the largest Chrysler shareholder, will make an additional profit of well over a billion dollars.

Top executives of Chrysler will get significant jobs in the merged company as well as huge financial payoffs—over $100 million for CEO Robert J. Eaton, and more than $20 million each for the seven other Chrysler executives directly involved in the merger.

Daimler Benz is under the wing of Germany's largest private bank, Deutsche Bank, which owns 22% of the stock. Also profiting from the deal is Kuwait, which owns 12% of Daimler Benz's stock.

As in the domestic financial mergers, Wall Street is very much involved with both Chrysler and Daimler Benz. But the merged company, Daimler-Chrysler AG, will be a German corporation, with operation centers in both countries. There is little doubt that the strings will be pulled from Stuttgart.

Obviously, it is very important for the United Auto Workers and the corresponding union of German auto workers to coordinate their actions to protect their members in both countries. The companies estimate that by the year 2000 the "synergies," that is, elimination of duplication of facilities, will amount to $3 billion and could cost the jobs of 60,000 autoworkers.

The $48 billion takeover of Amoco by British Petroleum (BP) is expected to set the stage for further mergers among the oil companies to deal with the 40% drop in the price for crude oil, now selling for about 30 cents per gallon. (Compare that with what you pay at the gas pump!) The pre-announced job cuts of 7,000 from this merger are probably a fraction of the job losses to come, considering the $2 billion per year in extra profits the merged company expects to make by cutting costs.

JP Morgan & Co. has long been symbolic of Wall Street power. But the amazing rumors of a possible takeover of Morgan by Deutsche Bank cannot be wholly discounted. As noted, Deutsche Bank is the leading stockholder of Daimler Benz, which is taking over Chrysler. (How the strands of international dealings intertwine!)

In the recent period, direct investments of European corporations in the United States have exceeded foreign direct investments of U.S. corporations. That is, French, German and Dutch companies have considerably larger holdings in the United States than American companies have in their countries. European capitalists' funds for investment are relatively larger, while the U.S. markets are growing faster. Japanese corporations, with $123 billion invested in the United States, have three times the U.S. corporate investment in Japan.

However, the total direct foreign investments by the U.S.—concentrated in Asia, Africa and Latin America—is greater than investments by foreign countries in the United States.

Up to now, the financial crises wracking more and more developing countries have not threatened U.S., European and Japanese corporate holdings in oil, textiles, auto, computer parts, etc., which take advantage of the prevailing poverty-level wages.

What is needed, of course, is a revolutionary resolution of the crises, which would likely involve repudiation of foreign debts and expropriation of capitalist corporations. U.S. governmental policies and actions focus on preventing such revolutionary solutions. But, while for the moment minimizing American corporate losses, these policies are making the crisis worse, thus increasing the need for a revolutionary solution.

5/15/1999

Bombs Boom, Stocks Zoom

The looming war economy promises a bonanza for big business. As the bombing of Yugoslavia started, the stock market took off—jumping 10% through early May. The Dow Jones index, which had been stuck below 10,000 for some time, reacted, not only reaching 10,000 but zooming past 11,000.

The Clinton-Albright-NATO aggression against Yugoslavia was brewing for the last 6 months. Anticipating the assault and the war orders to come, corporate sales and profits soared. Profits had been expected to stagnate or decline in the first quarter of 1999, but, in fact, for 100 large corporations they increased 18% over the same period in 1998.

The 300 members of the Business Council, the top moguls of monopoly capital, recently met. At a press conference of its nine-member executive committee—the heads of Citigroup, General Electric, Eastman Kodak, etc.—Sanford Weill, the Citigroup CEO, who was paid more than $100 million last year, summarized the unanimous sentiment of the group:

"This is really the best of times," he said, as other members of the committee smiled and nodded. "I don't think anyone at this table has seen better times," he added as he lauded seemingly unbridled economic expansion.

Quite a change from 6 months earlier when a number of CEOs fretted that impending profit squeezes would cause them to cut capital spending and hire fewer workers!

Current optimism is attributed to the fast economic growth during the past two quarters, indications that the world financial crisis is easing, retail sales are rising, and skimpy wage increases lag behind rising productivity.

But the underlying restorative was preparation for the assault that finally exploded in the cowardly bombing of Yugoslavia where, as the number of air raids increase, a number of non-military targets—hospitals, power grids, TV stations and now, the Chinese Embassy—have been hit and scores of civilians killed. And what about the attempts to assassinate the president of Yugoslavia and other leaders?

The payoff for industry came a couple of weeks ago, when Clinton and the Republican Congress made an emergency appropriation of $13 billion to pay for the war through September. Because of the balanced budget deal reached in 1997, the money will be taken from the Social Security surplus and the already underfunded federal authorizations for education, health, poverty and hunger programs.

For the stockholders and top brass of the mega-corporations, the $13 billion pays big dividends and accords uncounted billions of "collateral damage" to Yugoslavia's economy. So, by all means, let us be realistic about the motivation for the "humanitarian" aggression against Yugoslavia and Iraq: There is money to be made!

THE OPIUM POPPY

CIA and FBI

3/12/1967

The Multi-Millionaires Who Control the CIA

A chain of exposés has disclosed the vast scale and scope of big business collaboration with the CIA, has emphasized how the rich help the "Department of Dirty Tricks." But millionaires do nothing without expecting a more than proportionate return. Charity and patriotism are invoked only when they are good investments. Thus, to the well known use of "charitable" foundations as a tax-dodging device, we must add the use of underground activities and subversion at home and abroad.

For generations, employers have bribed pliable labor leaders, organized assassinations of militant workers, and financed far-right organizations. They carried out their own diplomatic and political interventions in countries they wanted to rob and exploit. And they still do all these things.

Now, however, they rely increasingly on the CIA. This way they can get much more "service" for their anti-labor, colonialist aims, and no longer have to pay for it. We do.

The CIA operates on a grander scale, with access to a bigger and more varied staff of murderers, liars, spies, and sundry skilled personnel than even the most powerful private corporation can muster. The CIA appeals to the misguided on the basis of patriotism, whereas the private corporation obviously acts only for its own profits.

The Dulles brothers, on their way towards becoming millionaires, spent most of their careers as agents of Wall Street bankers. John Foster finished as head of the State Department and Allen W. climaxed his career as chief of the CIA, directing the vast global network of foreign agents for the same Wall Street interests.

Ten years ago *Fortune* listed the 76 richest Americans, each with a fortune of over $75 million. Half a dozen appear directly or via an immediate relative in the incomplete list of CIA collaborators exposed recently. (Sometimes supermillionaires who help CIA on a given project are direct beneficiaries of that project; other times they are repaid through parallel CIA actions.)

Thomas Dudley Cabot, former president of the United Fruit Co. and chairman of the Cabot Corp. (carbon black trust), is the son and principal heir of Godfrey L. Cabot, listed among the 76. Thomas Cabot served as president of Gibraltar Steamship Co., a CIA dummy that operated the illegal Swan Island radio. Through this and other means Cabot was an active accessory to the CIA's Bay of Pigs invasion of Cuba. A major objective of that invasion was to restore millions of acres of Cuban soil to United Fruit.

A number of other representatives of the Boston aristocracy are involved in the CIA network, including the not-quite-so-rich Cabot Lodges. A United Fruit executive, Walter Turnbull, represented the CIA to contact Guatemalan militarist Ydigoras Fuentes to involve him in the CIA plot to overthrow the Arbenz Government for the benefit of United Fruit.

Roy A. Hunt is up with the du Ponts and Rockefellers in the 76 list. For many years president of Alcoa, this aged Mellon intimate is still a director, and one son is now a vice president, of the largest aluminum combine. The other son, Richard M. Hunt, gets some supplementary pin money as Assistant Dean at Harvard. Basically, this job is a front behind which Hunt heads the CIA's Fund for International Social and Economic Education, a branch for financing and organizing subversive activities among students and within unions in developing countries, principally in Latin America.

That's where the aluminum trust gets its bauxite, paying the workers and governments concerned about 1% of the ultimate value of the contained aluminum.

The CIA was active in recent coups and armed interventions in the Dominican Republic, using among other means students such as those financed through Hunt. The Dominican Republic is a major source of Alcoa bauxite.

It has been detailed how the CIA, through trade union stooges, organized the overthrow of the progressive Jagan administration in Guyana. Alcan, the U.S.-owned, Canadian-based aluminum company, is the largest foreign investor in Guyana, with big bauxite mines and an aluminum plant there. Alcan was once part of Alcoa, and there is still probably much interlocking stock ownership. Alcoa itself has large holdings in neighboring Surinam, and would face the prospect of having to pay more for Surinam bauxite if Guyana were able to reclaim its own resources.

Industrialist Henry Kaiser is another of the richest 76. The family-controlled Kaiser Corporation gave the CIA intelligence information derived from its last year's jeep-selling expedition to Eastern Europe. One direct repayment could be the licenses recently issued to sell jeeps to socialist countries. Formerly auto and truck sales were prohibited. But already the Kaisers have received a more important indirect payment: Kaiser Aluminum and Chemical is the largest U.S. investor in Ghana. Its position is rendered more profitable by the CIA-aided reactionary coup that overthrew Nkrumah last year.

Arthur A. Houghton, Jr., of Corning Glass, told *Fortune* that he was more interested in art than in business. Apparently he meant what Allen Dulles called "The Craft of Intelligence." For Houghton is president of the Foundation for Youth and Student Affairs, which is another of the top CIA fronts for subverting youth and religious organizations internationally. His cousin Amory is also a trustee of the Foundation. Both Arthur Houghton, Jr. and Amory Houghton, Sr.

are listed among those with over $100 million, derived from Corning Glass' monopoly patents.

The Houghtons are leading financiers of the Republican Party and hold directorships in many multi-billion dollar corporations, as well as trusteeships in Rockefeller and Morgan foundations. Amory Houghton, Jr. is a director of Dow Corning Corp., a joint company of Corning and napalm-making Dow Chemical.

The Houghtons are among the controlling inside group of the First National City Bank of New York, which, along with Chase Manhattan and Bank of America, moves in virtually everywhere that American imperialism establishes a foothold. Amory Sr. is currently a director, and Amory Jr. a member, of the trust advisory board of First National City. The Houghtons are truly global profiteers from CIA activities.

• • •

3/19/1967

The CIA Enriches the Rich

No U.S. corporate interests have received more services from the CIA than the Standard Oil companies with their $10 billion of foreign investments. And none is better represented in the top CIA hierarchy. Allen Dulles for decades headed Sullivan and Cromwell, top Wall Street law firm whose outstanding client is Standard Oil (N.J.).

Allen W. Dulles headed the CIA when it organized the coup against Iranian Premier Mossadegh, out of which the Standard Oil Trust was handed billions of dollars worth of oil that the Iranians had reclaimed from British exploiters. Kermit Roosevelt, known as "Mr. Iran" for his personal role in the CIA operation, was rewarded with a vice presidency in Gulf Oil, the Mellon company—another big winner from the Iran coup.

CIA plots to destroy the Sukarno regime in Indonesia began while Dulles was chief, and continued under the regime of John A. McCone, a Standard Oil of California director and large stockholder. This company, with its partner Texaco, was the main U.S. beneficiary of the ultimately successful reactionary coup. Sukarno's program of nationalizing oil was replaced with "incentives" for foreign investors.

Also active in the CIA network is the Pappas Foundation of Boston. Greek-born U.S. citizen Thomas A. Pappas controls it. Under the Truman Doctrine, Greece was the first victim of U.S. cold-war armed intervention, which resulted in establishment of a dictatorship under the kind of U.S. tutelage that has since become familiar in South Vietnam: putting low-wage Greek shipping at the disposal of the international oil cartel.

CIA aide Pappas, one-time special U.S. Ambassador to Uruguay, is temporary consul general for Greece in New England and, at the same time, is president of Esso Pappas, of Athens, of Hellenic Petrochemical Co., North Greece Ammonia Co., Salonika Refining Co., and others of the group.

The CIA, needless to say, is busy trying to defeat the movement for democratization of Greek life that the left and center are conducting. Victory of such forces would reduce the profits of Standard Oil and Pappas.

John Hay Whitney, recently revealed as a major CIA conduit, received much of his hundred millions plus as an heir of the Payne Standard Oil fortune, part of which he used to buy up control of the New York *Herald Tribune*. Whitney has been a partner of the Rockefellers in a number of postwar munitions enterprises, and allied with them and the Houghtons in Republican Party politics.

A trustee in Houghton's Foundation for Youth and Student Affairs is Francis T. P. Plimpton, partner in Debevoise, Plimpton & McLean, personal law firm of the Rockefeller family, and a trustee of U.S. Trust Co., which is controlled by Whitney and the Astors. Robert E. Blum (Abraham & Straus-Federated Department Stores), another trustee of this CIA front, is connected with the Rockefeller and Whitney interests through directorships in Equitable Life, Brooklyn Union Gas, New York Airways, and Lincoln Center of Performing Arts.

What happens to the funds the CIA turns over to foundations before they dribble into the hands of the ultimate CIA agents? The J. M. Kaplan Fund channeled $1 million for the CIA to labor schools and publishing houses in Costa Rica, the Dominican Republic, and Mexico, besides other money paid to the National Students Association, etc., in the U.S.

Jacob M. Kaplan, chairman of the Board of Trustees of the New School for Social Research, specialized for the CIA in financing "leftist" and "socialist" anti-Communist setups, those time-tried means by which the right-wing strives to split the left.

Through their CIA connections, big businessmen get access to the entire pool of information conned by the sprawling U.S. "intelligence community," information worth billions. The top capitalists have representatives on the Foreign Intelligence Advisory Board, a central control agency over the CIA and other intelligence branches. Among its members are munitions executive Frank Pace Jr., Corning Glass director Robert D. Murphy, again Corning Glass, Polaroid chairman Edwin H. Land, Bell Telephone research director William O. Baker, Rockefeller-connected hawk propagandist Gen. Maxwell Taylor, and newspaper owner Gordon Gray.

Richard J. Barber cites this board as a prime example of how big business gets rewarded for its collaboration with the administration in power:

> "One example is the Foreign Intelligence Advisory Board ... So great is its authority that it is informed in detail of the CIA's plans and methods of operation, precisely the information which will not be given to any Senator or Congressman who does not sit on existing oversight subcommittees.
>
> "Yet, with the present composition of the Board, such details are regularly disclosed to executives of American Telephone and Telegraph, the Polaroid Corp., and Corning Glass. Much other valuable information reaches Robert Kintner, a high

White House Staff aide, and former President of NBC." (*New Republic*, Aug. 13, 1966.)

CIA activities increase international tension, help speed up the arms race and add to the military budget. So munitions companies get repaid many times for collaboration with the CIA.

• • •

7/3/1971

Millions for Repression (FBI)

Press Item: House Appropriations Committee grants Hoover full FBI budget request, slashes Equal Employment Opportunities Commission.

Background: With increases over Nixon's original budget approved by the committee, total appropriations for what is ironically called "law enforcement and justice" in fiscal year 1972, which just began, will come to about $1,650,000,000.

Less than 10% of this is for general law enforcement—as against narcotics, racketeers, counterfeiters, etc. Less than 1% is for enforcement of the anti-trust laws. Nine-tenths of it is for repression. An additional billion dollars is for "reduction of crime," but not included in the budget category of "law enforcement and justice." The largest part of this, over $600,000,000, is for "crime reduction" by the Department of Defense—the repression of GIs by the military police, spying on civilians by Pentagon agencies, etc.

So it is valid to speak of $2.5 billion this year for war against the American people. Only 10 years ago, spending on "law enforcement and justice" was $300 million. It has multiplied five times in a decade.

The FBI is the lead agency of governmental repression. To millions of Americans, it has lost its TV gloss and stands exposed as a ruthless foe of all decent trends, all struggles of the American people.

The House Appropriations Committee not only gave Hoover everything he wanted, but even more than Nixon asked for. The amount approved was $334.4 million. That's $16 million more than Nixon's original budget request; it's $40 million, or 16.3%, more than was appropriated for fiscal 1971.

The long-term comparison is even more shocking. In 1948 the FBI appropriation was $35 million. Ten years later, in 1958, the FBI appropriation passed $100 million. In 1962 it was $127 million. In fiscal 1969, the last year for which Johnson was responsible, it was $220 million.

Other federal appropriations for repression have jumped even faster. The House Appropriations Committee also granted everything requested by the Law Enforcement Assistance Administration (LEAA), just shy of $700 million. This is the agency that specializes in beefing up local police departments for "control of civil disorders"—which means assaults on peace demonstrations, Black, Chicano, Indian, and Puerto Rican communities, mass picket lines of strikers, etc. It's also a boon for the corporations specializing in technically advanced weaponry.

The LEAA is a new program, which began with an appropriation of $60 million in fiscal 1969.

Matching the FBI in growth are the salaries of U.S. attorneys and marshals, and fees and expenses paid to government stoolpigeons. The former comes to $83 million in the present fiscal year, more than doubled under Nixon. The latter comes to $6.5 million this fiscal year, up 50% in the last three years.

One item in the 10%—for general law enforcement—not directly for repression is the $9 million appropriated to the Secret Service to protect "major" presidential and vice presidential candidates in 1972, commencing with the primaries. But why no protection for the "minor" candidates?

• • •

1/15/1994

Abolish the CIA

As President Clinton prepares the new budget that includes $29 billion for the CIA and related intelligence agencies, it might be well to ask the question: "Who needs the CIA, anyway?"

By way of answering, one might first answer another question: Who is R. James Woolsey Jr., the head of the CIA?

Woolsey is a classic example of the "revolving door" that under Clinton has been spinning faster than under even George Bush or Ronald Reagan. Woolsey's career has see-sawed between government and the private sector: a staffer on the Senate Arms Service Committee; a member of a Washington law firm representing military contractors; undersecretary of the Navy; arms control negotiator; director of Martin Marietta, a leading armaments profiteer. When Clinton took the reins of government, he appointed his good friend from the neighboring state of Oklahoma as CIA chief. The CIA, of course, provides uncounted billions in foreign orders for armament manufacturers and space equipment companies.

According to *The New York Times*, Woolsey lost out in his bid to succeed Les Aspin as Secretary of Defense because he had some differences in interpretation of issues with Clinton, but more to the point, because he had quarrels with Congress over the CIA budget.

Woolsey demanded an increase over and above the $29 billion allocated for the CIA, the National Security Agency, the National Reconnaissance Office, and other spy agencies. But with even the Pentagon taking some cuts and the CIA's main target, the USSR, no longer in existence, congressional leaders were in sharp conflict with Woolsey, finally lowering his budget a trivial $1 billion. The $28 billion he got, however, is more than the federal government spends for education, or for the environment, or for transportation.

So what is the motive for a huge CIA and related agencies budget now?

- Obviously, the cushy jobs of many bureaucrats. But Congress also had its orders—the instructions of its corporate and financial bosses.
- The former Soviet Union probably remains the main target: It is the only nuclear power capable of resisting U.S. imperialism, which is still trying to cripple Russia's armed forces; it is the most promising, previously untapped, target for the export of capital and source of superprofits; its vast natural resources and pool of low-wage, skilled workers are irresistible.

So far, however, American monopolies are losing out to those from West Europe. The former Soviet Union has more than doubled its trade surplus with the European Union (EU) since 1989, and its exports to the EU reached $20 billion in 1992—compared to less than $1 billion to the United States. While the former USSR has become a happy hunting ground for maquiladora-type operations of West European capitalists, U.S. monopolies are playing for bigger prizes: Exxon, Mobil and Chevron are all staking billions on the world's richest oil and gas fields, up for grabs with Yeltsin's blessings.

- With the more advantageous balance of forces, U.S. imperialism is homing in for the kill on the remaining socialist countries—notably Cuba, North Korea, and Vietnam. At this stage, the CIA is trying to stir up disaffection with Castro on account of the harsh conditions imposed by the U.S. blockade; the National Reconnaissance Office's spy satellites provide the "evidence" of nuclear weapons that Clinton is using as an excuse for his threats to invade North Korea; and the CIA is backing the MIA-POW organizations' claims of missing Americans in Vietnam.

The CIA and its related agencies are corrupt; are organizers of wars and assassinations; are instigators of coups and counterrevolutions; are involved in wholesale, illegal drug dealing. They perform no positive services. The CIA should be abolished.

• • •

3/15/1997

CIA's Interns: 'School of the Assassins'

The PWW's article by Julia Lutsky, "Shut down 'School of the Assassins'," was very timely. It referred to Rep. Joseph Kennedy's bill to that effect and featured the photo of a Los Angeles demonstration against the CIA's role as drug dealer bringing crack into U.S. cities. And it was timely because of *The New York Times* article that reveals that the CIA is keeping on its payroll most of its hired murderers and torturers.

The New York Times headline (3/3/97) is "CIA Breaks Links to 100 Foreign Agents," and I quote:

> "[The CIA] found . . . the violence and corruption of scores of those inform-ers so bad, and the quality of the information they provided comparatively so mar-ginal, that they were not worth the thousands or tens of thousands of dollars they were paid annually."

The *Times* reported that 1,000 of the CIA's foreign agents failed to meet the test of providing enough information to justify the murder and tortures of their victims. Apparently only 100 of the thousand have been fired, but 2,000-3,000 agents did pass the test, according to the article. That is, they fingered trade union-ists, Communists and peasant leaders accurately enough to "justify" the bombing of villages, the murder of whole families, and filling prisons with workers and peasants. The article notes:

"Throughout Latin America, Asia, the Middle East and Africa, the agency has long-standing official liaisons with military, intelligence and security ser-vices. Some of the officers of these services are violent or corrupt, but they are among the CIA's most valued informers."

Note that they **are** currently employed, not **were**.

"The agency also has had on its payroll people who are terrorists and drug dealers, or used to be terrorists and drug dealers. These people provide informa-tion that the CIA says is difficult to obtain elsewhere."

Again, they **provide** it, present tense.

> ". . . a Presidential panel, the Intelligence Oversight Board, reported in June that the CIA knowingly hired as paid informers Guatemalan military officers suspected of political assassinations, murder, kidnapping and torture.
>
> "Nor were these examples unique to Guatemala. They were repeated throughout Central America, where the CIA had been deeply involved in clandestine operations in support of pro-American governments and military regimes from the early 1950s onward."

Pro-American? Actually neo-colonial, subservient to Wall Street and engag-ing in overthrowing popularly elected progressive governments, abetted by U.S. troops, as in the Dominican Republic.

Pro-American? Certainly not pro-the-American-people. Not pro-U.S. work-ers. CIA operations in Central America, for example—in addition to slaughtering many thousands of peasants—forced many times more off the land to provide vir-tual slave labor for U.S. manufacturing corporations that had run away to a low-wage utopia. The goods produced there are then exported to the United States, cutting down jobs here. And these factors, in turn, force mass emigration to the United States, often at risk of lives, in the hope of getting work. Such jobs, if forth-coming at all, are on terms that further drive down conditions of all U.S. workers.

And now, of course, CIA operations are bearing fruit for the transnationals on an even larger scale, as subversive activities are certainly being expanded in the former socialist countries of Eastern Europe and USSR. And there will be constant replacements, reinforcements, enlistments for the thousands of goons currently being trained at the fascistic School of the Assassins at Fort Benning, Georgia, and at other such establishments not yet exposed.

Remember that neither the CIA, the FBI, nor the larger U.S. Intelligence Agency, nor the Army and Navy intelligence outfits, are mavericks operating on their own. They are all purposeful operations of the billionaire rulers of America, and are fully as important as the military establishment or the diplomatic corps in enforcing U.S. foreign policy.

BILLIONS for WAR

AMERICAN PEOPLE

Fred Ellis
May 6, 1952

Militarism

7/22/1961

Who Is Forcing Spurt in the Arms Race?

Washington war hysteria reached new peaks following Premier Khrushchev's speech announcing a sharp rise in Soviet military spending and an end to troop reductions. Secretary of State Rusk demanded a world-wide anti-Communist crusade; Gen. Norstad a NATO military buildup; President Kennedy more foreign aid—with the threat to forcibly impose capitalism where he can't buy it.

The President ordered a fresh study of defense needs, with the likelihood of a third rise in the military budget to follow. A massive publicity campaign seeks public support for this ominous course.

Americans should not be stampeded, should consider carefully Khrushchev's statement to judge for themselves whether he had to raise the Soviet military budget to meet western actions, as he claimed.

With the increase, Soviet 1961 defense outlays will total 12.4 billion rubles (new money), equivalent to $13.6 billion. The U.S. will spend about $49 billion. (Khrushchev spoke of $53 billion here, but that was for fiscal 1962 and probably included foreign defense support, civil defense, etc., omitted from the official U.S. total). The USSR avoids the colossal profiteering that inflates Pentagon procurement, and presumably gets more per ruble for its money. Still, they are spending a lot less, no matter what allowances are made.

What share of the national income goes for arms? The Soviet national income this year will approximate 156 billion rubles ($172 billion). Ours will be about $428 billion, but one-third consists of services not included in the Soviet national income concept. Calculated the same way, U.S. national income will be

$284 billion. Soviet military spending, therefore, will be 8% of their national income; ours will be 17% of our comparably calculated national income.

Now consider the trend. Khrushchev's increase was 3.14 billion rubles ($3.5 billion). The annual rate of U.S. military spending, spurred by Eisenhower's, and especially Kennedy's, speedups, has already gone up $3.5 billion in the last 12 months. *Fortune* estimates that a further rise of $3 billion per year is already assured through fiscal 1963, for a total of $9.5 billion—or almost three times the Khrushchev increase.

Kennedy's increase is on top of a gradual rise since 1955, when the Korean War demobilization was completed and a fresh, but slow, arms buildup began. Meanwhile, the USSR, striving to encourage disarmament agreements, was gradually cutting military outlays—by 13% altogether between 1955 and the present year, as originally planned. The Kennedy spurt in arms spending, and his evident intention to abandon disarmament negotiations, while threatening war over Berlin, caused the shift in Soviet arms spending.

Even so, the comparison with 1955 is as follows: Soviet spending now shows a rise from 10.5 billion rubles then to 12.4 billion in 1961; ours rises from $39.1 billion to $49 billion. Theirs goes up 2 billion rubles, ours 10 billion dollars. Theirs goes up 18%, ours 25%.

The Soviet action in ceasing to curtail the size of its armed forces also followed a U.S. lead in militarization. Under Kennedy, the size of the U.S. forces, which had been gradually declining, has already turned upwards: from May 1960 to May 1961, it increased 9,000, and a larger gain is scheduled.

Premier Khrushchev stressed the 13% rise in the FRG (West German) military budget. Yes, the USSR not only has to cope with the U.S. arms buildup, but also the still faster growing, neo-Nazi war drive. According to *Business Week*, FRG annual spending on military hardware is scheduled to rise 67%, and "West Germany is slated to become the largest military force in Western Europe—within the next two years."

Or sooner! For Norstad and Gen. Heusinger, who had served Hitler and now serves NATO, are using Berlin as an excuse to immediately put the West Germans in the van in NATO. According to a UPI dispatch from NATO headquarters, after the buildup, West Germany will have 12 divisions, the U.S. 8 divisions and brigades, and all other NATO countries combined another 10 in Western Europe.

Capitalist politicians, criminally irresponsible toward their own people, ignore the lessons of two World Wars, of the Nuremberg and Eichmann trials. The Soviet Union, a socialist humanitarian state, which suffered most from German militarism, cannot and will not.

Washington buries the news that Khrushchev accompanied his budget announcement with another impassioned plea for a peace conference on the Berlin question. Rusk responded with a denunciation of Soviet calls for negotiation.

Some conservative Americans retain their sanity. *The New York Times'* C. L. Sulzberger was shocked into full awareness of the seriousness of the situation, and called for international parleys over Berlin as "an alternative to autumnal suicide for the world."

Doubtless there will be many more such expressions in coming days.

Readers! Digest the facts shown here. Call for an immediate halt to the war-threatening military buildup of the Pentagon and the neo-Nazis; for the serious disarmament negotiations that President Kennedy promised to make his first order of foreign policy business when he was running for office.

• • •

12/15/1962

Global War Contractor No. 1: Lockheed

The Pentagon has just revealed that Lockheed Aircraft Corp. is now No. 1 munitions contractor of the U.S., and hence of the world.

Whence comes the power of this corporation, now in the public eye for its attempt, with White House assistance, to Taft-Hartleyize the union shop? Lockheed has risen fast by promoting and participating in the cold war. Its record employment was in World War II; but profit-wise, that holocaust was just a beginning:

Year	Sales (millions)	Profits after-tax (millions)	Employees (1,000's)	Sales per empl.	Profits per empl.
1943	$967	$ 8	94	$10,300	$85
1953	820	15	52	15,800	288
1962p	1,700	41*	80	21,200	513

*Includes special credit of $3 million.

Lockheed now does 2.5 times its peak World War II business, and double its Korean War peak. Profits are five times above 1943, with 15% fewer employees. Employment of production workers, represented by the Intl. Assn. of Machinists, has fared worse. Today, I estimate, only about 44,000 are production workers, as compared with perhaps 38,000 in 1953 and 76,000 in 1943. Sales per production worker have reached the phenomenal total of $40,000 yearly, or seven times average wages. I estimate their total wages are $270 million, or only 16% of Lockheed's sales, and 25% of its in-plant work (non-subcontracted).

Responding to the growth in profits and prospects, investors have bid up Lockheed stock from a market value of $55 million in mid-1953 to $400 million now, or seven times as much. Unlike stocks generally, this exceeds the 1961 bull market peak.

Profits Hidden

As with an iceberg, above-surface published profits are a deceptively small portion of the actual take. Because of the open-end situation on sales to the government, with the only serious hitches coming from taxes and labor demands, the aerospace companies have maneuvered profit concealment to its pinnacle.

A portion of the hidden profits is the catchall category of "administrative and general expenses." These jumped from $52 million in 1958 to $96 million in 1962. Depreciation multiplied five times in nine years.

A substantial portion of the phony accounting expenses are siphoned off in a hundred different ways by the inner clique: owners of the control blocks of shares, their relatives, trusted lawyers and bankers, favor-doers, close pals and toadies, company owners who sold out to them in mergers. They receive millions of dollars yearly in salaries, bonuses, expense accounts, retirement benefits and stock options. Already stock options granted, or authorized, cover one-tenth of the outstanding corporate stock.

The 1961 annual meeting voted, against significant opposition, to issue 300,000 more shares to the 271 favored top officers and executives (most go to the top 10).

Actually, only fractions of the insiders' "take" have ever been traced by outside investigators. All that is known is that characteristically this company, like others in the field, gets away with charges to the government often several times the actual production costs. Data for a typical P2V contract filled at Burbank, revealed in a 1956 hearing, showed that of the total price of $167,123,000 charged the government, $55,806,000 represented subcontracts and $111,317,000 represented work in the Burbank plant.

Of this sum, only $24 million represented raw materials and direct labor, while $77 million represented profits and overhead. No durable goods company with civilian customers would dream of getting away with a price equal to more them four times its direct costs. Obviously, in this situation, besides the very substantial $14 million admitted profits, much of the $32 million "administrative and overhead" costs, and much of the $21 million "engineering development and research" costs, on this old standard model of plane, was really concealed profit.

As a concession to one of the periodic eruptions of congressional concern over waste, the Air Force turned to competitive bidding on a few of the sales of spare parts previously made by "sole source" prime contractors. This was reported in a 1961 hearing. A bracket assembly, previously Lockheed's private baby at $11.11 each, went to the low bidder at 88¢. A $2.59 Lockheed bolt went under the hammer at 12¢. Some small company figured it could make a profit at 5% of Lockheed's price!

Lockheed officials are particularly pleased with Defense Secretary Robert S. McNamara because, among other things, he has instituted an "improved" incentive price system and has joined with airplane companies in resisting Renegotiation Board attempts to recover excess profits.

Militarism Boosted

The recent big jump in Lockheed business and profits was helped by accelerated war preparations. During the first two years of the Kennedy administration, the aerospace industries' military market has risen 44%. Said Chairman Gross in May 1961:

"The new administration's approach in the past few months has been refreshing," including high military spending both for all-out and for limited war. "It is a strong and wise policy, I think, and it has given our nation a new vigor and an improved sense of direction." It is "fortunate" that the new policy is in areas good for Lockheed. For all-out war, he cited the Polaris missile, with which Lockheed hit the jackpot. For limited war, he cited troop transports (Lockheed got the contract for the all-jet C-1141), the patrol plane, and the fighter, where Lockheed has the standard Starfighter.

"Even in the event of partial disarmament or arms control," he continued, "we have a program that contributes to the complicated inspection system that may be necessary to achieve our peace aims."

This sentence, I submit, exposes a real motive behind the tricky verbiage used by Wall Street lawyer Arthur H. Dean, U.S. disarmament negotiator, and others to justify "arms control" and "inspection" formulas. It is an attempt to appease the public demand for ending the thermonuclear war danger with a trick that will permit the munitions makers to continue receiving superprofits and the Pentagon to continue threatening mass annihilation.

Lockheed unabashedly advocates aggressive foreign policy and militarism, deplores any economies in the arms race.

Lockheed has also benefited from increasing its share of military business. During the Korean War, Lockheed ranked 8th among armament prime contractors. But by fiscal 1960 it was in second place, in fiscal 1961 in third place, and in fiscal 1962, finally, it reached the top of the heap.

So satisfied is Lockheed with military prospects that it has abandoned the civilian field.

• • •

2/16/1964

The Military Budget

The trend of military expenditures will have crucial importance in foreign and domestic policy. By it the world will gauge, in part, U.S. sincerity in disarmament conferences, influencing the possibility of effective compromises in the negotiations. It will strongly affect the amounts available for expanded federal programs in housing, education, etc.

Will the administration carry out Johnson's "peace drive," or his colonialist pretensions and McNamara's super-genocidal military strategy? Will it carry out

Johnson's "war on poverty," or tinker with it, as suggested in early messages, limited by the failure to free funds from a militarized budget?

The new budget provides clues. Military and related spending rises from $58.2 billion in fiscal 1963 to an estimated $62.9 billion in fiscal 1964.

Hard goods authority jumped sharply in 1963, and would have risen further this fiscal year, according to the original budget. But with tensions easing, and economy pressures growing, congressional authorizations actually only equaled the fiscal 1963 amount; and Johnson asked for $2 billion less in fiscal 1965.

Hanson Baldwin reports in *The New York Times* that the Pentagon feels squeezed by this procurement cut, and ultimately will require a sharp rise in buying new weapons for the undiminished armed forces. McNamara's hair-raising strategy suggests new programs in the tens of billions for anti-missile missiles and "civilian defense."

How can the American peace movement counter this and make the tentative munitions downtrend stick?

Important labor leaders have taken increasingly definite pro-peace and pro-disarmament positions, and connected them with labor's demands. The January *Bulletin* of the Industrial Union Department of the AFL-CIO states:

"Meanwhile, jobs remain the major problem of the U.S. domestic economy . . . . With cuts in defense, a great new opportunity faces the nation. The time has come to improve the quality of American life by allocating greater resources to the public sector and to the fight against poverty."

Joint activities by peace and labor organizations would bring millions of Americans into the struggle for peace, decisively multiplying the power of the struggle to counter the war drive of the militarists.

• • •

2/6/1966

A Field Day for War Profiteers

The administration combined its propaganda "peace offensive" with actions designed to prevent peace in Vietnam. An important war action was accelerated military procurement. Early in the "peace offensive" the administration realized its intention to submit the enormous supplemental appropriation of $12.7 billion. This finally went to Congress just as the ceasefire of the Vietnamese New Year was to go into effect.

In his State of the Union message, Johnson revealed the decisive military orientation of his budget. The Pentagon revealed its intention to draft and hire another 207,000 recruits, besides the 340,000 announced in mid-1965. The flow of armament orders approached a semi-mobilization pace.

The extent of the military buildup during its first stage—that is, before the "peace offensive"—is revealed by the following Commerce Department figures on monthly average new orders for defense equipment (millions):

1961		$1,828
1964		$2,260
1965:	first 10 months	$2,773
	Sept-Oct	$3,378

The increase in 1965 alone exceeded the cumulative gain in the previous 3 years. In the autumn, there was a sharp jump to a level 50% higher than in 1964 and 85% higher than in 1961.

Various reports reflect the new and higher stage of procurement in the last 2 months. The government has started to impose wartime priorities and command production orders. Military set-asides of aluminum have been raised to an annual rate of over a billion pounds. Copper exports have been forbidden. Twenty manufacturers were given mandatory orders to produce trousers for the military after insufficient voluntary bids were received. Priority assignments for deliveries have jumped to 150 monthly. Defense Department spending in the first 18 days of 1966, as reported in the *Daily Treasury Statement*, ran 37% above the first 18 days of 1965.

Business Week reports (Jan. 22), "Military spending for Vietnam will shoulder its way into every corner of the economy for a long time, sometimes pushing civilian dollars aside." Defense Department contracts in the period July-November 1965 ran 25% ahead of the corresponding 1964 period; but, since November, "Generals say that Army spending has doubled; the Defense Supply Agency reports that contracts for all service items are 90 percent above this time last year."

The government strives to develop new and more frightful weapons of mass destruction. General Telephone & Electronics Corp. mars its sponsored radio symphony programs with a sabre-rattling ad in which it boasts of attempts to develop military lasers (a potential death-ray weapon).

Business Week also adds two more to the list of corporate candidates for war criminal trials, identifying makers of the crop poisons used in the notorious "Operation Ranch Hand,"* recently denounced by scientists. These are the billion-dollar chemical giants Dow Chemical and Monsanto.

Business Week reports that only 40% of the Pentagon purchasing spree will go "directly" to the fighting in Vietnam. This supports my charge that the militarists are using the war in Vietnam as an excuse for a general increase in the militarization of the country, and as a screen behind which to prepare more and bigger wars of colonial conquest.

* Refers to use of defoliants in Vietnam.

4/23/1967

Anti-Personnel Bombs Are Profitable

"U.S. Aides Forecast Rise in the Bombing of Vietnam" reads the headline over a report of 68,000 tons of bombs dropped on North and South Vietnam in February, four times the Korean War rate and over twice the peak rate against Japan (*The New York Times,* 3/17).

Total bomb production is being cut to reduce excessive stockpiles. But output of the new fragmentation bomb, favorite of the Air Force, is mounting radically.

The March letter of 800 leading Catholics condemned "emphatically and un-ambiguously . . . (1) indiscriminate bombing which grossly destroys any suffi-cient distinction between combatant and civilian; (2) the horrible destruction of human life by means of napalm and fragmentation bombs. . . ." (*The Times,* 3/19).

U.S. military briefings boast of the effectiveness of these fragmentation bombs, used widely in both parts of Vietnam. The Air Force prefers the Bomb Live Unit BLU-26, which "was introduced in Vietnam about a year ago and is be-ing used in increasing numbers." (*Metalworking News,* 4/3). This year alone the Air Force is contracting for over $100 million of this single type of "anti-personnel bomb," a die cast sphere, 3 inches in diameter, containing 300 steel-aluminum pellets $\frac{3}{16}$ inches in diameter. Six hundred-seventy BLU-26's containing 200,000 of the steel-pellet killers are contained in one Cluster Bomb Unit, CBU-24 or CBU-29.

Life's Lee Lockwood reports from North Vietnam:

"Much of the outrage against U.S. bombing is directed at the use of anti-personnel bombs—particularly the CBUs . . . canisters which burst in the air, each scattering 300 baseball-sized explosives which detonate on impact, each spraying hundreds of pea-sized pellets at high velocity over a wide area. **The pel-lets are coated with napalm and stick when they hit**" (*Life,* 4/7).

These weapons are procured by the Deputy Director for Limited War (lim-ited!), Wright-Patterson Field, Dayton, Ohio. According to a *Metalworking News* story from that base:

"Reportedly, some die casters have shied away from the project. If the Air Force knows the reasons, they are not being discussed" (4/03).

An Air Force spokesman tried to justify use of the mass murder weapons thus:

"We are losing a lot of people and equipment in Vietnam because of the na-ture of the conflict. The BLU-26 is one of our most effective weapons." He said the Air Force is trying to develop better fuses to make them still more effective (*Ibid.*).

The "nature of the conflict" is a war of the U.S. military against the entire Vietnamese people, which it is trying to decimate. However, the Vietnamese people are taking a heavier toll of U.S. military lives and weapons than official Washington admits.

9/30/1967

Money, Missiles and Aggression

The morning radio reports that Washington will shortly announce the go-ahead for the multi-billion dollar Nike-X anti-ballistic missile system (ABM).

The propaganda buildup for this step started with the administration's hypocritical proposal to the USSR early this year to agree not to produce ABMs, while refusing to stop the U.S. buildup of offensive nuclear "overkill" capacity. Recently Washington has been publicizing inspired "intelligence" and "research" reports about the Russians "closing the missile gap." This is a transparent attempt to make people think we "need" the ABMs to protect ourselves. Any relationship to the real balance of military power is purely accidental.

Foreshadowing the big plunge, the Army let $231 million in R&D contracts on the Nike-X early in September. How large a production program is Johnson about to announce? If he acts according to his pattern, he will start with the $4-$5 billion "thin" defense and gradually escalate to the $40-billion plus "thick" defense.

Militarily this means intensified preparation for global nuclear war, and a further blow to prospects for serious disarmament talks. It fits Johnson's increasing alignment with the most sinister hawks. With the shadow of defeat looming ever larger in Vietnam, Johnson and his generals plan to avert or offset that defeat with even more destructive, dangerous aggression.

Economically, it is a fresh victory for the munitions giants. Their profit gains are slow, as an increasing share of the rising military budget must go for the routine supplies, payroll, and operating expenses of the escalating conflict. They clamor for a big new bonanza. Several billions were spent at earlier stages of the Nike program, producing equipment that couldn't do the job.

But it did create a scandalous profit pyramid, topped by Western Electric, the AT&T subsidiary, as prime contractor, and by Douglas Aircraft as main subcontractor. Most of the work was done by third-tier subcontractors. Douglas tacked another 10% for its profits onto that, often without even touching the goods produced. Each of these giants stands to make hundreds of millions in profits from the "thin" system, billions from the "thick" system.

AT&T, the world's largest corporation, has been slapped on the wrist by the FCC and may have to cut some long-distance telephone rates. It wants to make up that loss many times over. Douglas was taken over this spring by McDonnell Aircraft, the fast growing Pentagon-pampered munitions giant, the favorite weapons maker of the Rockefellers and chosen instrument of the Wall Street bankers to absorb Douglas. Those are forces Johnson obeys.

The President's 10% tax hike is in trouble, despite the all-out support of the dominant financiers, the establishment economists and George Meany (president of the AFL-CIO). A few big businessmen and some economists have stayed off the bandwagon; 99% of the voters have it in for any congressman who votes for this new robbery of their pockets. Rep. Mills (chairman of the House Ways and

Means Committee) and the conservative opponents are calling on the administration to cut spending instead. But Johnson calculates that with a fresh $5-$10 billion bill for "necessary" munitions that Congress dare not oppose, resisters will give in and "admit" that the tax hike is necessary to prevent inflationary chaos.

The ABM deal fits the administration's political pattern. It heads into a massive shelter program, increasing restrictions, forced drilling and "defense preparations" imposed on the civilian population. It is a step in the scheme for a garrison state. It blends perfectly with Johnson's speech to the police convention egging them on in their racist assaults against the Negro people.

The Nike-X program can be made to seem very logical: the USSR is erecting an ABM system to defend against our missiles, so we must erect one to defend against theirs. But this symmetry is illusory. The arms race is not everybody's fault. It is specifically the fault of the U.S. government, the world's aggressive power, which surrounds the USSR with nuclear bases, conducts a war of conquest in Vietnam, rebuffs all UN and other genuine disarmament initiatives. The Pentagon admits the Nike-X will not save scores of millions of Americans from near instant annihilation in the event of nuclear war. Actually, the main objective of the generals is to protect the offensive nuclear missile bases and military command headquarters, not the civilian centers.

• • •

10/21/1972

Peace Means Production

President Nixon's hatchetman Spiro Agnew charges that Sen. McGovern's military budget cuts would put 1.8 million munitions workers out of jobs. Nonsense! There aren't that many left! Nixon, the Pentagon and the armament corporations have accomplished the "miracle" of raising military budget authorizations to an all-time high, have collaborated to raise profits to record levels, while reducing employment in the munitions industries to the lowest level in 20 years.

In the officially designated "defense products industries"—aircraft, communications equipment, ordnance, missiles, etc.—employment of production workers declined 47%, and of white collar employees 29%, between 1968 and 1971. By the spring of 1972, man-hours of employment were down by one-third, and payrolls of production workers were down by more than one-fifth, while shipments were up by 10%, all in comparison with 1967.

Contrary to Pentagon propaganda, the huge military budget no longer directly provides a major part of private civilian employment. In June 1972 there were only 573,000 production workers and 540,000 other workers in the "defense products industries." That's why California, Connecticut and Washington, leaders in military production, are now also among the "leaders" in the rate of unemployment.

If Nixon is re-elected and puts over his intended increase in the direct military budget to over $100 billion per year, this will **not** mean more employment in the munitions industries, but it **will** mean more unemployment and inflation in the economy generally, because of the added financial drain.

In 1967 there was one production worker for each $23,630 of value added by manufacture in the munitions industries. But in 1971 there was only one production worker for each $40,620 of value added. The value of products per worker rose 71%, while wages per worker increased only 20%. Never was there so rapid a shift in values created from the worker-creators to employers, from wages to profits, and, in this situation, from all of the country's worker-taxpayers to the munitions profiteers.

What would happen if civilian business were substituted for military business, dollar for dollar? In contrast with the munitions industries, there was one construction worker for every $19,590 of value added in the construction industry in 1971, one production worker for every $21,060 of value added in production of construction materials, and one for every $24,360 of value added in manufacturing generally.

Thus, if construction work were substituted for munitions, blue-collar employment would be doubled; and if the substitution were made by government "force account" (under government control), without private contractor profits eating up a sizable chunk, employment would be tripled.

Shipments of "defense products" came to $44,205 million in 1971. This was the equivalent of 1,088,000 production worker jobs in munitions industries and in the plants of their subcontractors and suppliers. The same amount of money spent on construction sites would yield 2,256,000 jobs; for construction materials, 2,099,000 production worker jobs; and for manufactured goods generally, 1,815,000 production worker jobs. If the construction were done by government "force account," it would provide 25% more jobs, or a total of 3,008,000. Government health, education and recreation programs would yield even more jobs for the same number of dollars.

A glaring example of the lack of employment potential in the aerospace industries followed the award of a $2.6 billion contract to North American Rockwell for the space shuttle. The corporation estimates that at the peak, in three years, there will be a net increase of only 5,000 jobs. Grumman, one of the losers in the competition, will lay off 1,500; and McDonnell Douglas, another loser, will lay off 11,000 in the next two years. So the net effect of another $2.6 billion of government spending will be a loss of 7,500 jobs! And that's the way it will be with all the grandiose big spending programs of the administration for new bombers, missiles, submarines, etc.

McGovern promises to cut the military budget $30 billion, and to provide civilian programs with a higher job content. And, indeed, the overall prospect would be somewhat better than under Nixon. But not decisively. McGovern's program is insufficient to make a major dent in the unemployment situation, and his overall approach to foreign policy casts doubt on whether major cuts in military spending actually will take place. A prime example is his statement that "We must continue to retain sufficient American power" in the Middle East.

A Hall-Tyner administration would solve the problem of unemployment in the munitions industries and everywhere else:

- By nationalizing munitions industries and retaining all their employees at useful civilian work.
- By spending the entire sum now going for military purposes to meet the needs of the people, providing millions of additional jobs.
- By raising minimum wages to $5.00 per hour [from $1.60], and minimum family (of four) incomes to $6,500, while rolling back monopoly prices and shifting the tax burden from the poor to the rich. This would vastly increase the consumer market and thereby add more millions of jobs.
- By guaranteeing employment at regular wages, without any spending limit, to all able to work, in government enterprises and projects set up to provide the goods and services needed by the people, especially the poor and oppressed.

What about the hundreds of thousands of scientific and technical workers already let out of the munitions industries? A Hall-Tyner administration would hire them all to help solve the problems of the environment, of mass transportation, of urban planning and housing; to provide health and educational services on an expanded and qualitatively higher level. Indeed, there would immediately appear a shortage of engineers, scientific workers and technicians, rather than a shortage of jobs for them. A Hall-Tyner administration would multiply the training of new technical and scientific workers to make possible the full realization of its overall program.

• • •

7/19/1975

Pentagon Corruption: CIA style

The most serious and extravagant bribes are associated with the military-industrial-intelligence complex. When Grumman sold F-14 planes to Iran, it charged double the price charged to the Pentagon, and surely a goodly chunk of the extra went to Iranian collaborators. In the Middle East, armament contractors are "forced to sign on a local sales agent at 6 to 10% commission rates" (*Electronic News*, March 17). And that's just the "legal" surface of the corrupt swamp of the arms business.

The Pentagon, through its Defense Security Assistance Agency, has become the main international sales agent for U.S. weapons makers. It distributed $0.8 billion in 1965, $1.5 billion in 1970 and $3 billion in 1974. And then the agency really moved into high gear, collecting $8.3 billion in new orders in fiscal 1974.

Other export orders of U.S. death merchants brought the total to $10 billion. Already in 1973 the U.S. accounted for 54.4% of all international arms sales, according to U.S. government estimates, and obviously that percentage is going up.

The Pentagon and its CIA ally are not only selling armaments, they are selling war and fascism. They strive to involve other countries in the aggressive plans of imperialism and to strengthen the most reactionary regimes, from South Korea to Chile. Along with the armaments go thousands of U.S. servicemen, in and out of uniform, under the pretense of training the recipients in use of the weapons. The arms merchants send in their huge crews, and the CIA is amply represented. This practice is pursued with special intensity in the Middle East, in an attempt to re-establish or strengthen neo-colonialist domination in a new, highly militarized version.

In Western Europe the arms drive is directly connected with the attempt to use NATO to prevent the reduction of forces in Europe, to reverse the trend towards detente and East-West cooperation and to find new excuses to inflame the international situation. An unidentified Senate staff aide said of the arms business:

"The State Department sees the sales as . . . a way of penetrating the decision-making process in various countries through American advisers who go along with the arms. The Pentagon's interest is that the provision of arms . . . develops a relationship with our military, and provides the United States with leverage" (*The New York Times*, 6/22).

For many years Northrop Corporation had on its payroll Kermit Roosevelt, the CIA agent who organized the overthrow of the anti-imperialist Mossadegh government [Iran, 1953], and also "owned" the late General Paul Stehlin, ex-Chief of Staff of the French Air Force and a vice president of the French National Assembly. Stehlin was forced to resign from that position when he wrote the French president promoting the plane of his American employers over that of the French firm.

Most significant was Stehlin's use of anti-Soviet propaganda to promote cold war thinking and the arms race. Here's what he wrote "Dear Tom" Jones, president of Northrop, in 1973:

". . . The press will inform on the comparative strength of forces between East and West. That is what I have already done in a book, just published . . . , *La Force d'Illusion*. The purpose is to show the decline of NATO and to warn against the increasing superiority of the 'Warsaw Pact' military forces. You could and should take advantage of that situation to engage in a press campaign so that . . . you have a solution to offer with the P53-Cobra concept . . ." (*The Times*, 6/7).

Stehlin's political line screams of CIA orchestration. The only question is whether he was an "unwitting" CIA agent, with Northrop and Hughes "cutouts," or a "witting" collaborator with the CIA "station" in France. Certainly many of the NATO top men and supporting politicians in Western Europe are CIA-owned.

His important connection was as vice president of Hughes Aircraft's French subsidiary, which will supply the armament system for the YF-16 contract. The Hughes outfits are second to none in direct and dirty involvement with the CIA—from Castro assassination attempts to the Soviet sub-hijacking operation.

The most brazen domestic propagandist for the arms manufacturers is U.S. Defense Secretary James R. "First Strike" Schlesinger. He must be considered as the collective agent of the U.S. munitions crowd as a whole and the stellar purveyor of the CIA line.

The whole gang is becoming more desperate, more extravagant with our money, more reckless, as the people of the world deal them smashing blows, and the world balance moves in favor of socialism and national liberation.

We do not know how much of the bribes paid by U.S. arms merchants to foreign buyers are subtracted from their superprofits, and how much is paid by the CIA through the corporations as "cutouts."

In any case, the hundreds of billions of dollars sucked out of the people of the United States and other capitalist countries to pay for the armaments, and the bribes and payoffs that go with them, have become a serious drain on mass living standards. Still worse, they pose an ominous danger to world peace, to the existence of humanity.

The scandals of the munitions makers, the Pentagon and the CIA must spur intensification of the peace struggle, especially in the United States.

• • •

3/23/1977

The Ominous Buildup in Weapons Procurement

Here are the most important facts about the long-term armament buildup started under Ford and being continued under Carter.

Department of Defense, Military,
Budget Authority, 1976-1982
(billions of dollars)

Fiscal Year	Total	Weapons Procurement
1976	$96	$21
1977	108	28
1978	119	32
1979	134	39
1980	145	44
1981	156	48
1982	166	52

In 6 years the Pentagon's spending authority is scheduled to increase by $70 billion, from $96 billion to $166 billion.

The most rapidly increasing part of the military budget is that for procurement of weapons—of missiles, airplanes, tanks, submarines, carriers, electronics. In this fiscal year alone, the budget authority for procurement is 32% more than the year before. Carter has not changed that. By 1979, the procurement budget is $39 billion, almost double the 1976 figure of $21 billion; and by 1982 it is $52 billion, or two and one-half times the 1976 figure. By contrast, the peak procurement budget during the Vietnam War, when billions of dollars worth of weapons were being destroyed and replaced, was $24 billion.

The fact that the increase in procurement is so spectacular results from the entry into serial production of an array of qualitatively completely new weapons, weapons with new dimensions of capability for mass destruction of people. But these are the very weapons that are threatening to cancel the existing SALT I agreement, and threatening to prevent conclusion of a new SALT II agreement. They are the very weapons that must trigger further spirals of the arms race, multiplying the danger of catastrophe.

Also increasing very rapidly, although not so fast as procurement, is the budget for research, development, test and evaluation. The 1982 projected budget is $15.7 billion, up from $9.5 billion in 1976. That means accelerated preparation of future generations of new weapons, a continued striving for "superweapons" with which to conquer the world. Hitler tried that too.

I want to call special attention to the budget for "atomic energy defense activities." That means the production of atomic bombs, under the jurisdiction of the Energy Research and Development Administration. That is in addition to the procurement by the Defense Department. Authority for atomic bombs and missile warheads went up from $1,682 million in 1976 to $1,935 million in 1977, and is budgeted at $2,380 million in 1978. That's an increase of 41% in just two years.

Carter did not cut that section of the budget one cent.

Several times President Carter has declared his hope to completely eliminate nuclear weapons. That's very eloquent. And in words, it seems finally to respond to the call of the Soviet Union, ever since the beginning of the atomic age, for eliminating atomic weapons and prohibiting their use. But why, then, does Carter continue, at the previously designated all-out pace, accelerating production of atomic warheads? Why doesn't he reduce their production, or better yet stop it altogether?

Isn't it understandable for the Soviet Union, the socialist countries, and the developing countries to consider his eloquent generalities demagogy? Isn't it evident that this contradiction between words and actions is creating a tense situation in the world?

No president has talked more about human rights than Jimmy Carter. But the U.S. military budget poses a clear and present danger to the most elementary human right—the right to existence.

• • •

6/16/1978

The Detente Majority

The *Wall Street Journal* (5/26) says Carter is preparing to veto various civilian budget appropriations to reduce the deficit, but adds: "McIntyre and Blumenthal press hard for cuts of as much as $5 billion—mostly in military spending." McIntyre is the budget director, Blumenthal the treasury secretary.

This illustrates a vital point: the basic support for detente is exceptionally broad, extending across the entire range of social classes, including capitalist. Blumenthal was chairman of Bendix Corp. which, incidentally, continues to do considerable military business.

The powerful pro-war forces are very narrowly based. They include the most aggressive reactionaries among the very rich; the militarists, like Zbigniew Brzezinski, national security adviser. When Carter claims "public opinion" may prevent SALT-II ratification, he is referring to this vicious clique, which owns all-too-many members of Congress and of his own administration.

The influential May 15th Harris poll, showing overwhelming popular support for detente, disarmament and trade with socialist countries, demonstrates the broad base of the peace sentiment. On the most general question, "Do you favor detente?" the vote was 71% to 15% in favor. Among "executives" it was 73 to 16 in favor, about the same. Among those with incomes over $25,000, the vote was 82 to 14, somewhat stronger.

Union members are also strongly for detente and trade, despite the contrary propaganda of AFL-CIO leaders Meany, Shanker, et al. They voted 74 to 13 for detente, i.e. by a wider margin than the average, or executives.

Union members are particularly aware of the value of jobs for trade with socialist countries. They had much higher favorable percentages of those polled on the trade questions—including the restoration of most favored nation treatment to the USSR—than the average. By more than four to one, unionists, in effect, are for repeal of the anti-detente Jackson-Vanik and Stevenson amendments.

Another feature deserves special mention. Vehement anti-Soviet elements among Zionists falsely claim to speak for the entire Jewish community. They have not been able to destroy the progressive trend among the vast majority of Jewish people who voted 81 to 6 for détente. (Note not only the high favorable percentage, but the low negative percentage.) On one issue the anti-Soviet Zionists had some effect—the connection of trade discrimination with Jewish emigration. On eliminating this discrimination, the overall vote was 64 to 21 in favor, among Jewish people 70 to 22 in favor—again a larger percentage in favor, but this time a significant minority opposed.

• • •

2/19/1981

Four Minutes to Midnight

In 1976, the last fiscal year before Carter took office, the "national defense" budget authority reached $100 billion for the first time. In fiscal 1982, the last budget prepared by Carter, it reached $200 billion! Most of that acceleration has been in the last 2 years: the figure for 1980 was $145 billion.

Reagan's office has already publicized plans to increase the 1982 budget to $224 billion, which would represent an increase of $80 billion in just two years. **That means a tripling of the military budget in just 9 years**. During the 9 years of the Vietnam War escalation, from 1960 to 1969, the military budget did not quite double, let alone triple. Of course, inflation is faster now; but it is precisely the tripling of the military budget that is one of the prime causes of the near-runaway inflation—rather than its result.

Make no mistake! **This is a preparation-for-war budget**.

The United States is in the early stages of a Vietnam-type war of intervention against El Salvador.

The drive for establishment of more bases and permanent military intervention in the Persian Gulf area becomes increasingly insistent.

The Reagan administration shows every sign of intensifying the effort to mobilize Western Europe as the prime launching pad for a first-strike nuclear attack on the Soviet Union.

Reagan's appointments have been made as if he were selecting a war cabinet. General Alexander Haig, running the State Department, personifies the military-industrial complex. As NATO chief he consistently opposed the development of détente; and in recent years, as president and chief operating officer of United Technologies, he guided one of the most successful corporations to profit from the arms buildup of the Carter administration.

Haig, like National Security Advisor Allen, believes the only diplomacy that counts is aiming a gun and brandishing a nuclear bomb.

Vice-president George Bush, who took his share of a Wall Street fortune to Texas and became part of the rightwing Texas oil and banking gang of multi-millionaires, is notorious for his advocacy of nuclear war as acceptable policy.

To help finance the monstrous escalation of military spending, in fact, big business and the administration are, from the first days of the new regime, mounting a major campaign to radically slash Social Security, unemployment insurance, Medicare, food stamps, school lunches, and all the measures that provide minimal protection to the working people of this country, measures won through years of mass struggle.

The *Bulletin of the Atomic Scientists* has sounded the alert to the increased war danger by moving its Doomsday Clock forward to 4 minutes to midnight. A year ago the hand was moved to 7 minutes to midnight from 10 minutes to midnight.

But editor Bernard T. Feld, by distorting the Soviet position to be consistent with his "two superpowers" theory, reduces very seriously the effectiveness of his opposition to nuclear war. He talks of "the acceptance of counterforce first-strike by both sides" and "the flat unwillingness of either the United States or the Soviet Union to reject publicly, and in all circumstances, the threat of striking the other first."

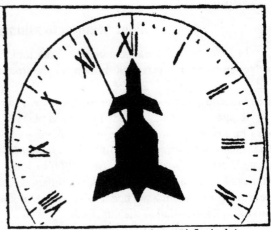

Four Minutes to Midnight

I find it hard to believe that Dr. Feld is ignorant of the frequent Soviet statements opposing first-strike policies, or of Brezhnev's declaration of May 1978:

"As for the Soviet Union, it, I repeat, is not thinking of 'making a first strike.' On the contrary, everyone knows very well our official proposal to all the participants in the all-European conference, including the United States, to conclude an agreement not to be the first to use nuclear weapons against each other. It is also common knowledge that the NATO countries reject this proposal, making it rather transparently clear that they are reluctant to give up their plans for delivering the first strike at our country. Who then is threatening whom?"

Soviet Foreign Minister Gromyko, in his 1980 "menu" of disarmament proposals to the United Nations, expanded this proposal to: ". . . conclusion by all states participating in the European Security Conference of a treaty on not being the first to use nuclear or conventional armaments against each other."

The U.S. media almost completely suppress these and other Soviet peace and disarmament initiatives. And U.S. representatives are devoting all their efforts at the current Madrid meeting on European security to shrieking anti-Soviet epithets and refusing even to discuss proposals for cooperation in any field.

Professor Feld, why do you support suppression of the facts? Yours is an influential publication. Why do you not help to push the Doomsday Clock back from midnight by breaking the Pentagon censorship and informing the American scientific community of the Soviet proposals?

268

11/22/1978

Guns Over Butter = Inflation

An Associated Press reporter put it straight to Carter at Kansas City: In drawing up our budget "it's a basic choice between guns and butter . . . is it true . . . that you've decided to let the whole military budget grow by about 3% faster than the rate of inflation while ordering" a $4-5 billion cut in social programs?

Carter answered with a long-winded and evasive equivalent of "yes." With inflation running at more than 10%, a 3% increase would bring it to 13%.

Carter reverses the train and the engine: It's not inflation that's pushing the military budget, it's the military spending that's pulling inflation. This year's 10% inflation is the speed given by last year's 10% rise in the military budget. And Carter's 3% add-on, to 13%, is like putting an extra engine on a train going on a down grade.

1/28/1987

Military Spending: Now You See It, Now You Don't

To see how the Pentagon has come to dominate actual government activity, we have to examine monies really spent, rather than what is put in the budget document.

Federal spending consists of two parts: (1) spending for goods and services, that is, for real government actions and operations; and (2) financial transactions involved in collecting money and passing it on to recipients—such as collection and distribution of Social Security taxes, collection of general taxes to pay out interest to bankers, and aid to state and local governments. The first part is decisive.

Spending for goods and services is divided between "defense" and "non-defense." During Reagan's 6 years, spending for so called defense, actually for militarism, jumped from $132 billion to $283 billion, a spurt of 114%, or 13.6% per year compounded. In 1986, the year just ended, the increase was 9.3%.

Bearing in mind the slower rate of inflation, the real rate of defense spending increased 7.8% in 1986, faster than the six-year compound average of 6.5%.

Meanwhile, real spending for non-defense goods and services in 1986 was just the same as in 1980, and lower than in 1985.

In 1986, defense spending of $283 billion for goods and services compared with only $88 billion for goods and services for other purposes, including pileups of surplus farm commodities and hidden military spending, as in the space program. Defense spending accounted for 77% of all federal spending for goods and services.

• • •

2/11/1987

Star Wars Strategy: First Strike, Not Defense

Most criticism of the Star Wars program, mislabeled "Strategic Defense Initiative" (SDI), has been on the grounds that it will not work technically, causing the waste of hundreds of billions of dollars without protecting either people or weapons.

Such criticism fails to expose the essence of SDI, which has nothing to do with defense and everything to do with planned first-strike nuclear aggression, with the drive of the Pentagon and White House for military superiority over the USSR and for world domination. That's just as insane and infinitely more dangerous—in the nuclear age—than Hitler's drive for the same ends.

A Union of Concerned Scientists (UCS) book against Star Wars (*Empty Promise*, by John Tirman) exposes the political and strategic essence of this evil program, excerpts of which have been published. Tirman writes:

"It is no secret that the Reagan presidency is marked by an undiluted disdain for arms control," which has to be concealed by "lip service" to the notion of nuclear disarmament because "the desire for arms control is simply too strong in American political culture to ignore."

SDI is central to the administration's political position—aggression, not defense:

"The new emphasis on space was consonant with the administration's fixation on war fighting capability, the doctrine that envisions the United States fighting a protracted, global nuclear war" requiring space weapons of various types. He quotes from a leaked "Defense Guidance" report of the Pentagon: "We must achieve capabilities to . . . apply military force from space if that becomes necessary."

This line, Tirman notes, "handed a carte blanche to the military to delve into the space weapons business without restraint."

All-out anti-Sovietism is the key to policy and profits, he admits: "SDI involves an attitude toward the Soviet Union, a posture of non-cooperation and competitiveness that extends into every sphere of U.S.-USSR relations. Those who knew Star Wars could cost hundreds of billions—and that the Soviets would have to react . . . foresaw an economic rivalry that the United States was bound to win. The . . . Russian economy will be disabled by the space arms race. The United States will have the pleasure of harassing the Soviets with superior technology and, perhaps, a public relations edge as well. At the same time, the U.S. defense industry will benefit handsomely, with an accelerated shift of national resources from social needs to military use."

The thrusts "to dominate space and badger the Soviets" are rationalized by the "use of technology as the main tool of policy." By leveraging the supposed U.S. "innate" superiority in technology, the United States can establish "permanent . . . military superiority" and avoid the "poisonous alternative: diplomacy."

In Tirman's opinion, there is "no doubt" that proceeding with SDI will "wreck the ABM Treaty . . . and any chance for future weapons limitation." And he stresses that Star Wars will fail politically, strategically and economically, as well as technically:

"The scientific community is balking at the program, and the most prestigious scientists and academic departments are resolutely refusing to participate, denying SDI their sorely needed talent."

Economically, Tirman adds, the Soviets can counteract it with "many . . . cost-effective measures."

I may add that the Soviets say the Cold War has slowed their progress seriously. But, despite it, they have made tremendous social and economic progress in contrast to the deterioration in our own country. And they will continue to gain, even if forced to cope with SDI.

Tirman continues that strategically, "It is extremely provocative to the Soviet Union, which views it as a component of a U.S. first-strike capability; and it will drive the offensive and defensive arms race to new heights of frenzy and peril."

He accuses Washington of lying to the U.S. people about SDI intentions. "And the very economic health and strategic security of the nation is increasingly placed in jeopardy with every day that Star Wars is allowed to proceed," he writes, anticipating that it will some day collapse of its technical contradictions and mismanagement.

But we cannot rely on that. The defeat of SDI requires millions of Americans, including the labor and peace movements, to focus on it. It must be one of the targets of the April 25 demonstration in Washington, and it should be a key issue in electoral struggles and pressure on Congress.

● ● ●

3/14/1992

Military Budget Cuts: True or False?

If you read the headlines in the newspapers you might think:

A: The Bush administration is offering major cuts in military spending.

B: The "cold war" is over and the menace of nuclear bomb destruction is ended.

C: The U.S. and Russia are now friends; only small wars and interventions are projected.

D: Conversion is required to use idled facilities and provide employment for laid off personnel.

The first three points are illusions, propagated by the White House and the media, which are totally refuted by the Bush administration's budget for fiscal year 1993! The fourth point is absolutely true, though the government has other plans entirely.

Let's analyze the actual budget data:

A. Bush claims to have cut the military budget $42 billion. That sounds encouraging. But it's a fake. They count a cut of $6 billion in the first year over and over, seven times, even though there are no further cuts! And, when Representative Aspin, for the Democrats, talks of cutting twice as much, it's by using the same trick, multiplied by two.

What's really in Bush's budget? His projections, which don't include Iraq War outlays, call for a cut of $3 billion in 1993, another billion in 1994, then increases in the next 3 years, so that by 1997, excluding Iraq War expenses, spending would be higher than in 1992.

Moreover, "International Affairs" and "Space"—overwhelmingly military—steadily increase throughout the period.

How high is military spending? It depends on whose figures you accept. The administration admits to $313.6 billion for 1991, falling to $303.8 billion for 1993. But the budget says that the Commerce Department and the General Accounting Office each estimate that military spending is some $20-$30 billion more than the Bush administration claims. The budget report also says that if they were to apply the budgeting system used by the State of California, plus the accounting industry's Generally Accepted Accounting Principles, the total for 1993 would be $506 billion!

B. Despite the "end of the cold war," the administration intends to raise the Atomic Energy Commission's budget for making atomic bombs from $8.1 billion in 1989 to $11.7 billion this year and $14.4 billion by 1997.

The military and the dominant sectors of U.S. monopoly capital, not satisfied with their frightful nuclear arsenal, fantasize about an invincible America, which alone would be shielded from the counter-bombing and the global radiation firestorm they could unleash.

C. What are the targets? Most media publicity emphasizes "safe little wars," making it clear that U.S. imperialism intends to use its military might to enforce its "right" to global domination. But these "easy" wars—killing a hundred thousand or so civilians at the cost of few American lives—would require a budget of $30 billion, not $300 plus billion. The Pentagon's real plans are based on other scenarios, revealed by *The New York Times*:

"Out of the former Soviet Union or some combination of powerful nations, a new . . . superpower emerges to threaten U.S. interests, calling for a total mobilization for global war in the year 2001." The imperialists claim Communism is dead, but they know better. Their goal is still the same, the destruction of socialism, the permanent enslavement of the working class, regardless of any cost in human life.

On Feb. 26, the Associated Press reported, "CIA Director Robert Gates yesterday ranked instability in the former Soviet Union as the #1 threat to U.S. interests abroad. 'I think it would be premature to take our sights off a country that still possesses 30,000 nuclear weapons.' " He obviously realizes that Yeltsin may not be able to force the Soviet peoples and their military to give up this means of self-defense.

D. Plants that produce for the military-industrial complex—General Motors and other corporations—want to make higher and higher profits with fewer workers. We should take seriously Senator Nunn's warning that even with the continued vast expenditures, ". . . more than two million military-related jobs will be lost by 1996." Conversion on a huge scale is needed.

• • •

9/7/1996

Dole, Clinton and the Military Budget

Bob Dole, addressing the Republican Convention, stressed his "crystal clear difference" with Clinton on military matters:

"And on my first day in office I will put America on a course that will end our vulnerability to missile attack and rebuild our armed forces. . . . On my first day in office, I will also put terrorists on notice: If you harm one American, you harm all Americans. And America will pursue you to the end of the Earth."

This is a brazen claim that the United States can and will police the world!

The Republican Party platform favors expansion of military spending with special emphasis on two ultra high-cost and deadly areas:

1. Star Wars: Endorsement of "the Defend America Act of 1996, introduced by Senator Bob Dole, which calls for a missile defense system for all 50 states by the year 2003."

This project is a blatant giveaway to the military contractors, and is also an attempt to hoodwink the public, to convince Americans that they can be protected from reprisals in a nuclear war that Washington would start.

2. Nuclear weapons and testing: "To cope with the threat of the proliferation of weapons of mass destruction . . . by rogue states . . . will require the continuing maintenance and development of nuclear weapons and their periodic testing. The Clinton Administration's proposed Comprehensive Test Ban Treaty (CTBT) is inconsistent with American security interests. . . ." (*The Times*, 8/13/96).

Dole's fixation on nuclear weapons is shown by his campaign promise to protect the jobs of the 15,000 workers in New Mexico who are developing and producing nuclear weapons, while the jobs of the other 70,000 Energy Department employees would be drastically slashed and government employees generally subject to major downsizing. Dole's position in fact encourages the spread of nuclear weapons and revives the environmental damage caused by nuclear testing.

Bill Clinton, at the Democratic Convention, denied that it was the intention, or within the ability, of the United States to police the world. But the military budget for fiscal year 1996 proposes increases to the year 2000, and it contains aggressive boasts and threats that Clinton, in his acceptance speech, to some extent echoes.

However Dole goes much further than Clinton with a brazen imperialist, really fascist claim that the United States is the world leader, and the President of the United States ". . . by virtue of the country's status, becomes in effect the leader. . . . Also, the President, in addition to being the leader, sort of the world leader, the No. 1 leader, he's also President of the United States."

Thus the job for which he is campaigning becomes a sort of second fiddle to his pretensions of being Czar of the whole world. And how he would use that power is indicated by his pressure on Clinton to bomb/invade Iraq—while the President is still deciding what action to take to "punish" that country (*The Times*, 9/2).

The Budget of the United States for FY 1996, under the caption "Contributing to International Peace and Security," states: "The military services no longer face the prospect of a world-wide war with the Soviet Union." Since former budgets emphasized preparations for such a war, the logical follow-up would be a reduction in military spending to a small fraction of current levels. Instead, while civilian entitlement programs are mercilessly slashed, authorizations for the military are being increased. The rationale?

"When our interests call for it, the U.S. is prepared to deploy unilaterally or participate in multinational efforts to settle internal conflicts and bolster new democratic governments. Thus our forces are prepared for rapid overseas deployment for such activities, as well as for participating in peacekeeping, peace enforcing, and other operations to support our national security goals."

This is a clear statement that the United States intends to enforce its domination of the world. How can so extreme a conclusion be drawn?

First, other sections of the *Budget* make clear that this policy is applicable anywhere in the world: there are no geographical limitations. As Secretary of State Warren Christopher put it: "I am perfectly—personally—prepared to see the United States use force, not only there [Bosnia] but any place around the world." (4/27/93)

Second, the terminology "help settle internal conflicts" aims to vindicate U.S. readiness to interfere militarily in the internal affairs of any country.

Third, the intention to bolster new democratic governments is a demagogic and hypocritical justification of the U.S./CIA practice of organizing and controlling elections to legitimate the installation of thugs and murderers, the lackeys of the United States, who dislodged by military means the previous, popularly elected leadership.

Our "national interests" turn out to be, politically, anti-Communism, pro-imperialism, anti-working class; any regime that favors interests of the transnational corporations: oil companies seeking to extend their monopoly control; TNCs seeking to "downsize" U.S. production, to replace U.S. workers with dollar-a-day labor in low-wage countries; corporate giants, like Coca Cola, aiming for control of world markets while driving out of business national (soft drink) companies.

The Budget admits: "Our defense budget, which is significantly higher than that of any other nation, supports one of the world's largest military forces, with a superior level of quality and talent."

And why is it a "defense" budget when there is no threat to the United States, nor any possibility thereof? Up until some time after World War II, there was a War Department. Today the term "Offense Department" and "Offense Budget" would be more realistic.

The Budget also stresses the advantage of being able to fight two local wars simultaneously, and being able to involve only a small fraction of U.S. military might in such actions. The prosaic language of the budget conceals the barbarism of these military aggressions: in the past decade there were the bombings of Iraq and Libya; the provision of state-of-the-art weapons and the training of armies of ruffians and mercenaries in countries targeted for attack—e.g., Afghanistan and Russia; the attempt to starve the people of both Iraq, with its anti-Communist dictator Saddam Hussein, and Cuba, with its Communist leader Fidel Castro. In re Iraq, the international oil cartel wants to regain ownership of the nationalized Iraqi oil industry; and as for Cuba, U.S. TNCs in nickel, sugar, ranching want to profiteer from ownership of its rich natural resources and to exploit the labor of its people. With the recently enacted Helms-Burton Act, the children of Cuba will be increasingly victimized.

As for our real "national interests," this crucial area is determined by government bureaucrats with no pretense of input from the American people. The U.S. Budget is drafted by officials in the Pentagon, State Department and intelligence agencies. To reflect our vital national interests, its provisions must be reversed by changing the balance of power in Congress and then by the exertion of mass pressure on Clinton to turn toward a real policy of peace.

• • •

1/16/1999

Military Budget Soars

According to the analysis in the *Washington Post*, ". . . responding to demands by the nation's top military commanders," President Clinton will authorize military spending in the fiscal year 2000, which begins in October 1999, at $296 billion. That means that an all-time high of military spending will occur in 2001. Further, Senator John Warner (R, VA), incoming chair of the Armed Forces Committee, says that Clinton's increase "falls way short" of the demands of the Joint Chiefs of Staff and that Congress will appropriate accordingly.

The implications for civilian programs are grave: appropriations for natural resources and the environment, education and training, health care, housing, commerce, etc. will all suffer. Combined military and civilian "discretionary" spending is limited, by congressional decree, to $565 billion in 2000. The higher military spending will thus necessitate a $27 billion reduction in previously planned non-military programs. That's 9%, not allowing for inflation! Add to that curtailments and taxes that Congress is likely to enact in response to Clinton's fraudulent campaign to "save social security," and the outlook for the American people is gloomy. ‿

As is the outlook for the world that is facing the rising military threats from the Rambos in the Pentagon and Congress.

THE POWER BEHIND THE THRONE

Oil

2/10/1973

Is There a Fuel Crisis in the U.S.?

With the cold snap in parts of the country early in January, the press suddenly discovered an "energy crisis." Schools in Denver were shut down. Boatloads of grain on Midwest waterways were stalled for lack of fuel. Flights from Kennedy were canceled. Landlords found a new excuse for not heating apartments.

Senator Henry Jackson, Washington State's man from Boeing, called the energy crunch "the most critical problem, domestic or international, facing the nation today."

Newsweek warned that the solution "may well strike at the very heart of the American life-style. Consumers inescapably will see their bills for electricity, heating and gasoline raised ever higher—and they could conceivably find these necessities being rationed." *Newsweek* predicted blackouts, brownouts, worsened pollution, and even diplomatic repercussions: "The U.S. could ultimately find itself alienating its Israeli allies as it tries to improve relations with the Arab nations that control most of the world's oil reserves" (1/22).

The *Wall Street Journal* warned of consumer prices for oil doubling by 1980 (1/23).

The long-run problem is real. The immediate shortage is not.

The United States recklessly consumes mounting quantities of fuel of all sorts. With 6% of the world's population, it uses one-third of the globe's energy output. Consumption of oil and gas has even gone beyond what can be supplied by the huge U.S. reserves. Oil imports reached 19% of total consumption in 1972 and are expected by the industry to reach 35% in 1973—and evidently this will be exceeded, as imports reached 44% of consumption in mid-January.

U.S. production of oil peaked two years ago and is gradually declining despite capacity pumping in the Texas fields, previously kept shut down part of the time to keep up prices. Output of the more efficient natural gas has also peaked.

For some time, oil and gas companies have campaigned for higher prices, in order, they say, to provide an "incentive" for stepped up exploration and drilling within the United States.

The cry of shortages, combined with Phase III regulations, opened the way for the start of escalating prices. Beginning January 22, the big companies raised the price of home heating oil and gasoline one cent a gallon. The Cost of Living Council, while cracking down on New York hospital workers and West Coast longshoremen, offered no objections.

The short-term "shortage" is largely contrived, and partly brought on by oil company tactics. Some may have resulted from faulty distribution by the companies; others may have been faked for purposes of company propaganda. Significantly, no big companies were forced to curtail production.

Distributive margins absorbed as profits by the oil companies have been rising steadily. The price of oil at Oklahoma wells is now $3.51 [$14.09] a barrel. Imported oil, even with transport cost, is nearly $1 per barrel cheaper. But the average price to final consumers is $13 per barrel, and still pointing upwards. All in all, it seems as if the oil companies put over their recent price increases just in time to beat a widespread realization that the "shortage" was over.

Meanwhile, oil imports have shot up. It seems probable that by the end of February, stocks of petroleum products will actually exceed the 1972 level.

A particularly sinister feature of the situation is the corporate propaganda campaign for dirtier fuel, linked to the supposed shortage. Thus New York City was pressed into accepting high-sulphur fuel oil by the Texaco Company.

There is also the fact that tremendous economies in fuel consumption are possible. The U.S. military, directly and through its munitions makers, continue to consume as much as one-fifth of the energy supply of the United States. Enormous quantities of electricity are used in production of aluminum, alloy steels, rare metals, and above all, nuclear bomb material. This could well be drastically cut.

With the capitalist world recovering from the economic slump centered in the United States, demand for oil is soaring. Under such conditions, temporary tightness in fuel supplies is not unusual, and the pinch in the U.S. and its use to hike prices have been matched elsewhere. This is especially true of the developing countries, and India is engaged in a struggle with the oil monopolies over the sharply rising prices.

The effect of economic conditions was aggravated by oil company tactics in the struggle against producing countries. Early in 1972, Iraq Petroleum Co., the Anglo-American monopoly, cut in half output at the Kirkuk fields, the largest in Iraq. This was done in reprisal for Iraq developing its own oil output, with Soviet help, on the North Rumeila field. When Iraq Petroleum refused to restore output, Iraq nationalized the Kirkuk field. Since then, the U.S. and British companies have attempted to organize a capitalist world boycott of Iraqi oil, with partial success, keeping Iraqi output well below normal. Similarly, in reprisal for Venezuelan preparations to take over ownership of national oilfields in the 1980s, the companies reduced output in that country.

Output cuts in these two major producing countries significantly affected the global supply-demand balance. The administration and the oil companies resisted until well into winter demands of New Englanders for removal of limitations on the import of fuel oil to the Northeast, although earlier action would have done much to avert spot shortages.

Negotiations with the Soviet Union for long-term supply of liquefied natural gas are crucial for augmenting the U.S. supply. But when the U.S. companies were on the verge of an agreement, President Nixon ordered them to delay action until further notice—part of his futile campaign to get the USSR to press the Democratic Republic of Vietnam to yield to his terms.

For the long run the fuel shortage is real only in relation to the drive for superprofits of the U.S. and British oil monopolies. They aim to maintain control of the world's oil; to get it cheaply from the countries of the Middle East, Africa, Latin America, and Asia; to sell it to consumers at increasingly higher prices.

• • •

10/6/1973

The Oil Profits Gusher (Domestic)

Now that the winter heating season is at hand, there are renewed threats of a fuel-oil shortage. Exxon Corporation raised the wholesale price of gasoline another cent a gallon; and the cost of living council approved retail price increases in gasoline, diesel fuel, and fuel oil. Simultaneously there is press agitation about a possible withholding of supplies by Saudi Arabia.

Earlier this year (*World Magazine*, 2/10), I exposed the phony nature of the fuel shortage. That is now fully confirmed. The latest figures, for the month of July, show a spectacular escalation in U.S. consumption of gasoline and other petroleum products. For the year to date, consumption is up 7.5%; and for the month of July alone, 10%. Every day in July, the United States consumed 1.5 million barrels more than a year ago, a rise nearly equal to the entire daily production of Canada or Indonesia. One has to go back over 20 years to find a two-year period of increase comparable, on a percentage basis, to the last two years.

Nevertheless, petroleum stocks have been gaining throughout the year. As of the latest week, stocks of gasoline and household heating oil were actually above the year earlier level, when they were regarded as being in surplus. But the shortage propaganda has been played to the hilt by the big oil companies. They have increased their prices to consumers mercilessly, and 30 companies reported a 49% rise in profits in the first half of the year. Exxon alone cleared over a billion dollars, one-third of a billion more than last year.

John C. Winger, the Chase Manhattan Bank's apologist for the oil companies, writes in the bank's monthly publication on oil: "In their efforts to cope with a worldwide shortage of petroleum, the companies have operated at capacity rates. And in response to the basic law of supply and demand, prices have risen all over the world as the shortage has evolved. The increase in net income is, of course, a logical consequence of expanded operation and higher prices."

An accurate account would admit that the manipulated pseudo-shortage was used as a cover by the oil monopolies to put over higher prices throughout the capitalist world so as to make outrageous profits.

The ads of the Mobil man to "dive into the pool—the car pool" are not actually meant to cut petroleum use, any more than Con Edison's "save a watt" campaign is meant to cut electricity use. In both cases the object is to create an atmosphere in which it is easier to raise prices, and both companies have been getting away with it.

Where is our expanded petroleum consumption coming from? Domestic production is on the downgrade, despite strenuous efforts to raise it. So all the increase in consumption is supplied from imports, which by now account for over one-third of the oil used. It is coming from Nigeria, Algeria, Libya, Iran, Saudi Arabia and other Persian Gulf countries, and from Indonesia. And, despite the devaluation of the dollar, and despite cries that the producing countries are robbing us, the average price of imported crude during the first 6 months of 1973 was up only 8% over the same period of 1972. Moreover the average price of crude oil was 80¢ a barrel less than that of domestic crude, so the shift to more foreign crude tended to lower overall costs. Yet consumer prices for gasoline went up 10.5%, showing the added profiteering margin.

• • •

12/19/1973

Oil's Exorbitant Expectations

Chase Manhattan Bank, financial center of the world oil cartel, has spelled out the goals of the industry's policies, which are being faithfully carried out with full cooperation by the administration in Washington.

Having increased sensationally in 1973, profits of 30 oil companies are estimated by Chase Manhattan to come close to $10 billion this year, after taxes and interest. Their goal, as published in the latest issue of the bank's monthly, *The Petroleum Situation*, is to double those profits to $20 billion in four years, by 1977; quadruple them in another four years, to $40 billion in 1981; and redouble them again in a third four-year interval, to $80 billion in 1985. This represents an 18% per year compound rate of increase.

No industry, or even large company, has even come close to such a high rate of profit increase over an extended period, not even IBM. If the goal is realized, the oil giants alone will make more profits in 1985 than all U.S. corporations did in 1973.

The total profits they project, in the 16-year period 1970-1985, are $755 billion. But this is in addition to hundreds of billions that would be paid out as interest to bankers, and more hundreds of billions as booty to the huge corporate bureaucracy of the oil companies.

Here is Chase Manhattan's argument:
1. There is plenty of petroleum in the world to meet constantly expanding energy needs. But huge quantities of capital are needed to get it, transport it to consuming countries, and refine it. . . . That capital can only be

supplied through profits. And profits can only be increased by higher prices.

2. There hasn't been enough capital invested in the petroleum industry heretofore. There is a deficit of investment. Therefore, investment has to be increased very fast to make up for the past deficit and expanding future needs. That is why profits have to increase 18% per year.

This whole argument pushes the logic of monopoly capitalism to the edge of insanity.

It **assumes** that the U.S. and related cartel members will continue to have virtually unlimited access to all parts of the capitalist world for oil.

It **assumes** that a rational policy will want to continue to expand consumption of petroleum in the industrialized capitalist countries at past rates.

It **assumes** that working people will tolerate a situation where they will have to pay out up to a quarter of their incomes for petroleum products—an assumption implicit in these fantastic profit goals.

And this "logic" is accompanied by threats against even the remnants of official restraint on prices:

"For a long time representatives of government have insisted that consumers must be protected by controlling the price of energy. But how can consumers possibly be protected when the controls lead to a shortage of energy? Even today, many politicians still maintain that the controls must be continued—they say it would be politically unrealistic to allow energy prices to rise in response to economic laws. But, as the shortage worsens, aren't they even more likely to be swept out of office by angry consumers, unable to obtain enough energy for their own needs and also suffering from the adverse economic consequences of the shortage?"

All of the assumptions of this "logic" are false. And the desired multiplication of petroleum prices has nothing to do with textbook economic laws of supply and demand, but only with the manipulations of monopolies, the basic economic law of state-monopoly capitalism: maximum profits at the expense of the people, through exploitation of labor, through suppression of minorities and peoples in other countries, and through militarism and war.

It is perfectly obvious that the Democratic and Republican politicians have no intention of even trying to interfere with this program.

And it is also obvious that attention must be focused on a fundamental solution to the threat: the Communist program for nationalization of the entire energy industry, putting it under control of a democratically chosen and representative council, and using it to meet the needs of the people, with full regard to the consideration of nature and improvement of the environment, and with respect for the rights of other peoples.

• • •

4/19/1979

Carter's Energy Message

Anticipating President Carter's energy message, oil shares rose rapidly on the stock market during the first days of April. Carter surpassed the stockholders' expectations—and the public's fears. His announced measures will:

- Provide a bonanza to the oil companies of $17 billion per year, minimum, by 1982;
- Increase costs to consumers by $34 billion per year, in addition to the higher costs accruing from rising world oil prices and from other recent measures of his administration;
- Aim at an ultimate increase in domestic oil production of 5% and reduced consumption, through conservation, of 1%;
- Result in slowing, not stopping, the increase in oil imports in quantity, with a faster rise in cost;
- Provide for giveaways of government oil to the oil companies, plus billions in energy research and development contracts;
- Reduce environmental protection.

For Carter to call this "sacrifice by all" is blatant hypocrisy. The centerpiece of the plan is the decontrol of oil prices. This is supposed to stimulate the companies to produce more domestic oil by opening new wells and by operating at full capacity at existing wells. This calculation is dubious. Beginning in January 1980 and continuing until October 1981, 3% of "old oil" will be reclassified as "new oil" each month, and its price more than doubled. At that time all controls will lapse and the companies will be able to charge what they want. The incentive to keep oil in the ground, or to pump it very slowly, will be stronger than ever with the assurance that controls will really end in October 1981—and with much higher prices of world market oil.

According to the published administration calculation, the ultimate saving from Carter's trivial conservation measures will be 250,000 barrels per day, about 1.3% of present consumption. The combined official estimates of production increase and consumption curtailment come to a million barrels a day by 1985. But this falls short of matching the growth in use from population growth and economic activity.

More fundamentally, nothing in the Carter program reduces the control by the oil companies over production and distribution. There is nothing to defeat their permanent strategy of maintaining a tight supply situation whenever possible; nor to change the conditions of the last 6 years, which make it easy for the companies to do so. Thus the Carter plan, like previous plans since the time of Nixon, will end with larger, not smaller, oil imports; with frequent artificial shortages and hardships for the people; and with much higher prices being posed as the only "solution" each time. But a much greater increase in supply could be obtained at **no cost** to the public while maintaining and tightening price controls over oil products:

- By confiscating and operating the shut-in wells through a public company;
- By cutting by 50% the consumption of oil by the military and armament industries.

The public is cynical and angry. What is necessary is to convert this mood into active struggle for a really radical approach to the energy situation—putting an end to oil monopoly profiteering.

• • •

6/5/1979

The Gas Shortage Conspiracy

Yes. People's suspicions are correct. The gasoline crunch is a corporate-government conspiracy. This year's new supply has exceeded last year's every month up to and during the first week of June, the latest week for which figures are available.

The local shortages, resulting in the gas lines, which began in California in April, had to be contrived. I do not know how it was arranged, but it spread panic and served as an excuse to effect shortages in many places in May and June. The oil companies did this by cutting their May refining activity, and especially their production of gasoline. They cut their shipments of gasoline to dealers by even more, 9.8% in comparison with May 1978.

James Schlesinger, secretary of the Department of Energy, and the Pentagon combined to create still more problems. The government continued to put substantial quantities of crude oil into a special, extraordinary, unjustifiable military reserve; and the energy department set up a system of allocations, as in wartime. It allocated 10% of May's actual gasoline output to priority users, the main ones being the Pentagon and agriculture. In such a situation "priority" users always take more than they really need. Then 5% of output was set aside for distribution by state governments, as compared with 3% earlier. So more gasoline went to local bureaucracies, to companies close to them, to favored dealers.

Next, Schlesinger decreed extra shipments to dealers with a record of sales growth. Many of these were stations selling unbranded gasoline, which had attracted customers by offering a few cents off the going price. Now, with the aid of government, these stations have "pioneered" in dollar gas and such outrages as the $1.57 per gallon in California and in sections of New York.

A leading business report tells its readers that there is no evidence of a real shortage, because crude oil inventories are higher than usual, and that the apparent shortage of gasoline is caused by business firms and gasoline stations storing unusual amounts in their facilities. (Exact quote not permitted).

The shortages are focused in metropolitan areas with heavy concentrations of workers, of Black and Hispanic peoples. Congress refuses to authorize even a standby rationing system that might provide some degree of equity.

The lack of order in distribution encourages all the petty meanness by which some dealers sell gas to "favorite" customers only. All this increases the general tension and deteriorating quality of life. What is the purpose?

The oil companies, by eliminating the last semblance of competition and taking advantage of the absolute need of millions to obtain gasoline to get to work and to shopping centers, have removed customary restraints on their profiteering. Many dealers are going all out also. And this is mainly at the expense of workingclass purchasers.

The administration collaborates with the oil monopolies partly because of the intense interlocks between the oil companies and the government apparatus, and because of the many senators and representatives beholden to the oil lobby. Schlesinger has just about abandoned all pretense of putting ceilings on gas prices.

But there is more to it. This cooked-up shortage is in accord with the energy strategy of state monopoly capitalism. It aims to adapt to the weakening grip of U.S. imperialism on the capitalist world's oil reserves by curtailing consumption at the expense of the working people and in ways that increase monopoly profits.

• • •

4/19/1984

Monopolizing More Oil

Reagan's virtual scrapping of the anti-trust laws has spurred a record merger boom. There are almost daily announcements of new takeovers running into hundreds of millions, or billions of dollars. The ultimate cost in employment will run into millions of jobs, as the merged corporations shut down "redundant" shops, especially those with militant union locals.

The 10 largest corporate mergers in history, dollarwise, have taken place since 1979; nine of them since Reagan took office. That's not counting still pending steel mergers. The 10 largest involved a combined cost of $61 billion, about half of which represented immediate profit to the stockholders of the companies taken over, from the doubling of their share prices. But the owners of the takeover corporations expect to gain still more from the long-run profits derived from control of still larger monopolies and the power that goes with it.

Seven of the 10, including the 4 largest, involve acquisition of oil companies. Five of these 7 are by other oil companies; the other 2 are by duPont and U.S. Steel. The drive to get control of more deposits of oil and natural gas reflects the fact that the oil industry remains the most profitable of all, and that anti-imperialist revolutions have weakened the grip of the transnationals on the capitalist world's richest reserves, in the Middle East. Also, major holdings in Africa and Latin America were nationalized.

The economic crisis, with a decline in physical capital investment, left huge sums available for takeover investments. It stimulated giants like duPont and U.S. Steel—facing increasing global competition and, for steel, a grave structural crisis—to use their own and their bankers' capital resources to buy major stakes in oil where the sure billions in profits lie.

The wave of oil mergers tightens monopoly control, resulting in wider price spreads, as this past winter when the price of household fuel oil zoomed to as much as double refinery prices. Gas stations are being closed down by the tens of thousands, presaging rising gasoline prices. Refinery workers, oil and gas drillers, service station people, are all losing jobs, while the companies use the shutdowns to drive against oil workers' unions.

For decades capitalist oil has been dominated by the "Seven Sisters" cartel— Exxon, Royal Dutch Shell, British Petroleum, Mobil, Texaco, Standard Oil of California and Gulf. Five of them are controlled through U.S. money-center banks, the other two from London and Rotterdam.

Now they will be six, since the biggest merger of all will be the pending $13.2 billion takeover of Gulf by Standard Oil of California. The Mellons, who controlled Gulf for generations, reduced their holdings in recent years, but retained a 5% share that, with the holdings of allied Wall Street groups, was sufficient to retain control. However, they decided to take the profits from selling out, and to yield control.

The California billionaire Getty family owns more than 50% of Getty Oil, which has more oil reserves than any other independent, and more than some of the Seven Sisters. The Getty family, beset with internal feuds, elected to sell. In the second largest merger, Texaco will take over Getty for $10.1 billion, beating off the bid of an independent Texas company, Pennzoil. Texaco doubles its own oil reserves through this takeover.

Major gainers from the takeovers are the Wall Street banks and investment houses, which negotiated terms and set up the multi-billion dollar loans to finance the mergers. Prominent in the process was Chase Manhattan, traditional Rockefeller bank of the oil companies. Sharing in the lucrative, oil-secured loans are banking syndicate members in money centers from San Francisco to Boston.

When Reagan and his cohorts send warships to the Persian Gulf, their sole purpose is to prevent a possible loss of profits to the oil cartel. And when Margaret Thatcher sends her warships to supplement Reagan's, she is protecting British Petroleum and Royal Dutch Shell. Above all Reagan and Company fear more far-reaching revolutions in this area, which will win genuine people's control over these massive reserves and put an end to the Pentagon's aims to reestablish bases there for aggression against the Soviet Union.

Thus the struggle for peace in the Middle East is intimately connected with the anti-monopoly, workingclass struggles against the transnationals and their political representatives in the U.S.

"He can't be disturbed now, he's preparing Phase 3."

Politics: Government Policy

8/23/1964

Johnson's Backers

The 1964 election brings with it the first major shakeup in the pattern of financial forces behind big party candidates in nearly 30 years. The $100 million that big business pours into presidential campaigns is high-powered money. It is played for a bigger bite into the $100 billion federal budget, for more diplomatic, military, and foreign "aid" help for the $50 billion of private foreign investments. It seeks the very top posts of power in America: the Cabinet, the National Security Council, the "Special Group," and a direct line to the White House.

Drowning the public in an ocean of campaign propaganda, the billionaire owners of the two parties strive to herd voters into line. Fortunately they do not have things all their way. Labor, civil rights, peace movements—operating with a tiny fraction of the big business financial resources—exert a substantial influence because their programs correspond to the real interests of the majority. Sometimes major party groups ally themselves with people's forces and make policy concessions to win their support. The Roosevelt Democrats reached the high point of such a relationship.

As the 1936 campaign formed, most top Wall Street tycoons who had traditionally supported the Democrats moved to the Republicans. Democratic financing was divided among lesser lights of the big money:
- Wealthy second-tier Wall Street houses—Brown Brothers Harriman; Dillon Read; Lehman-Goldman Sachs.
- Southern latifundists, cotton and tobacco dealers and processors.
- Some Texas oil, Rocky Mountain mining, and West Coast industrialists.
- Consumers goods and construction capitalists wanting more mass purchasing power and more public works.
- Jewish and Irish Catholic capitalists, excluded from the summits of high finance.

This motley crew has financed and largely controlled the Democratic Party ever since. Their control wasn't shaken even in 1944, when the unions put up most of the money and carried the campaigning lead. These groups are tied in with and dependent upon the top bankers by a thousand business connections. They are one with the giants in opposition to labor, support for foreign expansion, hostility to socialism. They don't strive to overthrow the Rockefellers, Morgans and duPonts, only for places closer to the head of the table.

So the Democrats, when in power, have left control of foreign and military affairs to the main Wall Street groups. Postwar secretaries of state included Acheson, a Morgan man, and Rusk, a Rockefeller man, for the Democrats; Dulles and Herter, both Wall Street aristocrats close to the Rockefellers, under the Republicans.

Beginning as a representative of Texas interests, in Washington Johnson established important ties with eastern financiers and became known to big business generally as a "reliable" politician. This eastern support, added to his southern backing, made him Kennedy's leading contender for the 1960 nomination.

Despite the desertion of many former Texas supporters, Johnson maintains a significant base there. Herman Brown, big Texas construction-natural gas man, a veteran Democratic contributor, is a friend.

For decades Johnson's personal finances have been handled by Edwin Weisl, senior partner in Simpson, Thacher and Bartlett, general counsel for Lehman Brothers. Other connections also suggest that Johnson's most intimate ties are with men close to this house, which has expanded in scope and relative position since World War II.

In addition, he has won the support of some top Wall Streeters, who for decades were solidly Republican. Henry Ford II declared for Johnson long before Goldwater's nomination seemed certain. That event has led more capitalists into the Johnson camp. Doubtless they are seriously interested in defeating Goldwater. At the same time they will strive to push the Democrats further to the right, to make that party even more like the "liberal" wing of the Republicans.

• • •

8/22/1970

The Multi-Billion Dollar Question:
Does Capitalism Need War To Survive?

This is the text of a broadcast delivered by Mr. Perlo over radio station WBAI-FM in response to several letters from "World Magazine" readers asking him to comment on the Silk columns.

Some important columns about war economy have been written in *The New York Times* Sunday financial section (7/19, 7/26) by Leonard S. Silk, and syndicated in many papers across the country. He quotes from a recent book of Professor Robert Eisner showing the enormous cost of the Vietnam War.

Eisner says that if men in the armed forces had been in civilian life instead, they would have earned $82 billion more; that the cost of the dead and wounded to the nation was $23 billion. Added to the budgeted expense of $113 billion, this makes a total of $219 billion. That's Eisner's estimate of the 5-year cost in lost opportunities, in the shifting of resources away from better use.

Silk generalizes that war and militarism damage the economy. He doesn't deny a powerful military-industrial complex pushing it, but claims that the financial community and much of the business community not directly involved in war contracts find that the cost of war in taxes outweighs its profits, and have come to oppose the war and excessive arms expenditures.

He says:

"The notion of a local dependence on a specialized kind of industry producing military goods should be made obsolete by government willingness to plan substitute kinds of expenditure or to make other provisions for readjustment of the industrial mix. . . . The long postwar record of economic growth and full employment of Western European countries and Japan, whose military budgets are a minor fraction of that of the United States in relation to national income, shows that peace and prosperity in capitalist societies are by no means impossible to attain."

I haven't seen Professor Eisner's book. It seems to be a good one. I agree with much of what Mr. Silk writes about, except the notion that smooth prosperity is possible indefinitely for capitalism under any condition. Listeners to my broadcasts know that I have stressed many of these points. I made an analysis parallel to Eisner's in my book *Militarism and Industry* published 7 years ago.

Yet I have to disagree with Silk on two major points not directly connected with Eisner's work.

First, Silk uses his analysis to attack Marxism on utterly false grounds. It's almost as if he figures that he can get away with a strong argument against war economy if he clears his political skirts by delivering a blast at Marxism at the same time.

He begins his article:

"The old Marxist charge that capitalist economies depend on war to provide prosperity and full employment dies hard. Not only orthodox Communists but radicals of the New Left take it as axiomatic that the military-industrial complex controls the nation's basic foreign and domestic profits and wages through the expansion of the capitalist system."

The Florida *St. Petersburg Times* headlines its syndicated reprint:

"Was Karl Marx right? Do capitalist economies really need a war to exist?"

This typical head shows how frivolous, how irresponsible capitalist publicists, economists and politicians get when they want to attack Marx. Anything goes.

Of course, it's utter nonsense. Marx didn't even write about war economy. It wasn't important when he wrote *Capital*. It didn't figure in his basic analysis of capitalist economy.

Marxists have always contended that war was harmful to the economic interests of the working people. Marxists have made a specific analysis of the effect of war on the U.S. economy over the past 30 years.

Here, in capsule form, is the analysis of Marxists, of Communists:

It took the Second World War to pull the U.S. out of the long depression and stagnation of the 1930s. U.S. capitalism gained from this war, for the **special** reason that it was remote from the scene of battle, suffered no war damage, collected tens of billions in gold in payment, seized military bases in many lands and used its power to open them up for domination by U.S. big business. That the war harmed most capitalist countries economically is incontestable. It ended up eliminating capitalism altogether from a number of them.

Since World War II, continued large military budgets, global interventionism and war have been increasingly harmful to the domestic economy generally, and especially to the economic interests of workers. Cold war politics enabled big business to shift tens of billions in taxes from themselves onto workers, to increase the share of profits at the expense of wages. The militarized economy has brought about a marked deterioration in public services. It has contributed to the rapid loss in the relative economic status of the United States, not only in relation to socialist countries, but in relation to other capitalist countries. It has strengthened reactionary and racist political elements.

All this has reached a climax in the Vietnam War, with an absolute reduction in the real wages of the average worker, and with the first wartime economic depression in history.

Certainly there are many who say that labor benefits from armaments. Establishment propaganda stresses the theme, with Labor Department statistics exaggerating the number of jobs dependent on the military budget. Some union officials support the most hawklike foreign policy and are right in front demanding armament contracts for their employers. Some ultra-leftists delight the ultra-right by claiming the working class has been co-opted by the capitalists and the military-industrial complex.

There are workers whose immediate jobs are financed out of the military budget, and many more who have the illusion that their jobs are dependent on it. Yet workers are not, by and large, hawks. They are not the silent majority of whom Silk speaks. Herbert Aptheker has analyzed the available polls, and indicates that the workers have consistently shown the highest percentage of votes against the Vietnam War.

The Marxist contention that the war program hurts labor is proven to the hilt by the Vietnam War.

The particular characteristic of Marxists, of Communists, is that they aren't satisfied with analyzing evils. They organize the fight against evils. The American Communists spearheaded the fight against militarism and the arms race, the fight for disarmament, when that was a tough fight indeed, when most leaders of the U.S. Communist Party were put in prison for it.

True, some self-styled revolutionaries of the ultra-left or Maoist persuasion theorize that capitalist economy depends on armaments, that any cut in the armaments would bring about a deep insoluble economic crisis. The most savage attacks against my book *Militarism and Industry* came from those quarters. They spread a spirit of pessimism, of defeatism, the idea that war cannot be stopped, that armaments must continually increase, that it is hopeless to seek any change.

Pretending to be for a revolutionary overthrow of capitalism, they would render it impossible to mobilize the forces needed for a real revolution by stopping the struggle on immediate issues, especially the most urgent issue of peace. By posing as revolutionaries, they confuse honest people into a distorted concept of Marxism, and make it easier for enemies of Marxism to attack that distorted version as the real thing.

There is another basic weakness in Mr. Silk's analysis. He concedes that there is a powerful military-industrial complex pushing the arms race for its own profits. But he wrongly believes that this grouping, narrowly conceived, is the decisive force behind the arms race, and that Marxists think so.

Administrations in power have manipulated armament contracts for economic reasons, stepping them up to stimulate the economy, and slowing them down to cool the economy. Top officials have used contracts to pay off particular big corporations. But that hasn't determined the main trend. The arms race is not conducted primarily for domestic economic reasons, nor primarily for the profits of munitions makers. Big business orders the arms race, and the foreign policy that depends overwhelmingly on U.S. military might. Big business dictates the objectives of that foreign policy: to destroy Communist and anti-imperialist governments, to prevent their formation, to open up all areas possible for investment by U.S. corporations, to insure the maximum profitability of these investments, to establish bases from which to attack or threaten other lands with those ends in view.

The top men of the financial establishment are the key formulators of foreign policy. They determine the approximate scale of the armament budget. Their munitions holdings, however, are relatively small in comparison with their total economic stake, at home and abroad. The decisive policy voice is not of capitalists who are limited to munitions industries and their Pentagon associates.

Men like Rockefeller and Lovett, Acheson and Dulles, Harriman, Forrestal and Gates are the ones who decree the policy and its implementation, the men who finance the McDonnells and Packards, who hire the Douglas MacArthurs and Maxwell Taylors. Their key holdings are multinational corporations of oil, metals, electronics, automobiles, banking. The profits from foreign investments have multiplied many times since World War II, and far exceed the profits from munitions contracts, large as they are. The foreign policy has hurt the American economy, but it has paid off handsomely to its architects.

The profitability of foreign investments is determined mainly by U.S. military and political influence, which permits U.S. firms to operate unhindered, with super-low wages in outright neo-colonies like Taiwan and South Korea, and lower-than-U.S. wages in countries of the NATO alliance and U.S. military bases. Resistance to U.S. domination is rising in all parts of the globe; and wherever it leads to the expulsion of U.S. military and political domination, the profitability of U.S. private investments is curtailed, from Peru to Libya to Ceylon.

An outstanding example is provided currently in the Middle East. Washington spokesmen are becoming increasingly frank about their real objectives. They care no more for the security of the people of Israel than they do for the freedom of the Greek people. Their concern is for the multi-billion oil profits of Standard Oil, Texaco and Gulf, which are threatened by the growing anti-imperialist trends in the Arab countries. It's not even a matter of oil supplies. Relatively little flows from that area to the U.S. Nor is the flow of oil to Western Europe and Japan at stake. It is a matter of who will get the main profits from that oil, and nothing else.

A particular weakness of part of the opposition to the military-industrial complex is the tendency to consider this grouping in isolation from the more powerful forces of which it is a part. One sees the weakness in much congressional criticism of excesses and cost overruns in the armament program—which fails to attack the whole concept of a big military program, and often even asserts that its objective is to more effectively support the military and foreign policy objectives of the U.S. government.

The weakness also appears in much opposition to the Vietnam War, especially in the business opposition to which Silk gives so much credit. That opposition is to this one war, because it is a failure. It is often an appeal to extricate the country from that war in order to strengthen the U.S. armed forces and existing general foreign policy as a whole. Business opposition to the war is welcome, and its recent increase is a hopeful sign. But it is necessary to realize its limits. These men say, in effect, let's give up in Vietnam—our forces commit atrocities, we act like bad sports and bullies, we are turning the whole world against us, we are alienating our youth from the capitalist system. Let us pursue our foreign objectives more in accord with American traditions, cleanly and decently.

But it is the policy that leads to the atrocities. The pursuit of big business objectives led to U.S. atrocities in the Philippines in 1900, to Belgian atrocities in the Congo, to Hitler's atrocities throughout Europe, to South African apartheid, and to U.S. atrocities in Indochina. This doesn't forgive any war criminals who are personally and directly responsible for atrocities, including all postwar presidents of the United States. It doesn't make it any the less crucial to end this particular war, to get U.S. troops out of Vietnam—not only for the sake of the heroic people of Vietnam, but because defeat of U.S. imperialism in Vietnam will be a severe blow to U.S. imperialism globally. Such a rebuff will make it more difficult for U.S. imperialism to prevent the liberation of other peoples, including in the United States itself.

It is necessary to understand what the real attitude of Marxists is on this question, because we have an important part to play in the united front of all peace forces, of all anti-imperialist forces, in the United States and in the world.

• • •

10/23/1971

Children, 'Yes'; Bombs, 'No'

A two-page advertisement appeared in the editorial section of the Sunday *New York Times* of September 26. I suppose it cost $20,000 or more. That could not have mattered less to the 17 signers, who represent a wealth of $200 billion.

The first page of the ad consisted mainly of a picture of a new-born babe, a "disarming little thing"; the rest of the ad attempts to convince readers that he is a menace who should not be permitted to come onto this earth. The ad calls on readers to take three actions:

1. To urge President Nixon to spend $200 million per year, and to use all his authority, to hold down the population.
2. To urge Congress to pass a resolution favoring policies to bring about zero population growth in the United States.
3. To urge the Commission on Population Growth and the American Future (John D. Rockefeller III, Chairman) in its next report to President Nixon to recommend a policy of population stabilization (zero growth).

The main argument is that "People pollute!" Indeed, that people are the main cause of pollution. But it is capitalism and monopoly profiteering and war that destroy the environment and pollute the air and water. For example, U.S. Navy vessels pollute the oceans more than all U.S. merchant vessels.

The ad says that the cost of cleaning up our environment over the next 5 years will be $105 billion, an amount that could be financed with little more than a year's military spending.

The argument is hypocritical. The main sponsors of this ad were urging population control 20 years ago, when nobody was talking or thinking about pollution. They control the biggest oil and chemical companies, which lead in industrial pollution because they have refused to use some of their excess profits to take the necessary protective measures. They are using the pollution issue because it is so popular today. They aim to transfer that popularity to their anti-people cause. At the same time, they are trying to deflect concern from any effective struggle against real pollution.

Their ad claims: "Our cities are packed with youngsters—many of them idle and victims of drug addiction." But they oppose full employment programs; and the government, in which they and those like them have decisive influence, actually encourages the use of drugs and collaborates with drug growers and distributors, from their puppet tribesmen in Laos to the racketeer pushers in the United States.

They say "twin clouds (are) threatening mankind's survival on earth—the population bomb and the atom bomb." But they **oppose** banning the bomb and **propose** banning people! They have been the main force behind the developers and promoters of the atom bomb; they approved its use against the Japanese people. They oppose prohibition of the atom bomb and destruction of stockpiles. Some of them are profiting directly from production of atom bombs.

They try to inspire fear by listing the huge quantities of goods the baby will consume in a lifetime, but ignore the much larger quantity he will produce. The United States, and the earth, can comfortably support many more people than now live here.

To equate the atom bomb with people as a menace, and in particular with the newborn babies and the youth of the cities, demonstrates a particularly vile depth of misanthropy, of anti-humanism, and—as will be seen—of racism.

Who are the signers of the ad?

There are George Champion, retired chairman of the Chase Manhattan Bank, and Frank W. Abrams, retired number one man of Standard Oil (New Jersey). These are leading executives of the Rockefeller corporate empire, and the Rockefellers have been leading the global campaign for the reduction of population ever since World War II.

John D. Rockefeller III, chairman of Nixon's advisory commission on population, has been the family member most involved in this campaign, and it is his commission that made the outrageous statement that population growth "is an intensifier or multiplier of many of the problems impairing the quality of life in the United States."

Also among the signers are William F. May, chief executive of the American Can Co., and Hugh Moore, retired head of its Dixie Cup subsidiary. They are executives of the Morgan big business empire.

Then there is Lammot duPont Copeland, retired big wheel of the duPont chemical monopoly; General William H. Draper Jr., former Ambassador to NATO and a Dillon Read man; and Robert S. McNamara, the ex-Ford "whiz kid," now president of the World Bank and, as former Secretary of Defense, bearer of major responsibility for destroying the Vietnamese environment through genocidal warfare against the people and the land.

The 17 signers also include a window-dressing of academic, medical, religious and political figures of the establishment, as well as one well known conservationist.

What is the real purpose of the ad and the stop-the-baby campaign? It is essentially diversionary and genocidal.

It aims to divert the attention of people of good will from the struggle against imperialism, against war, against colonialism, against capitalist exploitation, against racism—to the false issue of overpopulation. But its genocidal character is even more sinister. Because of the stepped-up racist drive of the Nixon administration and big business, Washington's prime policy makers are stepping up the anti-people campaign.

Population control is directed especially against the Black people, the Chicanos, the Puerto Ricans and the Indians, as well as against poor whites in Appalachia and other depressed areas. It is accompanied by propaganda for "voluntary" sterilization and attempts to set the stage for compulsory sterilization of welfare clients.

Birth control information and free supplies of contraceptives are desirable objectives. But the policy of zero population growth, the intent actually to cut the population of Black and other oppressed peoples, is a vicious policy that should be vigorously opposed and exposed.

2/19/1977

U.S. Hypocrisy on Human Rights

In the United States today, the press, Secretary of State Cyrus Vance, and even President Jimmy Carter berate the socialist countries, often on the grounds of infringement of human rights.

But there is a recognized criterion for judging the performance of a country in its race relations: the International Convention on the Elimination of All Forms of Racial Discrimination. Adopted by the UN General Assembly in 1965, it went into effect in 1969, having been ratified by the governments of the requisite number of countries.

As of 1976, it had been ratified by about 100 countries, including all of the socialist countries in the United Nations except China and Albania, most capitalist and most developing countries. While the U.S. representative to the UN didn't dare vote against it, and even signed it, the United States has never ratified it, nor has it ever been presented to Congress for ratification. Similarly the U.S. government has refused to ratify—and hence be bound by—the convention against genocide, the two covenants on human rights, and the convention facilitating punishment of war criminals. Let's look at some of the provisions of the anti-racism convention, *which are now part of international law.*

Article 2
1. States Parties condemn racial discrimination and undertake to pursue by all appropriate means and without delay a policy of eliminating racial discrimination in all its forms and promoting understanding among all races, and, to this end:
   d) Each State Party shall prohibit and bring to an end . . . racial discrimination by any persons, group or organization.

If the United States were to abide by the Convention, there would have to be an end to the de facto discrimination by virtually every corporation and government body in the country. Discrimination would have to be abolished in education, housing, jobs, thearts, sciences and professions—in all phases of life in the United States today.

---

   e) Each State Party undertakes to encourage . . . integrationist multiracial organizations and movements and other means of eliminating barriers between races, and to discourage anything which tends to strengthen racial division.

This would require government support of all organizations supporting Black liberation, Chicano liberation, Native American liberation, the cause of Puerto Rican and Asian-American people, etc.

> 2. States Parties shall . . . take, in the social, economic, cultural and other fields, special and concrete measures to ensure the adequate development and protection of certain racial groups or individuals belonging to them, for the purpose of guaranteeing them the full and equal enjoyment of human rights and fundamental freedoms.

Actually, there have been a handful of local regulations requiring the hiring of Blacks up to their percentage of the population—e.g., in Jackson, Mississippi, municipal employment. But the counteroffensive against affirmative action has overturned some of these decrees, often using the "reverse discrimination" argument, and the move towards affirmative action has almost stopped. But Article 1, paragraph 4, specifies that affirmative action measures "shall not be deemed racial discrimination," thus discrediting the "reverse discrimination" cop-out.

> **Article 3**
> States Parties particularly condemn racial segregation and apartheid and undertake to prevent, prohibit and eradicate all practices of this nature in territories under their jurisdiction.

But in these United States, segregation in housing and education is, if anything, increasing; and the federal government not only is not taking decisive action against it, but even, in many instances, is supporting it. Under this article, President Jimmy Carter would be required to eradicate the crudely segregationist practice of his own church and of Attorney-General Griffin Bell's clubs.

> **Article 4**
> States Parties condemn all propaganda and all organizations which are based on ideas or theories of superiority of one race or group of persons of one color or ethnic origin . . . and to this end. . . .
> a) Shall declare an offense punishable by law all dissemination of ideas based on racial superiority or hatred, incitement to racial discrimination, as well as all acts of violence or incitement to such acts against any race or group of persons of another color or ethnic origin, and also the provision of any assistance to racist activities, including the financing thereof.

This provision spells out a major point in the Communist Party's election campaign platform: **make racism a crime**. It would outlaw all the hate mail and telephone calls, the vicious propaganda of a Shockley. It would severely punish the mobsters who attack Black schoolchildren and homeowners.

296

> b) Shall declare illegal and prohibit organizations, and also organized and all other propaganda activities, which promote and incite racial discrimination, and shall recognize participation in such organization or activities as an offense punishable by law.

This would outlaw the Ku Klux Klan, ROAR, and all the other overt or covert racist outfits.

It is well to remember, of course, that the USSR and other socialist countries have and enforce explicit laws in conformance with Article 4. And even Britain, a capitalist country, has recently passed a law, in partial conformity with this convention, prohibiting certain kinds of racist propaganda.

Article 5 refers to civil rights and economic, social and cultural rights, and specifies that these should be open to all, without discrimination as to race, color or national or ethnic origin. In particular . . . **a) The right to equal treatment before the tribunals and all other organs administering justice.**

As to that, compare the treatment and sentence of a Patricia Hearst, or a Claudine Longet, to that of Ruchell Magee or Gail Madden [white versus Black].

Then there is . . . d) The right to freedom of movement and residence within the borders of the States.

Well, take Lake Forest, Illinois, a suburb of Chicago. It is only one example of a town closed to Black people. Fancy residential areas all over the United States are de facto closed not only to Blacks, Puerto Ricans, Chicanos, Native Americans, but some also to Jews.

> e) . . . The right to work, to free choice of employment, to just and favorable conditions of work, to protection against unemployment, to equal pay for equal work, to just and favorable remuneration.

The gross discrimination against Blacks and other minorities on all these counts is an accepted fact in the United States. In *The Economics of Racism* I have documented the wage and job differentials between the minority peoples and whites, although all workers are partly deprived of these rights. For example, the median wage of the average Black male worker is one-quarter below that of the average white male worker in the same job.

> (v) The right to education and training.

But segregated schools, with inferior facilities and equipment, plus inadequate teachers and staff, provide substandard education to Black and Spanish-speaking pupils in U.S. schools. There is the added factor that classes are conducted in English, ignoring the potential for greater abilities if Spanish were also used in Puerto Rican and Chicano neighborhoods.

Article 7

States Parties undertake to adopt immediate and effective measures, particularly in the fields of teaching, education, culture and information, with a view to combating prejudices which lead to racial discrimination and to promoting understanding, tolerance and friendship among nations and racial or ethnical groups, as well as to propagating the purposes and principles of the Charter of the United Nations and of various UN conventions dealing with human rights.

This would require a whole set of new textbooks and curricula in U.S. schools, plus special media programs on a sustained basis. And it would require really mass distribution of documents, such as this UN Convention, which are essentially suppressed in the United States.

One provision of the Helsinki accords, to which the U.S. government is committed, is relevant to the issue of racism. Needless to say, this section is **not** one the U.S. publicizes!

In the "second basket," item 6 of the Economic and Social Aspects of Migrant Labor calls on participating states:

". . . to ensure equality of rights between migrant workers and nationals of the host countries with regard to conditions of employment and work and to social security, and to endeavor to ensure that migrant workers may enjoy satisfactory living conditions, especially housing conditions."

Migrant workers are also to have an equal break at getting other jobs in the event of unemployment, and **the right . . . to receive . . . regular information in their own language.**

The gross violation of this provision was highlighted recently when 150,000 Florida fruit and vegetable workers, almost all migrants, were thrown out of work without unemployment insurance, without sources of food and shelter, without any prospect of another job. Of course, virtually all of these migratory workers are Black and/or Spanish speaking.

• • •

1/19/1984

Democrats' 'Jobs for the Future'

The Democratic Party's pamphlet *Jobs for the Future*, prepared by a senatorial task force headed by Senator Edward M. Kennedy, aims to win votes in the 1984 campaigns. But it fails to present a program that would provide jobs for the millions of unemployed; nor is it likely to be effective in defeating Reagan. Aside from some rhetoric, it does not really differ fundamentally from the big business line pursued so aggressively by the Reagan administration.

The pamphlet gives some facts on how workers' conditions have worsened and how the country's foreign trade position and economic effectiveness have deteriorated—under Democrats, as well as Republicans. But it advances no clear, decisive program for reversing these declines.

Agreeing that government policy is crucial, it adopts the slogan, "Neither Central Planning nor Aimless Drift." Comprehensive central planning is, of course, impossible in a capitalist society; but forceful government planning is possible and necessary to formulate, enact and carry out a program to provide the 15 million additional jobs that are required in the U.S.

All capitalist governments do, as the pamphlet says, intervene in and regulate the economy to some extent. And the Reagan administration, in its planning and regulation, is far from "aimless." It definitely aims, with exceptional aggressiveness, to aid the drive of big business to increase the exploitation of labor, to destroy the trade unions, to restore fully racist discrimination. It aims to expand the areas controlled militarily and politically by U.S. imperialism as modern slave markets for U.S.-owned transnational corporations. Above all, it aims to build up a nuclear superiority with which to launch a first strike to destroy the USSR—a plan that must be stopped to prevent destruction of all humanity.

Incredibly, the Democratic Party's report doesn't even mention the soaring military budget and aggressive actions of the Reaganites, which are at the heart of the deteriorating conditions of most in the U.S.

It mentions declining real wages since 1973, but has no proposals to reverse the decline. On the contrary, it proposes to make it easier for employers to cut wages by offering to continue payment of partial unemployment insurance to unemployed workers who accept wage cuts as a condition for reemployment. Such payments, in effect, are subsidies to corporations at labor's ultimate expense. It doesn't even mention the Reagan administration's anti-union drive nor its extreme racism and increasing discrimination against Blacks and Hispanics, let alone propose to do anything about these evils.

In any effective job program, organized labor has to play a major role. But the Kennedy Commission limits unions to representation on a quadripartite advisory council with "no power to override regulations or change laws." The unions, the Congressional Black Caucus and most progressive groups recognize that any program to reduce unemployment must include a provision that the federal government directly supply jobs to restore the infrastructure, operate industries abandoned by private companies, etc. The Democratic program proposes only a trivial "community service" (make-work) job program in distressed communities, for workers over 55 who have exhausted their unemployment insurance.

The pamphlet's main proposals are for standard big business benefit:

Investment incentives. The Democrats want to "improve" the very liberal Republican investment incentives by encouraging state investment agencies—which operate mainly to stimulate runaway shops—and by encouraging research and development by continuing Republican-enacted tax credits and amending antitrust laws to permit monopolistic R&D ventures. There is no plan to slash the military R&D diversion of more than half the country's skilled researchers and resources, the main reason for the U.S. lag behind other countries in civilian product improvement. There is no proposal for a major federal R&D program, coordinated with nationalized enterprises in steel and other key sectors, to revive basic industry.

Job training, better targeted to growing occupations, is certainly worthwhile. But it doesn't create a single job. It helps particular workers get jobs, but its overall social effect is the provision of government subsidies to private firms that traditionally trained their workers at their own expense, which is why big business supports such programs. Nor is there social merit in the proposal that workers in "declining industries" be encouraged to resign and receive unemployment benefits while enrolled in approved training programs. That avoids dealing with the need to revive basic industries and to prevent transnationals from moving their production abroad.

Foreign trade does play an increasing role in economic life. Opposing protectionism in words, the Kennedy Commission proposes particular protectionist measures as combating "unfair trade practices." Its main focus is on export promotion, but along standard lines of government advice to industry.

There is no proposal for ending the economic warfare against the USSR and other socialist countries, which effectively bars U.S. goods from the world's most rapidly growing markets. Nor for ending U.S. imperialist aggression, which hampers the revolutionary changes necessary for the well-being of the billions of people in Latin America, Africa and Asia—changes that would open up markets unprecedented in world history.

The bankruptcy of this Democratic Party program shows the importance of widely publicizing the Communist Party candidates and their concrete, effective program for providing 15 million jobs through public works, nationalizing key industries, slashing the workweek, raising wages and benefits, ending discrimination, providing labor with a major role in economic management, and opening trade with socialist and developing countries.

$$\bullet \ \bullet \ \bullet$$

7/2/1994

Crime Pays—but for Whom?

For the past 15 years, at least, the U.S. policy makers have made **crime** a key political issue. With their control of the media, they have persuaded masses of people that crime is the main problem facing the country. Their objectives are:

- To divert the working class from the struggle for jobs, for labor's rights, for all the required social needs that are deteriorating and neglected.
- To foment racism and thereby justify the police, immigration, etc., offensive against African Americans and Latinos.
- To prevent united action, social and political, of minority peoples and labor.

- To ensure election of far-right candidates to office—e.g., Reagan and Bush, Wilson in California, Giuliani in New York—and to drive the country in the direction of fascism.

Yes, the United States is surely the crime capital of the world. But—and this may be a surprise—there is less crime now than before racist politicians elevated fear of crime to fever pitch during the Reagan campaign in 1980. Since 1975, the crime rate has fallen 30%. However, the number of people imprisoned has multiplied four times between 1970 and 1991, and by now has reached an estimated 1.5 million—the highest in the world in relation to population.

How come? The rightward shift of political power has increased convictions and sentences. A series of federal and state laws now include severe sentencing requirements.

"In the 1980s, draconian sentencing laws were used to combat the drug problem . . . 60% of inmates in federal prisons and 20% in state prisons are there on drug charges." (*Business Week*, 12/13/93). Many convictions are for trivial possession, an offense that never puts rich users in jail.

President Clinton is giving priority to new crime legislation, which would intensify the drive toward a police state, with its sharp edge against the working class, with a veritable ripping through African American and Latino communities. This drive profits the capitalists by weakening labor, thereby facilitating greater exploitation of workers. It would also generate a shift of tax and spending policies that favor capital versus labor—plus the fact that billions will flow into the pockets of a special sector of corporate America—the direct profiteers from the sums that will be spent for repression.

Total spending for cops, prisons, courts, etc., have gone up as follows: 1954—$2.1 billion was spent; in 1970—$8.6 billion; in 1990—$76 billion! A rising share of the total goes to corporate contractors for prison construction, high-tech police equipment and management of privatized prisons.

A *Wall Street Journal* lead feature (5/12) was headed: "Triangle of interests creates infrastructure to fight lawlessness—cities see jobs; politicians sense a popular issue—and businesses cash in.

"These . . . interests are forging a new 'iron triangle' similar to . . . that of arms makers, military services and lawmakers formed three decades ago." Despite declining Pentagon orders, armament manufacturers are reaping rising profits through accelerated munitions exports and, especially, "conversion" to weapons of repression.

"Westinghouse Electric, Minnesota Mining & Manufacturing Co., General Dynamics . . . have created special divisions to retool their defense technology for America's streets." Sandia National Laboratories, a major research and development center for nuclear weapons, is experimenting with blinding and deafening sprays.

Goldman Sachs, Prudential Insurance, Merrill Lynch are "competing to underwrite prison construction with private, tax-exempt bonds—no voter approval required." New specialist corporations have made it to the Big Board. Corrections Corp. of America just broke $100 million in sales. "Its founders and officers include big contributors to both major parties."

Further, the item noted, ". . . Businessmen stood up and cheered in Massachusetts when . . . Sen. Edward Kennedy announced that Fort Devens, slated for closure, would be converted to a federal prison.

The latest federal budget hammered social programs, which would deter crime, but jumped anti-crime spending by 21%—including a 5-year 68% rise in federal prison construction and maintenance! The new anti-crime package, which Congress is expected to pass soon, will force even sharper increases. Clinton wants it to include the notorious "three-strikes-and-you're-out" proposal for mandatory life sentences.

Taxes

6/24/1962

Bitter Tax Medicine

The almost paranoiac animosity of many business executives towards President Kennedy, erupting after the steel price episode, may be dissolving or moderating as Wall Street and Washington get together to put over a piece of fiscal grand larceny.

By the built-in conditions of law and administration, there has been a gradual shift of the tax burden from rich to poor, continuing in this regime. Also, the NAM regularly urges reduction in corporate and upper-bracket taxes. Prospects for such cuts were enhanced when Kennedy espoused the argument that they were desirable to stimulate investment, economic growth and employment. He and his advisors worked out their own fancy way of doing it: through the Kennedy-Dillon program introduced in 1961 and now on its way to passage. As feared, the balancing "loophole closing" features have all but vanished, leaving a $2.5 billion bonanza for corporations—the $1.5 billion in tax credit against new machinery expenditure going through Congress, and the $1 billion from faster depreciation regulations about to be issued by the Treasury.

Early in June, attempting to assuage business hostility, restore confidence in the stock market, and forestall a new recession, Kennedy and Treasury Secretary Dillon unveiled the main features of the major tax "reform" they will introduce in 1963. Dillon announced the corporate and individual tax cuts, without mentioning rates. The *Wall Street Journal* revealed that under tentative plans the corporate rate will drop from 52% to 50% or less, and the top individual rate from 91% to 65%. Cuts will narrow with incomes. The under $2,000 bracket, split in half, will apparently be cut from 20% to an average of 17.5%. Of course, nobody actually pays anywhere near 91%, but the proportions of change are meaningful.

The result will be a bonanza of up to 100% in the after-tax income of the very rich, but perhaps 1% in the after-tax income of the poor.

Well, it looks as if everybody is getting **something** out of the deal. Big business lobbying seems to have succeeded in preserving "freedom" for expense account racketeering, foreign tax haven manipulations, and the like, minimizing

loophole closing possibilities. So what are the catches? Here is one: the total package will mean a net cut of $5-6 billion in government tax receipts, offsetting the new revenue levies. What will these be?

Dillon let the cat out of the bag about the administration's new approach, which is an old one for his financial class. He said that "any reduction will cost the government revenue, and will bring with it the need to broaden the base of our tax structure so as to offset the reductions in whole or in part." No decisions have been made on "the form and extent of possible offsetting measures to broaden the income tax base."

Thus taxes paid by workers, especially those with low wages, will be increased, either through lowering income tax exemptions or through sales taxes, or other devices to "broaden the base"—euphemism for raising mass taxation. Benjamin Javits, brother of the Republican Senator, has openly called for a turnover tax to make up for upper income tax revenue losses.

Business seems pleased with these proposed further concessions, but asks for still more. U.S. Steel chairman Blough claims Kennedy's depreciation regulations will be insufficient, and demands, in essence, a better-than-wartime deal to permit super-fast depreciation of old and new property, which would cut U.S. Steel's bill by perhaps $50-75 million yearly.

The New York Times suggests that the big cut scheduled for 1963 might well be enacted right now. Thus, the market drop and anti-Kennedy propaganda may be used to create an atmosphere of alarm permitting a $5-10 billion tax steal this year, with the administration going along because this is its ultimate program anyhow. Whether administered in two doses or one, the medicine is bad.

It is prescribed on the false diagnosis of economic difficulties, and the claim that such tax policies will stimulate economic growth and employment. Moreover, Kennedy has openly adopted the cold war Keynesian line that a permanent government deficit ensures steady growth and wards off recessions.

The policies in question will not accomplish such economic ends in the short run, and will worsen economic stagnation and unemployment in the long run, while hastening dollar devaluation and a faster run-up of living costs. They will enrich the haves, and impoverish the have-nots.

Corporation boards have organized stockholders to lobby for their kind of tax program. It is high time for labor to do likewise.

• • •

8/20/1967

The 10% Surtax

If Johnson's 10% addition to income taxes becomes law, the federal government will take $100 billion out of workers' paychecks next year, including 50¢ out of every dollar of added wages.

Johnson tries to sugarcoat the surtax by saying the tax burden will be less than before he came into office. It will be less—on his Texas oil cronies, on the munitions merchants, multinational corporations and Wall Street banks.

But the burden on labor is already far heavier than before Johnson. Labor is now paying 50% more taxes than prior to Kennedy's assassination. If Johnson has his way, labor's tax bill when the next president is elected in November 1968 will be almost double that when Johnson was sworn in 5 years earlier.

The figures follow:

Federal Taxes Withheld Year	Billions	Percent of Wages & Salaries
Fiscal 1963	$53.6	17.7%
Fiscal 1965	54.5	15.8
Fiscal 1967	77.5	18.9
Calendar 1968 (with the surtax)	101.8	22.1

The peak tax load on labor during World War II was about 11%; and during the Korean War, 14%. Over 35% of the increase in payrolls during the last two fiscal years was taken by Washington to pay for the Vietnam War. The $23 billion rise in the annual tax burden approximated the cost of the war in fiscal 1967.

So Johnson has succeeded in making labor pay the entire cost of his dirty war.

Suppose Congress enacts the 10% surtax and proposed social security tax boosts. Then in calendar year 1968 the federal government will withhold $101.8 billion, or 22.1% of estimated wages and salaries. The rise over fiscal 1967 will eat up half the estimated increase in annual payrolls. And the amount of the hike means Johnson wants to raise Vietnam War spending to $45-$50 billion yearly.

What does this mean to the individual worker?

A 6% increase will leave him with the same take-home pay as formerly. And then he will still have to cope with higher state and local taxes, which are also going up faster than ever because of the Vietnam War. With what is still left, he will have to pay the inflating consumer prices, already going up at an admitted 3.6% annual rate, and likely to rise faster if the tax increase goes through.

The 5% annual wage increase pattern forming over the past year will not be enough to prevent a substantial drop in real take-home pay. To meet higher living costs, higher state and local taxes, and Johnson's proposed tax increases will require annual wage increases of 10-15%.

If Johnson has his way.

But he need not have his way. This surtax can be beaten more easily than 10-15% annual wage increases can be won. It can be beaten despite Meany's anti-labor action in supporting it. Congressmen have been receiving heavy mail against it, including letters from "hawks." Rep. John E. Hunt (R-NJ) reported a big "hawk" majority in a poll of constituents. But 87% voted against Johnson's surtax to pay for the escalation!

This is a time and occasion on which enough of them can be convinced to send Johnson and his Vietnam War to their most crushing domestic defeat.

• • •

3/4/1969

The U.S. Tax Apparatus in 1969

Note: This is a condensed version of the series of seven columns on Nixon's 1970 Budget. It appeared in March and April of 1969. Duplications and some descriptive material were eliminated, but no relevant data were omitted, and no facts were changed.

Losing Your Wages Down the Tax Drain

Everybody complains about taxes, but nobody knows what to do about them. Nobody but the rich, who have had the laws stacked to let them off lightly. Big tax chunks are taken out of people's paychecks. Sales and excise taxes, open and hidden, blow up already inflated prices. Homeowners—most American families—pay crippling real estate taxes. The bills come from Washington, the State Capitol, City Hall, and school districts.

Taxes soar much faster than people's incomes. Indignation mounts as stories of wealthy individuals and giant corporations avoiding taxes are publicized. Public opinion has made tax reform a major domestic economic issue before Congress. Proposals are advanced by Congressmen, unions, government officials.

At the same time, people are fed misleading propaganda concerning the cause of high taxes, who pays and who doesn't pay.

Let's analyze the data about the colossal swindle imposed by a small exploiting minority upon a large working majority. But first, let's briefly review the history of the income tax in the United States.

The income tax was originally a progressive tax, levied according to ability to pay. It was urged by Marx and Engels 120 years ago; it was promoted by American reformers and fiercely resisted by American capitalists. At first, when finally enacted, it was paid almost wholly by capitalists and other rich people and corporations. Only a handful of highly paid workers paid any income tax.

Workers were protected by personal exemptions higher than the average wages then prevailing, and by a liberal tax credit against earned income.

Since the start of World War II the capitalists have gradually turned the income tax around. They were able to keep cutting the personal exemption until now, in real terms, it is about one-fifth of what it was before World War II. The earned income credit was removed and a dividend credit was substituted, as well as numerous other "loopholes" through which property income escapes taxation. Withholding taxes from workers' paychecks was initiated on an arbitrary "pay-as-you-go" basis, while capitalists continue to figure their own tax on the "honor" system, and they pay after they receive their income.

What Is the Situation Now?

Between 1929 and 1968 total tax payments to all U.S. governments—national, state and local—increased 23 times. Of course prices, incomes, and population also rose. So, to measure the tax burden, we must compare tax payments with the national income.

In 1929 taxes took 13% of the national income.

In 1939 taxes took 21%.

In 1945, at the peak of World War II, taxes took 29%.

In 1968, after 4 years of Vietnam, taxes took 37%.

The burden of taxes is higher than ever before. It is nearly three times as high as in 1929.

Who Pays the Taxes?

Two-thirds of all taxes are paid to the federal government: taxes paid by workers—income taxes and employment taxes deducted from payrolls, excise taxes and customs taxes; and those paid by men of property and their corporations—individual income taxes not withheld from paychecks, corporation income taxes, estate and gift taxes, and certain taxes on property and property income.

In fiscal 1941, just before the U.S. entered World War II, workers paid 45% of the taxes, capitalists 55%; in fiscal 1968 workers paid 66%, capitalists 34%. And according to the budget for the coming fiscal year, 1970, workers will pay 68%, capitalists 32%. Workers will pay more than twice as much as capitalists.

The federal government expects to collect $196 billion in fiscal 1970. Workers are to pay $133 billion, capitalists $63 billion. If the burden were distributed as in 1941—45% paid by workers, 55% by capitalists—the workers would pay $45 billion less, and the capitalists $45 billion more. Thus American workers are being swindled out of $45 billion per year through shifting of the tax burden from the rich and corporations. And the same development has taken effect in re state and local taxes. Workers now pay about 40% of their income in taxes. About two of every five wage and salary dollars go down the tax drain, directly, or hidden in the cost of purchases.

Where Do the Taxes Go?

The federal budget schedules total spending of $195.3 billion for fiscal 1970, which begins July 1st of this year. It classifies $81.5 billion as "national defense"; but many other budgeted items are actually for military purposes, direct and indirect. Fully one-third of these items are to support the Vietnam War, the rest carry over from past wars. Actual military spending will be well above the $115.3 billion budgeted, if the Vietnam War continues.

Big business subsidy and "pork-barrel" projects are scheduled to get $16 billion under the captions "commerce and transportation," "agriculture," and "national resources." Provision for social security payments, including Medicare, is $46.1 billion. In effect, this vast insurance system is paid for by the workers, and operated by the government.

The remaining $19.5 billion of welfare programs, broadly speaking, is financed out of general revenues. They are grouped under "community development and housing"; "education and manpower"; and "health and welfare." Far from all of this is really for people's welfare. Even so, it amounts to only 10% of the total budget, or 17% of the military budget. The public assistance program—the "welfare" that reactionaries often blame for higher taxes—comes to only $4.5 billion of the $19.5 billion, or 2.3% of the overall budget.

Besides outright subsidy programs, most of the military spending consists of profit-heavy orders for big business, and the $16 billion budgeted for interest is pure profit for the bankers.

Taken all in all, the federal budget has become a vast class-biased taxation machine for transferring money from labor to capital, from the poor to the rich. That and the military are the main parts of the budget.

Withholding Taxes and the Vietnam War: The Hidden $80 Billion

There was a time when workers were hit mainly by indirect taxes—sales and excise taxes. Today the biggest chunks are taken by direct taxes, which the workers never see. The government keeps quiet about the income tax withheld from workers' pay. The President's Budget Message, which is published in all the newspapers, doesn't give the figure, which is on page 496 of the detailed document, *The Budget of the United States Government, 1970*. The complete document is available only through the Government Printing Office in Washington.

This semi-secret figure—the individual income taxes withheld from workers' paychecks—is set at $79,800,000,000 in fiscal 1970. Imagine it, about $80 billion to be withheld from workers' wages. An additional $20 billion-plus will be withheld for social security payments. Thus a total of over $100 billion will be taken out of workers' paychecks directly by the federal government, and more billions will be taken by state and city governments.

In fiscal 1965, just before masses of troops went to Vietnam, federal income taxes withheld from workers' paychecks came to $36.8 billion. The $79.8 billion projected for fiscal 1970, just 5 years later, is 117% more.

Individual income taxes paid by capitalists in fiscal 1965 totaled $16.8 billion and are projected at $23.4 billion in fiscal 1970. That is an increase of 39%, or one-third the percentage increase borne by workers. Gross corporation income taxes amounted to $26.1 billion in fiscal 1965, and are projected at $39.2 billion in fiscal 1970, for an increase of 50%.

In fiscal 1970 "other" income taxes and corporate income taxes combined will come to $63 billion. The $80 billion to be withheld from workers' paychecks is $17 billion more. We have already crossed the divide where the working class carries the main burden of the federal income tax.

The War Surtax

The trade unions' priority demand is for repeal of the Vietnam War surtax. They call on President Nixon to keep his campaign promise to let the tax expire in mid-1969. However, *The New York Times* reports:

"Mr. Kennedy [Treasury Secretary] said the surcharge on business and personal incomes was tied directly to United States involvement in the Vietnam War, which Administration calculations say will continue at present levels for the next 22 months." (2/17)

Thus, Kennedy confesses that Nixon lied while campaigning, and intends to continue to put a big wartime financial burden on the workers' shoulders. Moreover, comparing real tax rates for fiscal 1965 with those of fiscal 1970 shows:

The effective surtax on workers, by fiscal 1970, will be 45%, not 10%.

The effective surtax on capitalists will be zero.

The effective surtax on corporations will be zero.

State and Local Taxes

Passage of proposals up before state legislatures this year will raise state taxes nearly $5 billion, or 13%. Similar increases in local taxes are being levied, and they hit workers and the poor hardest—sales taxes, income taxes with rate structures that make them virtual payroll taxes, hikes in realty taxes directed almost exclusively against small homeowners.

State and local **sales tax** collections reached $19.3 billion in 1967, after doubling in only 8 years. State and local **income taxes** tripled in the same 8 years, reaching $6.3 billion, most of it paid by workers. **Property taxes** reached $26.7 billion, not quite doubling in 8 years.

The share of property taxes paid by small homeowners and renters has escalated. During the 10 years 1957-1967, taxes paid on residential properties increased 135%, from $6.8 billion to $16.1 billion. By now, the average tax on a one-family home is $400 nationally, and $500 in metropolitan areas. Workers pay most of the residential property tax, as homeowners or as passed on to them in rent by landlords.

$45 Billion Tax Avoidance

The U.S. Budget Bureau estimates that next fiscal year corporations will pay an average of only 39.5% on their admitted profits, instead of the paper rate, including surtax, of 52.8%. The U.S. government will lose $12.8 billion by this.

Just two examples:

Standard Oil (N.J.): 1967 federal income taxes of $166 million on profits of $1,439 million before such taxes, for a rate of 11.5%. That was higher than usual. In 1962 it paid only $8 million on $849 million, or 0.9%.

Standard Oil of California: 1967 federal income taxes of $6 million on profits of $428 million, for a rate of 1.4%.

Every large corporation deducts from its revenues large amounts of hidden profits disguised as fictitious expenses. So the actual profits are much larger than reported, and the actual tax rate lower.

The U.S. government devotes much of its huge military machine to protecting the foreign investments of U.S. corporations. But hardly a cent of the ten billions of profits now being made annually on these investments comes into the Treasury as income tax.

A low rate, 22% (before surtax), on the first $25,000 of profits, is supposedly to help small business. A recent Treasury study shows that big corporations avoid large sums by dividing their tax returns into as many as 500 little pieces, claiming the lower rate on each of them.

Using official government data, estimates of the amount of taxes avoided through the major corporate income tax loopholes comes to $45 billion.

How to reclaim the $45 billion:

- Retain the 10% surtax on corporations.
- Cancel the investment credit, and all other special credits for corporations.
- Fully tax all profits on foreign investments, with no allowance for payments made to foreign governments. Often these are payoffs in exchange for anti-labor laws that keep wages at a fraction of the U.S. level.
- Tax all operating profits, less deductions only for strictly limited, necessary, overhead items.
- Limit depreciation allowances to the old, straight line rates. Eliminate all depletion allowances, "intangible drilling," and other trick deductions of the oil and mining companies.
- Allow no deductions for salaries, "travel and entertainment expenses," bonuses and stock options to corporation officials and top executives.
- Allow no deductions for advertising, corporate donations, research and development and capital investment.
- Allow no lower rates or non-taxation for special groups of corporations or special types of income.
- Limit the 22% small corporate rate to legitimate small business operations.

Foundations and Trust Funds

Hundred-millionaire and billionaire families set up supposedly charitable foundations to avoid taxes on all the monies turned over to them. The $3 billion Ford Foundation was set up for the avowed purpose of evading the estate tax when the family fortune moved from one generation to the next.

The "founding" families retain effective control over the money, using it for business or political purposes. The Hughes Medical Institute, for example, is manipulated by Howard Hughes to reduce taxes paid by his huge armament firm.

Posing as "do-gooders," foundations also meddle in other countries' affairs.

They use slogans of "population control," "land reform," and even—the acme of hypocrisy—"tax reform!" Their purpose is to strengthen regimes providing profitable conditions for U.S. corporations owned by the same millionaires who control the foundations.

Foundations collect very substantial dividends and interest, all tax-free. Proposals currently before Congress would place an inadequate tax of 20% on such income. Foundation incomes should be taxed at the corporate rate.

Representative Wright Patman's Banking and Currency Committee showed that by 1967 the bank-managed trust funds of the super-rich reached $180 billion, 10 times as large as the sum in foundations

Trust funds are important. They are the core of the spider web through which a small group of financial tycoons, owning the principal banks, monopolize the economic life of the United States.

They are also an important mechanism for tax evasion. They are supposed to pay regular individual tax rates, and their rich owners would pay in the top brackets. However in 1965 the trusts and estates, which are part of the bank-operated trusts, paid a tax of only $659 million, or 7.7%, on reported income of $8,512 million.

... and other ploys

The rich and their corporations also play off one state and township against another. They set up plants where they are offered the lowest taxes, or even subsidized with tax-exempt industrial bonds. They close down plants in places that maintain reasonable taxes on business property. They set up their legal residences where income and estate taxes are lowest, and where they are able to bargain down their real estate taxes.

A people's tax movement cannot yield to such threats. A real struggle over local taxes can win concessions, and also provide the spark that ignites a major national tax struggle.

What's to be done?

Tax reform is urgently needed. Demand should include homestead exemptions for small homeowners; higher taxes on big industrial and commercial properties; elimination of sales taxes and taxes on labor income; increased taxes on wealthy individuals and on corporations; taxes on extraction of mineral and forest wealth, on inheritances, on banking and stock exchange transactions. However, the exact demands have to be worked out in terms of the particular tax problems of each area.

American workers produce more than enough to provide every worker with a real income of $10,000 per year, plus differentials for skill.

Our program eliminates the federal income tax on workers and employees with incomes under $10,000, and sharply cuts it for workers' incomes above that level:

End the war surtax: This is the first step. It requires enough public pressure to persuade a majority of Congress not to vote for its extension. Then it will die June 30, saving individual taxpayers $8 billion.

Raise personal exemptions: Personal exemptions should be raised to $3,000 for a single person, and $1,500 for each dependent. That approximates, in real terms, the pre-World War II exemptions. In addition, Congress should provide for an automatic increase each year in proportion to rising living costs.

The higher exemptions will save taxpayers $40 billion in the coming fiscal year.

Tax credit for wages and salaries: During the decade 1934-1943 there was a 10% tax credit on earned income. Congress should enact a 10% credit applicable to the first $10,000 of a person's wage or salary income—a tax credit, not a deduction. Thus, a worker making $9,000 per year would first calculate his tax, and then subtract $900 from the tax to determine what he actually has to pay.

This tax credit will save workers $20 billion, over and above what they will save from the higher exemptions.

Remove war excises: Congress should repeal (or not renew) the $9 billion of manufacturers' and users' excise taxes on autos, tires, gasoline, telephone bills, airline tickets, etc. Most of these were introduced as wartime emergency taxes, but kept on indefinitely. The big business demand for a value added tax should be rejected. No additions should be made to existing alcohol and tobacco taxes.

Freeze social security deductions: The combined social security deductions are scheduled to go up from 9.6% to 10.4%, and the ceiling of application from $7,800 to $9,000 in the new budget. Congress should not enact these increases. This will save taxpayers $3 billion at an annual rate. All future increases in social security benefits should be paid out of general revenues, with no increase in wage withholdings.

Taken together, our proposals will save taxpayers $80 billion, 90% by workers.

• • •

4/1969

How the Rich Avoid Taxes

Newspapers do not carry ads for courses in robbery and embezzlement.

But plenty of ads advise executives and businessmen to send $100 and learn 100 ways of getting away with tax evasion. Wealthy alumni are urged to contribute to their alma mater and let Uncle Sam pay 70% of the bill via tax deductions.

A half million accountants and lawyers make their living figuring out how the rich and their corporations can get away with the most taxes, and acting as buffers for them in dickering with Internal Revenue agents.

Here are a few of the main ways rich individuals avoid income taxes:

- Capital gains: The rich in 1967 admitted capital gains of $28 billion, but paid taxes, mainly at a reduced rate, on only $14 billion.

- Phony farms: The rich call their country estates "farms" and the cost of living in luxury on them "farm losses." In 1967, 101 persons in the million plus bracket reported "farm losses" averaging $75,000 each.
- The expense account racket: There are no statistics on this vast opening. I estimate that at least $15 billion of rich men's living expenses are charged to business accounts. Most of this avoids taxes twice, by the corporation and by the capitalist.
- Fantastic deductions or non-inclusions in income for "charitable contributions," tax-exempt interest, oil depletion, and many other items.

• • •

4/10/1971

Taxes and You (What's Left of You)

Year by year, the workers' share of the tax payments increases, the share of the capitalists decreases. For the present 1971 fiscal year, tax collections are off because of mass layoffs and the economic slump, and because of effects of the 1969 Tax Reform Act, reducing rates. But let's see whose payments were cut how much.

Withholdings from workers' paychecks were lower by less than 1%!

Other individual tax payments—by capitalists and other non-workers—were lower by 9%!

Corporation tax payments were 17% lower!

Thus an additional few percent will be added to the workers' share of the federal tax burden and a like percentage taken off the capitalists' share.

The "Tax Reform" Act of 1969 was passed as a result of a mass "tax revolt." Unions lobbied Congress. Groups of individuals picketed internal revenue offices. Hundreds refused to pay all or part of their tax, as a political protest against its use in the Vietnam aggression.

Originally the idea was to ease the burden on the workers, and to close the glaring loopholes of the rich and the corporations. But in the end there was a "compromise." Workers' taxes were cut a little, but the taxes of the rich and the corporations were cut more. Moreover, the cut for workers was merely temporary.

One trick of the income tax system is a fixed personal exemption, which is important for lower and middle-income people, unimportant for the rich. As wages rise in proportion to living costs, the real value of the exemption declines. The reform provided for a gradual increase in exemptions, but living costs are increasing faster; so by 1973, when the reform is complete, the real exemption will be less than it was in the first place. At the same time, the withholding rate for social security will be considerably higher. So by 1973, under present laws, workers will have a larger percentage bite taken out of their paychecks than in 1969, at the height of the Vietnam War. Meanwhile, all the tax cuts enjoyed by the rich will be retained, and are being steadily expanded, as new tricks are discovered and old ones pushed further.

There was special indignation in Congress in 1969 over the many millionaires who pay no federal income tax at all. Much publicity was given to a reform supposed to make certain that everybody paid at least a 10% tax—obviously a ridiculous rate for a multi-millionaire like David Rockefeller, who admits he has no tax to pay—but claims he pays a small tax, just to be patriotic.

But the proposed reform was watered down, and ended up with a number of new loopholes. Here is what has happened so far. In 1967 there were 155 persons with incomes over $200,000 who paid no tax. In 1969 there were 301 persons with incomes over $200,000 who paid no tax. Rep. Henry Reuss (D-WI) was quoted as saying that the "reform" makes it easier than ever for the rich to avoid taxes. He predicted that in 1970 again "hundreds of wealthy non-taxpayers" will get off "scot-free."

There was also much controversy over excessive depreciation and depletion charges by corporations and holders of oil royalty rights, luxury farms, etc. After lengthy maneuvering a slight cut was made in the most notorious device, the 27% oil depletion rule.

But early in 1971 Nixon delivered another big bonanza to the rich. He ordered the Internal Revenue Service to arbitrarily permit corporations and private business generally to increase by 20% their depreciation deductions. He didn't ask Congress' permission. He never does any more, for anything. "I-am-the-law" Nixon decided it. By official estimates, it will save corporations $4.4 billion in taxes, which means, in the long run, it will add $4.4 billion to the workers' tax burden.

These days most corporations keep a triple set of books:

One set is for the tax collector. It shows very little profit, so as to provide very little taxes.

Another is for the published annual report. That usually shows a higher profit, so as to encourage investors to buy stock in the company. But when wage negotiations are coming up, it often shows the same as the report to the tax collector, or even a more gloomy picture, so as to provide an argument against workers' wage demands.

The third set of books is the detailed analysis of "cash flow" for the controlling executive committee, and for the confidential use of the corporations' bankers and selected large private and institutional stockholders. That shows, in one way or another, the real profit picture.

The one sure way to radical tax reform is to have a socialist revolution. There are no big capitalists in socialist countries, and very low or non-existent individual income taxes. However workers can win considerable concessions under capitalism. That takes a real tax revolt. Real mass action to stop outrageous taxes on workers, and to make the corporations pay.

• • •

5/6/1982

Polluted Harbor

Reaganite publicists are expert at perfuming filth linguistically. Consider the phrase "safe harbor." Doesn't it make you think of something clean and good and peaceful?

Treasury Secretary Donald F. Regan, former head of the country's biggest stock-promotion operation, now uses "safe harbor" to identify the newest and crudest tax swindle yet—the tax leasing deals authorized by Congress last year.

The Economic Recovery Tax Act of 1981, otherwise known as ERTA, legalized a ploy that was formerly a serious offense: using a "wash sale" to evade taxes. It is a "wash sale" when somebody sells something and immediately buys it back for the same price to get a tax advantage from the sale.

ERTA made the swindle safe—hence "safe harbor"—and into that harbor the biggest monopolies sailed with nearly $10 billion of our money.

Here's how it works [company names invented]. Consider the Multirow Farm Combine Corporation that purchased $150 million of new production machinery in 1981. Under previous ERTA provisions, it could cut its taxes by perhaps $100 million through investment credits and fast depreciation on the new machinery. But, thanks to the aftereffects of Jimmy Carter's anti-Soviet grain embargo, profits were less than usual. And through various other deductions allowed—interest payments to bankers, super salaries to its top brass, and tax credits for its foreign operations—it didn't owe any federal income tax for 1981.

So the chief executive of Multirow turned to a tax pilot: "Find me a corporation to pay me good money for $100 million of tax savings I cannot use." The pilot found a perfect recession-proof corporation—Universal Personal Services, Inc., one of the Big Three in coffins. Universal made plenty in 1981; its growth rate was unchecked. It didn't buy new machinery: the old plant made fine coffins. It might even have to pay $100 million in federal income taxes. Horrors!

The pilot brought manna from heaven, if not for Universal's customers, at least for its stockholders. He guided Universal into a "safe harbor" for that $100 million.

So: Multirow "sold" its new machines to Universal. Universal left the machines in Multirow's factories to produce combines, but "leased" them back to Multirow. The contracts provided that each year Universal had to pay a "purchase installment" to Multirow exactly equal to the "rent" Multirow had to pay to Universal.

In short, it was a net zero transaction. A "wash sale."

Except that on the books, Universal now "owned" the equipment and could claim the $100 million in tax breaks for its "investment." For that privilege it paid Multirow a "down payment" of $70 million. The end result: the U.S. Treasury lost $100 million in taxes. Multirow got an extra $70 million free and clear. Universal saved $28 million it would otherwise have had to pay. The other $2 million went to the "pilot" for his services. And the chief executives of both companies could boast of helping President Reagan's objectives—"taking the government off the backs of business" and reducing wasteful spending for "welfare cheats and loafers."

The Treasury Department prepared statistical analysis of about 2,000 "safe harbor" leases concluded in 1981. They estimated that there were "wash sales," or the equivalent, on property worth $19.3 billion, on about three quarters of which "tax benefits" of $6.8 billion were shown. Extending this proportionately, and adjusting to the total tax savings from a reduced "present value" on part of them, brings the indicated total to $9.3 billion.

Of this, about $2 billion went to the "lessors"—the superprofitable oil, machinery and financial companies that "bought" the properties. Some $7.1 billion went in "down payments" to the "lessees"—the auto, lumber and paper, chemical and metal companies that didn't have enough profits. And about $150 million went to the "pilots" who arranged the deals.

Not all the tax saving takes place this year. It's spread out for up to 10 years. If the law isn't changed, the amount of the swindle will mount yearly. Treasury calculations, covering about three quarters of the total, show "savings" of $3.2 billion this year, rising to $9.4 billion by 1986 and going up faster and faster.

Remember, in the final analysis **we**, the working people of the United States, pay this through higher taxes, through reduction in government services, and even, in part, through inflation caused by government deficits.

At that, the "safe harbor" racket is only a small part of the hundreds of billions of dollars that the corporations and the rich evade and avoid yearly through legal and illegal methods, according to government figures of "tax expenditures" and Internal Revenue Commissioner Roscoe L. Egger Jr.'s estimates of illegal tax evasions, almost all by capitalists.

The "safe harbor" is so corrupt, it raises such a stench, that there is a move in Congress to eliminate it. But the balance there suggests that the most that can be expected this session is a cosmetic "limitation" on its application.

Still, there remains the possibility that a taxpayers' suit against it, if filed, would win in the courts if backed by enough mass protest to force the swindling corporations to cough up the back taxes they avoided through this device.

• • •

12/30/1982

Unfair Taxes

President Reagan's proposal for taxing unemployment insurance benefits was hastily withdrawn in the face of a storm of protest. A nationwide poll published in house-to-house advertising weeklies showed a three-to-one majority (75%) against it.

What most people do not realize is that unemployment insurance is already taxed. A recent column in the *New York Post* prompted me to investigate.

The extent to which unemployment insurance is taxable depends on the amount of other income the worker and/or spouse got during the year. Prior to 1982, the provisions were such that perhaps half the workers who suffered periods of insured unemployment did not have to pay a tax on the benefits, and most of the others were taxed on only part. But in 1982, Congress, following the orders of Reagan and big business, made the terms much stiffer. I won't try to explain here the complicated formula, but I will give examples of workers who, next April, will have to pay income tax on all the unemployment insurance benefits they received in 1982. (The percentage of unemployment insurance to be taxed will depend on the amount of income received outside the benefits.)

A married worker with two children was employed 6 months and earned $6,000. He got $3,000 in unemployment insurance for the other 6 months. His spouse, employed all year, earned $15,000. So their total income was $24,000—surely a tight squeeze with a family to provide for. But that amount was, of course, reduced by several thousand dollars as a result of the taxes withheld from their $21,000 wages. And now this family will have to pay additional taxes, at a higher rate, on every cent of the $3,000—the unemployment benefits—about $588.

A single worker, employed part of the year, got $15,000 in wages. He received unemployment benefits of $3,000 for the rest of the year, and he also will have to pay income taxes on all of the $3,000—about $678.

The *Post* columnist suggested that workers had better pay up, implying that the IRS, "understaffed" when it comes to millionaire tax evaders, may go hard after taxes due from unemployed workers.

About 12 million workers received unemployment insurance some time in 1982. At a rough estimate, 3 million will pay income tax on all of it; 6 million on part of it, say one-half of it on the average; while only 3 million will not be taxed on any of their unemployment insurance, mainly the hungry and the homeless who exist in deepest poverty.

Shouldn't the 75% of those polled who voted "no" to taxing unemployment insurance let the new Congress know, decisively, that they insist on the repeal of all taxes on unemployment benefits?

And the next goal of big business is to increase Social Security taxes on workers, both retirees and employed. There is a serious drive by the administration to tax old age and disability pensions. An additional aim is to raise the Social Security taxes withheld from employed workers' paychecks while reducing the size of the pensions.

Remember these facts:

Through payroll taxes deducted from their paychecks, workers have paid all their lives for future pension benefits. To tax those benefits is, in large part, double taxation.

Almost all other countries finance Social Security, in part or wholly, through general revenues, in addition to or instead of employer/employee contributions. A modest federal contribution, amounting to 5% of Reagan's escalating military budget, would assure balance throughout this decade.

Old age disability pensions are miserably low. Basic old age pensions average only one-third the wages of employed workers.

Capitalist executives and officials, who are behind the drive to cut workers' Social Security, pay Social Security taxes on only a fraction of their salaries. They get their main, rapidly rising pensions from corporate surplus profits. Thousands of corporate bureaucrats are getting pensions in six figures; and the corporations' experts find tax shelters to enable the executives to avoid paying a large part of their taxes.

The big-business/government attack is two-pronged. It immediately aims at both employed workers, through higher taxes, and at retirees, through lower pensions that would be taxed. Thus there is strong motivation to unite trade unions and senior citizens' organizations to fight the entire two party attack on the social insurance of the working class, to press for doubling benefits and to require employers to pay all costs.

• • •

11/3/1988

Taxes: Grand Larceny

Early this month, representatives of the nation's top corporations met in Hot Springs, Va., to draw up budgetary recommendations to the incoming president and Congress. The recommendations: raise taxes on workers and slash Social Security benefits and other socially beneficial programs. They agreed that any deficit-cutting package should, for "political reasons," include tax increases as well as spending cuts. Their preference runs to a sales or value-added tax, the most costly form of regressive taxation.

For cost cutting, the businessmen's prime target is Social Security. Because most other social programs have already been carved up, Social Security is ripe for the picking. Cuts have already been made in it, and the 33 million who are affected have not been effectively organized to prevent the takeaways. Nor have there been active protests by the 110 million currently employed workers who will suffer later from the present cuts, and who are already paying extra Social Security taxes passed during the Reagan-Bush years.

According to *The New York Times*, the businessmen "support George Bush: but they don't believe him when he says he won't raise taxes . . . 'I think Bush will come around to seeing the need for taxes,' said International Business Machines Corp. Chairman John Akers, 'We'll leave it to the English majors to figure out how he can word it.'"

Tax cuts for billionaires

The super rich are not concerned with Bush's hypocritical promise that he won't raise taxes. They gloat about the 8 years of Reagan-Bush tax giveaways, and they are confident that their gains will remain secure—and be augmented.

The richest 400,000 Americans, about 4 out of 1,000 income tax payers, had an average adjusted gross income of about one million dollars and an actual average personal income of at least $1.5 million in 1986. They paid, in total, $154 billion, $64 billion less than they would have paid in 1980, before the Reagan-Bush slash in the top tax rate from 70% to 50%. In addition, they saved tens of billions through new loopholes.

Then the Reagan-Bush Tax Reform Act of 1986 cut the top rate from 50% to 28%—except for a small part of the income of the very wealthy taxed at 33%—saving the capitalists another $72 billion. The cuts for the super millionaires totaled a saving of $136 billion per year.

Bush has come out for radically reducing the capital gains tax in what Dukakis estimates as a further $40 billion bonanza to millionaires.

The cuts in corporate taxes have been almost as drastic. The 1986 cut from 46% to 34% in the rate for all but small businesses saved corporations $40 billion, and they gained much more by the wide loopholes opened up by Reagan-Bush, aided by congressional Republicans and right-wing Democrats since 1980. Restoring 10 percentage points to the corporate share of taxation would bring in an additional $110 billion to the federal government.

Architects of the loopholes

The 1986 corporate tax cut was rationalized as being offset through partial closing of some loopholes—mainly by putting a small tax on former freeloaders. But most large corporations gained from the lower tax rates. Moreover, the law was riddled with $5 billion of special exceptions maneuvered by members of the Senate for their big business constituents.

Sen. Daniel P. Moynihan (D-NY) was the eagerest beaver. According to one report, "In addition to obtaining a number of special exceptions for public projects in New York, Senator . . . Moynihan . . . obtained special exceptions for a brokerage firm in New York and a group of five doctors in Rochester.

"Senator Moynihan, one of the leading supporters of the tax revision effort in the committee, requested and received more exceptions than any other senator."

And he was duly rewarded. The big business Tax Foundation gave him its 1987 Tax Foundation's Distinguished Public Service Award at its 50th Anniversary Dinner.

There is nothing remotely democratic about the auction process by which Congress sells out the American people to friends and supporters. For the 1986 legislation, it was all finalized behind closed doors by two men: Rep. Dan Rostenkowski (D-IL) and Sen. Bob Packwood (R-OR). In the current wheeling and dealing, Packwood has been replaced by Sen. Lloyd Bentsen (D-TX), candidate for vice president on the Democratic ticket. But Rostenkowski carries the ball. He functions as chairman of the House Ways and Means Committee, which in 1986 masterminded dozens of giveaways.

The New York Times reported, "In reality, they are special favors inserted in the legislation personally on the last day of drafting by the committee chairman,

Rep. Dan Rostenkowski . . . Altogether, the special tax breaks would cost the Treasury $2 billion to $3 billion a year in lost revenue, more than twice what the government spends on cancer research."

According to journalist David E. Rosenbaum, Rostenkowski outdid his predecessors in this "typical" dirty dealing.

The same Washington actors put over hundreds more giveaways in what is deceptively called the Technical Corrections Act of 1988, passed late in the last session of Congress. Under the headline, "Tax-break sweepstakes, Round No. 2," the *Philadelphia Inquirer* gives details, focusing on the steel industry, notably LTV.

The IRS has ruled that LTV owes $130 million for failure to fund its pension plans. If repaid, the company could finally be forced to pay pensions owed to thousands of workers laid off when LTV used the Chapter 11 Bankruptcy device. LTV has made more than a billion dollars of reported profits after tax in the last 2 years and still refuses to pay workers who remain jobless and are struggling to feed their families.

Under the pressure of earlier exposures, Rostenkowski and Bentsen have stopped some giveaways, but there remains in the bill a special provision blocking the IRS from collecting the $130 million from LTV.

Taxes and the elections

One way or another, American workers face a heavy increase in their tax burden next year, hidden as additional deductions from paychecks and pension checks, through the proposed high excise and sales taxes.

A Bush-Quayle victory will make this very difficult to prevent. It is the big business community, overwhelmingly Republican, that has launched the campaign for raising taxes on workers and reducing taxes on capitalists—a bare month before the election. It is Bush who has openly called for lowering taxes for the rich by cutting the capital gains tax.

Dukakis, in his campaign oratory, has favored more social equity in taxation. Further, a larger percentage of Democratic than Republican legislators favor taxing the rich and cutting taxes on workers.

A wait-and-see attitude on the part of the majority is almost certain to bring bad tax news in any prospective post-election environment.

● ● ●

6/6/1992

Tax Reform = Tax the Rich

Vast sums of money are required to finance the many programs necessary to provide a decent life for all Americans. The largest potential source of these funds is a program to **tax the rich**. In addition to raising needed money, such a program would serve to partially redress injustices resulting from the enormous giveaways to the wealthy and the corporations over the last 30 years. While the Reagan-Bush administrations have been ruthless in acting to shift the tax burden from the rich to the poor, the current process began when the top tax rate on the highest incomes was reduced from 90% to 70%. In 1981 Reagan, with the cowardly consent of Congress, cut the rate to 50% and to 28% in a second round of giveaways to the rich. Meanwhile, the total tax burden on working people escalated.

This discriminatory tax structure is a major factor behind the widely publicized fact that the rich have gotten richer, the poor poorer; and middle-income workers have been pushed towards—even into—real poverty. It also does much to explain why the number of people reporting annual incomes of a million dollars or more multiplied a hundred times—from 600 in 1970 to 60,000 in 1989.

Last December I wrote a letter to *The New York Times* proposing a modest tax reform that would yield $100 billion yearly. It attracted much attention and was followed by many other letters supporting the demand for taxing the rich.

But *PWW* readers are interested in more than "modest" reforms. The following proposal is more in line with present needs and possibilities. It would also restore the "New Deal" progressivity that was in effect for almost 20 years. This proposal eliminates federal income tax for most of the working class; cuts taxes in half for better paid workers and some in the middle class; leaves unchanged taxes on most of the middle class; and fully restores progressive tax rates on capitalists. The estimated net yield to the federal government would be hundreds of billions per year, far more than the current total generated by income taxes on individuals.

Income Group	Number of Tax Payers	Tax Rate		Revenue Change ($Billion)
		Present	Proposed	
Under $25,000	70,000,000	7%	0%	-$50
$25,000-$50,000	30,000,000	12%	6%	-60
$50,000-100,000	15,000,000	14%	14%	0
$100,000-$200,000	2,500,000	20%	50%	100
$200,000-1,000,000	900,000	24%	70%	150
$1,000,000 and over	100,000	25%	90%	400

Most of the increase would be paid by the super-rich—those with annual incomes of more than a million dollars—who represent fewer than one out of a thousand of the population.

•

Notes: The term "income," as used in this column, refers to the official definition of "adjusted gross income" for tax purposes. This excludes much of the income of the rich, such as tax-exempt interest, expense account income, etc.

The number of taxpayers in various income groups for 1992 are estimates based upon past trends.

Cities, States, and Regions

7/16/1961

Michigan's Misery: a 'One-Crop' Economy

In March, 422,000 Michigan workers, 14.2% of the labor force, were totally unemployed. The General Motors bastion of Flint had 23.2% unemployed, the national top spot; Detroit and Lansing, with around 15% unemployed, were runners up for that dubious distinction among cities having over 100,000 in the labor force.

With the seasonal spring revival, Michigan unemployment dropped to 9.8% in May, but not much further improvement is to be expected. The state may face a long-run prospect of 10% or more unemployed. Why is its situation twice as bad as the national average?

Michigan is a "one-crop" state—automobiles. In 1954, half of its million factory workers were in autos or in supplier industries, like special tools and dies and metal stampings. No other major industrial state is so tied to a single industry.

For 50 years Michigan, aside from crises, prospered because autos were a "growth industry." It became a leader in wage rates, and its population increased as auto companies scoured the land for labor.

Since 1953 all that has changed. Michigan employment has declined 10%, while the national average increased 5%. In 1953 per capita income in Michigan was 19% above the national level, but by 1959 it was only 4% higher. Adjusted for changes in living costs, it fell 3% in those six years, the worst showing of any state. This year Michigan's per capita may be below the national average, which is pulled down by subnormal southern incomes.

Reasons:

- Automobiles are no longer a growth industry. Any further rise will not exceed that of the total economy. The share of autos in the consumer's dollar has reached its maximum, and may decline.
- The industry has decentralized rapidly, with plants moving to the Far West, the South, and to other northern states. Between 1954 and 1958 alone, Michigan's share of auto industry employment fell from 53% to 43%.
- The U.S. share of the world auto industry is on the downgrade. In passenger cars, we have shifted from a net export to a net import basis.

- The shift in the character of war has reduced the tank-automotive sector to marginal importance. Michigan munitions employment fell from 200,000 in 1953 to 40,000 in 1961, while the munitions-financing tax drain on the state's people continues to rise.

Because of its mass-production character, the automobile industry has been particularly suited to employment-cutting automation.

A fine example of the anarchy of capitalism! But we can't leave it at that. The auto magnates are the particular villains of this story. Their greed has never been bounded by consideration for the human beings they exploit. While on the up-grade, they used their influence with officials and banks to discourage the entry into Michigan of other industries. They saw to it that the hundreds of thousands recruited from the South, Negro and white, would be tied to the automotive Big Three, with no escape in times of model changeover or prolonged slump in this feast or famine industry. They made Michigan a one-crop state.

By building a powerful union despite violent company-inspired repression, the auto workers overcame the one-industry strategy and won economic improvements. So the companies took a new tack. After World War II they moved more and more of the industry outside of Michigan. Leaving the workers they had lured there high and dry, they turned to domestic areas with weak or non-existent unions, low taxes and social services.

More, taking advantage of lower overseas wages and Marshall Plan-NATO concessions to U. S. companies, Ford and General Motors tripled their foreign output in ten years, each approaching a million units abroad in 1960. They are the Big Two of the rest of the capitalist world as well as the United States.

The new post-war tactics certainly paid. Before-tax profits of the three largest companies, including ailing Chrysler, rose from $781 million in 1947 to $2,879 million in 1960. General Motors' profits went up from $500 million in 1947 to $2 billion in 1960, besides another $93 million paid out in bonuses and stock splits to officials. With the highest profits of any manufacturing company in history, General Motors and its duPont owners are flourishing out of the hardships of Michigan workers.

The capitalists, politicians, and professors of the state have only weak ideas for coping with this situation. If things are left to them, Michigan could join the coal areas of West Virginia and Pennsylvania, and New England textile towns in chronic depression.

• • •

3/9/1963

California's Growth Outpaces Workers' Gains

With 17.5 million people, California will probably become the most populous state in 1963. Let's take a look at the recent 1960 Census data about it.

The Golden State grew rapidly for most of its 165 years, with different lures bringing immigrants at different times. In the last decade there was a record gain of 5 million, sparked, as in the previous decade, by mushrooming munitions industries and military bases.

Employment in aircraft-missiles and shipbuilding doubled—from 105,000 in 1950 to 224,000 in 1960. Jobs in fabricated metals, largely on military subcontracting, jumped from 53,000 to 179,000. Employment in the electrical and electronic group, prominent in missiles and space, leaped from 27,000 to 147,000. These three groups account for two-fifths of California's factory employment, more than half the Los Angeles area's total, and 75% of San Diego's.

Then there are places like the Mojave Desert, all of which has become part of a "Metropolitan Area," if you please, thanks to the military bases dotting it.

The Bank of America, in its latest annual report, links California's growth to the defense-space market, speaks of the state's pre-eminence in this field and expresses confidence that there will be "continued expansion in this vital area of the state's economy." Doubtless militarism has helped this No. 1 bank to obtain assets of $13.4 billion, including a record-for-any-bank $2.3 billion overseas. But has it brought corresponding gains to California working people?

In the Los Angeles area, the munitions manufacturing capital of the world, the median earning of males was $5,684 in 1959. That was one or two percent higher than the corresponding figures for Chicago, Detroit and Cleveland, located in the least militarized central industrial region. The slight Los Angeles advantage reflects the higher proportion of professionals employed in munitions.

On balance, militarism has brought no decisive advantage to California labor. Nor have armaments eliminated unemployment. Despite their growth trend, munitions factories experience sharp fluctuations in employment as much as civilian industries.

Nor have California munitions manufacturers contributed, on balance, to equality in employment and residence opportunities. Non-whites comprise 8% of the state's labor force, but only 5% of those employed in the industrial groups where armaments are concentrated. The general figures show that the traditional color differentials are no less than in other industrial states. Non-whites with income had a median of $3,515 in California, 69% of that for whites. In Illinois the median was $3,613, or 71%; in Michigan, $3,728, or 75%; and in Ohio, $3,433, or 70% of that for whites.

The non-white population redoubled in the last decade, passing 1.25 million, with Negroes approaching 900,000. But sharp segregation patterns persist. The adjacent Los Angeles area cities of Compton and Lynwood have 40.1% and 0.3% non-whites, respectively. Some fast-growing munitions centers virtually exclude Negroes.

The 90,155 residents of Burbank, Lockheed's capital, include only 302 non-whites. The same proportion, 0.3%, applies to El Segundo, Douglas' secondary center. The population quintupled since 1950 at Sunnyvale, site of Lockheed's Polaris plant. But only 1.7% of its 52,000 people are non-white. North American has important factories at Bellflower (0.5%), and Downey (0.7%). Northrop has them at Anaheim (0.7%) and Hawthorne (0.9%) non-white.

After the Census was taken, the arms program had the fastest buildup since the Korean War. But this hasn't brought economic stability to California. Factory employment declined in 1961, and increased only 5% in 1962. Then new layoffs hit at the turn of the year, especially on the Skybolt and the B-70. The *Wall Street Journal* (1/23) reports on thousands laid off by Douglas, Northrop, and North American, and the difficulty of finding new jobs for them because "there's an oversupply of semi-skilled workers in this area."

There are bound to be economic problems when California disarms. But, so far as the vast majority of its inhabitants, including munitions workers, are concerned, the state will benefit, economically as well as in peace of mind, from an end to the cold war and the establishment of a modern peacetime economy.

• • •

5/11/1963

Chicago's Negro Ghetto

Almost one-fourth (900,000) of Chicago's 3.6 million people are Negroes, almost as numerous as those in New York, a city twice as large. Chicago's Negroes have a long history of participation in basic industry. But today they face a particularly bitter and difficult battle for their right to live and to work.

Illinois finally obtained a limited Fair Employment Practices law in 1961, but its effect is still peripheral. Employment is trending downwards in industries where Negroes obtained a reasonable share of jobs over long years of struggle—packinghouse and steel; while they have been kept out of most factories in the new and rising industries—e. g., electrical equipment and chemicals.

Trade unionists explained to me, on a recent visit, how the main heavy industry employers utilize automation and speedup to squeeze out Negroes, along with women, young and older workers.

A faction among taxi drivers still strives to force Negroes off the roads. I arrived just after a fresh mob attack on a Negro's home. Chicago is notorious for these outrages. Gangs in the thousands, many of them youthful hoodlums, carry out the burning and smashing of homes bought by Negroes, and of those of white real estate men who sell to them.

The Negro people fight back; and, in and around Chicago, there are important instances of Negro-white unity, including joint campaigns to establish and maintain integrated communities, and election of integrated boards.

Who is behind the segregationist gangs? Who stirs up prejudices? The exact line of control has not been exposed, but the Chicago Urban League rightly puts the finger on the real estate-banking crowd, which imposes residential segregation by "rigidly enforced institutional practices," including "(1) real estate brokers who refuse to show property or sell to Negroes; (2) professional real estate organizations which exclude Negroes and punish whites dealing with them in white areas, and (3) banks and lending institutions which refuse to make mortgages available to Negroes in areas outside the Negro ghetto."

By such rigid segregation the banker-real estate racists collect the highest rents in the country from both whites and Negroes. Median rents for 1960 were: Chicago, $88; Los Angeles, $78; Detroit, $77; New York, $73 ; Philadelphia, $65. University of Chicago Professor Taeuber calculates that 93% of Chicago's Negroes would have to change places with whites to create an integrated pattern.

The Urban League has mapped Negro residence in Chicago. The great majority of Negroes live in the areas having over 90% non-whites, which occupy only 5-6% of Chicago's entire area. Most of the remainder live in adjacent areas becoming part of the ghetto, with 50-90% Negroes occupying only 2% of the area. Hardly any Negroes, except for house servants, live in the more than 90 % of the total, which the Urban League calls, perhaps ironically, "white ghettoes."

Since the median Negro family income of $4,700 was only two-thirds of the white $7,200, the burden on Negroes of Chicago's super-high rentals was unusually onerous. Their median rental was 22.5% of income, which means that in tens of thousands of cases, Negroes had to pay one-third or more of their income for rent.

The Chicago story can be repeated, with varying details of discrimination and intensity of segregationist outrages, in every city of the land. A test of elementary decency in government today is its action to support the constitutional and human rights of the Negro people. The Chicago government rates zero—or perhaps a little minus for police brutality.

• • •

5/25/1963

Who Are the Real Rulers of Birmingham, Ala.?

President Kennedy identified the "business community of Birmingham" as the responsible ruling party that he hoped would offer concessions to the "justifiable needs of the Negro community." In Birmingham, as never before, it became clear that southern racism today is enforced not by some backward "colonel" vaguely associated with plantations, but by modern capitalists—manufacturers, merchants and bankers.

They derive the extra profits from low wages of Negroes, live in luxury provided by squads of Negro servants paid a pittance. They forbid Negroes to use the schools or to vote, and they order the police to unleash dogs and fire hoses, and jam the jails with Negroes. The old plantation lords have merged with the new masters.

The real rulers of Birmingham are tycoons centered in New York, Pittsburgh and Chicago, using southerners as hired executives in their corporations. The top industrial company in Jefferson County (where Birmingham is) is U.S. Steel, with its integrated Tennessee Coal & Iron installations in Bessemer, Fairfield and Birmingham proper. Police Commissioner "Bull" Connor was regarded as U. S. Steel's servitor when he specialized in "anti-Communism" in the union organizing days. Today he serves the same interests striving to repress the heroically struggling Negro working people.

DuPont has a powder and acid plant in Birmingham. It has shifted the balance of its activities to the South, and it is notorious for the two-to-one segregated wage scale it used constructing the H-bomb works near Savannah. Chicago-owned Armour has a packing plant and a fertilizer plant in Birmingham. Recently meat packers have reimposed the southern differential, with wage cuts in many plants, while employment of grossly underpaid Negro workers in fertilizer factories is notorious.

U.S. Pipe & Foundry has nine plants in Jefferson County. Its dominant shareholders are the Colgate family of New York (Colgate University) and its fiduciary agents, the First National City and Manufacturers Hanover Banks. The Pullman Corporation, controlled by the Mellons and Chicago bankers, has a freight car factory in Bessemer.

The largest industrial company with important local ownership is Vulcan Materials, a merger of building material and related enterprises, including Birmingham Slag Company, in which the Ireland family of Birmingham has the top jobs. Chairman Charles W. Ireland is a director of the First National Bank of Birmingham and of other local commercial and civic institutions. But behind Ireland stand New York directors of Morgan Guaranty Trust, Goldman Sachs, Continental Can, and St. Joseph Lead.

The variety store chains, often the focus of integration struggles, are also owned by northern bankers and capitalists. The *Birmingham News*, which printed anti-Negro editorials during the struggle, is owned by New York-based newspaper magnate Samuel I. Newhouse.

The Alabama Power Company is owned by the Southern Corporation, one of the offshoots of the Morgan utility super-holding company of the 1920s, the United Corporation. It is still run by and for the same Wall Street financial interests, with the collaboration of an all-Alabaman board of directors. Southern Bell Telephone has the lowest wages and highest profits of the Rockefeller-Morgan dominated American Tel & Tel system, and one of its directors is chairman of Birmingham's Liberty National Life Insurance Company.

The corporate interests control the politics of the South. V. O. Key, outstanding authority on American political parties, wrote that utilities are influential in politics throughout the South, while the main southern financing of the Democratic Party is from oil interests in Texas, textile mills in South Carolina, and coal, iron and steel in Alabama, etc. He claims the main source of funds for the party in Alabama is U.S. Steel and its satellite firms.

Segregation and discrimination, coming out of slavery, have been taken over, are managed and profitably used by the new national aristocracy of monopolists who run the government and economy of the entire country. Meanwhile the Negro people have become the most exploited section of the working class in all corners of the land.

Eliminating the southern oppression of Negroes is a requirement of the entire nation, not only because the Constitution demands it, but because it involves the most fundamental national social forces and interests.

• • •

4/21/1968

Baltimore's Oligarchy

An inbred and exclusive clique of 133 businessmen and lawyers controls Baltimore, its government, its commerce, its culture, education and social institutions. In turn, this select corps of interlocking and overlapping corporate agents is dominated by a half-dozen men who emerge at the apex of the Baltimore community.

Power in Baltimore is consolidated on, and spreads out from, the boards of the city's five major commercial banks—the Equitable Trust Co., the First National Bank of Maryland, the Maryland National Bank, the Mercantile-Safe Deposit & Trust Co., and the Union Trust Co."

All this is not from a leftist publication, but from two full-page spreads by Frank De Filippo in the *Baltimore News American* (12/17-18/1967). He continues:

To a startling degree, these men and institutions influence and help decide: how much money city and state government will spend and how it will be spent; what city and state construction projects will be undertaken; what interest rates Baltimoreans will pay on money borrowed for a house or a new car; what new businesses will be started.

They select governors, mayors, senators and congressmen. They select university presidents and fix curricula in colleges and schools. They control virtually all communications outlets in Baltimore. And with their wives they even decide what art will hang on the walls of Baltimore's galleries and museums.

I don't know who De Filippo is, or what magnates' quarrel led the owners of the *News American* to print the articles. But I have checked enough of the details to attest to the writer's accuracy. And I salute him for a bold and timely job.

Lenin showed how modern monopoly capitalism is dominated by a small financial oligarchy, centered on the great banks, joining under single control the operations of finance, industry, and government. Propagandists for American big business, liberal and radical super-sophisticates deny that any such pattern exists here.

Recently William Domhoff freshly proved it on a national scale. Now De Filippo has shown it for a big city. Every major city in America is run exactly the same way, with only minor structural variations. And here we have the key to understanding everything that goes on: in labor relations, the decay of the cities, foreign policy, Vietnam, the draft, and most urgently of all, race relations.

Possibly today there's a token Negro among the 133 bank directors, although I wouldn't bet on it. Perhaps a few of the 133 press for "social reform . . . for Negroes," as the author claims for Cardinal Shehan, the only non-banker among the top six.

What is certain is that lawyer-banker William L. Marbury, another of the six, recently "led the fight and authored a minority report opposing the U.S. Attorney General's guidelines for abolishing discrimination in the selection of Federal juries."

Another certainty is that the all-white six at the top of the power pyramid have complete control over every significant financial institution in Baltimore. They thereby determine exactly what housing will be built, who will get mortgage money and reasonable insurance rates, who will get federal aid, what landlords will be helped to keep their all-white apartment dwellings in good repair.

They plan the ghetto boundaries, mastermind the realty men's blockbusting, finance and set up the slumlords' rapid depreciation tax swindles, arrange the "Negro removal" operations for thruways, high-rise luxury buildings, and other deals they have going. They determine that the ghettos shall have inadequate and inferior schools and hospitals, and that construction contracts shall be let to concerns without black craftsmen. They manipulate the party hacks, select or approve the police chiefs and set the policy for keeping the blacks in their place.

There is nothing unusual about Baltimore. That's how American cities are run.

• • •

5/5/1968

The South

Thirty years ago Franklin Roosevelt called the South the nation's #1 economic problem. Since then industrialization has progressed rapidly, regional agriculture has been modernized, life has been urbanized, growth has been more rapid than in the North. But the present march of hungry people on Washington dramatizes how much of the past remains. The South is still the seat of the country's worst social problems and the base of extreme reaction.

Among the Black people oppression and super-exploitation are general, starvation and imprisonment are common, and death by murder an ever present danger. White working people are generally poorer and have less democratic rights than elsewhere in the country.

The working class comprises the majority of the modern South's population. Some of the impact of the region's social evils on labor is presented in the special issue of the *Monthly Labor Review* for March, titled "Southern Labor Comes of Age." Rupert P. Vance, in the introduction to this Labor Department publication, writes:

When one comes to consider the status of the worker and his job, the South con-
ventionally remains the home of nonunion labor, the differential wage, racial discrimination, and the lower standard of living.

Despite the soft-toned treatment of an official publication, the magazine reveals that these characteristics have not been moderated.

Ray Marshall brings out the unchanged lag of the South behind the rest of
the country in union organization, as well as the relative decline in unions nation-
wide:

Nonfarm Workers Organized (%)

	1939	1953	1964
North	21.5	34.1	29.5
South	10.7	17.2	14.4

The momentum of New Deal organizing efforts continued through the
1940s. By 1953, 34.1% of northern nonfarm workers and 17.2% of southern non-
farm workers were organized. But by 1964 these percentages had declined alarm-
ingly, to 29.5% in the North and 14.4% in the South. Throughout, the South has
remained only half as well organized as the North.

Marshall attributes the southern losses to the failure of the AFL and CIO
(before their merger) to follow through on postwar southern organizing drives; to
the defeats of textile, railroad, tobacco, and construction workers in major strikes;
to operation of Taft-Hartley and other anti-labor legislation, federal and state; and
to racism.

He claims that where unions take a "forthright equalitarian racial position"
they usually gain membership, and cites a Georgia Teamsters official who gave
this as a main reason for growing from 1,500 to 9,000 members in 12 years up
to 1964:

> .... our union does not equivocate or pussyfoot on the race question. On the
> job and at the hall all members are union brothers. ...

H. M. Douty finds wage differentials averaging 21% against southern workers in manufacturing, and about the same in trade. He finds the differential unchanged for 60 years, and predicts: "It is unlikely that southern wage differentials
will disappear in the near future despite a growing industrial society."

Emory F. Via presents devastating facts about job discrimination against
southern Negroes. They comprise 20% of the southern labor force, but hold only
8.9% of the jobs in textiles, the region's largest industry. And they hold only 0.7%
of the white-collar jobs and 2.3% of the skilled jobs in textiles.

Other industries show a similar picture. In food industries things are a little
better, partly because of traditional employment of Negroes in slaughterhouses
and other undesirable jobs, and partly because of relatively good work done by the

Packinghouse Workers and Meatcutters unions. But still, the pattern of discrimination remains sharp. With 23.2% of the total jobs, Negroes hold only 2.3% of the white-collar and 13.8% of the skilled jobs.

Via rightly, although mildly, puts much of the blame on government officials for systematic failure to uphold the law, and for carrying out discriminatory policies themselves. In Mississippi, where Negroes are 40% of the population, they have only 10.7% of the federal jobs, only 3.2% of the federal white-collar jobs, and 5.0% of the postal field service jobs, hopelessly concentrated in the lowest paid grades in each category.

Via also rightly blames many union officials for the extreme discrimination. Although he fails to state the primary responsibility of employers, his article, taken together with other material in the issue, brings out important and dramatic evidence on this score.

• • •

11/20/1971

Michigan Diary

Michigan is one of the strongholds of racism and red baiting. The old divide and rule tactics, in crude form, are still practiced by General Motors and Ford, as it was during the 1930s before the UAW defeated the Black Legion and Father Coughlin. Now it centers around the issue of school busing. The Ku Klux Klan and like minded elements are getting tremendous publicity for their propaganda campaign to give the impression that the overwhelming majority of white Michiganders are racists. But that is not the fact. In Pontiac, where the racists burned school buses to try to halt integration, white UAW members, with the approval of the Local, mobilized to protect the remaining buses and the children going to integrated schools.

9/28/1978

Native Alaskans Threatened by Uncertain Future

Alaska's media pay little attention to the rest of the country, still less to the rest of the world. Driving into Alaska from Canada's Yukon Territory, the welcome sign does not say: You are entering the United States. It says: You are entering Alaska!

The dramatic scenery surpassed our high expectations. We were struck with the state's enormous resources and, with an area more than double that of Texas, with only 0.7 persons per square mile, its great potential for growth.

But Alaska cannot avoid the problems of U.S. capitalism: exploitation of labor; large-scale unemployment; monopoly plundering of oil, lumber, and fish; prices 65% higher than in the "lower 48." The two largest cities, Anchorage and

Fairbanks, are surrounded by huge military bases, established during World War II, then expanded and currently maintained as seats of potential anti-Soviet aggression. The Defense Department remains the state's largest employer, with more uniformed and civilian employees than all manufacturing and mining establishments put together.

Currently Congress is debating disposition of the land and natural resources of Alaska. Will it be turned over to monopolies for unrestricted plunder? Will it be frozen into a "forever wild" environmental paradise, or become a shooting gallery for wealthy trophy hunters? Or will there be a controlled, balanced development with consideration of the needs of the working people, insofar as that is possible within a still capitalist United States? Will it be a base for aggression and war, or a bridge to peaceful cooperation with the world of socialism?

The crucial question, governing other issues, is the outcome of the struggle against racism in Alaska. Oppression of the 65,000 native people is as severe as racism in the lower 48 states, even though there are differences in form. The struggle of the native people—for equality, for land, for national rights and heritage—is highly organized, with its particular methods and particular goals. While not challenging the capitalist basis of U.S. society, these goals objectively support non-exploitative, cooperative production relations; cooperation rather than confrontation with the Soviet Union.

Numbers of whites first entered Alaska in the 1880s, the beginning of the imperialist epoch, bringing disease and slaughter to the native peoples. The Census showed a 23% decline in the native population in 10 years. Even by 1950 the native population was no larger than it was 70 years earlier, and probably much smaller than 1880's actual population.

Between 1900 and 1962, use of native languages was barred, and children caught speaking in their own tongues in the schools had their mouths washed out with soap.

The 1956 edition of the *Encyclopedia Americana* enumerates the major populated areas of Alaska, inhabited by Eskimos, Aleuts, Athabascans, Tlingits and other native peoples, and then adds these amazing words:

> Racial discrimination in Alaska is unknown, and is in reality illegal. The fact that Indian and Eskimo children attend their own schools largely is due to geographic conditions . . . there is no discrimination when it comes to employment of Indian or Eskimo persons. They have proved to be excellent machinists, electricians . . . and vessel operators. In the professions they have attained considerable recognition as attorneys, physicians, and legislators. Native girls have found their place as clerks, stenographers, cashiers, and nurses.

The *1970 Census of the United States*, with just released social and economic statistics for Alaska, gives the lie direct to this bland concoction. It reveals the extreme racial discrimination that has not eased in the past decade.

The 1970 Census, the latest, showed per capita annual income of Alaskan natives at only $1,475, or 36.4% of the $4,061 per capita income of non-natives. The $1,475 was less than the U.S. per capita income of Blacks, Chicanos, Puerto Ricans, or Native American Indians, and far, far less in real terms, in view of the 65% higher level of prices in Alaska. Moreover, the differential between natives and non-natives is even worse than indicated because two-thirds of the natives live in the villages, where prices are 50% higher than the very high prices in the urban areas, where most of the non-natives live. Natives are three-fourths of the population in the bitterly cold north and northwest of Alaska.

An Interior Department report speaks of housing as "the most serious and intractable of the problems . . . in Native Alaska," related to the "harsh climates, the low level of income . . . and the uniquely high costs of transportation, construction and heating . . . Native housing is over-crowded and for the most part lacking in the standard amenities and facilities . . . about two-thirds of all native dwellings . . . were deficient in standard plumbing and sanitation facilities." Many lacked phones, electricity, and water. And those native villages with electricity usually depend on cooperative-owned small diesel generators producing energy at the frightful cost of 25-35 cents per kilowatt hour, with the Rural Electrification Administration, instead of subsidizing these costs, demanding still higher rate increases.

Age-adjusted death rates of natives are nearly double those of non-natives. There is a terrible toll from accidents, especially among the native fishermen, lumber workers and hunters, who are forced to work with inadequate equipment and safety provisions.

The native youth are passing through a crisis as the old individual family-subsistence way of life is squeezed out by monopoly seizure of fish and forests, as the oil pipeline and other growth areas—and modern education—open up new opportunities for white Alaskans that prove mirages to so many of the native youth. This has resulted in a tragic epidemic of suicides. Among native youths aged 20-24, the annual suicide rate jumped from an already excessive 47 per 100,000 a year in 1965-69 to 170.6 per 100,000 a year in 1970-1973.

A new report shows that natives and Blacks in Alaska receive sentences five times as long as whites for identical crimes.

But Alaska could not escape the influence of the anti-colonial, anti-imperialist liberation struggles around the world, of the civil rights struggles in the United States. And, in Alaska especially, there was the powerful impact of the tremendous forward strides and complete liberation of the northern peoples of the USSR—some of them speaking the same Inuipiaq, Yupik, and Aleut languages—in direct contact across the Bering Strait.

U.S. imperialism was forced to relax its pressure on the native peoples: they were permitted written languages; their tongues were taught in some of the schools; medical care improved; the native population doubled since 1950. Some natives obtained jobs in the federal and state government and in lower-paying private firms.

Congress passed the Alaska Native Claims Settlement Act (ANCSA), in 1971 which revoked all existing native claims to land and compensation in return for a payment of $962 million in cash and 42 million acres, about 11% of Alaska's land. The cash is gradually being turned over to 13 native regional corporations and scores of village corporations. But scarcely an acre of the land, the most important part of the settlement, has been handed over.

The regional corporations have invested the money received in various hotel and office building construction projects, in tankers and in a cement plant, and they have obtained some oil company construction contracts. These activities have given employment to a certain number of native workers, but have not as yet made any significant change in the general condition of the native people.

The waters of southeast Alaska are teeming with salmon. Even at the monopoly-paid prices to fishermen, perhaps one-tenth of what the ultimate consumer pays, the catch with free-floating nets is quite lucrative. A few years ago the state passed a limited-entry law, granting permits for commercial salmon fishing to a certain number of fishermen, based on a complicated point system. The Tlingit and Haida peoples, the best fishermen, who historically depended on salmon fishing, were largely excluded. Nor can they afford the $60,000 going price for a permit! So, with a few exceptions, they are relegated to working as wage fishermen for permit holders, or to subsistence fishing under the restrictions that limit them to the catch they can personally consume.

The federal government claimed ownership of virtually all of Alaska's 375 million acres at the time of statehood. The state was permitted to select 104 million acres, about two-thirds of which has been chosen and, for the most part, turned over to state ownership. The hopes of the native people for a decent livelihood depend on their getting their 42 million acres and their right to use its forests, its mineral, animal and aquatic wealth.

The racist Bureau of Land Management of the Interior Department has been the most flagrant saboteur. Monopoly corporations, trophy game hunters, and other special interests have filed claims for "easements"—that is, the right to trespass on the natives' lands, which ties up the land in administrative procedures and in the courts. Some environmental groups are demanding that parts of the natives' chosen lands be taken from them for "wilderness" purposes, although the native peoples rightly claim that they have proven themselves the perfect environmentalists, with their centuries-long harmonious interaction with nature.

The native corporations, capitalist in form and striving for high profits and dividends, for the most part have been unable to compete successfully against experienced monopoly capital. Some of them have been hoodwinked by private capitalists, misled by expensive corporate consultant outfits. Some, notably the Northwest Alaska Native Corporation (NANA), have done reasonably well. But in general, the prospect of significant dividends to the native people from these corporations is slim for many years to come.

Each native was issued 100 shares of stock in their regional corporations. Transfer or sale of these shares is prohibited until 1991. With equal stockholding, then, for the present these corporations are essentially a type of cooperative. An official of the Sealaska Corporation, a native corporation with its headquarters in Juneau, told me of their education campaign to try to convince the native people to hold on to these shares after 1991, to resist the inevitable attempt of big non-native capitalists to take over control, especially of those corporations that have good financial prospects.

Meanwhile, Sealaska has a race with time, to get the 240,000 acres of great timberland it has selected so that it can start to provide employment for its thousands of working people, to procure a decent standard of living from the sale of the timber, the establishment of sawmills, etc., before the 1991 deadline.

Building and receiving mutual support from other oppressed peoples' movements, from the working class and from the peace movement, the native peoples of Alaska can win important concessions from racist monopoly capital, and move towards a better life, towards realizing for Alaska the great future it offers for all of its people.

Personalities

3/21/1970

Senator Moynihan Unmasked

Daniel Patrick Moynihan, counselor to Nixon on race questions, has delivered to his boss a memorandum claiming that black people have made "extraordinary progress" and urging a period of "benign neglect" of what has been the "central domestic political issue."

Moynihan starts with details of alleged dramatic gains of black people in income and education. He follows this with his customary mass slanders of black people for illegitimacy—quote—"social pathology," crime and arson. He engages in name calling against the black liberation movement. He ends with recommendations for "benign neglect," for—quote—"research on crime," and, finally, for Nixon to build up a black Ambassador as the leader of a black "silent majority."

Moynihan's economic claims provide the foundation for his argument that the material problems of black people are essentially solved, and hence can be safely ignored. And also for the implication that there is no justification for what he regards as the outrageous behavior of black people, and every justification for a tough administration policy towards them.

I will discuss his economic claims. Let me bring up to date the key figures on the relative economic status of black people, which Moynihan avoids.

The median income of black families of two or more was 60% of that of whites, up from 57% in 1945, at the end of World War II, and in 1952, at the peak of the Korean War. Black families have gained 3 percentage points in 23 years and three wars, or at a rate that would bring equality by the year 2275—in over three centuries.

And even that slight gain was won not by the benign neglect, or benign action, of the government, but by the struggles of black people themselves, aided by their allies among white people, and by the influence of world movements against racism and imperialism. Moynihan attempts to get around this basic fact with a number of statistical swindles. Let's focus on the one he emphasizes most:

"Young Negro families are achieving income parity with young white families. Outside the South, young husband-wife black families have 99% of the income of whites! Thus, it may be that this ancient gap is finally closing."

This figure is incredibly misleading, and deliberately so.

Moynihan's figure refers to families in which the husband is between 14 and 24 years old. The Census published national figures for such families, showing black families in the category receiving 88% of the income of white families. The figure for families outside the South was especially prepared for Mr. Moynihan.

Now, let's see what's wrong with Moynihan's figure.

1. Why leave out the South, where more than half of the blacks still live? Obviously, just to sweeten the dish artificially.

2. Only 5% of blacks in the 14-24 year age group are part of husband-wife families in the North. The statistic, therefore, has no representative value so far as the economic status of black youth.

3. The Census counts as a family only those couples who have their own apartment or private house. A couple doubling up with parents or other relatives is not regarded as a family. The proportion of young black couples forced to double up with relatives is three times as great as the corresponding proportion of young white couples. The ones regarded as families are the better off ones, who have made it enough economically to set up their own apartments despite the special obstacles facing black people.

4. The Census excludes from income gifts, money borrowed, inheritances, etc. Nowadays a substantial proportion of young white couples are students, who depend for finances in whole or in part on support by parents, government guaranteed bank loans, and scholarship contributions to tuition. These young couples, who are really much better off than young working couples, appear in the statistics to have little or no income.

   There are relatively fewer black students who can afford to set up households as married couples depending on such aid. On the other hand, welfare payments, which are received in disproportionate amount by black people because of their more frequent poverty, are included in income by the Census Bureau.

5. Among white young couples the majority of the wives do not work; but among the young black couples the majority of the wives do work. Thus, the closer approach to income equality was achieved in part by two people working instead of one, with the difference in income per worker considerably more.

6. The white families include most Puerto Rican and Chicano families, and these national groups tend to marry young. They are victims of discrimination, like black people, so their statistical inclusion with whites cuts down the real difference.

7. The relatively few black youth able to set up housekeeping as married couples are almost always those able to get regular, full-time jobs. Outside the South, it has long been true that starting wages for blacks are not very much lower than average starting wages for white workers. However, it has been and continues to be true that whites get promotions much more rapidly, while the majority of black workers are

stuck forever at or near their starting point. Thus, a lower differential in income at younger ages does not establish anything about the time trend in the racial differential as a whole.

• • •

2/20/1971

Henry Kissinger

The State Department is in eclipse. Foreign affairs are run by President Nixon and his special advisor, Henry Kissinger. That well known fact is stressed in the excellent *New York Times* series on the foreign policy of the Nixon administration.

This partnership might seem puzzling. William P. Rogers, the Secretary of State, is an old friend of Nixon; but the President never knew Kissinger, who was a political opponent of his in 1968. Kissinger, according to *The Times*, had a "tart, partisan bitterness" toward Nixon.

Where did Nixon find him? Why did he give him such supreme power?

And power it is. Kissinger spends hours with Nixon privately, almost daily; he is part of and often chairman of every major committee that meets with Nixon. He has fancy White House quarters and a staff of 110. He runs the National Security Council and the network of special committees under it, including those controlling military programs, Strategic Arms Limitation talks (SALT), Vietnam operations, and the Washington Special Actions group, which might be called the brink-of-war committee. He also chairs the "40 Committee" for Covert Action, a secret bunch that plots all the dirty tricks of imperialism, from the Bay of Pigs and similar sneak attacks to assassination of political opponents.

One basis of Kissinger's position is the conformity of his politics to Nixon's. German born, and very conscious of it, Kissinger has the revenge-seeker's hatred of the Soviet Union. No few refugees from Hitler Germany, as well as Nazis taken prisoner by U.S. forces, became particularly active servants of U.S. imperialism's attempt to take over where Hitler left off in trying to destroy communism and conquer the world.

Wernher von Braun and his team of Nazi missile makers put the United States in the missile-space race with the Soviet Union. Kissinger is trying to do a comparable job in foreign policy. And there is no need to qualify the comparison on the grounds that Kissinger is a Jew. He represents those German Jewish capitalists whose only criticism of Hitler was that he was anti-Semitic.

Kissinger came to this country at the age of 15, in 1938. His well-to-do family sent him to Harvard, his brother to Princeton. While Henry became a big political wheel, his brother W.B. became an armament-oriented manufacturer. After Henry Kissinger made it with Nixon, W.B. was made president and chief executive officer of Allen Electric and Equipment Corp. of Chicago.

Henry Kissinger graduated from Harvard summa cum laude in 1950 and immediately became a government consultant on military and foreign policy issues. With his PhD degree in 1954, he was made director of nuclear weapons and foreign policy research for the Council on Foreign Relations. This is the top private foreign policy group of America's most powerful tycoons. In 1956 he became director of the Rockefeller Brothers' Special Studies project. This project worked out the Rockefeller Group's basic cold war policy manifestos, which in large part were adopted by successive administrations in Washington.

On every issue Kissinger is on the side of aggression, confrontation and war. He opposes withdrawal of U.S. troops from Western Europe. He inspired the campaign against the easing of relations between the USSR and West Germany. He is the author of NSSM Memo 99 on American objectives in Southeast Asia and Vietnam over the next 5 years, prepared for discussion with the Pentagon.

In short, he envisages a permanent war of conquest in Southeast Asia. He is an advocate of the notorious "positions of strength" policy, and denounces the proposal for a rapid withdrawal from Vietnam as "an elegant bugout."

Hard-line cold warriors are no rarity in academic and political circles. Kissinger is especially hard-line, energetic, and able. He was picked by the Rockefellers, three of whom are overseers of Harvard, and they are a leading force on the Council of Foreign Relations. And ever since 1956, Kissinger has been the family's chief foreign policy adviser. He was right-hand man to Nelson Rockefeller during the 1968 Republican nomination campaign, when Nixon won out.

Why did Nixon then pick his chief rival's emissary as his own key man after Kissinger had let the world know how little he thought of Nixon?

We do not know the mechanics of how it was arranged. But we do know that Rockefeller men have been in charge of the foreign policy of the United States continuously for 18 years—Dulles, Herter, Rusk, and now Kissinger. C. Wright Mills* explained the principle of selection of key government officials in this way: "As in the private corporation, the rule is the co-optation of one's own kind by those who have taken over the command posts."

The Wall Street Establishment finances the major candidates, Nixon as well as Eisenhower as well as Kennedy as well as Johnson. No man can be elected, within Establishment-controlled parties, without its approval, without certain commitments and deals. And the most influential single force in the Wall Street Establishment these days is the Rockefeller-Standard Oil-Chase Manhattan Bank group. Apparently it is understood that they are to have foreign affairs, regardless who wins out in primary and final election skirmishing, and regardless of the personal fate of an individual Rockefeller running for office.

But what about Secretary of State Rogers? Isn't he Establishment? Certainly. But his law firm, his corporate connections, his clients, are on the second level of importance. Kissinger worked for the top circle. One may say that this arrogant, dangerous man is the choice of the bigwigs of the oligarchy, the Wall Street Establishment, to be their instrument on the spot for direction of the foreign policy of the United States. To be more exact, he represents the most reactionary groupings within that oligarchy, and especially the Rockefeller-Standard Oil-Chase Manhattan Bank group.

* C. Wright Mills is author of *The Power Elite*.

• • •

10/9/1971

Your Friends at Chase Manhattan, Standard Oil, Ludlow and Attica

The world is still in shock from the results of Nelson Rockefeller's signal for the murderous assault on defenseless, mainly Black, men at Attica prison.

But this act is characteristic of the entire policy of the Rockefellers. This multi-billionaire clan has a history of three generations of economic and political piracy—with violence against working people, racism, aggression and war their hallmark:

* The 19th century war against small businessmen and farmers in the formation of the Standard Oil monopoly.
* The Ludlow massacre of the Colorado miners in 1914.
* The collaboration with I.G. Farben in helping Hitler prepare for genocidal warfare in the 1930s.
* The period since World War II, when their power and the scale of murder they sponsored have put their past exploits in the shade.

The five Rockefeller brothers of the third generation, besides sharing the six square mile Tarrytown estate and partnership in ventures of the Rockefeller Brothers Fund, have a rough division of labor in advancing the overall interests of the clan. John D. III, the eldest, is the foundation man; Nelson is the chief political representative; Laurance is the corporate promoter; Winthrop, recently governor of Arkansas, worked directly in the oil industry and posed as the family's paternalistic "friend of the Negro"; David, the youngest, is the family banker.

The Rockefeller clan today, buttressed by allied Standard Oil families, is the most powerful economic and political grouping of American big business. It controls corporations with assets of around $100 billion. The financial kingpin of its empire is the $25 billion Chase Manhattan Bank; the industrial foundation consists of the Standard Oil companies. Other well known entities within its realm are the Metropolitan and Equitable Life Insurance companies, the Bank of New York, Eastern Airlines, National Lead Co., Borden Co., Southern Railway. It has a major share of power in the AT&T telephone trust.

The Rockefeller group has gained more than any other from the overseas expansion of U.S. imperialism since World War II. Chase Manhattan now has $7 billion in foreign deposits, comprising 40% of its total deposits.

•

Last year Standard Oil companies took 9 million barrels of oil per day out of the earth of countries in Asia, Africa, Europe, Latin America and Canada, nearly equal to total production by all companies in the United States. Its foreign profits, after taxes—as incompletely reported—came to $1.33 billion.

Since World War II, the Rockefeller clan has had the leading role in most coalitions dictating to Republican presidential candidates, and its representatives have occupied key cabinet and advisory positions in Democratic as well as Republican administrations. Rockefeller men—John Foster Dulles, Dean Rusk and Henry Kissinger—have been in charge of foreign policy under Eisenhower, Kennedy, Johnson and now Nixon. Nelson Rockefeller has been official advisor on Latin American policy under Roosevelt and Nixon, and unofficially dominant in the area throughout.

Since World War II, the Rockefeller Standard Oil-Chase Manhattan Bank group has led in promoting and profiting from racist aggression, genocidal attacks against non-white peoples, militarism, and anti-Communism.

In 1946 Leo D. Welch, treasurer of Standard Oil Co (N.J.), declared that the United States "must set the pace and assume the responsibility of the majority stockholder in this corporation known as the world. . . . Nor is this for a given term of office. This is a permanent obligation." Demanding "proper respect for our capital abroad," Welch called for that policy, which led to armed interventions, wars, and the setting up of hundreds of foreign bases. The records of U.S. and U.S.-supported aggression and Standard Oil-Chase Manhattan Bank penetration are synchronized throughout the postwar period.

1947: U.S. armed intervention and "advisors" in Greece. Thousands of Greeks killed, tens of thousands exiled, a dictatorship imposed. U.S. military bases established in Greece, Turkey, Saudi Arabia.

The payoff: Standard Oil and other U.S. companies' share of Middle Eastern oil multiplied, displacing British companies as dominant factor.

1953: CIA-organized coup overthrows progressive Mossadegh government in Iran; thousands killed by subsequent dictatorship.

The payoff: U.S. oil companies, principally Standard Oil, given 40% share of Iran's rich oil resources.

1961: Massacre of hundreds of Blacks by apartheid regime in Sharpeville, South Africa. John Foster Dulles, Rockefeller-associated lawyer, then head of U.S. delegation to the United Nations, acted to block strong UN action against South Africa and its seizure of Namibia, making possible apartheid policy and Sharpeville. Chase Manhattan Bank led syndicate of U.S. banks bailing out racist government of South Africa from financial crisis following Sharpeville, saving the regime from overthrow.

The payoff: Dulles' law firm's client, American Metal Climax, greatly expanded holdings in South Africa, Namibia. Chase Manhattan Bank gained important interest in the Standard Bank, with over 1,000 branches in South Africa and Rhodesia.

1965: U.S. Marine invasion overthrows democratic regime in the Dominican

Republic, reinstates dictatorship, prevents land reform. Large-scale political murders continue to this day.

The payoff: South Puerto Rican Sugar Company, major industrial enterprise on the island, wholly dominated by Rockefeller financial interests. Two years later the Rockefellers sold the company at a big profit to the Gulf & Western Industries conglomerate.

1967: U.S. backs Greek colonels' coup, destroying incipient democracy.

The payoff: Standard Oil (N.J.) built and expanded the Esso-Pappas refinery and petrochemical works near Salonika. Rockefeller group insurance companies provided main financing for Greek shipbuilders, who are principal big business force in colonels' regime.

1965-1971: U.S. intervention in Vietnam escalated to full-scale war. Over a million Vietnamese killed by U.S. forces.

The payoff: Standard Oil (N.J.), earlier the principal U.S. business interest in Vietnam, vastly expanded sales for war purposes and got puppet-government approval for big refinery; Chase Manhattan Bank built the first U.S.-owned bank branch in fortress-like building in Saigon. Standard Oil companies now preparing, along with other oil companies, to bid for offshore leases, while the U.S. fleet remains in control of surrounding waters.

•

The Rockefellers, personally and through their hired men, have given public support to every aggressive turn in U.S. foreign policy, from the Truman Doctrine to the Vietnam War. They have persistently worked for higher military budgets, and especially for development and promotion of genocidal weapons. During World War II, E.V. Murphree, a top Standard Oil (N.J.) research official, chaired the planning board that organized the industrial mobilization for atomic bomb production. Standard Oil played a leading part in developing napalm and provides much of the gasoline used in the preparation of these civilian-killing bombs.

After World War II Laurance Rockefeller, with participation of his brothers, specialized in building up munitions companies, including several involved in nuclear weapons development. The prize investment, however, was in McDonnell Aircraft (now McDonnell Douglas), makers of the Phantom Jets, which have killed hundreds of thousands of Vietnamese and many Arabs.

Frederick Seitz, president of Rockefeller University, and Detlev Bronk, its former president, were two of the handful of non-governmental scientists Defense Secretary Melvin Laird could dredge up in support of the ABM, against the overwhelming majority of prominent scientists.

John D. Rockefeller III organized, financed and became president of the Population Council, which works for "solving" the problems of poverty in other countries by reducing their population. The Council boasted that it sponsored 850,000 abortions in Japan in 1953. For 20 years John D. III was chairman of the Rockefeller Foundation, which has spent $45 million since 1963 for the reduction of population. This drive for "population control" has nothing in common with desirable health measures. It is promoted by the Rockefellers as a **substitute** for social reform, for the revolutionary changes that can free billions of people from poverty and starvation.

The Rockefeller Brothers Fund, Inc., sponsored the 1958 report, prepared under the research directorship of Henry Kissinger, calling for a rapid increase in the military budget, a schedule that was implemented almost in toto in the first half of the 1960s.

In 1963, when seeking the 1964 Republican presidential nomination, Nelson Rockefeller demanded a tougher anti-Communist foreign policy; attacked Kennedy for being "soft" on Cuba; called for a more aggressive, interventionist policy toward Latin America; opposed negotiations with the USSR and moves toward a nuclear test ban.

A newspaper advertisement in September 1965 supported the bombing of North Vietnam and mass invasion of South Vietnam. It was signed by 47 individuals, mainly big businessmen. Of these, 11 were of the Rockefeller group, headed by David Rockefeller. In 1968 David Rockefeller called for a $10 billion tax increase and a multi-billion slash in civilian spending to finance further escalation of the Vietnam War, claiming "we must be prepared to shoulder this kind of financial burden when necessary in defense of freedom." He is chairman of the Council on Foreign Relations, the principal foreign policy body of U.S. big business. As such he was decisive in appointing as editor of its journal, *Foreign Affairs*, the notorious Vietnam warhawk William P. Bundy.

Michael L. Haider, a top Standard Oil (N.J.) official, was chairman of Radio Free Europe, the war-provoking CIA-funded broadcast and espionage center, from 1966 to 1968.

The Rockefellers have played a demagogic role with respect to the Black people. They have been the leaders in trying to channel activity into conformist and segregated lines. Rockefeller brothers have acted as financial angels and chairmen of the boards of the National Urban League and the United Negro College Fund. More recently, they have played the "Black capitalism" game to the hilt, appointing a Black director to the board of Equitable Life Assurance Society, and publicizing the appearance of Black women tellers at the counters of Chase Manhattan branches.

But the Rockefeller companies have one of the worst records for racism of any in the country. Despite gains due to recent struggles, Black workers had only 3.9% of the jobs in the petroleum industry in 1968. These were almost all in the lower-wage categories. Only 0.3% of the officials and managers, 0.7% of the professionals and 2.2% of the craftsmen were Black. Black employment in the petroleum industry has declined sharply since 1950, while increasing in most basic industries.

Only a few years ago, the Chase Manhattan Bank was among those subject to sharp criticism by an official investigation into racist hiring practices. The recent hiring of Black women tellers and other clerical employees was virtually forced by the shortage of white people for low-paying clerical jobs and by the desire to cut salary costs by substituting lower-paid women for men.

The Rockefellers' Metropolitan Life Insurance Company persistently enforced a racist, segregationist policy in its housing developments in New York City, evicting tenants who attempted to break the Jim Crow pattern. David Rockefeller, as chairman of Chase Manhattan Bank, has been powerful in New York City affairs, leading in the bankers' syndicate that hamstrings city finances and insures deteriorating services and conditions for the Black and Puerto Rican population. As president of Morningside Heights, Inc., he pushed the eviction of hundreds of working people, including many Black and Puerto Rican, to make way for expensive high-rise and university buildings.

Governor Nelson Rockefeller, immediately on taking office, put through a soak-the-poor tax program, which hit the Black and Puerto Rican people most heavily. And more recently he has slashed welfare payments, promoted no-knock police entry, and taken other repressive steps directed most sharply against the minority groups.

For the Rockefeller clan, bloody repression of any people's revolt against intolerable conditions is a standing rule, as is special oppression and exploitation of colored peoples, in the United States and abroad. These drives of the Rockefeller Standard Oil-Chase Manhattan Bank group inevitably lead to genocidal policies and practices—and yield billions of extra profits.

To them the murder of 42 at Attica is but a minor incident in their global antipeople profit drive. But to millions of Americans it has been an eye-opener, awakening them to the need to struggle against racism and genocide at home and abroad in the international aggressions and wars abetted by the Rockefellers and other leaders of U.S. imperialism.

• • •

9/28/74

The $100 Billion Rockefeller 'Myth'

Nelson Rockefeller used his confirmation hearings [for U.S. vice president] this week to try to shoot down what he called the "myth" of his family's financial power and the Rockefeller Empire. With the reduction in mass living standards, soaring corporate profits, and superhigh interest rates, people are again seeing the great financial oligarchies as sources of oppression and poverty.

Rockefeller wants to divert that.

But the Rockefellers remain one of the handful of billionaire families, and his own testimony bears this out. Moreover, the Rockefellers remain part of the financial industrial oligarchy that in fact dominates the economic and political life of the country; and his testimony, despite all it conceals, provides evidence on this score.

Rockefeller concedes that his personal fortune is $218 million; and the wire services, commenting on his testimony, place the combined wealth of the Rockefeller Brothers at more than $1.5 billion. But these are minimal figures.

Nelson Rockefeller, because of his divorce if for no other reason, probably has less than the other brothers. And vast amounts are stowed away in holding companies, foundations, and other devices.

The Rockefeller family wealth was estimated by Menshikov (*Millionaires and Managers*, Moscow, 1973) at $6-$10 billion, and other independent estimates are consistent with this. But that's only a fraction of the wealth controlled or dominated by the Rockefeller family and its allies, consisting mainly of the families of the partners of the original John D. Rockefeller in the Standard Oil Trust.

This group is one of the two largest of the eight to ten financial-industrial empires that dominate the U.S. economy, as well as its political life. The assets controlled by the Rockefeller group in 1956 were estimated at $61 billion, slightly less than the Morgan group assets. Later data confirm that this has expanded to more than $100 billion.

At the hearings, Rockefeller conceded that he, his brothers, his sister, and their direct descendants own 2.54% of Chase Manhattan Bank, 2.06% of Standard Oil of California, 1.75% of Mobil Oil, 1.07% of Exxon—the last three being parts of the original Standard Oil Trust. But he insisted "we have no control of any kind over the management or policies of any of the oil companies." (He didn't dare say it about Chase Manhattan, where his brother David is Chairman of the Board.)

But the percentages Rockefeller conceded hide the bulk of the holdings. There are the holdings of the families of his aunts, Alta Prentice and Edith McCormick, who linked the Rockefellers with the Chicago financial grouping. There are the billions of family-controlled holdings of investment-type companies, holding companies, charitable foundations, universities, controlled by the Rockefeller family.

Then there are the holdings of the Harknesses, Pratts, Brewsters, and other descendants of the partners of John D. Rockefeller Sr., in Standard Oil. All of these are combined into assets that easily exert effective domination over a wide range of corporations.

Centers for coordinating these holdings include Rockefeller Brothers Inc., the trust department of the Chase Manhattan Bank, and other banks with major Rockefeller influence.

It is widely recognized that 5% is sufficient to exercise effective control over any of the multibillion dollar corporations. The Chase Manhattan Bank, alone, has more than 5% of the holdings in 26 important corporations, and David Rockefeller has refused requests for details. We do know that Exxon, the largest chunk of the original Standard Oil trust, continues to be No. 1 in the Chase Manhattan portfolio, as it is in Nelson Rockefeller's personal holdings.

Congressional studies in the 1930s showed that the Rockefeller group holds 40% or more of the stocks of the main Standard Oil companies. Doubtless it is less now, because they have shifted assets to other corporations, but it is still ample for control.

Nelson Rockefeller's disavowal of power partly rests on a phenomenon of U.S. monopoly capitalism: the tendency of different groups of financial rulers to pool their interests into huge coalitions or even supergroups.

As early as the teens of the present century, John Moody, the chronicler of the trusts, wrote in *Masters of Capital* of a tendency of the Rockefellers and Morgans to merge into a single supergroup. Recently Menshikov, in his book, takes account of this tendency by apportioning shares of control in major corporations among various financial groups.

Rockefeller said he will turn his securities over to the Morgan Guaranty Trust Co. to administer as a "blind trust"—that is, without informing him of the details. He avoids charges of keeping it in the family by not turning it over to Chase Manhattan. But there is nothing abnormal in Rockefellers using Morgan financial services: Morgan Stanley & Co. is the traditional investment banker for the Standard Oil companies.

The Morgan and Rockefeller groups, while rivals in some respects, collaborate overall in promoting the interests of U.S. monopoly capital, and cooperate directly in a number of business arrangements and monopolistic cartels.

Nelson Rockefeller's diversification of holdings has followed a pattern traditional among the centimillionaire and billionaire families. These groups have made IBM the favorite "growth stock" among those "in the know." By now, his holdings of IBM are third only to his stock in Exxon and Rockefeller Center. Similarly, the Morgan bank, while leading by far in IBM holdings, also has a significant stake in the Standard Oil companies.

The Rockefellers, then, remain the leading financial group in the condominium of interests running the oil companies, while the Morgans remain the leading financial group in the conglomerate dominating IBM.

There is indirect evidence that much of the Rockefeller diversification took place in the late 1960s. His dividend income declined from a peak of $5.3 million in 1966 to a low of $2.3 million in 1970—and then jumped back to $3.4 million the following year.

During this period, also, he reported very large capital gains. Presumably he sold substantial blocks of Standard Oil stock, paying relatively high dividend yields, and bought IBM and other "growth stocks" paying very little in dividends.

The advantage of the billionaire over the petty bourgeois investor is also brought out. Being on the inside, and knowing what will happen, he can judge when to buy and sell. Thus Rockefeller had capital gains in 8 out of 10 years, and only trivial losses the other two years. The ordinary small investor or speculator, on the other hand, generally ends up behind.

His losses are the gains of the Rockefellers.

• • •

1/2/1982

Who Is Nitze?

Washington never did put Al Capone in charge of cleaning up crime. But it did put Paul Henry Nitze in charge of negotiation with the USSR on reduction of medium range missiles in and around Europe. His real assignment is not to agree, but to talk enough to distract the West European peace movement and keep NATO governments in line for introduction of the first-strike Tomahawk cruise missiles and Pershing II missiles.

Nitze, a cold-blooded hawk, is known for his arrogance, "toughness," and hard, unsmiling countenance. Secretary of the Navy in the Johnson administration, he directed the scorched earth policy of U.S. troops against the land and people of Vietnam. When press photographers caught U.S. marines burning a peasant village in August 1965, Nitze justified the operation as a "defense" of the U.S. airbase at Danang, and admitted that he had ordered the marines to burn all huts in places that neither American nor puppet forces could occupy continuously. These services earned him promotion to Deputy Secretary of Defense.

Nitze is an advocate of nuclear blackmail who resigned from Nixon's disarmament negotiating team in protest at its attempt to reach agreement. In 1957 he helped write the Gaither Committee report that featured the big lie of the "Soviet missile gap," used by Washington to set off the punishing nuclear arms race of the 1960s. In the 1970s, he was policy committee chairman of the warhawk Committee on the Present Danger.

What is Nitze's background?

After graduation from Harvard and before World War II, Nitze worked 10 years at Dillon Read, one of the 17 Wall Street investment banking houses prosecuted after World War II for conspiracy to monopolize the capital markets and to promote super-monopoly mergers. During the pre-war period, Dillon Read led the syndicates floating loans to Germany, which included, of course, the bankers who financed Hitler.

Nitze became a vice-president at Dillon Read, an inner member of the Wall Street investment banking cartel. This house, like Brown Brothers, Harriman & Co., is peculiarly important in supplying Republicans to run elected Democratic administrations for Wall Street. Like C. Douglas Dillon and others before him, Nitze fits this pattern.

Nitze first moved to Washington, along with other Wall Streeters, during World War II to take over the vast properties financed by the war effort. Appointed head of corporations dealing with global mineral and raw material supplies, Nitze was able to facilitate the major postwar expansion of Dillon Read and other Wall Street associates in this area. Then, in 1944-46, he became vice-chairman of the Strategic Bombing Survey, the U.S. industrial espionage enterprise that set the terms for the revival of West German heavy industry under the old Nazi magnates in partnership with Wall Street.

After World War II, Dillon Read was the financial adviser and chief investment banker for the South African apartheid regime and for Engelhard Industries, which had the largest mining stake in South Africa.

At the start of 1950, Nitze was appointed to the key post of Director of the State Dept.'s Policy Planning Staff, under hawk Dean Acheson. There he helped plan the genocidal war against the Korean people, which provided a model for the war of conquest later waged against Vietnam. He was appointed Navy Secretary by Kennedy.

While his career stems from Dillon Read, Nitze's fortune gushes from still richer springs. In December 1932, while millions of Americans faced starvation, Nitze hit the jackpot by marrying Phyllis Pratt, heiress to one of the dozen original Standard Oil fortunes. According to the TNEC study of 1939, the Pratt family owned 1.72% of the shares of Standard Oil (NJ), and other oil stock, with a present value of hundreds of millions of dollars.

The Rockefeller-Standard Oil group has been in the forefront of the most belligerent, aggressive sections of big business, actively involved in economic warfare against the Soviet Union and other socialist countries, and with the largest stake of any group in neo-colonialist foreign investments.

Paul Nitze is a formidable foe of peace. But the sabotage of the Nitzes can be overcome by mounting struggles against the Reagan war program, for detente and disarmament.

• • •

7/19/1997

George Soros: Playing God

Establishment propagandists call regimes they approve of "democratic," those they oppose "authoritarian"—distinctions that have no relation to the actual character of a government.

Hungarian-born George Soros, who has accumulated a fortune of between $2.5 and $5 billion while living in the United States, has spent more than $1 billion over the past ten years to aid and abet in the destruction of socialism and the imposition of capitalist "democracy" in the former USSR and the countries of Eastern Europe. This year he expanded his operations from 24 to 40 countries, where he employs 1,300 agents.

Now, however, Soros' activities are being challenged. He has been accused of shielding spies, violating currency laws, and tax evasion in several countries, including Croatia and Albania, where, according to *The New York Times* of July 10, his "democratic" activities anger "the world's authoritarian rulers."

His most serious confrontation has been in Belarus where the bank accounts of the Soros Foundation have been seized and the foundation fined $3 million for tax violations. Soros says he would "like to continue working in Belarus but we will not play by Mr. Lukashenko's rules."

The Times describes Aleksandr Lukashenko as the "popular but autocratic" president of Belarus who won an "overwhelming" victory in 1994 running on a platform calling for rebuilding the USSR, ending corruption and preserving some of the gains of socialism.

But Soros, who, as quoted in the most recent issue of *Forbes* magazine, sees himself as "some kind of a god, the creator of everything," acts as though he is not subject to the laws of the countries where he operates.

The trouble is, neither does the Clinton administration, which, taking the same stance, has suspended an aid program meant for Belarus. And similar reprisals have been taken by governments in Western Europe and by the World Bank.

The same *Times* article says that Soros' "quiet confidence" in his counter-revolutionary activity is the result of "his access to any world leader, including President Clinton . . . just a phone call away."

One is forced to ask: Since Clinton was elected president in 1996 with the support of only 28% of the electorate, and Lukashenko won an "overwhelming majority," where is the real democracy, where the authoritarianism?

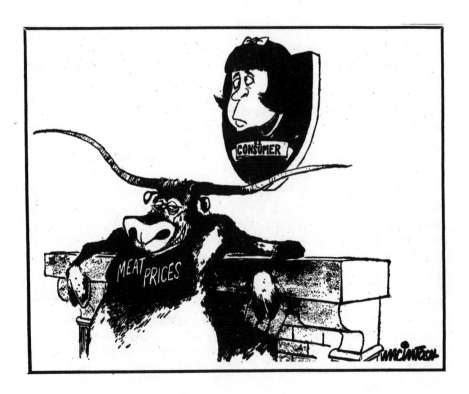

Agriculture

8/14/1973

Feeders of Steers Starve Consumers

Despite the wailing from the giants of the meat industry, the cost of producing a butchered and trimmed steak is only 6 cents a pound more today than in 1972. And that's steak for which you pay $1.89 a pound—about 60 cents more than you paid last year.

Feedlot operators—the people who fatten the cattle before turning them over to the packing houses—are selling steers for twice the cost of production. Of the $700 paid by the packer for a feedlot steer at Chicago, $350 is profit for the big feedlot operator and the ranchers, investors and bankers associated with him.

These facts and more were calmly confirmed by William H. Webster, a Greeley, Colorado feedlot operator, in a telephone interview with the *Daily World* yesterday. In an earlier interview published in *The New York Times*, he described himself as a spokesman for the American Cattlemen's Association.

His purpose, he said, is to defend himself and his associates from "consumer groups and irate shoppers." He blames high prices on "the Soviet wheat deal" and the "abnormal increase" in beef consumption. But his facts tell a different story.

Webster is no peasant. At present, the 45,000 cattle he feeds annually will bring in $30 million when delivered in Chicago, of which $15 million are profits for him and his associates.

Webster is a contract operator, with a computer to keep precise track of feed consumption so he can accurately bill his customers. These are, he said, even bigger businessmen—ranchers and investors who own the cattle, "living as far away as New York, for whom the cattle may be just one of a variety of investments."

A calf grows on a ranch for a year until he is a 700-pound steer. Then Webster gets him and feeds him intensively—even keeping him up nights with bright lights—to add another 450 pounds in five months. The tens of thousands of animals on Webster's 220-acre spread are jammed into nine pens where, to rest from the constant feeding, they have no room to lie down except on piles of their own dung.

This inactive, superfed existence makes prime tender steaks, so the steer "finished" on the feedlot is worth much more, pound for pound, than the one left on the ranch until slaughter time. Webster gave the *Times* many examples of the increased cost of feed, and he summarized: "It now costs . . . more than 30 cents to put a pound on a steer or heifer, compared with 23 cents a year ago."

In our telephone interview, however, Webster told me that the 30 cents includes all internal costs of operating the feedlot—feed, labor, vaccination, depreciation, the computer, billing, etc. Moreover, he expects that his actual costs will not exceed 30 cents a pound because of the bumper corn crop. He uses husked corn from nearby eastern Colorado and Nebraska.

The 7 cents per pound increase at the feedlot comes to 3 cents a pound when applied to the entire 1,150 pounds at which the steer leaves Webster's spread. Because of weight loss in slaughtering and trimming, this is the equivalent of a 6.2 cents cost increase per pound at retail (with adjustment for packinghouse byproducts).

But the BLS (Bureau of Labor Statistics) reports a 22 cents per pound rise in retail beef prices over the past year, or three times the cost increase. With the expected further rise when the beef ceiling is lifted on Sept. 12, we may end up with an actual increase of 50 to 60 cents a pound, or up to 10 times the cost increase of raising the animal.

So most of the increase in retail prices consists of profits. And it is of little concern to the consumer how that is divided among big feedlot operators, ranchers, packers, railroads, chain outlets, capitalist investors in feedlots and ranches, and bankers who charge them all record interest rates.

In the case of Webster and his rancher and investor associates, however, it is clear that the profit is huge. As against the cost of 30 cents a pound at the feedlot— and certainly less at the ranch—the price of cattle at the Chicago Mercantile Exchange on August 10 was 58.5 cents per pound. However, feeder cattle—one year old sold to feedlots—were selling for 70.2 cents per pound, indicating the price feedlot operators expect to get when the beef price freeze is lifted.

Moderate and low-income consumers are suffering an "abnormal decrease" of beef consumption, rather than the "abnormal increase" that Webster claims accounts for the price rise. Agriculture Department statistics show that in the first half of 1973, per capita consumption of beef declined three pounds and all red meat seven pounds in comparison with the same period of 1972. Obviously, consumption has declined much more since then. It is not excessive demand but a monopoly-organized reduction of supply that creates conditions under which the superhigh prices can be charged.

Webster reveals that the Agriculture Department has been helping organize big ranchers and feedlot operators to hold back production. "For years," according to the *Times* interview, "the Federal authorities cautioned ranchers not to increase their herds by more than 2 percent a year . . . to avoid gluts of beef on the market."

Of course, the small farmer with 45 head of beef cattle, without access to feed on favored terms, is squeezed. He is not responsible for the extortionate retail prices. But so many small farmers have already been forced out that the agribusiness giants like Webster monopolize the supply of beef and, in collaboration with the Agriculture Department, determine the price.

Referring to Mr. Webster's accusation about Soviet wheat purchases, the

USSR accounted for about one-eighth of the grain and soybean exports ordered from last year's crops and less than 5% of U.S. grain and soybean production.

• • •

7/16/1974

The Strawberry Children

Henry Jackson, the warmonger, has the reputation of being a "liberal" on domestic affairs. He has a 100% accolade from fellow ultra-rightist George Meany.

Jackson is taking a leading role in a campaign to preserve child labor in agriculture in northwestern states for at least one more year, and if he has his way, indefinitely.

Under the amended Fair Labor Standards Act, employment of children under 12 in agriculture is illegal. For many decades after child labor in general was made illegal, it continued in agriculture, where the most exploited sections of the working class—mainly Black, Chicano, Puerto Rican and immigrant labor—were employed. The frightful conditions to which these workers have been subjected, the particular tragedy of their children, have been exposed in innumerable hearings, reports, and newspaper articles.

Now, in a minimal reform move, an elementary step in the direction of humanity, children under 12 will no longer be forced to work as berry pickers.

Senators Henry Jackson and Warren G. Magnuson of Washington State immediately went into action on behalf of the exploiters of child labor in the northwest. They urged Senator Gaylord Nelson of Wisconsin, chairman of a migratory labor subcommittee, to arrange for suspension of the ban on using child labor for berry picking for a year, while the situation was "studied" at first hand. The senators argued that the use of children for berry picking "has been traditional in the Northwest . . . and is generally viewed as non-exploitive." [sic]

Editorially supporting them, the *Seattle Times* chastised the senators for being caught napping and letting the law be passed in the first place.

Not only has child labor in the berry fields been traditional, but more than half of the workers have been children under 12.

Shades of Charles Dickens!

Backed by this senatorial pressure, an Oregon strawberry-farm owner went to court demanding an injunction against the Fair Labor Standards Act. On June 22 a Federal District panel in Portland, OR issued a temporary injunction granting the growers' request. Collaborating with the owners, U.S. District Attorney Sidney Lezak is in no rush to have it reversed by the full District Court or by appeals: He says the case is unlikely to be heard until the growing season is over. So once again the children will be exploited on the berry fields.

Meanwhile the strawberry-farm owners, Jackson, and his cohorts can get to work on Congress in the attempt to make up for their earlier "carelessness" and will try to get Congress to pass a special law to authorize child labor in the berry fields.

• • •

6/10/1986

Washington's Slaughter of Cows

Over the next 18 months 1 million cows and 600,000 young dairy cattle will be slaughtered, under the auspices of an Agriculture Department program to reduce milk production by 12 billion pounds. Fourteen thousand farmers will be driven out of business.

Those 12 billion pounds would supply one pint of milk daily for a year to the 13 million U.S. children officially classified as under the poverty line, and to the 20 million even hungrier children in nearby Mexico and Central America.

With prices constantly rising and more people poverty-stricken, the market demand for milk and dairy products has been falling further behind the increasing supply.

So the U.S. Government is buying up more milk each year through its price support program. Storehouses are crammed with dried milk products. Last year Washington bought 13.2 million pounds—roughly 9% of output—for $1.7 billion.

To reduce the "surplus," the government offered to buy out many dairy farmers. The object was to reduce milk output by nearly as much as the 1985 "surplus." Farmers would be paid an amount related to their milk production on condition that they slaughter or export all their cattle, close down their cow barns and get out of the business for 5 years. The dairy farmers were invited to submit bids for the amount they wanted to be paid for the milk they might have produced with the cows they would kill. The bids ranged from $3.40 to over $1,000 per hundredweight. The Agriculture Department accepted all bids up to $22.50. Only 14,000—a third of the farmers—bid within those limits. The remaining two-thirds got nothing.

In addition to the government buyout, farmers will get some income from the sale of their slaughtered cattle. In all, in exchange for the destruction of all their capital, they will be paid an amount equal in value to about one and a half year's output. That's not much better than a bankruptcy sale.

Many farmers who accepted the program feared they were going under financially and wanted to be sure they got something out of it. Many who bid too high figured that if they got anything less, they would not be able to pay off their heavy loans. Now they're stuck with those debts and must battle to meet the rising costs of equipment for modern high-intensity dairy farming. In addition, all remaining dairy farmers must pay what amounts to over a 3% tax on the milk they sell, to cover part of the cost of buying out the farmers whose bids were accepted.

What will be the results? Last year's milk production was a record high. It jumped higher in the early months of this year. Even with the killing of cows, it is estimated that 1986 milk output will be even higher than last year. By next year, big farmers will add enough additional cows to fully maintain output at or above previous levels. Dairy farming will increasingly be limited to large capitalist farmers.

The Agriculture Department will continue to pay over $10 billion yearly to dairy companies for all the milk consumers can't buy because the monopoly prices are too high.

The sharpest slash in milk production, about 20%, will be in the South, which produces less than it consumes. It is the area with the largest number of children, especially Black children, whose parents are too poor to buy milk.

What alternative is there? Lane Palmer, editor in chief of the *Farm Journal*, headed a U.S. delegation that visited Soviet collective and state dairy farms. He wrote that Americans who are told about food shortages in the USSR are surprised to learn the USSR "is the world's largest milk producer. That's right. The USSR topped 100 million tons of milk in 1985, whereas the U.S. produced 65 million." (*Farm Journal*, Dairy Extra, April 1986).

The Soviets produce 50% more milk than the U.S. They don't talk of surpluses, and no children go hungry. They send some dairy products as aid to Third World countries. Instead of challenging the Soviet Union in missiles, the United States should challenge them in milk production. Farmers here should be encouraged to produce food rather than destroy it. Milk and other dairy products should be provided free by the government to all families of unemployed and to people living in poverty.

All milk not consumed here should be sent as aid to African and Latin American countries where the need is acute, to be distributed under United Nations auspices. The cost would be just a fraction of what could be saved if the United States accepted Soviet disarmament proposals.

• • •

9/23/1987

Apples: A Case Study in Exploitation

The fall season begins when we get fresh, tart, juicy New York apples that make splendid applesauce and apple pies. For the several months of fresh apples, if lucky, we get them for an average of 50¢ per pound.

The following details come from *The New York Times* (9/6), certainly not biased in a pro-labor direction.

New York farm workers tend orchards and pick more than a billion pounds of apples a year, second only to Washington State in quantity. Jamaican immigrants, here for 3 months to pick the apples, are permitted to enter for this purpose by the U.S. Immigration and Naturalization Service on the grounds that not enough U.S. citizens are willing to do the work. The 1,550 Jamaicans are augmented by 300 migrant workers from the South.

That's 1,850 workers picking, perhaps, 1.2 billion pounds of apples in the two and a half month season. Each worker picks, on the average, 650,000 pounds of apples, or more than $300,000 worth at retail.

The Jamaicans are paid 60¢ a bushel, or 1.5¢ a pound of apples. When we buy them at Mike's fruit and vegetable stand for 50¢, Linford Stewart, the Jamaican quoted in *The New York Times* story, gets just 3% of what we pay. Add liberally for the work done by farm maintenance workers, truckers, handlers at the store, etc., and we're talking of a labor cost of perhaps 5¢ per pound. That leaves 45¢ for those who exploit the labor. They are getting nine times as much as the workers; and doubtless the most exploited are the pickers.

We are told that the immigrants, besides a guaranteed $5.03 per hour, are given free transportation from and to Jamaica, and free housing while on the job. If New York is like most other states, farm workers' housing varies from miserable to horrible.

Two organizations, Farm Workers Legal Services and Migrant Legal Action Program, are suing the government to provide more adequate wages and better conditions.

Why are the Jamaican workers willing to do it? Because, the employers say, they can take back home $2,000 from their months of toil. That's vital for a family's survival in Jamaica, a neo-colony of imperialism.

Naturally, the employers are happy with the program. They get highly skilled workers who have no rights and no possibility of organizing and fighting for a more reasonable share of what they produce. Yes, the law requires proof that this isn't taking jobs from U.S. workers. James Russo, a growers' representative, says, "We spent $3,000 in advertising . . . to recruit local workers and didn't even get one."

It may be true that it is difficult to recruit local workers at the height of the tourist season, but it is also true that not very far away, in New York City, tens of thousands of youth search in vain for summer jobs. Did the U.S. Department of Labor advertise summer jobs picking apples in the country, at decent wages, with enough time off; with free transportation to and from the city; with free, decent housing? And would it see to it that these promises were kept? Of course not. Naturally, the employers couldn't drive U.S. workers so hard—workers who could, and probably would, form unions to better their conditions.

Apples are one of many agricultural and industrial products now produced in the U.S. by millions of rightless immigrants, who constitute a source of superprofits for employers and are used to pull down wages and working conditions for all U.S. workers, while keeping unemployment high.

Chronological Index

1968

1969

1970

1971

1972

1973

1974

1975

1976

Chronological Index

Chronological Index

Index

Index

Index

Index

Index